NEW DOCUMENTS ILLUSTRATING EARLY CHRISTIANITY

A Review of the
Greek Inscriptions and Papyri
published in 1980-81

by

S.R. Llewelyn
with the collaboration of
R.A. Kearsley

The Ancient History Documentary Research Centre
Macquarie University
1992

The Ancient History Documentary Research Centre (Director: E.A. Judge, Professor of History) within the School of History, Philosophy & Politics at Macquarie University fosters research and professional development in association with other organisations interested in the documentation of the ancient world.

Committee for *New Documents Illustrating Early Christianity*
P.W. Barnett (Chairman), P. Geidans, E.A. Judge, A. McComb, J.A. Shepherd

Editorial Consultants

G.W. Clarke, Director, Humanities Research Centre, Australian National University.
G.H.R Horsley, Senior Lecturer in Religious Studies, La Trobe University
M. Lattke, Reader in Studies in Religion, University of Queensland.
J.A.L Lee, Senior Lecturer in Greek, University of Sydney.
K.L. McKay, formerly Reader in Classics, Australian National University
G.R. Stanton, Associate Professor in Classics & Ancient History, University of New England.
M. Wilcox, Senior Lecturer in History, Macquarie University.

This volume has been produced with the support of a Macquarie University Research Grant and the Australian Research Council.

Editorial correspondence should be addressed to Dr S.R. Llewelyn, School of History, Philosophy & Politics, Macquarie University, NSW 2109, Australia.

Business address: The Ancient History Documentary Research Centre, Macquarie University, NSW 2109, Australia.

SUGGESTED CATALOGUING DATA:

Llewelyn, S.R.

New Documents Illustrating Early Christianity, Volume 6. A Review of the Greek Inscriptions and Papyri published in 1980-81.

Bibliography.
Includes index
ISBN 0 85837 763 2
ISBN 0 85837 771 3 (pbk)

1. Bible. New Testament — Language, style. 2. Inscriptions, Greek. 3. Manuscripts (Papyri).
4. Greek language, Biblical. 5. Church History — Primitive and early church.
I. Macquarie University Ancient History Documentary Research Centre. II. Title.
PA 810 1992 487.4

Typeset by the Ancient History Documentary Research Centre.
Printed by Southwood Press, 80-82 Chapel Street, Marrickville, NSW 2204

TABLE OF CONTENTS

Introduction i

List of Works Read ii

Abbreviations vi

Textual Sigla vii

Acknowledgements vii

The Family

1 Paul's Advice on Marriage and the Changing Understanding of Marriage in Antiquity 1

2 A Woman's Behaviour *E.A. Judge* 18

3 Women in Public Life *R.A. Kearsley* 24

4 The Allotment after Death and Paul's Metaphor of Inheritance 27

5 The Revocation of Wills and Gal.3.15 41

Slaves and Masters

6 The Sale of a Slave-Girl: The New Testament's Attitude to Slavery 48

7 A Petition Concerning a Runaway: Paul's Letter to Philemon 55

8 'He gives authority to his slaves, to each his work ...' Mark.13.34 60

9 'If you can gain your freedom': Manumission and 1Cor.7.21 63

10 The Slave of God (Rom. 6.22) and Sacral Manumission 70

11 Manumission in Thessaly and at Delphi 76

Business Transactions

12 'Even the winds and the waves obey him' Matt.8.27: Acts of God in Shipping Contracts 82

13 Self-Help and Legal Redress: The Parable of the Wicked Tenants 86

14 'Having cancelled the bond which stood against us': Col.2.14 and the *Cheirographon* 105

Roman Administration

15 'And everyone went to his own town to register' Luke 2.3 112

16 The Provincial Census and Jesus' Birth in Bethlehem 119

17 The Preservation of Status and its Testing 132

18 Petitions, Social History and the Language of Requests 140

The Army

19 Name and Status: A Veteran seeks Tax Exemption 147

20 Claudius Lysias (Acts 22) and the Question of Paul's Roman Citizenship 152

21 A Soldier's Letter Home 156

22 The Size of the Roman Garrison in Jerusalem 159

Judaica

23 The Goliath Family at Jericho *R.A. Kearsley* 162

24 A Work Contract of Jewish Soldiers 164

TABLE OF CONTENTS

Ecclesiastica

25	Ammonios to Apollonios (*P. Oxy.* XLII 3057): The Earliest Christian Letter on Papyrus?		169
26	The Epitaph of Aberkios: The Earliest Christian Inscription?	*R.A. Kearsley*	177
27	Monastic Orthodoxy and the Papyri of the Nag Hammadi Cartonnage		182

Magic, Medicine and Cults

28	Ailments and Remedies	*R.A. Kearsley*	190
29	The Mysteries of Artemis at Ephesus	*R.A. Kearsley*	196
30	Ephesus: *Neokoros* of Artemis	*R.A. Kearsley*	203
31	Angels in Asia Minor: The Cult of Hosios and Dikaios	*R.A. Kearsley*	206
32	Acts 14.13: The Temple Just Outside the City	*R.A. Kearsley*	209

Appendix

Statistical Tables 211

Indexes

Subjects		213
Words	Greek	217
	Latin	218
	Hebrew	218
Greek and Latin Writers		219
Papyri and Ostraca		220
Inscriptions		222
Old Testament, Qumran and Rabbinic Literature		224
New Testament		226

INTRODUCTION

The sixth volume of *New Documents Illustrating Early Christianity* (*New Docs* 6 [1992]) represents something of a departure from the earlier volumes in the series. The former volumes were undertaken largely to look at the feasibility of rewriting MM. That has now become a joint project of Sydney (J.A.L.Lee), La Trobe (G.H.R.Horsley) and Macquarie Universities independently of the New Documents project. A glance at the table of contents should show that the project now has a slightly different emphasis. The documentary evidence is used to illustrate and open up for discussion areas of social history which bear on the history of the early church and the study of the NT in particular. Depending on its primary focus each entry is grouped under a larger thematic heading, e.g. the family, slaves and masters. Independent miscellaneous philological notes are no longer made. This is not to say that such notes are absent altogether. They are now subsumed under the topic which is the focus of each entry.

The range of documents sampled in *New Docs* 6 is those which were first published or significantly re-edited in the years 1980-81. Of course, exceptions will be found. For example, where a document earlier published is under discussion because of its relevance to an entry's topic, it is included and translated to save the reader having to search elsewhere. Again, when a document first published since 1970 illustrates a theme or topic under discussion, it is considered sufficiently recent to be included. Working with texts published over a two-year period has provided a larger range than that used in former volumes. This has obvious benefits for it extends the choice and permits the grouping of the documents under larger thematic headings. Documents have been selected because of their interest, even if tangential, to the history of the early church. If the document does not have a direct bearing on this history, the connection is mediated through its topic or theme. For example, **§15** is prompted by a newly published house-by-house census declaration. The document's text is given and translated. The entry then discusses the nature and workings of the Roman provincial census and its relevance to Luke's dating of Jesus' birth. The connection between the document and the NT is the topic of the provincial census. Another determining factor in the choice of documents has been their date. A general cut-off date of AD 200 was chosen. However, if a later document illustrates an earlier practice or bears on a related field, such as the cartonnage of the Nag Hammadi texts in **§27**, it may be used either in its own right or to illustrate the theme and topic under discussion. It is difficult to employ any hard and fast rules in the selection process as this would place an undesirable restriction on the direction and scope of discussion.

A change has also been made in the translation of documents. In order to assist the reading of the Greek text, the translation has attempted to reflect as far as practicable the formal structure of the document. This means that the translation is line-by-line, with doubtful and restored readings marked by *sigla* in the English translation. Naturally, one cannot translate the Greek document into flowing English if at the same time one pays strict regard to formal structures. Thus something of a compromise has resulted. For example, the indication of doubtful and restored readings can only be an approximation. Again not all documents can be rigidly translated line-by-line. Words and expressions may need to appear on different lines in the Greek and English texts for syntactic reasons. Where this occurs to a significant degree the reader will be alerted to the fact by a continued indentation of the English translation, e.g. see *P. Amst.* 40 *ll.*24-28 in *New Docs* 6 **§1**. Resumption of line-by-line translation is indicated by the cessation of indentation. It is hoped that all these devices will help the non-Greek reader to use the documents in a more critical fashion, knowing what the text actually says and what the editor has restored to it.

In all this the entries have been written with a specific reader in mind. *New Documents Illustrating Early Christianity* seeks to elucidate its subject by better understanding its historical and social milieu. The assumed reader is thus the NT researcher, teacher or student. A number of entries deal in part with statistical matters. Data and tables are presented and an interpretation of them offered. However, it is not necessary that the reader understand all this (particularly the tables given in the footnotes) in order to understand the entry's argument; an understanding of the interpretation will suffice. Nevertheless, the presentation of the data in whatever form is necessary as it is the basis on which the interpretation has been made. Where the data concerns the NT, I have made use of an electronic text (UBS 3) kindly supplied by CCAT (Center for Computer Analysis of Texts at the University of Pennsylvania).

List of Works Read

Adrassus	*The Necropolis of Adrassus (Balabolu) in Rough Cilicia (Isauria)*, by E. Alföldi-Rosenbaum (Vienna 1980).
ANRW	*Aufstieg und Niedergang der römischen Welt* II, 7.2, ed. H. Temporini (Berlin 1980).
BE	*Bulletin épigraphique*, by J. and L. Robert, in *Revue des études grecques* 93 (1980), pp.368-485; 94 (1981), pp.362-485.
BGU XIV	*Ägyptische Urkunden aus den Königlichen Museen zu Berlin, Griechische Urkunden* XIV: *Ptolemäische Urkunden aus Mumienkartonage*, ed. W.M. Brashear (Berlin 1980).
Bickermann, *Studies*	E. Bickermann, *Studies in Jewish and Christian History* II (Leiden 1980).
C.Ord.Ptol., 2nd ed.	*Corpus des ordonnances des Ptolémées*, ed. M.-Th. Lenger (Brussels 1980).
Festschr.Vittinghoff	*Studien zur antiken Sozialgeschichte. Festschrift Friedrich Vittinghoff* (Cologne 1980).
FiE IX/1/1	*Forschungen in Ephesos* IX/1/1. *Der Staatsmarkt. Die Inschriften des Prytaneions. Die Kureteninschriften und sonstige religiöse Texte*, by Dieter Knibbe (Vienna 1981).
Freyne	S.Freyne, *Galilee from Alexander the Great to Hadrian, 323 BCE to 135 CE,* (Delaware 1980).
Friedman	M.A.Friedman, *Jewish Marriage in Palestine* (New York 1980).
Griechische Epigramme	A. Wilhelm, *Griechische Epigramme*, aus dem Nachlass edd. H. Engelmann and K. Wundsam (Bonn 1980).
Hachlili	R. Hachlili, 'The Goliath Family in Jericho: Funerary Inscriptions from a First Century A.D. Jewish Monumental Tomb', *BASOR* 235 (1979), pp. 31-70.
Holder	P.A. Holder, *The Auxilia from Augustus to Trajan* (Oxford 1980).
I. Ephesos III-VII, 2	*Inschriften griechischer Städte aus Kleinasien* 13-17, 2. *Die Inschriften von Ephesos* III-VII, 2, edd. H. Engelmann, R. Merkelbach, D. Knibbe et al. (Bonn 1980-81).

I. Kalchedon	*Inschriften griechischer Städte aus Kleinasien* 20. *Die Inschriften von Kalchedon*, ed. R. Merkelbach (Bonn 1980).
I. Kyzikos	*Inschriften griechischer Städte aus Kleinasien* 18. *Die Inschriften von Kyzikos und Umgebung* I, ed. E. Schwertheim (Bonn 1980).
I. Nikaia II, 1	*Inschriften griechischer Städte aus Kleinasien* 10,1. *Katalog der antiken Inschriften des Museums von Iznik (Nikaia)* II, 1, ed. M. Şahin (Bonn 1981).
I. Sestos	*Inschriften griechischer Städte aus Kleinasien* 19. *Die Inschriften von Sestos und der thrakischen Chersones*, ed. J. Krauss (Bonn 1980).
I. Stratonikeia	*Inschriften griechischer Städte aus Kleinasien* 21. *Die Inschriften von Stratonikeia* I. *Panamara*, ed. M. Şahin (Bonn 1981).
I. Xanthos	*Fouilles de Xanthos* VII. *Inscriptions d'époque imperiale du Létôon*, by A. Balland (Paris 1981).
Kotansky	R. Kotansky, 'Two Amulets in the Getty Museum: a gold amulet for Aurelia's epilepsy; an inscribed magical stone for fever, chills and headache', *J. Paul Getty Museum Journal* VIII (1980), pp. 181-88.
Le Bohec	Y. Le Bohec, 'Inscriptions juives et judaïsantes de l'Afrique romaine', *Antiquités africaines* XVII (1981), pp. 165-207.
Medizinische Rezepte	*Medizinische Rezepte und Verwandtes*, edd. H. Harrauer and P.J. Sijpesteijn (Vienna 1981).
Misc.Pap.	*Miscellanea Papyrologica*, ed. R. Pintaudi (Florence 1980).
Naour, *Tyriaion*	*Tyriaion en Cabalide: épigraphie et géographie historique* (*Studia Amstelodamensia* XX), by Chr. Naour (Zutphen 1980).
Neumann/Untermann	*Die Sprachen im römischen Reich der Kaiserzeit*, edd. G. Neumann and J. Untermann (*Beihefte der Bonner Jahbücher* 40, Cologne 1980).
O. FayJouguet:	P. Jouguet, 'Ostraka du Fayoum', *BIFAO* 2 (1902), pp.91-105.
O. Leid.	*Greek Ostraka. A Catalogue of the Collection of Greek Ostraca in the National Museum at Leiden*, edd. R.S. Bagnall, P.J. Sijpesteijn and K.A. Worp (Zutphen 1980).
P. Amst. I	*Die Amsterdamer Papyri* I , edd. R.P. Salomons, P.J. Sijpesteijn and K.A. Worp (Zutphen 1980).
P. Bodmer XLV + XLVI	A. Carlini and A. Citi, 'Susanna e la prima visione di Daniele in due papiri inediti della Bibliotheca Bodmeriana: P.Bodm. XLV e P.Bodm. XLVI', *MH* 38 (1981), pp.81-120 and pll. 114.
P. Charite:	*Das Aurelia Charite Archiv*, ed. K.A. Worp (Zutphen 1980).

P. Haun. II	*Papyri Graecae Haunienses* fasc. II : *Letters and Mummy Labels from Roman Egypt*, ed. A. Bülow-Jacobsen (Bonn 1981).
P. Köln III	*Kölner Papyri*, edd. B. Kramer et al. (Opladen 1980).
P. Köln ägypt.	*Kölner ägyptische Papyri* I, edd. D. Kurth, H.-J. Thissen and M. Weber (Opladen 1980).
P. L. Bat. XX	*Papyrologica Lugduno-Batava* XX: *Greek and Demotic Texts from the Zenon Archive*, ed. P.W. Pestman (Leiden 1980).
P. L. Bat. XXI	*Papyrologica Lugduno-Batava* XXI: *A Guide to the Zenon Archive*, by P.W. Pestman et al. (Leiden 1981).
Pleket	H.W. Pleket, 'New Inscriptions from Lydia', *Talanta* 10-11 (1978-81), pp. 74-91.
PME	*Prosopographia militiarum equestrium quae fuerunt ab Augusto ad Gallienum* III. *Indices*, by J. Devijver (Leuven 1980).
P. Mich. XIV	*Michigan Papyri* XI, ed. V.P. McCarren (Chico 1980).
P. Mil.Vogliano VII	*Papiri della Università degli Studi di Milano* VII: *La contabilità di un' azienda agricola nel II sec. d.C.*, ed. D. Foraboschi (Milan 1981).
P. Nag Hammadi:	*Nag Hammadi Codices. Greek and Coptic Papyri from the Cartonnage of the Covers*, edd. J.W.B.Barns, G.M. Browne and J.C. Shelton (Leiden 1981).
P. Oxy. XLVII	*The Oxyrhynchus Papyri* XLVII, edd. R.A. Coles et al. (London 1980).
P. Oxy. XLVIII	*The Oxyrhynchus Papyri* XLVIII, edd. M. Chambers, W.E.H. Cockle, J.C. Shelton and E.G. Turner (London 1981).
Proc XVI Cong.	*Proceedings of the Sixteenth International Congress of Papyrology*, edd. R.S. Bagnall et al. (Chicago 1981).
P. Strasb. 701-720	*Papyrus grecs de la bibliothèque nationale et universitaire de Strasbourg*, ed. J. Schwarz (Strasburg 1980).
P. Strasb. 721-740	*Papyrus grecs de la bibliothèque nationale et universitaire de Strasbourg*, ed. J. Schwarz (Strasburg 1981).
P. Tor. Amenothes	*L'archivio di Amenothes figlio di Horos. Testi demotici e greci relativi ad una famiglia di imbalsamatori del II sec. a.C.*, ed. P.W. Pestman (Milan 1981).
PTA 27 (Early LXX)	*Papyrologische Texte und Abhandlungen* 27:*Three Rolls of the Early Septuagint: Genesis and Deuteronomy*, ed. Z. Aly, with preface, introduction and notes by L. Koenen (Bonn 1980).
P. Turner	*Papyri Greek and Egyptian, edited by various hands in honour of Eric Gardner Turner on the occasion of his seventieth birthday*, edd. P.J. Parsons and J.R.Rea (London 1981).

PUG II	*Papiri dell' Università di Genova* II, ed. L.M. Zingale (Florence 1980).
P. Ups. Frid	*Ten Uppsala Papyri*, ed. B. Frid (Bonn 1981).
P.Vatic. Aphrod.	*I papiri Vaticani greci di Aphrodito*, ed. R. Pintaudi (The Vatican City 1980).
P. Wash.Univ. I	*Washington University Papyri* I: *Non-Literary Texts (Nos. 1-61)*, ed. V.B. Schuman (Chico 1980).
Robert, *Asie Mineure*	L. Robert, *A travers l'Asie Mineure. Poètes et prosateurs, monnaies grecques, voyageurs et géographie* (Paris 1980).
SB XIV, 1	*Sammelbuch griechischer Urkunden aus Ägypten* XIV, 1 , edd. H.-A. Rupprecht et al. (Wiesbaden 1979).
Scritti Montevecchi	*Scritti in onore di Orsolina Montevecchi* (Bologna 1981).
SEG	*Supplementum Epigraphicum Graecum* XXX (1980 [1983]); XXX1 (1981 [1984]).
Sheppard	A.R.R. Sheppard, 'Pagan Cults of Angels in Roman Asia Minor', *Talanta* 12-13 (1980-81), pp. 77-101.
SIG/L	*Sylloge Inscriptionum Graecarum et Latinarum Macedoniae*, ed. M. Demitsas (reprinted Chicago 1980).
Strobel, *Montanisten*	A. Strobel, *Das heilige Land der Montanisten* (Berlin 1980).
TAM V,1	*Tituli Asiae Minoris* V. *Tituli Lydiae*, fasc. 1, ed. P. Herrmann (Vienna 1981).
Velkov, *Bulgaria*	V. Velkov, *Roman Cities in Bulgaria. Collected Studies* (Amsterdam 1980).
Versnel	*Faith, Hope and Worship. Aspects of Religious Mentality in the Ancient World*, ed. H.S. Versnel (Leiden 1981).
Weitzmann, *Symposium*	*Age of Spirituality. A Symposium*, ed. K. Weitzmann (New York 1980).

Abbreviations

Abbreviations follow standard conventions, except where altered for clarity.

Journals - as in *L'Année philologique*.

Papyrological works - as in S.R. Pickering, *Papyrus Editions held in Australian Libraries* (North Ryde 1984); ibid., *Papyrus Editions: Supplement* (North Ryde 1985).

Epigraphical works according to generally used conventions (see LSJ), preceded where necessary by *I.* (e.g. *I. Ephesos*).

Ancient authors, biblical and patristic works - generally as in LSJ, BAGD, and Lampe (see below).

Some other abbreviations used in this volume:

BAGD	Bauer, Arndt, Gringrich and Danker, *A Greek-English Lexicon of the New Testament and Other Early Christian Literature* (Chicago 1979[2]).
BDF	Blass, Debrunner and Funk, *A Greek Grammar of the New Testament and other Early Christian Literature* (Chicago 1961).
CIJ	J.B. Frey, *Corpus Inscriptionum Judaicarum* (2 vols; Rome 1936, 1952); vol. 1 repr. with Prolegomenon by B. Lifshitz (New York 1975).
CPJ	V.A. Tcherikover, A. Fuks, et al., *Corpus Papyrorum Judaicarum* (3 vols; Cambridge [Mass.] 1957-64).
Deissmann, *LAE*	G.A. Deissmann, *Light from the Ancient East* (Grand Rapids 1980[4]).
Jastrow, *Dictionary*	M. Jastrow, *A Dictionary of the Targumim, the Talmud Babli and Yerushalmi, and the Midrashic Literature* (New York 1950 repr.).
Lampe	Lampe, *A Patristic Greek Lexicon* (Oxford 1961, repr.),
LSJ/LSJ Suppl.	Liddell/Scott/Jones, *A Greek-English Lexicon* (Oxford 1940[9], repr. with supplement ed. E.A. Barber 1968).
LXX	Septuagint (Rahlfs' edition).
MChr and Mitteis, *Chrest.*	U. Wilcken – L. Mitteis, *Grundzüge und Chrestomathie der Papyruskunde* (Hildesheim 1963), II 1 and 2.
MM	Moulton and Milligan, *The Vocabulary of the Greek Testament* (London 1930; repr.).
MT	Masoretic Text
NT	New Testament
OT	Old Testament
PSI	*Papiri greci e latini* (*Publicazioni della Società Italiana per la ricerca dei papiri greci e latini*), edd. G.Vitelli, M.Norsa et al. (Florence 1912 -)
Stud.Pal.	*Studien zur Palaeograhie und Papyruskunde*
Taubenschlag, *Law*	R.Taubenschlag, *The Law of Greco-Roman Egypt in the Light of the Papyri* (Warsaw 1955).

Textual sigla used are as follows:—

α̣β̣	—	letters not completely legible
. . . .	—	4 letters missing
...	—	indeterminate number of letters missing
[αβ]	—	letters lost from document and restored by editor
[±8]	—	about 8 letters lost
‹αβ›	—	letters omitted by scribe and added by editor
«αβ»	—	editorial correction of wrong letters in the text
(αβ)	—	editor has resolved an abbreviation in the text
{αβ}	—	letters wrongly added by scribe and cancelled by editor
⟦αβ⟧	—	a (still legible) erasure made by scribe
\`αβ´	—	letters written above line
$\overline{\alpha}$	—	letter stands for a numerical equivalent
v., vv., vac.	—	one, two, several letter spaces left blank (*vacat*) on document
m. 1, m. 2	—	first hand (*manus*), second hand
front / back	—	writing along the fibres / across the fibres of a papyrus sheet

Acknowledgements

In addition to the writing of eight entries R.A. Kearsley has contributed to the production of *New Docs* 6 (1991) in many ways. She has been involved in the project at all stages and levels of its development, i.e. the reading and selection of the documentary material, researching, correcting and advising on draft entries and the final production of the volume. Appreciation is also expressed to E.A. Judge for the freedom and encouragement he has given to both of us in the writing of the entries. His support, however, has extended beyond this. Besides contributing one entry in the present volume he has read and constructively commented on most other entries as well. E.A. Judge, C.B. Forbes and M. Wilcox were the successful applicants for the two awards (Macquarie University Research Grant and Australian Research Council) from which this project is funded. Special thanks are also extended to the editorial consultants: G.W. Clarke of the Australian National University, G.H.R. Horsley of La Trobe University, M. Lattke of the University of Queensland, J.A.L. Lee of the University of Sydney, K.L. McKay, G.R. Stanton of the University of New England and M. Wilcox of Macquarie University. Besides offering the many constructive ideas which are acknowledged in the relevant entries, they have spared me from making numerous *faux pas* by their helpful comments, and directed me to relevant literature and examples. Finally, I would like to express my thanks to R. Cook, P. Geidans and E. Lewis of the Ancient History Documentary Research Centre, who have helped in various ways in the production of this volume.

S.R. Llewelyn

THE FAMILY

§1 Paul's Advice on Marriage and the Changing Understanding of Marriage in Antiquity

Provenance unknown — First century AD

Ed.pr. – R.P. Salomons, P.J. Sijpesteijn and K.A. Worp, *P. Amst.* 40 (Zutphen 1980), pp.80-82.

The papyrus measures 12 x 9.5 cm. The top of both columns is broken off. Space is left at the bottom of each column. The space between the columns changes. The text runs parallel to the fibres. The back of the papyrus is blank.

(Column I)

[γυ-]	
ναικὸς [αὐτο]ῦ̣	... of [his w]ife,
Θαισοῦτο[ς] τῆς	Thaisous, also called
καὶ Διδυ[μα]ρίου	Didymarion,
ἀδελφῆς̣ [N]ιννοῦ-	his sister, to Ninnous,
τι τῇ καὶ Σερ̣απιάδι	also called Serapias,
παρθένῳ οὔσῃ	being a maiden
ἐγδεδομένῃ ὑ-	given in marriage by
π' αὐτοῦ Βακχύλο̣υ̣	him, Bacchylos,
καὶ συνερχομένου	and being united with
αὐτῷ Διδύμῳ πρὸς	him, Didymos, in
γάμον φερνὴ ἀρ-	wedlock, a dowry
κολ(λημ) λ̅θ̅	Kollema 39
κ̣[ο]λ(λημ) κ̅β̅	Kollema 22
κολ(λημ) κ̅γ̣̅	Kollema 23

(Column II)

. .] . [	
Θὼθ λ [. . . .]υ̣τη̣. ηηλ̣( )	Thoth 30 ...
ἑκουσίως θ̅ μέρος ∠̣	willingly a 9th part of a 1/2
μέρους τῶν οἰκοπέ-	share of the building blocks
δων τῇ γυναικὶ αὐ-	to his wife,
τοῦ Νιννοῦτι τῇ	Ninnous, also called
καὶ Σεραπιάδι Ἥρωνος	Serapias, daughter of Heron,
ἀστῇ πρὸς ἃ ὀφείλι	citizen, for what he owes
αὐτῇ ἀφ' ὧν περι-	her from
έλυσεν αὐτῆς ἐν	her father's
τῷ οἴκῳ αὐτοῦ	unsecured loans
πατρικῶν ψει-	which he repaid her in
λῶν δανείων.	his house
λ̅θ̅	39

....

8 ἐκδεδομένη 10 συνερχομένη 12 φερνήν 23 ὀφείλει 25 αὐτῇ 27-8 ψιλῶν

A central question in the discussion of the dowry has been the relationship between the two systems of προίξ and φερνή. H.J. Wolff, 'Marriage Law and Family Organisation in Ancient Athens', *Traditio* 2 (1944), pp.43-95, has described the socio-political function of marriage in the democratic πόλις. The function of legitimate marriage (i.e. marriage by ἐγγύη and ἔκδοσις) was to secure for any offspring the rights of succession and citizenship. The προίξ, usually consisting of money or real estate, was a transaction from the bride's father's οἶκος to her husband's οἶκος which provided for her maintenance and succession of property through the female line. J. Modrzejewski, 'La structure juridique du mariage grec', *Scritti in onore di Orsolina Montevecchi* (Bologna 1981), pp.231-68, discusses the areas of continuity and change as Greek marriage evolved from its classical function of providing the citizens for the city-state to its colonial function of preserving Hellenistic culture and identity. A thorough discussion of the changing nature of marriage is also found in G. Häge, *Ehegüterrechtliche Verhältnisse in den griechischen Papyri Ägyptens bis Diokletian* (Köln-Graz 1968). Several aspects of the new φερνή-system can be cited by way of example.

1. Increasingly marriage became an agreement between the spouses. Whereas the family's κύριος had once had control over the arrangement and conditions of marriage, this now gave way to a joint participation of the intending spouses with or without the involvement of their respective κύριοι. Four related changes are also relevant: a) the bride's mother could be involved in the ἔκδοσις; b) a self-ἔκδοσις by the intending wife, though exceptional (e.g. *P. Giss.* I 2 and *P. Oxy.* XLIX 3500 – cf. *P. Dura* 30 outside Egypt), became possible; c) legitimate marriage no longer required a separate act of betrothal or ἐγγύη, a procedure which according to J. Modrzejewski, op. cit., pp.243-7, was also connected with the transfer of κυριεία over the woman; and d) the husband's legal relationship to his wife (i.e. his status as κύριος) was now conceived to be one of guardianship (Häge, op. cit., pp.23-6, and J. Modrzejewski, op. cit., pp.247-58, 264-7).
2. The dowry could be given by a person other than the family's κύριος, e.g. the bride's mother (Häge, op. cit., pp.26-7, and J. Modrzejewski, op. cit., pp.264-5).
3. The bride was conceived as having brought the dowry into the marriage. The dowry was given to the bride who then brought it into the marriage (Häge, op. cit., p.27).
4. The dowry on termination of the marriage was returned to her (rather than to her οἶκος) or in the case of her death belonged to her estate (Häge, op. cit., pp.89-99).
5. The dowry itself was substantially made up of the bride's personal effects (e.g. clothing, jewellery, utensils etc.). Slaves (unless personal servants) and land were excluded from the φερνή (Häge, op. cit., pp.36-62).
6. In the classical law of Athens on the termination of a marriage by the husband's death the wife either a) stayed in her husband's οἶκος (now her son's house) or b) returned to her father's οἶκος or c) changed to another οἶκος altogether by remarriage. From an analysis of 25 testaments H.-A. Rupprecht, 'Zum Ehegattenerbrecht nach den Papyri', *BASP* 36 (1985), pp.291-95, observes a reduction in the wife's options. Indeed, by making particular provision for the wife's continued maintenance through gifts and rights of usufruct[1] most testaments indicate, it is argued, that b) was no longer the viable option that it had once been under classical law. Rupprecht finds in this further evidence for the diminished role of the οἶκος.

In view of these changes Häge concluded that the φερνή-system as practised by the Greeks in Egypt no longer functioned like the προίξ-system of Athens to transfer property[2] through the female line (Häge, op.cit., p.129). Z.M. Packman, 'Return of a Dowry', *P. Coll.Youtie* II (Bonn 1976), p.449, takes an opposing stance. She argues that 'the φερνή of Graeco-Roman Egypt was, like the προίξ of classical Greece, a device for the transmission of family goods through the female line'. For Packman this explains why there are so few receipts for returns of dowries from widows and why in *P. Yale.inv.*1535 a receipt is only issued for

---

1 E.g. *P. Ups.Frid* 1 *ll.*15f. in *New Docs* 6 (1992) §4.

2 See H.-A. Rupprecht, 'Ehevertrag und Erbrecht', *Miscellània Papirològica Ramon Roca-Puig* (Barcelona 1987), pp.307-11. However, note *P. Ups.Frid* 1 and the discussion of *ll.*17-18 in *New Docs* 6 (1992) §4 n.38. The προίξ appears to be distinct from the φερνή, for it was paid on the death of the mother and not on the marriage of the daughter. As such, it represented a monetary payment to a daughter from her mother's estate (i.e. the property which the mother had brought into her marriage) and thus can be described as a testamentary transfer of property through the female line.

the returned παράφερνα. In the case of widows, it is assumed that the majority probably had children and that for this reason property rights would have fallen to their progeny. However, the anomaly observed by Packman (i.e. the paucity of widows' receipts as opposed to receipts of divorced wives) is better explained in terms of the widow's continued maintenance from her husband's estate. Since she did not receive back her dowry but continued to be maintained from her husband's estate, there was no reason for her to issue a receipt.[3] The divorced wife, however, left her husband's house and received back her dowry. The marriage was annulled and the husband no longer had an obligation for her maintenance. In this context the issuing of a receipt for the returned dowry was legally significant, for it indicated the fulfilment of the husband's obligation on the marriage's termination.

Another anomaly might also be mentioned here. It concerns the census-declaration of a child's inherited property by the surviving parent. M. Hombert - Cl. Préaux, *Recherches sur le recensement dans l'Égypte romain* (Leiden 1952), p.61, note that whereas census-declarations by a mother for her children occur (cf. also *SB* XIV 11577), there are no similar declarations by a father for his children. Since there must have been cases where children inherited from their deceased mother, Hombert - Préaux explain the anomaly by the chance survival (or better non-survival) of documents.

In law the dowry was considered to be the husband's property. In reality, however, the issue was not so simple. There are several points to consider: a) on the termination of marriage the husband had to repay the dowry (Häge, op.cit., pp.89-99) – to this end the value of the dowry was always recorded in the marriage settlement (Häge, op.cit., pp.36-40); b) clauses in some marriage settlements conceded a joint dispositional right over the dotal property (Häge, op.cit., pp.65-9); c) other clauses restricted the husband's right of disposal, i.e. the property could be alienated neither to the wife's detriment nor without her guarantee (Häge, op.cit., pp.70-2); and d) the use of certain terms indicates that the dowry remained the wife's property (see Häge, op.cit., pp.72-4, and his discussion of ἀποδιδόναι, ἀπέχειν and στέρεσθαι).

According to Häge, op.cit., pp.75-91, and Modrzejewski, op.cit., pp.261-4, the dowry not only formalised the conjugal bond in a symbolic way but it also played a regulatory role in marriage. It regulated marriage in two ways. First, the dowry was fundamental to the husband's obligation to maintain his wife. In other words, it gave to the married woman some security and right against neglect. Second, in Ptolemaic Egypt and in Alexandria until the end of Augustus' time[4] penalties for breach of contract were based on the value of the dowry. Depending on circumstances the wife might be deprived of her dowry or part thereof (see στέρεσθαι τῆς φερνῆς below) or the husband compelled to repay both the dowry and a 50% penalty.[5] For example, *BGU* IV 1050, an Alexandrian marriage settlement from the time of Augustus, stipulates of the husband:

> τὸν Διονύσιον ἀπεσχηκότα τὴν προκειμένην φερνὴν τρέφειν καὶ ἱματίζειν τὴν Ἰσιδώραν ὡς γυναῖκα γαμετὴν κατὰ δύναμιν καὶ μὴ κακουχεῖν αὐτὴν μήδ' ὑβρίζειν μήδ' ἐγβάλλειν μήδ' ἄλλην γυναῖκα ἐπεισάγειν ἢ ἐκτίνειν τὴν φερνὴν σὺν ἡμιολίᾳ κτλ
>
> **Dionysios having received the aforementioned dowry will maintain and clothe Isidora as a married wife to the best of his ability and will not treat her badly nor insult nor**

---

3 The right of the pregnant wife or wife with children to continued maintenance on the death of her husband is found also at Athens (see D.M. Schaps, *Economic Rights of Women in Ancient Greece* [Edinburgh 1979], p.81) and in Jewish law (see R. Yaron, *Gifts in Contemplation of Death* [Oxford 1960], pp.174-6). The right to maintenance and the right to the payment of her *kethubah* (כתובה) were mutually exclusive alternatives in Jewish law.

4 J. Modrzejewski, op. cit., pp.261-4, argues that the dowry still played a regulatory role in the later period. For divorcing a wife without cause the husband paid the 50% (or 100%) penalty, unless he paid the dowry's value immediately. On the other hand, if a wife initiated the divorce, the simple value of the dowry was returned within a period varying from ten to sixty days. Again, the 50% penalty applied if the dowry was not returned within the prescribed period.

5 In Jewish law a 50% penalty above the value of the dowry also applied. See Yaron, ibid., p.174.

repudiate (her) nor take another wife or he will repay the dowry with half as much again etc.

and of the wife:

τὴν δὲ Ἰσιδώραν μήτε ἀπόκοιτον μήτε ἀφήμερον γείνεσθαι ἀπὸ τῆς Διονυσίου οἰκίας ἄνευ τῆς Διονυσίου γνώμης μηδὲ φθείρειν τὸν οἶκον μήδ' ἄλλῳ ἀνδρὶ συνεῖναι ἢ καὶ αὐτὴν τούτων τι διαπραξαμένην κριθεῖσαν στέρεσθαι τῆς φερνῆς κτλ

Isidora will neither sleep apart nor be absent for a day from Dionysios' house without his knowledge nor will she ruin his house nor live with another man or if she is convicted of doing any such thing she will be deprived of her dowry etc.

Häge, op.cit., pp.132ff., discusses several important changes which occurred to marriage settlements and the dotal system in the Roman period.[6]

a. The dowry was conceived no longer as having been brought into the marriage by the bride but as having been appointed to the husband for his wife, i.e. ἐπὶ τῇ θυγατρί or ἐφ' ἑαυτῇ (pp.139-40).

b. The joint dispositional right of husband and wife was replaced by a restriction on the husband's right to dispose of particular property or by the use of guarantors to secure the dowry (pp.148-160, 177-181).

c. Clauses governing marital duties were simplified, i.e. it was now stated that the married couple should live together blamelessly – συμβιούτωσαν οὖν ἀλλήλοις ἀμέμπτως οἱ γαμοῦντες (pp.160-2). However, some marriage settlements also emphasised the husband's obligation to maintain his wife, e.g. καὶ χορηγείτω ὁ γαμῶν τῇ γαμουμένῃ τὰ δέοντα κατὰ δύναμιν – 'and let the husband furnish his wife with necessities to the best of his ability'.

d. Penalty clauses regarding non-compliance with marital duties (see the examples from *BGU* IV 1050 cited above) were removed from the marriage settlement (pp.160-5). Penalties now only applied in instances where the dowry was not returned within the prescribed period.

e. The parents of either spouse appear to play a more important role in the marriage of their children. For example, there are cases where the husband's parents take part in the marriage settlement (p.133).[7] Also one can cite cases of divorce where the dowry was returned to the wife's parents rather than to the wife herself (pp.167-8).

f. A right of πρωτοπραξία was ceded to the wife. This placed the wife above other creditors in securing the repayment of her dowry (pp.169-70).

g. Marriage settlements began to record a bride's παράφερνα. Consisting of such items as clothing, jewellery etc. the παράφερνα remained the bride's personal property and as such were distinct from the dowry proper (pp.211-23).

h. Marriage settlements also began to record another category of property called the προσφορά. It remained the property of the wife or her parent, but the husband had a right to its usufruct for the duration of the marriage. The προσφορά consisted of such property as land and slaves (pp.250ff.).

i. There was an increased incidence of unwritten marriages, i.e. ἀγράφως συνεῖναι (pp.164-5). On the legal validity of an unwritten marriage and the constitutive role that cohabitation played in marriage see H.J. Wolff, *Written and Unwritten Marriages in Hellenistic and Postclassical Roman Law* (Haverford 1939), pp.48ff. and S. Allam, 'Quelques aspects du mariage dans l'Égypte ancienne', *JEA* 67 (1981), pp.124-5 (cf. also marriage by cohabitation in Roman law).

What was the cause of these numerous changes to Greek marriage in the Roman period? Several of them – **a, b, e, g, h** and **i** – are ascribed by Häge to the influence of Egyptian

---

6 For the use of the dowry under Roman law see J.F. Gardner, *Women in Roman Law and Society* (Beckenham 1986), pp.97-116. The Roman dotal practice is similar to that described above. The dowry was paid by the wife's family to the husband's family as a contribution to her maintenance. It was bound up with the maintenance of social status between families. The dowry was conveyed into the property of the husband or his *pater*; however, it was viewed as part of the wife's patrimony and so possession was similar to a duty of stewardship or right of usufruct (i.e. it remained a charge on the estate). The wife in free marriage remained in the *potestas* of her own family. Therefore, on termination of marriage, whether by death or divorce, the dowry or *dos profecticia* was returned to her family. The husband had no obligation to maintain his divorced wife. She was either maintained by her family or supported by the dowry. However, deductions could be made against the returned dowry (e.g. deductions for expenses incurred in the necessary maintenance of a dotal asset, deductions of 1/5 for each child born of the marriage). A premarital agreement could be made specifying the retentions.

7 As with point **b**, the participation of the husband's parents could have acted to secure the dowry.

custom. See also S. Allam, ibid., pp.125-8, for the influence of Egyptian custom on Greek marital practice in both the Ptolemaic and Roman periods. Of course, Greek custom also exerted an influence on the practices of Egyptian marriage (see below). Be that as it may, many of the changes listed here manifest a degree of coherence among themselves. For example, Häge relates **a** and **b** to changes in the nature of the φερνή and the appearance of the παράφερνα. Since the goods of a more personal nature were now included in the παράφερνα, the dowry was more likely to be seen as a sum handed over for the duration of the marriage to off-set costs (Häge, op.cit., p.180). Other points of coherence can be seen in several other developments. For example, the listing of the παράφερνα and προσφορά in deeds of marriage shows an increased acknowledgement of the wife's independent property rights, just as the right of πρωτοπραξία, the restriction on the husband's right to dispose of property and the use of guarantors secured her claim over the dowry itself.

P. Mich. XV 700 (reproduced below) illustrates several aspects of Greek marriage in the Roman period. In particular it is worth noting that: a) all penalty clauses are absent from the settlement; b) the dowry appears to be given for the bride, though one hastens to observe that the reading is not secure at this point; and c) the expression of marital duties is simplified. Since the bride acts with a *kyrios* who is not her father, it is reasonable to conjecture that her father was already dead. Also it will be noted that though the matter was transacted through a bank and Chairemonis acted with a *kyrios*, the arrangement was between the spouses themselves.

Oxyrhynchus ? 5 Nov. AD 143

Ed.pr. – P.J. Sijpesteijn, 'Marriage Contract in the Form of a Bank Diagraphe (*P. Mich. inv.* 6551)', *ZPE* 34 (1979), pp.119-122 (= *P. Mich.* XV 700 [Zutphen 1982], pp.30-2).

The papyrus sheet measures 18.5 x 10.0 cm. The text is described as 'extremely difficult to read on account of the many holes and abrasion'. Below the last line 10 cm of papyrus are left blank.

[᾿Αντίγραφον διαγραφῆς] ἀπὸ τῆ̣ς̣ . . [τραπέζης]	[A copy of the *diagraphe*] from the .. [bank]
[± 15 letters ἔτου]ς̣ ζ Αὐτοκράτ[ορος]	[*name of banker* in year] 7 of Imperat[or]
[Καίσαρος Τίτου Αἰλί]ου ῾Αδρ̣[ι]α̣ν̣οῦ ᾿Αν̣τ̣[ωνίνου]	[Caesar Titus Aelius] Hadrianus Ant[oninus]
[Σεβαστοῦ Εὐσεβοῦς] ῾Α̣θὺρ η̄ Χαιρημ̣ο̣[νὶ]ς̣	[Augustus Pius], in the month of Hathyr 8, Chairemon[is],
[(name of father) τοῦ] Σ̣ω[κ]ράτους μ̣ε̣τὰ κυρίο̣υ̣ [τοῦ ἑαυ-]	[daughter of N, son of] Socrates, with [her]
[τῆς συγγενοῦς Σ]αραπίωνος τ̣[ο]ῦ̣ Σεύθου Πασίω̣ν[ι]	[relative] Sarapion, son of Seuthes, acting as guardian, to Pasion,
[(name of father) ἀπέ]χ̣ε̣ι̣ν α̣ὐ̣τὸν̣ π̣α̣ρὰ τῆ̣ς̣ Χαιρημ̣ον[ί]δο[ς]	[son of N]. (It is acknowledged ?) that he has received from Chairemonis
[φερ]νὴν [ἐφ'] ἑ̣α̣υ̣τῇ̣ ἀ̣ργ(υρίου) (δραχμὰς) τεσσαράκοντα	[as dowry for] herself forty silver drachmae
[καὶ] κιτῶ̣νος λευκοῦ δραχμὰς εἴκοσι· κ[αὶ]	[and] twenty drachmae of white fabric. [And]
[συμ]β̣ι̣ώ̣σ̣ουσι ἀ̣λλήλοις τ̣ο̣ῦ Πασίωνος ἐπιχορη-	they will live [with] one another, with Pasion supplying
[γο]ῦ̣ντο̣ς̣ α̣ὐ̣τῇ̣ τὰ̣ δέοντα̣ π̣άντα κα[ὶ] τ̣ὸν ἱμα-	her with all necessities and clothing

[τισ]μὸν ὡ̣ς̣ ἐ̣π̣ὶ̣ [γ]υ̣ν̣α̣ικὶ γαμ̣ε̣[τ]ῇ	as for a married wife
κατὰ δύναμιν τοῦ	according to the capacity of his
β[ί]ο̣υ· καὶ ἐ̣π̣ὶ̣ τ̣οῦ χωρισ̣μοῦ	livelihood. And in the case of divorce
ἀπο̣δώσει ὁ Πα-	Pasion will return
σ̣ί̣ω̣[ν] τῇ Χαιρ̣η̣μονίδι τὴν προκιμένην	to Chairemonis the aforementioned
φερνήν,	dowry
τὸ[ν] δ̣ὲ̣ κιτ̣ῶ̣ν̣α̣ ἐν τῇ ἴσῃ διατιμήσει.	and fabric to the same assessed value.

....

9 χιτῶνος 14 προκειμένην 15 χιτῶνα

P. Mich. XV 700 was a receipt in the form 'A to B; B has received from A' issued through a bank – the banker's name is now lost as also is the word 'bank' itself. It also constituted the agreement according to which the payment was made. In it a receipt and description of the dowry is given; the parties agree to live together; the husband promises to maintain his wife and on divorce to return the dowry to her. As such the document must be classified as a *selbständige Diagraphe*.[8] Sijpesteijn, op.cit., p.119, states that to the best of his knowledge a marriage settlement in this form is otherwise unattested.

Deeds of divorce show a similar twofold function of receipt and agreement, though in mirror image to *P. Mich.* XV 700. In other words, a receipt was issued for the returned dowry and by agreement the marriage was declared to have ended. H.-A. Rupprecht, *Studien zur Quittung im Recht der graeco-ägyptischen Papyri* (Munich 1971), pp.43-51, analyses the following formal elements in such deeds of divorce:

a. the agreement that the marriage is at an end;
b. the permission to remarry;
c. the confirmation of the dowry's return (and return of other property);
d. the declaration that the written marriage settlement is void.

There was, however, considerable variation between such deeds. Special clauses could also be added, e.g. the agreement of each party not to proceed against the other and the specification of penalties for breach of agreement.

Greek and Egyptian Matrimony

The Egyptian dowry was an alimentation capital paid to the husband for the maintenance of his wife. In consideration of this capital the husband made yearly payments (in cash and/or in grain) to his wife and pledged his own property as a guarantee of it (Häge, op.cit., pp.104-6, and P.W. Pestman, *Marriage and Matrimonial Property in Ancient Egypt* [Leiden 1961], pp.115-7, 133-6 and 143-150 – on Type B) and C) marriages see pp.32-50). As such it differed considerably from the Greek dowry and offered greater security to the wife. The wife's maintenance was based on the sum paid rather than on the husband's ability to pay as in the Greek dowry (Häge, op.cit., pp.107-8). For the Greeks who lacked a similar custom the Egyptian dowry resembled a loan made to the husband and was so described by them, e.g.

---

[8] For a full discussion of the *diagraphe* see P. Drewes, 'Die Bankdiagraphe in den gräko-ägyptischen Papyri', *JJP* 18 (1974), pp.115-119. According to H.J. Wolff, *Das Recht der griechischen Papyri Ägyptens* (Munich 1978), pp.95-105, the *diagraphe* developed from being no more than a copy of the bank's entry (=*unselbständige Diagraphe* – the actual transaction was documented by another instrument, i.e. *syngraphe*, *synchoresis* or *cheirographon* as at *P. Turner* 17 *l*.13 in *New Docs* 6 [1992] §14) to its becoming an instrument documenting both the bank's procedure and the transaction itself (=*selbständige Diagraphe* as in the above example). The development appears to have occurred spontaneously (i.e. without governmental legislation to judge from regional differences) at the end of the first century AD. For this reason Wolff (p.105) advises caution in accepting a usage of the *diagraphe* outside Egypt itself.

δάνειον in *P. Tebt.* II 386 (12 BC) and δεδανεικέναι in *P. Tor.* 13 (136 or 83 BC) – see also Häge, op.cit., pp.108-125. However, there was no distinct term used in Greek to denote the Egyptian dowry itself. Like the Greek dowry, it was also called φερνή. However, a formal differentiation was made between their respective standards of valuation. The Greek dowry, which was paid in silver drachmae, was called an ἀργυρικὴ φερνή. The Egyptian alimentation capital, the value of which was stated in *deben* (χρυσοῖ), was called instead a χρυσικὴ φερνή (Häge, op.cit., pp.191-2).

Though the Greek and Egyptian dotal systems influenced each other, they continued to exist side by side as functionally distinct institutions (see Häge, op.cit., pp.188 and 206-7). In particular, the Egyptian dowry retained its function as an alimentation capital secured by the husband's property and promising fixed maintenance payments to the wife. No doubt, custom and the greater legal freedom and financial security afforded the female were the reasons for its continued use.[9] But that is not to say that individuals did not seek to use both systems.[10] For example, parties to some Egyptian marriage settlements give their origin as Greek (Pestman, op.cit., p.169). In *P. Mich.* II 121 recto II ii (AD 42) which is an abstract of an Egyptian deed of maintenance or συγγραφὴ τροφῖτις, both an Egyptian alimentation capital valued at 21 χρυσοῖ (= 420 silver drachmae) and a Greek dowry valued at 200 silver drachmae were paid (Häge, op.cit., pp.183-5). Also the entries in the *grapheion* register *P. Mich.* II 121 verso XII *ll.*3-4 (AD 42) and the text of *P. Mich.* V 340 recto I/II (AD 45-6) show that parties could execute two deeds, an Egyptian συγγραφὴ τροφῖτις and a συγγραφὴ Ἑλληνική (Häge, op.cit., pp.188-91). Alternatively, an Egyptian might only execute a Greek marriage.[11] A Greek marriage was usually written in the form of a ὁμολογία or acknowledgement between the parties. In making a Greek deed it was usual for an Egyptian to assume the fictitious designation of Πέρσης, τῆς ἐπιγονῆς (Häge, op.cit., p.198);[12] more generally the designation indicated that the party obligated by an agreement (e.g. the lessee, the borrower, the

---

9 See Pestman, op.cit., pp.151-4, 162-4 and 182-4, on the legal freedom of Egyptian women to own and to deal in property without a guardian. In time the freedom was lost under Greek influence and Egyptian women began to act with a κύριος. For an evaluation of the economic penalty entailed in divorce and the protection afforded the wife see S. Allam, op.cit., pp.119-124, and Pestman, op.cit., pp.155-160.

10 The dispute between Dionysia (a Greek given in marriage by ἔκδοσις) and her father Chairemon (a former gymnasiarch) indicates the degree to which Egyptian laws might apply more generally to Greeks living in the *chora.* H.J. Wolff, *Written and Unwritten Marriages*, p.64, observes on the dispute: 'It is precisely *P. Oxy.* II 237 that shows the extent to which Greek and Egyptian elements had fused in one Greco-Egyptian common law; we find the Greek institution of *ekdosis* in closest connection with the application of rules of native origin'.

11 There were several institutions of private law in operation from the Ptolemaic period. See H.J. Wolff, 'Plurality of Laws in Ptolemaic Egypt', *RIDA* 7 (1960), pp.191-223, for a discussion of their development. The language in which the deed was written determined the legal institution to which it was subject. Parties could thus avail themselves of the institution which best suited their interests by the choice of the deed's language. The decree of Euergetes II (*P. Tebt.* I 5 *ll.*207-220 dated 118 BC) is important in the discussion of this issue for the Ptolemaic period. For a criticism of the decree's interpretation see J. Modrzejewski, 'Chrématistes et laocrites' in *Le monde grec* (Brussels 1975), pp.699-708. The coexistence of parallel legal institutions continued into the Roman period as well. Wolff (p.194) observes of the Roman period: 'all the peregrine institutions of private law, irrespective of their Egyptian or Greek origin, were equally available to all the peregrine inhabitants of the country'.

12 For a discussion of the meaning of Πέρσης, τῆς ἐπιγονῆς in documents of the Ptolemaic period see J.F. Oates, *The Status Designation:* Πέρσης, τῆς ἐπιγονῆς (*YCS* XVIII, 1962). In the earlier period, he argues, τῆς ἐπιγονῆς indicated that the person was a civilian and Πέρσης that the person had some claim to Greek status but lacked a specific ethnic. In the later period, the expression Πέρσης, τῆς ἐπιγονῆς indicated a hellenizing Egyptian. P.W. Pestman, 'A proposito dei documenti di Pathyris II: Πέρσαι τῆς ἐπιγονῆς', *Aegyptus* 43 (1963), pp.15-53 and *P. L. Bat.* XXII (Leiden 1982), pp.56-63, argues instead for the expression's military provenance. Formerly it had designated a person as the 'son of a soldier' and thus as a possible recruit to active service. However, from the beginning of the first century BC the designation was assumed by debtors as a legal fiction in Greek deeds.

vendor or in the case of marriage the husband etc.) became ἀγώγιμος or liable to seizure of his person and without rights of asylum. Its socio-economic effect was that the creditor was provided with greater security in his dealings with the debtor class. In the case of marriage the designation secured the wife's claim to her dowry. But why would an Egyptian wish to contract a Greek marriage? Häge, op.cit., pp.187 and 195, suggests two reasons: a) the desire to assimilate to the practices of the ruling and socially higher stratum of society; and b) the prevalence of mixed marriages and the desire of parties to retain their own customs.

Another feature that Häge comments on is the supplementary raising or πρόσδοσις of the Greek dowry. The discussion centres on *P. Mich.* V 340 recto I/II (cited above). In that case Häge, op.cit., pp.189-91 and 193, argues that both an Egyptian and a Greek dowry were paid and that the supplement to the Greek dowry brought its value up to par with that of the Egyptian dowry. One document in the material culled for 1980/81 appears to concern such a supplementary increase of a Greek dowry. As with *P. Mich.* XV 700 reproduced above, it will be noted that the deed acknowledges a transaction between the spouses themselves.

Tebtunis? AD 59/60

Ed.pr. – B. Frid, *P. Ups.Frid* 2 (Bonn 1981), pp.21-30.

Only the left side of eight lines from the beginning of the deed survive. Half of each line is lost. The sheet measures 8.2 x 36 cm and shows 13 folds. Portions of the text reconstructed by the editor in his commentary have been added.

	Ἀντίγραφον ὁμολο̣γίας γάμου.	Copy of an agreement of marriage.
	(ἔτους) ϛ̄ Νέρωνος Κλαυδίου	(In year) 6 of Nero Claudius
	Καίσα̣ρος Σεβαστοῦ Γερμανικοῦ	Caesar Augustus Germanicus
	Αὐ̣τοκ̣ράτο[ρ]ο̣ς μη[νὸς Καισαρείου	Imperator, in the month [of Caesareion
	κᾱ ἐν Τεβτύνει τῆς Πολέμωνος	21, in Tebtunis of the district of
	μερίδος τοῦ Ἀρσινοΐτου νομοῦ	Polemon of the Arsinoite nome
	ἐπὶ Ἰουλίας]	(as though) before Julia]
2	Σεβαστῆς. Ὁμολογεῖ Κρο[[.]]νίων	Augusta. Kronion, son of
	Πετεσούχου Πέρσης τῆς ἐπιγονῆς	Petesouchus, Persian of the descent,
	ὡς ἐτῶν πεντήκ̣οντα μέ[σο]ς	aged about fifty years, medium (height),
	μελίχ̣ρως μα̣[κροπρόσωπος	honey skin, [large face,
	εὐθύρ̣ινος οὐλὴ πήχει δεξιῶι τῆι	straight-nosed, scar to right forearm,
	ἑαυτοῦ γυναικὶ Θαήσει τοῦ N ὡς	acknowledges to his wife, Thaesis,
	ἐτῶν]	daughter of N, aged about]
	τεσσαράκοντα ἐννέα μέσηι μελίχρωι̣	forty-nine [years], medium (height), honey
	μακροπροσώπωι εὐθύρινι οὐλῆι	skin, large face, straight-nosed, scar in
	γεν̣είωι μέσωι μετὰ κ[υρ]ίου τοῦ	the middle of her chin, with her
	ἑ̣[α]υ̣τῆς σ̣[υγγενοῦς N τοῦ N ὡς	[kinsman N, son of N, aged about X
	ἐτῶν .. μέσου μελιχρώου]	years, medium (height), honey skin,]
4	μακροπροσώπου εὐθύρεινο̣ς οὐλῆι	large face, straight-nosed, scar to his left
	μήλωι ἀρ̣ιστερῶι ἔχειν παρ' αὐτῆς	cheek, acting as guardian, that he has
	ἐν προσδ̣όσει διὰ χειρ̣[ὸς ἐξ οἴκου]	received from her in cash X silver
	ἀργυρί[ου δραχμὰς .. ἧς ὁ Κρονίων	[drachmae] in addition to the other
	εἴληφε παρὰ τῆς Θαήσεως ἐφ'	dowry [which Kronion has received
	ἑαυτῆι]	from Thaesis for herself]

	ἑτέρας φερνῆς κατὰ συνγραφὴν	in accord with the Egyptian
	Αἰγυπτίαν τροφεῖτιν	agreement of maintenance
	τετελειωμένην ἐν τοῖς ἔ[μ]προσθεν	executed formerly
	[χρόνοις διὰ τοῦ αὐτοῦ	[through the same
	γραφείου ± 88]	office ...]
6	ἣν καὶ συγχωροῦσι ἀμφότεροι ὅ τε	which they also agree, both
	Κρονίων καὶ ἡ Θαῆ[σι]ς κυρίαν	Kronion and Thaesis, to be and to
	εἶναι καὶ μ[ένει]ν καθό[τι	[remain] valid just as
	γέγραπται ± 77]	[written ...]
	τοῦ Κρονίωνος ἐπιχωρηγοῦν[τος	Kronion providing
	αὐτῆι πάντα τὰ δέοντα καὶ	[her with all necessities,
	ἱματισμὸν καὶ τὰ ἄλλα ὅσα καθήκει	clothing and other objects which are
	γυναικὶ γαμετῆι κατὰ δύναμιν τοῦ	fitting for a married woman according to
	βίου ...]	the capacity of his livelihood ...]
8	ἐν τοῖς κ. [...]	in the [...]

....

3 οὐλή   4 εὐθύρινος, οὐλή   5 συγγραφήν, τροφῖτιν   7 ἐπιχορηγοῦντος

P. Ups.Frid 2 is yet another example of the influence of differing customs on marital practice. On the one hand, Kronion acknowledges the receipt of a supplementary increase to a Greek dowry (the referent of ἑτέρας φερνῆς in *l.*5). Two considerations lead the editor to this conclusion: a) the present deed is in the form of a ὁμολογία (*l.*2 but especially the heading Ἀντίγραφον ὁμολογίας γάμου at *l.*1); and b) the dowry was apparently valued in silver (*l.*4). Despite the fact that the dowry itself is not referred to as the ἑτέρας ἀργυρικῆς φερνῆς (cf. *P. Mich.*V 339 *l.*5), it is argued that its valuation in silver can be inferred from the supplement. On the other hand, the Egyptian element of the document cannot be ignored. In particular, it is noted that the original deed was a συγγραφὴ τροφῖτις (*l.*5). Also, like other Egyptian parties to a Greek deed Kronion bears the ethnic Πέρσης τῆς ἐπιγονῆς (*l.*2). It thus appears that the συγγραφὴ τροφῖτις of Kronion and Thaesis originally included the payment of both an Egyptian and Greek dowry (as with *P. Mich.* II 121 recto II ii cited above) and that *P. Ups.Frid* 2 represents a supplement to this latter payment.

Marriage or Divorce?

We turn now to a discussion of the papyrus which heads this present entry. The use of the term κόλλημα in *ll.*13-15 and of the number 39 in *l.*29 of *P. Amst.* 40 tell us that the document was probably an extract from the records of the βιβλιοθήκη ἐγκτήσεων or Registry of Real Property.[13] But what circumstance would have required the taking of the extract? If the answer to this question were known, then some light might be thrown on the relationship between columns I and II of the document. The reconstruction of the papyrus' context is difficult, a task not helped by its mutilated condition. Nevertheless, the editors make the following suggestions:

[13] The term κόλλημα was employed to describe each papyrus sheet inserted in the official τόμος. For example, each census-declaration occupied a sheet of papyrus which when submitted to the authorities was glued to other census-declarations to form a τόμος. See M. Hombert - Cl. Préaux, *Recherches sur le recensement dans l'Égypte romain* (Leiden 1952), pp.132-5; also Taubenschlag, *Law*, pp.222ff. *P. Amst.*40 was an extract from such a τόμος.

i. The missing portion at the top of the first column and *ll.*1-5 concern the consent of Bacchylos' wife and sister Thaisous, alias Didymarion, to the transaction.
ii. Bacchylos and his wife had obtained from Heron, Ninnous' father, unsecured loans. They now refund the loans, pay his daughter's dowry and make a gift of a parcel of building land.
iii. The transaction appears to have been between Bacchylos and Ninnous' husband, Didymos (see τῇ γυναικὶ αὐτοῦ *ll.*20-21).
iv. Heron, the father of Ninnous, was probably dead since Bacchylos provides the dowry.
v. Ninnous was probably a citizen of Alexandria (see *l.*23).

Ninnous was given in marriage (ἐγδεδομένη *l.*8) with a dowry valued in silver (φερνὴ ἀρ[γυριοῦ] or perhaps ἀρ[γυρικὴ *l.*12 ?). These considerations indicate that the marriage was Greek. The difficulty for the editor's construction lies in the relationship between Bacchylos and Ninnous. How is one to construe a relationship which involved the extending of unsecured loans and the giving of a dowry? Indeed, it is not even clear whether Bacchylos is the subject of the finite verbs in *ll.*23-25. Several further observations can be made.

a. In the absence of a father the obligation to provide a woman's dowry fell to her nearest male relatives, e.g. brothers, paternal uncles etc. Thus in *SB* XIV 11575 (third-century AD), Aurelius Hatres writes to Aurelia Apia that he will provide her daughter with a φερνίκουλον (note the use of the Latin diminutive ending). The ed. pr., *ZPE* 21 (1976), pp.26-7, observes: 'It is not a rich dowry, and one may suppose that Apia is a woman living in modest circumstances for whom Hatres, possibly in view of a close family relationship, has thought it his duty to facilitate the marriage of her daughter.' In the case of *P. Amst.* 40 it may also be assumed that Bacchylos was a close relative of Ninnous.

b. In the above discussion of the Greek dowry we observed that the husband could be restricted in his right to dispose of particular property and that this acted as a form of security against the dowry. If the dowry were composed, in part at least, of restricted property, does this explain the assumed need for Thaisous' consent? I do not think so. First, it is not clear whether the lost lines at the beginning of the document do indeed speak of her giving consent. To all intents and purposes, the first column of *P. Amst.* 40 appears to be the summary of part of a marriage settlement. Indeed, the text may have read: 'from Bacchylos and Thaisous ... to Ninnous ... for marriage a dowry of X silver drachmae etc.' A comparison with the marriage settlement *CPR* 27 (= *MChr* 289) is informative:

ἔχειν τὸν Ἰσίδωρον παρὰ τοῦ Π[ασίωνος] τοῦ καὶ Ἰσιδώρου [ἐπὶ τῇ ἐπιτροπευομένῃ αὐτοῦ Θαισ]αρίῳ [Ἡρ]ακλείδου παρ[θ]ένῳ οὔσῃ συνερχομ[ένῃ αὐτ]ῷ πρὸς γάμον φερ[νὴν χρυσ]οῦ μνα[ιαῖα τρία] κτλ

Isidoros (acknowledges) that he has received from Pasion, also called Isidoros, for his ward Thaisarion, daughter of Herakleides, being a maiden and being united with him in marriage, a dowry of [three] gold minae etc.

It thus appears likely that Bacchylos and his wife both gave the dowry. Second, the fact that Thaisous is at the same time Bacchylos' sister and therefore shared the same relationship to Ninnous seems to offer a more coherent reason for her participation here.

c. The editors, apparently aided by the use of ἑκουσίως in *l.*18, conclude that the 9th part of a 1/2 share in building blocks was additional to the repayment of the loans and therefore a gift. However, two points suggest that this may not be the case. First, the use of πρὸς ἃ ὀφείλι (= in respect of, for)[14] rather than πρὸς οἷς ὀφείλι (= in addition to) implies that the part share in the building blocks constituted a repayment. Second, ἑκουσίως can occur with reference to a loan repayment made before its due date, e.g. *P. Oxy.* VIII 1132: ὁμ[ολογῶ] ἀπέχειν παρὰ σοῦ ἀποδιδ[ό]ντο[ς ἑκου]σίως πρὸ προθεσμί[α]ς κτλ – 'I acknowledge that I have received from you repaying willingly before the appointed time

14 See *P. Köln* III 147 *l.*8 and *P. Turner* 18 *l.*14.

etc.' We may tentatively conclude that the part share in the building blocks was used to repay the unsecured loans.

d. Since the pronoun αὐτοῦ (*ll.*20-1) needs an antecedent, Didymos (i.e. Ninnous' husband) and not Bacchylos may well have taken out the loans which he now repays before their due date. A clear advantage arises from this interpretation of column II, namely, both columns now concern financial obligations (i.e. a dowry and unsecured loans) owed by Didymos to Ninnous. In turn this offers a better point of connection between the two columns.

e. The adverb ἑκουσίως gives no clear indication of what type of document is involved. It is used (often in conjunction with αὐθαιρέτως) in leases (e.g. *BGU* XII 2133), variations of lease (e.g. due to a natural disaster – *P. Oslo* 3), oaths (e.g. *BGU* XIII 2245), guarantees (e.g. *SB* XII 10786 and XIV 11548), divisions of property (e.g. *P. Oslo* 31), the selection of a woman's κύριος (e.g. *SB* I 2133), receipts (see *P. Oxy.* VIII 1132 above) and divorces (e.g. *P. Mich.* V 340). Only the last two uses appear applicable in the present context. As column I concerns marriage, priority of consideration might be given to the suggestion that column II deals with divorce. Divorce in the Roman period was either by ἀποπομπή (if initiated by the husband) or ἑκουσία ἀπαλλαγή (if initiated by the wife), e.g. *P. Ryl.* 154 (see further Häge, op.cit., pp.165-7):

ἐὰν δὲ διαφορᾶς αὐτοῖς γεναμένης [χ]ωρίζονται ἀπ' ἀλλήλων, ἤτοι τοῦ Χαιρήμονος ἀποπέμποντος τ[ὴ]ν Θαισάριον ἢ καὶ αὐτῆς ἑκουσίω[ς ἀ]παλλασσαμέν[η]ς [ἀ]π' αὐτοῦ κτλ

if a difference arise and they separate from one another either by Chairemon's sending Thaisarion away or her willingly releasing herself from him etc.

Problems arise with the suggestion of divorce. First, its viability rests in part on the fragmentary nature of *l.*17, i.e. it is unclear whether ἀπαλλασσαμένη actually occurs. Second, the expression in question (i.e. ἑκουσίως ἀπαλλασσαμένη) occurs in deeds of marriage rather than deeds of divorce. Also the post-positioning of the adverb, as required here, is unusual. Third, it is unclear what part in the deed of divorce column II would play, e.g. it cannot be Ninnous' receipt for her dowry for several reasons: the loans appear to have been made to Didymos before Heron's death and thus before his marriage to Ninnous; the property is not such as would be contained in a dowry; column II does not conform to the *cheirographon* form, i.e. it cannot be a receipt issued by Ninnous to Didymos. Fourth, there is a grammatical difficulty. A reading of ἀπαλλασσαμένη in *l.*17 requires that its subject not be specified till *l.*20.

What of the other possibility? The first point to be made is that column II cannot be a receipt in the form of a *cheirographon* from Ninnous to Didymos. The dative case of Ninnous shows as much. The most probable form is that of the bank *diagraphe* where the name of the debtor is in the nominative case and the name of the creditor or receiver of the payment is in the dative. See further P. Drewes, 'Die Bankdiagraphe in den gräko-ägyptischen Papyri', *JJP* 18 (1974), p.98. However, again the suggestion meets with difficulties. First, according to the usual form of the *diagraphe* the designation of the document as a *diagraphe* of X's bank follows the date. In *l.*17 the date of the document is given as Thoth 30. However, in the remaining portion of *l.*17 there is neither room for nor are the surviving traces of the letters consistent with a designation of the bank. Second, the cancellation of the loans is described as occurring in his house (*ll.*25-6) rather than through a bank. For these reasons the form of column II must remain problematic.

Despite these formal difficulties, the contents of column II present themselves as a statement by the debtor (necessarily in the objective form due to the use of the third person) that he has repaid the loans owed to Ninnous. An action to occasion the issuing of such a statement might conceivably be Ninnous' making of a complaint against her former husband, Didymos (e.g. *P. Oxy.* II 281-282 dated AD 20-50 and AD 30-35 respectively).

Jewish and Christian Marriage

The above discussion provides an interesting background against which to assess the treatment of marriage in the NT and in Paul in particular. A preliminary caution, however, is necessary. In antiquity different legal systems ran in parallel and each could and did exert an influence on the other. The evolving nature of Greek marriage and the influence of parallel legal traditions and social customs on it has already been described. A similar phenomenon can also be observed in the case of Jewish marriage. For example, the influence of non-Jewish practice is attested to in the right of the wife to initiate divorce (see below). The editors of *P. Colon.* XII, a *kethubah* (כתובה) or Jewish deed of marriage dated AD 417, also point to several areas of convergence between this deed and Greek marriage in Egypt (see especially p.13 and the relevant lines in the commentary). Indeed, we find that Greek law may be referred to in the Jewish deed of marriage itself (e.g. *P. Yadin* 18 *ll.*16, 51 of AD 128). Again, non-Jewish courts could even be used to exert duress on a recalcitrant husband, e.g. *m. Git.*9.8. Added to this factor is the further complication that Jewish marital practice was itself evolving during the period under discussion. M.A. Friedman, *Jewish Marriage in Palestine* (New York 1980), p.8, comments that the crystallisation of its *halakah* only occurred during the Tannaitic period and even then two separate traditions (i.e. the Palestinian and Babylonian traditions) emerged. Several changes in Jewish marriage may be noted.

a. In the OT the father gave his daughter in betrothal (e.g. Gen.34.12; Ex.22.16-7; 1Sam.18.25; Tobit 7.12-14). The Mishnah continued to affirm the father's *potestas* over his minor daughter – see *m. Ket.*4.4 and J.R. Wegner, *Chattel or Person? The Status of Women in the Mishnah* (Oxford 1988), pp.20-39. In particular, note the references at *m. Ned.*11.10 and *m. Yeb.* 13.6 to a father's betrothing of his daughter whilst still a minor. A similar *potestas* over the minor son was also assumed, e.g. *m. Ket.* 9.9 and *Mek. Nez.* 3. However, both the son betrothed as a minor (*m. Ket.* 9.9) and the daughter betrothed as a minor by her mother or brother (*m. Yeb.* 13.1, 2 and *t. Yeb.* 13.1) could repudiate the contract. What of the minor daughter betrothed by her father? Though the *kethubah* itself was addressed as a unilateral proposal by the groom to his bride (e.g. see *m. Qid.* 2.1, 3.2, *P. Colon.* XII *ll.*6-7), betrothal became more an agreement between them, the father waiting till his minor daughter was old enough to declare her mind. At twelve and a half years (plus one day) a girl was emancipated and could then marry at will. On the subjects of consent, proposal and acceptance in marriage see Friedman, ibid., pp.131-61, 179-81, 216-7. There was also a decline in the use of levirate and polygamous[15] marriage and corresponding changes in *ḥaliṣah* (חליצה – on this procedure see *m. Yeb.* 12.6). See further Z.W. Falk, *Introduction to Jewish Law of the Second Commonwealth* (Leiden 1978), vol.2, pp.317-22.

b. The *mohar* (מהר) or bride price[16] paid by the bridegroom to the bride's father was replaced by the *kethubah* (also known as the פורנא = φερνή) or bill obliging the sum's payment (on

[15] Deut.17.17 (applied more generally) was important in the argument against polygamy. See, for example, *CD* 4.19-5.5, *y. Sanh.*2.6 (reproduced in part at *New Docs* 6 [1992] §5) and D. Daube, 'Violence to the Kingdom', *The New Testament and Rabbinic Judaism* (New York 1973), pp.297-300.

[16] Since tradition and scholarship support an Egyptian provenance for much of the LXX, a question arises concerning its understanding of the dowry. The first point to note is that the term προίξ does not appear in the LXX itself. The term φερνή, however, does appear and is used to describe the *mohar* (מהר) or bride price (Gen.34.12, Ex.22.16-7). On one occasion *mohar* is translated by δόμα (1Sam.18.25). The *mohar*, however, is a different procedure from the φερνή of Ptolemaic Egypt, for it is paid by the husband to his father-in-law and not vice versa. Gifts were made to the Hebrew bride by her father on marriage and by way of inheritance (Gen.31.15, Jos.15.18-20, 1Kings 9.16, Tob.8.21) but there is no one term to describe them. There are only two occasions when the LXX uses φερνή as a payment by the father of the bride to her husband (Jos.16.10 and 2Macc.1.14).

divorce or death) to the wife and secured by a pledge over the husband's property (cf. *P. Yadin* 18 *ll.*16-19; 21 *ll.*11-12).[17] Jewish law set a minimum amount. The pledge assured the payment of the agreed sum, also called *kethubah* (the term denoted both the deed and the agreed sum), to the wife but she stood behind other creditors of the estate (*m. Git.* 5.1-3; cf. the wife's right to πρωτοπραξία in the Graeco-Roman law of Egypt). Like the dowry in Ptolemaic Egypt, the *kethubah* was used to penalise the spouse who was either at fault or initiated the divorce (e.g. *m. Ket.* 5.7, 7.6, *t. Ket.* 12.1).

c. In the OT period, there had been a separation between the husband's and wife's property. This changed under Greek influence according to E. Bickerman ('Two Legal Interpretations of the Septuagint', *RIDA* III [1956] = *Studies in Jewish and Christian History* [Leiden 1976], pp.201-215). The bride now brought property into the marriage either as *ṣon barzel* (צאן ברזל) or *melog* (מלוג). The *ṣon barzel* property was valued (*m. Ket.* 6.3) and recorded either in the *kethubah* itself or in addition to it and became the property of the husband. On divorce either the property itself or the amount of its valuation was returned to the wife. The *melog* property (usually immovable property), however, remained the property of the bride or her father and was not recorded in the *kethubah*. The husband, however, had right of usufruct of this property but was neither responsible for any loss nor benefited from any increase in its value. On the husband's rights over property acquired by the wife after marriage see *m.Ket.*8.1. Concerning the *kethubah* and dowry see further Friedman, op.cit., 239-311 and M. Gil, 'Land Ownership in Palestine under Roman Rule', *RIDA* 17 (1970), pp.25-29. On divorce the total amount (*kethubah* + dowry) was paid to the wife. On the predecease of the husband there were two possible courses of action: the widow could either be provided for out of his estate, in which case she did not receive her *kethubah*, or she could return to her father's house (or remarry) and seek her *kethubah* (*DJD* II 116, *m. 'Ed.* 1.12, *t. 'Ed.* 1.6, *m. Ket.* 4.12, 12.3-4; also Friedman, op.cit., pp.427-43). The wife did not inherit from her husband. Where a husband died without heirs his property went either to the levir or to his father and agnates, *m. Yeb.*4.7. On the other hand, the husband might inherit from his wife if she died childless (*m. B.Bat.*8.1, *m. Ket.* 9.1 and *b. Ket.* 84a). However, as this constituted a clear loss to the bride's family, stipulations in the deed of marriage tended to regulate this contingency (cf. *m. Yeb.*4.3; see also Friedman, op.cit., pp.391-418). Where a wife had surviving children, they inherited from her.

d. There was a change in the terminology of marriage. In the OT the concept of 'acquisition' described the husband's function in marriage. The husband paid the *mohar* and was said to have acquired his wife (קנה – Ruth 4.5, 10). The transaction could also be likened to a sale (מכר – Gen.31.15). Thus the husband became his wife's master (בעל – Gen.20.3, Deut.21.13, 22.22, 24.1; see also E.G. Kraeling, *Brooklyn Aramaic Papyri* 2.4, 7.4, A. Cowley, *Aramaic Papyri* 15.4) and she could be listed among his possessions (Ex.20.17).[18] Though the rabbis could still speak of the woman as 'acquired' like other

---

Both uses are peculiar in that they involve gentile marriages (Pharaoh and Antiochus). The mention of the dowry in LXX Jos.16.10 has no direct parallel in the MT but does parallel 1Kings 9.16 and is called שלחים, i.e. 'that which is sent off'. It is also of interest to note that these dowries comprise money (2Macc.1.14) and land (Jos.16.10), i.e. items which did not usually form part of the φερνή of Ptolemaic Egypt.

17 The change from the actual payment of a bride price to the bride's father (*mohar*) to an obligation to pay the sum on divorce or death (*kethubah*) is found in Egyptian marriages also – see Type A) marriages in P.W. Pestman, *Marriage and Matrimonial Property in Ancient Egypt* (Leiden 1961), pp.15-20 and 108-114. Pestman identifies three stages in this development: a) the sum was handed to the father of the bride by the bridegroom; b) the sum was handed to the bride; and c) the sum is paid fictitiously and only on the dissolution of the marriage. The intervening stage (dated approx. 230 BC) is significant. It shows marriage to be an agreement between the spouses themselves. Stage c) seems then to follow from the nature of property rights within marriage.

18 How literally should the terminology be taken? It appears that Hebrew tradition grappled with the description of marriage and in many cases opted for the commercial language of sale. But the wife was not like other property. The husband could not sell her and if he wished to divorce her, he had to release her to herself, i.e free

property (see *m. Qid.* 1.1-6 and J.R. Wegner, op.cit., pp.42-5), there was nevertheless a shift in terminology and with it a change in related concepts – see especially points a) and c) above. Increasingly, the term *qidesh* (קדש - 'set apart') was used of betrothal and marriage. Jastrow, *Dictionary*, p.1319, describes it as 'the rabbinic term in place of the Biblical קנה'.

Several points of comparison and similarity can be drawn between Paul's response to the Corinthians' question on marriage (1Cor.7.1-16, 25-40) and the evolving concepts of marriage in contemporary practice. For example, we see that Paul also may have considered marriage to be an agreement between individuals (i.e. the husband and his wife). The decisions to marry (vv.8-10), to abstain (v.5) and to separate (vv.10-13, 15) are considered to belong to the marriage partners. However, as far as the παρθένος is concerned, Paul seems to indicate that the decision whether to marry or not lay with the male (1Cor.7.36-38).[19] In the OT a similar development can also be seen in the post-exilic period when marriage (used as a metaphor) began to be conceived as a covenant (ברית) between the spouses (e.g. Ez.16.8, Mal.2.13-16, Prov.2.17). Rabbinic law also assumed a mutuality, for the adult woman was free to accept or to reject marriage (see *m. Qid.* 4.9, *t. Yeb.* 13.1, and *DJD* II 19 *ll*.6-7, but cf. the wording of *m. Git.*9.3). A similar development can be argued for free marriages[20] in Roman law, i.e. either spouse could both initiate marriage and consent to divorce. However, for the woman who was not *sui iuris* the consent of her *paterfamilias* or *tutor* was also required. Since the woman was still under his *potestas*, he also could legally terminate the marriage – at least until the time of Marcus Aurelius. However, in both marriage and divorce it may generally be assumed that the *paterfamilias* respected the wishes of the woman.

The above discussion on the clauses in marriage settlements which relate to the obligation of the husband to his wife and the wife to her husband also provide a context for Paul's ruling that 'the husband should fulfil his marital duties to his wife, and likewise the wife to her husband' (1Cor.7.3). In Jewish law a mutual obligation was also placed on the married couple. For example, the wife was obliged to honour and serve her husband (*m. Ket.* 5.5 – cook, wash, suckle her child and work in wool) and could not avoid her duties by making a vow (*m. Ned.* 11.4)[21] and the husband was obliged to feed, to clothe, to honour and to have sexual intercourse with his wife (*DJD* II 20 *l*.3 ?, *m. Ket.* 5.8-9, *t. Qid.* 3.7, *Tg. Exod.*21.11). Since the maintenance of sexual relations was an obligation by Jewish law and failure to do so a ground for divorce (*m. Ket.* 5.6), abstention, as discussed by Paul, must result from an

---

her (Deut.21.14). Thus greater stress needs to be placed on the synchronic meaning of the term בעל (= husband) rather than upon its historical derivation. The same also applies to the term κύριος when used to describe the husband's authority over his wife in Greek law. In her study of the status of women in the Mishnah, J.R. Wenger, op.cit., pp.40-96, concludes that wives, like other dependent women (i.e. minor daughters and levirate widows), were considered as both chattels and persons. It is her thesis that the Mishnah treats a woman as chattel when the issue under debate is her sexual and reproductive function. It is this that the husband, father or levir owns.

19 The interpretation of 1Cor.7.36-38 is problematic. The male is variously understood as the girl's father or fiancé or spiritual guardian. See E.-B. Allo, *Première épitre aux Corinthiens* (Paris 1956), pp.184-7, J. Dauvillier, 'Le droit du mariage dans les cités grecques et hellénistiques d' après les écrits de saint Paul', *RIDA* 7 (1960), pp.149-64 and W.G. Kümmel, 'Verlobung und Heirat bei Paulus (1Kor 7, 36-38)' in *Heilsgeschehen und Geschichte* (Marburg 1965), pp.310-27.

20 Because of the declining use of marriage *cum manu*, free marriage will be used to illustrate and compare Roman law and practice. On the history and development of marriage *cum manu* see G. Hanard, '*Manus* et mariage', *RIDA* 36 (1989), pp.161-279.

21 A father could annul the vows of his minor daughter (see *m. Nid.*5.7 and *m. Ket.*4.4). Vows of self-denial made by a wife could be annulled by her husband, whilst other types of vows could not (see *m. Ned.*10.2, 11.1-2, *t. Ned.*7.1 and *CD* 16.10-13). However, the situation was different in the case of the oath made by an adult woman not under the *potestas* of another (see *m. Ned.*10.2, 11.10, *m. Nid.*5.7, 11.10).

agreement of both partners (1Cor.7.5). Parties to a *kethubah* expressed the marital obligation in the words 'according to the law of Moses and Israel', e.g. Tobit 7.13, *DJD* II 20 *l*.3, *CPJ* 128, *P. Yadin* 10 *l*.1 and 18 *l*.7, *m. Ket*. 7.6, *t. Ket*. 4.9, *y. Yeb*. 15.3.14d, *y. Ket*. 4.8.28d and *P. Colon*. XII *l*.8; see further Friedman, op.cit., pp.162-7. In other words, the law of Moses and Jewish custom formed the basis of obligation in Jewish marriage. On the other hand, Paul seems to have considered the basis of marital obligation to be the subjugation of each spouse to the other's control or *potestas* (1Cor.7.4)[22] and saw in this a possible hindrance to a proper concern for the Lord's affairs (1Cor.7.32-35).[23] Nor was there for Paul any difference in the status of the spouses before God (cf. 1Cor.11.11 and Gal.3.28). However, this did not mean that the marital obligations of the husband and the wife were the same nor that the husband was not the 'head' of his wife (1Cor.11.3; cf. Eph.5.21-33 and Col.3.18-19).

In the legal context of the papyri the situation is different again. Marital obligations arise from the transaction, and the liability of the parties is based on the dowry's sum (see above; cf. *P. Yadin* 18 *ll*.23-24 where a 100% penalty is envisaged in a deed of marriage from Palestine dated AD 128 – *m. Ket*.5.7 stipulated fixed, daily deductions from or additions to the *kethubah*). The husband became his wife's κύριος; however, the κύριος in marriage did not acquire the possession of his wife nor did he have dominion over her but acted more as her guardian (see above and the discussion of ἐκδιδόναι by H.J. Wolff, 'Marriage Law in Ancient Athens', *Traditio* 2 [1945], p.48). Before comparing the Pauline and Greek legal conceptions of marital relations it is important to note the differences between Greek legal conceptions on the one hand and ethical advice and marital practice on the other hand. It is perhaps in these latter domains that Paul's understanding of the husband as the 'head' of his wife finds better parallels. For example, see *P. Haun*. 13 (*ll*.31-4) in *New Docs* 6 (1992) **§2** where the husband's βούλησις is described as a νόμος to be engraved on the wife herself. The legal conception of marital relations was different again in Roman law. Here the wife in free marriage was not under the *potestas* of her husband but of her *paterfamilias*.[24] She was not even under the guardianship of her husband. On the death of her *paterfamilias* she became *sui iuris* and had a *tutor*, who was usually an agnate, appointed. She could own and manage property independently of her husband.

In Roman law divorce could be initiated by either spouse (the wife with the consent of her *paterfamilias* or *tutor*) or by the wife's *paterfamilias*,[25] and remarriage was actively encouraged. A divorce initiated by the wife, however, was contrary to Jewish law and practice. The wife could not initiate divorce but only the husband (*m. Yeb*. 14.1, *m. Git*.9.10 and *m. Ket*.7.6-7); however, under certain circumstances the husband could be compelled to divorce his wife (*m. Ket*.7.4-5, 9-10, *m. Git*.9.8, *m. Ned*. 11.12 and *m. 'Arak*. 5.6). The court might even use gentile legal procedure to secure the enforcement of its decision. Exceptions to *m. Yeb*. 14.1 are

---

22 The notion of *potestas* (ἐξουσιάζω – 1Cor.7.4) does not seem to arise in any concept of marriage as acquisition, i.e. קנה, but rather from the idea that by sexual intercourse the husband and wife 'become one body/flesh' (Gen.2.24; cf. 1Cor.6.16). This idea explains both the basis of *potestas* (i.e. one has *potestas* over one's own body) and its mutuality (i.e. the wife has *potestas* over the husband's body and vice versa). Further confirmation of it is found in the context of 1Cor.7.4 which speaks of sexual relations in marriage.

23 Cf. *P. Haun*. 13 (*ll*.29-31) in *New Docs* 6 (1992) **§2** – ἀρ̣έσκ̣ε̣ι̣ν̣ τε σωφρονοῦντι τῷ [ἑαυ]τῆς ἀν̣δ̣ρὶ ἐ̣π̣ιτελο̣ῦσαν τὰς ἐκε[ίνου βο]υ̣λήσεις.

24 In the case of *cum manu* marriage the wife was no longer under the *potestas* of her *paterfamilias* but under that of her husband.

25 Cf. J. Modrzejewski, op. cit., pp.258-61, H.J. Wolff, *Written and Unwritten Marriages*, pp.60-65 and *P. Oxy*. II 237 (pp.149,168-9,171 and 172-3), for the existence of the same paternal prerogative (ἀφαίρεσις) in Graeco-Egyptian common law. The prerogative appears to have been of Egyptian origin. The Romans sought, however, to restrict its perceived inhumanity (ἀπανθρωπία) by respecting the daughter's wishes in certain cases, i.e. if she were the child of an ἔγγραφος γάμος or given in ἔγγραφος γάμος.

found in the Aramaic papyri,[26] some Greek papyri[27] and even possibly the Talmud itself (see *y. Ket.* 30b, *y. B. Bat.* 16c and the discussion by Friedman, op.cit., pp.316-17). The Mishnah also seems to envisage the case where a wife initiates divorce by forgoing her *kethubah* (see *m. Git.*7.5 and the discussion by J.R. Wegner, op.cit., pp.136-7). After divorce the woman was free to marry again (*m. Git.* 9.2-3 and *DJD* II 19). Both 1Cor.7.10-11, 15 and Mark 10.12 are addressed to a community in which the wife had the right to initiate divorce. One may compare these verses with Matt.5.32, 19.9 and Luke 16.18 where no such right is assumed. However, unlike Greek, Roman and Jewish law[28] Paul did not recognise the right of a divorced spouse to remarry. The alleged reason for the prohibition was that remarriage constituted an act of adultery. Clearly, the validity of divorce itself was not recognised. In these matters Paul seems to be following the Jesus tradition (1Cor.7.10, Mark 10.11-12 and Luke 16.18) – Matt.5.32 (par. 19.9) is an exception in that it recognises divorce on the grounds of πορνεία. Clearly, both Paul and his tradition hold a view on marriage which is fundamentally different from that found in Greek, Roman and Jewish practice. It does, however, show an affinity with Qumran's Torah governing the king (see *11QTemp*.57.17-19).[29] Paul's and Jesus' (Matt.19.12) preference for celibacy also shows a point of similarity with Qumran.

The NT and Paul in particular make no mention of the dowry either as a social phenomenon or as a metaphor.[30] The former omission is interesting and two possible reasons can be suggested for it. First, a large proportion of Paul's audience may have belonged to the lower social classes in which unwritten marriage predominated. As such, dotal practice may have been outside his readers' social experience and thus required no comment. In this regard note P.J.Tomson, *Paul and the Jewish Law* (Minneapolis 1990), p.118, who suggests that τοῖς λοιποῖς at 1Cor.7.12 refers to those members of the community who had been married informally, i.e. by unwritten marriage. Second, its omission may be tied to the more general attitude to marriage and property. The issue can be clearly seen when one looks at the context of Paul's advice in 1Cor.7. Here Paul's whole discussion of and advice on marriage appears to have been motivated by a sense of the end-time. When Paul advised the Corinthians that it was better not to marry and only permitted marriage as a concession to the weakness of the flesh, he must have foreseen no need for the procreation of children. Indeed, when Paul did mention children, he only spoke of their sanctification through a believing parent. Such an attitude is consistent with a view that the end-time was imminent. More explicitly Paul wrote:

---

26 See *Brooklyn Aramaic Papyri* 2 *l*.9, 7 *ll*.24-25 and *Aramaic Papyri* 15 *ll*. 22-23. Falk, op.cit., pp.310-11, ascribes the difference at Elephantine to the presence of few women in the military colony and their corresponding respected status.

27 See *P.Yadin* 18 *ll*. 21-27 and possibly*DJD* II 20 *l*.6. The former shows elements from both the Jewish and Greek laws of marriage. Indeed the document states as much itself (cf. κατὰ τοὺς νόμους *ll*.7 and 39 and ἑλληνικῷ νόμῳ *ll*.16 and 51).

28 Remarriage was permitted expressly in the documents from Graeco-Roman Egypt (see above discussion of deeds of divorce) and in Palestine (Deut.24.2, *DJD* II 19 *ll*.6-7//17-19, *m. Git*. 9.3).

29 *CD* 4.19-5.5 and *y. Sanh*.2.6 are cited by Daube, op.cit., pp.297-300, as examples of the argument against polygamy and divorce. However, they appear only to deal with polygamy.

30 The omission of the dowry as a metaphor is surprising considering the NT use of the metaphor of marriage to describe the relationship between Christ and his church (e.g. 2Cor.11.2 and Rev.21.2). Perhaps it was not necessary for the authors to make explicit allusion to the dowry since it was so inextricably involved in the practice of marriage itself. An explicit use of the metaphor does, however, appear in later church writings. For example, Methodius, *Symp*.6.5, speaks of himself as an espoused wife to the Word who takes as her dowry the crown and wealth of incorruptibility from her Father – νυμφεύομαι τῷ Λόγῳ καὶ τὸν ἀΐδιον τῆς ἀφθαρσίας προῖκα λαμβάνω στέφανον καὶ πλοῦτον παρὰ τοῦ Πατρός. The metaphor could, however, be used in other ways. For example, John Chrystostom, *Hom*.18.4 *in Ac*., speaks of the obligation of estate owners in regard to the conversion of their rural labourers. He says that they should act towards the church as towards a bride endowing her for this mission – ὡσανεὶ γυναῖκα ἀγαγὼν ἢ νύμφην ἢ δοὺς θυγατέρα, οὕτω τῇ ἐκκλησίᾳ διάκειςο· προῖκα ἐπίδος αὐτῇ.

> Τοῦτο δέ φημι, ἀδελφοί, ὁ καιρὸς συνεσταλμένος ἐστίν· τὸ λοιπὸν, ἵνα καὶ οἱ ἔχοντες γυναῖκας ὡς μὴ ἔχοντες ὦσιν, καὶ οἱ κλαίοντες ὡς μὴ κλαίοντες καὶ οἱ χαίροντες ὡς μὴ χαίροντες καὶ οἱ ἀγοράζοντες ὡς μὴ κατέχοντες, καὶ οἱ χρώμενοι τὸν κόσμον ὡς μὴ καταχρώμενοι· παράγει γὰρ τὸ σχῆμα τοῦ κόσμου τούτου. (1Cor.7.29-31)

If in view of the imminent end-time marriage is not encouraged and the believers are called to review their attitude to property generally, any question or dispute over the dowry would tend to be subsumed under those concerns perceived to be of a greater and more immediate import.

Paul's idea of the sanctification of the unbelieving partner by the believing partner and the subsequent procreation of sanctified children (1Cor.7.12-16) also finds interesting points of comparison in the classical Athenian (i.e. from the time of Pericles) and Hellenistic laws, the OT and rabbinic law. In Athens, legitimacy and citizenship was reserved for the offspring of a marriage duly constituted between two οἶκοι. Indeed, marriage was for the procreation of such offspring, i.e. ἐπὶ ἀρότῳ παίδων γνησίων, an expression found in the Athenian ἐγγύη (see J. Modrzejewski, op.cit., p.259 n.115). In Egypt a similar tendency towards endogamy is seen amongst privileged classes of society. For example, in Oxyrhynchus the child became a member of the *gymnasium* class only if both its parents were also members (see further the discussion of this topic at *New Docs* 6 [1992] §17). Similarly in post-exilic Israel, Ezra and Nehemiah (Ezra 9, Neh.10.31, 13.23-28) applied a strict rule prohibiting marriage to individuals of another race. One can also note the clause in the Aramaic writ of divorce *DJD* II 19 *ll*.5-7 (cf. *m. Git*. 9.2) permitting the ex-wife 'to go and be married to any Jewish man you wish'. Further rules were set down governing intermarriage between members of different social castes and the status of their offspring (e.g. *m. Yeb*. 7.5, *m. Qid*. 3.12, 4.1-7, *t. Qid*. 4.15, 5.1-13). In a validly constituted marriage the status of the child was that of its father. If the marriage was invalid because it infringed the law of incest, the status of the child was that of a *mamzer* or bastard. If the spouses belonged to castes which were not permitted to intermarry or if one of the spouses was either a slave or a gentile, the child took the status of the inferior party or that of *mamzer*, depending on the particular circumstances. In the case of apostasy the other spouse could seek a divorce. These rules produced a similar tendency to endogamy especially among the priests and sages. Roman law also sought to regulate marriage between members of different social classes. *Conubium*, one of the conditions for *iustum matrimonium* and the legitimisation of offspring, was conditional upon the status of the spouses. See further J.F. Gardner, *Women in Roman Law and Society* (London 1986), pp.67-8, 138-144. The legitimate child took the status of the father whilst the illegitimate child took the status of the mother. By the *lex Minicia* (first century BC) the child born of a marriage without *conubium* took the status of the lower-status parent.

In a similar fashion Paul taught that the believer should not marry an unbeliever (1Cor.7.39 and 2Cor.6.14-16). The incompatibility of two theological constructs appears to have led him to this conclusion – to be married to an unbeliever (= to become one body/flesh with an unbeliever) and to be a believer (= to be in Christ). However, there is a degree of inconsistency between Paul's attitude to marriage occurring after conversion and his attitude to marriage occurring before conversion, for Paul not only recognised the validity of an existing marriage between the believer and non-believer (dependent on the consent of the latter) but also argued that the status of the spouse and the children derived from the believing partner – the non-believing spouse was sanctified by the believing spouse and their offspring were also sanctified (1Cor.7.12-16). Did Paul then allow divorce in the case where the non-believing spouse's consent was not given (see 1Cor.7.12-13)? D. Daube, 'Pauline Contributions to a Pluralistic Culture', *Jesus and Man's Hope*, ed. D.G. Miller and D.Y. Hadidian (Pittsburg 1971), pp.223-45, argues that since in Jewish thought conversion entailed the creation of a new person, former relationships (including marriage) were thought to have been terminated by conversion.[31] Thus if one partner wished to leave, he or she was free to do so. In other words, the question of divorce did not arise as the marriage itself no longer existed. However, in Paul's view the continued cohabitation[32] of the believing and non-believing partners constituted a new act of marriage. At 1Cor.7.14 Daube notes the play on the term *qidesh* (קדש), a polyseme meaning both to marry[33] and to sanctify. Perhaps Paul's argument is better seen as a piece of midrash, i.e. just as the husband *marries* his wife and the wife is *married* to her husband, so the husband *sanctifies* his wife and is *sanctified* by his wife. Because both spouses are sanctified the children also are sanctified. **S.R.L.**

§2 A Woman's Behaviour

Provenance unknown III AD

Ed.pr. – A. Bülow-Jacobsen, *P.Haun.* II 13 (Bonn 1981), pp.1-10 (= *P. Haun.inv.* 155).

In a third-century literary hand, with admixture of cursive forms, a *koine* paraphrase of the pseudo-Pythagorean letter of Melissa to Clearete was written on the back of an official document (unpublished). The first of the three more ancient letters of Theano begins in the same column before the papyrus is broken off. The editor assumes it is the fragment of a roll, so that several more columns may have followed, perhaps covering all three Theano letters. Aligned ahead of the papyrus text below are the corresponding parts of the edition of Alfons Städele, *Die Briefe des Pythagoras and der Pythagoreer* (Meisenheim am Glan 1980), nos III (Melissa) and V (Theano), pp.160 and 166. They match R. Hercher, *Epistolographi Graeci* (Paris 1873, repr. Amsterdam 1965), nos XI and IV, pp.607 and 603, whose texts are reproduced by H. Thesleff, *The Pythagorean Texts of the Hellenistic Period, Acta Academiae Aboensis*, Series A *(Humaniora)*, vol.30.1 (1965), under the names of the pseudo-authors. Translations of the Städele texts are supplied by A.J. Malherbe, *Moral Exhortation: A Greco-Roman Sourcebook* (Philadelphia 1986), 34-35. Brief reference is made below to the illustrative value of the Pythagorean letters for two aspects of NT studies, before taking stock of the linguistic novelty presented by the paraphrase.

A. The Perfection of Virtue in a Woman and her Children

The training of women and children (as of men) is concentrated as usual in the Greek ethical tradition upon 'adornment of soul' (τῆς ψυχῆς εὐκοσμία, *l.*41). The goal is 'perfection in virtue' (τελειοῦσθαι κατ' ἀρετήν, *l.*8). For both woman (*l.*28) and child (*l.*47), as indeed for a man (*l.*30), the guiding principle is moderation (σωφροσύνη). Relations amongst people are conducted basically with a view to the individual improvement of each in turn.

According to Mary Ellen Waithe, *A History of Women Philosophers:* vol. 1, *Ancient Women Philosophers 600 B.C.–500 A.D.* (Dordrecht 1987), these discourses reflect the effort to apply the Pythagorean norm of *harmonia* to each one's personal life (p.6). The 'realities of the social situation' (p.41) are to be ignored, and a woman's 'being naturally more inclined towards temperance' (p.43) will lead to her behaving justly even if her husband does not. Household management *(oikonomia)* provides an arena for the practice of ethical principle as much as the state does (p.xi).

---

31 According to Jewish law both the proselyte and freedman were thought to have lost their family ties and ancestry by conversion and enslavement respectively. The loss did not concern marital relations only. For example, children conceived before conversion were no longer thought to be related to their mother or to each other. For this reason they were not subject to levirate marriage (see *m. Yeb.* 11.2).

32 In Jewish law, sexual intercourse, like unwritten marriage in Greek law and marriage by cohabitation in Roman law, was a third method of marriage, after money and writ (see *m. Qid.* 1.1, *m. Ket.* 4.4, *m. Nid.* 5.4). The Rabbis, however, interpreted this as referring to the nuptials after a duly constituted marriage (Friedman, op.cit., pp.204-5) or as applicable to levirate marriage (*m. Qid.* 1.1).

33 Jewish marriage consisted of two stages, betrothal (אירוסין) and nuptials (נשואין). The term *qidesh* referred to the former, i.e. betrothal, but could also refer to marriage generally.

The 'domestic code' (*Haustafel*) that appears in several forms in the New Testament (notably Col. 3.18-4.1; Eph. 5.22-6.9; 1 Tim. 2.8-15, 6.1-2; Titus 2.2-10; 1 Pet. 2.18-3.7) seems, however, to be conceived on different lines. It shows a concern not so much for the orderly individual as for an ordered community under its head. There are reciprocal obligations between wives and husbands, children and parents, servants and masters, the husband-father-master being the focal point in these partnerships, though women of course are embraced by the terms 'parents' and 'masters'. Characteristic of the NT approach is the principle of mutual answerability ('be subject to one another out of reverence for Christ', Eph. 5.21) and the fact that each category (including slaves and children) is directly addressed. The use of the imperative, like the formal structure of the code, is also characteristic of the NT.

The relation of the NT *Haustafel* to the philosophic topic of *oikonomia* has been the subject of extensive discussion, analysed independently by D.L. Balch, 'The Household Codes' in D.E. Aune (ed.), *Greco-Roman Literature and the New Testament: Selected Forms and Genres* (Atlanta 1988), pp.25-50, by B. Witherington, 'The *Haustafel*', in *Women in the Earliest Churches* (Cambridge 1988), pp.42-61, and by P. Fiedler, 'Haustafel', *RAC* 13 (1986), cols 1063-73. See also D.C. Verner, *The Household of God: The Social World of the Pastoral Epistles* (Chico 1983), discussed by R.M. Kidd, 'The church as household', in his *Wealth and Beneficence in the Pastoral Epistles* (Atlanta 1990), pp.78-82.

While certain elements in the NT formulae parallel their Hellenistic and Jewish antecedents, what seems 'entirely new in ancient social history' (Balch, p.33) is the 'integrating power' of the NT church order built upon the household. The fact that this was never again so clearly spelled out as in the *Haustafeln* of Colossians and 1 Peter highlights the distinctiveness of the NT approach to domestic relations. Ethical development is displaced by social commitment, 'good bearing' (καλοκαγαθία, *l.*24, the classical ideal conspicuously absent from the NT) by 'good deeds' (ἔργα ἀγαθά, 1 Tim. 2.10), 'good order' (εὐταξία, *l.*36) by 'mutual subordination' (ὑποτασσόμενοι ἀλλήλοις, Eph. 5.21). The ideal of 'loving the good' (φιλοκαλεῖν, *l.*28) is refocussed in personal terms, 'working as for the Lord' (ἐργάζεσθε ὡς τῷ Κυρίῳ, Col. 3.23).

Although there are close similarities of detail between the letter of Melissa and the NT letters on the restraint of women's dress (*ll.*10-15, 24-26, compared with 1 Tim. 2.9, 1 Pet. 3.3), the justification for it is different. Melissa is concerned about the sexual implications of display, and with the need to be attractive to the husband (*ll.*20-22), whose will is the good woman's law (*l.*32). The NT *Haustafeln* refer to physical beauty only in the metaphor of the church as bride (Eph. 5.27) or in the figure of the 'inner man of the heart' (1 Pet. 3.4). The restraint of women's dress is desired because it goes with devotion to God (1 Tim. 2.10, 1 Pet. 3.5). The wife is subordinate to the husband because this is the pattern of relations set in creation (Adam was formed first, 1 Tim. 2.14) and in the line of women who hoped in God (like Sarah who called Abraham master, 1 Pet. 3.5-6).

B. Pseudepigraphy and Moral Authority

Are the (neo-) Pythagorean letters written by women, or by men using their names as a device? Women were noticeable in the original Pythagorean school of the sixth century. A thousand years later Iamblichus ends his study by listing 17 women after the 218 men known to have been Pythagoreans (*On the Pythagorean Life*, tr. G. Clark, Liverpool 1989, 267). Theano was Pythagoras' wife, and it may be assumed that the name was considered suitable for the daughters of later Pythagoreans. But Melissa, Clearete and Euboule are not in the list, and are ordinary enough Greek names, though hardly so common that one might choose them as typical. Someone wishing to claim antiquity and authority for his views might anyway have been expected to choose a famous name. Sarah B. Pomeroy, *Women in Hellenistic Egypt from*

Ed. Städele	P. Haun. 13	
Μέλισσα Κλεαρέτᾳ	Μέλισσạ Κ̣λεαρ[έτῃ]	Melissa to Clearete,
[χαίρειν]. Αὐτομάτ-	χ̣αίρειν. [α]ὐτομ̣[άτ-]	greetings. Of your own desire,
ως ἐμὶν φαίνῃ πλέ-	ως μοι φα̣ίνῃ [πλεί-]	it seems to me, you possess
ονα τῶν καλῶν ἔ-	ονα τῶν κ̣αλ̣ῶ̣[ν ἔ-]	most of what is good.
χεν· τὸ γὰρ ἐσπουδασμένως ἐθέλεν	χειν· τὸ γὰρ ἐ̣σ̣[πουδασμένως ἐθέλειν]	For your zealous [wish] to
τὺ ἀκοῦσαι περὶ γυναικὸς εὐκοσμίας	σε ἀκοῦσαι π̣ε̣ρ[ὶ γυναικὸς εὐκοσμίας]	listen to the topic of [woman's adornment]
καλὰν ἐλπίδα διδοῖ ὅτι μέλλεις	καλὴν ἐλπ[ί]δ̣α̣ δ̣[ίδωσι ὅτι μέλλεις]	offers fair hope [that you intend]
πολιοῦσθαι κατ' ἀρετάν. χρὴ ὦν τὰν	τελειοῦ[σ]θαι κατ' ἀ̣[ρετήν. χρὴ οὖν τὴν]	to perfect yourself in virtue. [It is necessary then]
σώφρονα καὶ ἐλευθέραν τῷ κατὰ νόμον	σώφρονα καὶ ἐλευ[θέραν τῷ κατὰ νόμον]	for the moderate and liberal woman to live [with]
ἀνδρὶ ποτῆμεν αἰσχύνᾳ κεκαλλωπισμέ-	ἀν[δ]ρὶ προσῖναι ἡσ[υχίᾳ κεκαλλωπισμέ-]	[her lawful] husband [adorned] with quietness,
ναν [ἀλλὰ μὴ πολυτερδῶς], ἦμεν δὲ τᾷ ἐσθᾶτι	νη̣ν̣ τῇ ἐσθῆτι λευ[κοείμονα καὶ κα-]	white and clean in her dress,
λευκοείμονα καὶ κα-		
θάριον καὶ ἀφελῆ, ἀλλὰ μὴ πολυτελῆ	θάρειον, ἀφελῆ ἀλ̣λ̣[ὰ μὴ πολυτελῆ],	plain and [not costly],
καὶ περισσάν·	ἁπλῆν ἀλλὰ μὴ ποι̣κίλην [καὶ περισσήν].	simple and not elaborate [or excessive].
παραιτητέον γὰρ αὐτᾷ τὰν ἁλουργῆ	παραιτητέον γὰρ αὐτῇ τὰ [±8]	For she must reject [...],
καὶ διαπόρφυρον καὶ τὰ χρυσόπαστα τῶν	καὶ διαπόρφυρα ἢ χρυσόπα[στα τῶν ἐνδυ-]	and garments shot with purple or gold.
ἐνδυμάτων. ταῖς ἑταίραις γὰρ τάδε χρή-	μ̣ά̣των. ταῖς γὰρ ἑταίραις τάδ̣[ε χρή-]	For these are used by call-girls
σιμα ποττὰν τῶν πλεόνων θήραν,	σ̣[ιμα] πρὸς τὴν τῶν π̣λειόν[ων θῆραν,]	in [soliciting] the generality of men,
τᾶς δὲ ποθ' ἕνα τὸν ἴδιον εὐαρεστούσας	τῆς δὲ πρὸς ἕνα τὸν ἴδιο̣ν̣ [εὐαρεστούσης]	but if she is to be [attractive] to one man, her own,
γυναικὸς κόσμος ὁ τρόπος πέλει καὶ οὐ-	γυναικὸς κόσμος ἐστι̣ν̣ ὁ τρό[πος καὶ οὐ-]	a woman's ornament is her manners and not
χ αἱ στολαί· εὔμορφον γὰρ τὰν ἐλευθέραν	χ ἡ στολή. εὔμορφον δὲ τὴν ἐλευ[θέραν]	her clothing. And a liberal and moderate woman
ἰδέσθαι τῷ ἑαυτᾶς ἀν-	καὶ σώφρονα ἰδέσθαι χρὴ τῷ ἑαυτῆ[ς ἀν-]	must seem good-looking to her own husband,
δρί, ἀλλ' οὐ τοῖς πλασίον. Ἔχοις ἂν ἐ-	δρί, ἀ̣λλ' οὐ τῷ πλησίον, ἔχουσαν μὲν [ἐ-]	but not to the man next door, having on
πὶ τᾶς ὄψιος ἐρύθαμα μὲν σαμεῖον αἰδοῦς	πὶ τῆς ὄψεως αἰδοῦς ἐρύθημα ἄμειν̣[ον]	her cheeks the blush of modesty rather
ἀντὶ φύκιος, καλοκαγαθίαν δὲ	φύκου καὶ ψιμιθίου, καλοκαγαθ[ί]αν δ̣[ὲ]	than of rouge and powder, and good bearing
καὶ κοσμιότατα καὶ σωφροσύναν ἀν-	καὶ κοσμιότητα καὶ σωφροσύνην ἀ[ν-]	and decency and moderation rather
τὶ χρυσῶ καὶ σμαράγδω. οὐ γὰρ ἐς τὰν	τὶ χρυσοῦ καὶ σμαράγδου. οὐ γὰρ ε[ἰ]ς τὴ̣ν̣	than gold and emerald. For it is not in
τᾶς	[τ]ῆ̣ς̣	

ἐσθᾶτος πολυτέλειαν	ἐσθῆτος καὶ τοῦ σ[ώ]ματος πολυτέλει[αν]	expenditure on dress and looks that
φιλοκαλεῖν δεῖ τὰν γλιχομέναν τᾶς	φιλοκαλεῖν δεῖ τὴ[ν] σώφρ[ον]α, ἀλλ' [εἰς]	the moderate woman should express her love of
σωφροσύνας, ἀλλ' ἐς τὰν οἰκονο-	οἰκ[ο]νο-	the good but in the management
μίαν τῶ οἴκω. ἀρέσκεν	μίαν τε καὶ σωτηρίαν [τοῦ οἴ]κου, ἀρέσκειν	and maintenance of her household, and pleasing
δὲ αὐτὰν τῷ αὐτᾶς ἀνδρὶ ἐπιτελέας	τε σωφρονοῦντι τῷ [ἑαυ]τῆς ἀνδρὶ ἐπι-	her own husband, given that he is a moderated
ποιεῦσαν τὰς ἐκείνω θελήσιας· αἱ γὰρ	τελοῦσαν τὰς ἐκε[ίνου βο]υλήσεις· ἡ γὰρ	man, by fulfilling his wishes. For the
τῶ ἀνδρὸς θελήσεις νόμος ὀφείλει ἄ-	τοῦ ἀνδρὸς βούλησι[ς νόμ]ος ὀφείλει ἐν-	husband's will ought to be engraved as law
γραφος ἦμεν κοσμίᾳ γυναικί, ποθ' ὃν χρὴ	γραφῆναι κοσμίᾳ γ[υναικί, πρὸ]ς ὃν χρὴ	on a decent wife's mind, and she must
βιῶν αὐτάν· νομίζεν δὲ προῖκα ποτενη-	βιοῦν αὐτήν· νομίζει‹ν› δὲ [πρ]οῖκα εἰσενη-	live by it. And she must consider that the dowry
νέχθαι ἅμα αὐτᾷ καλλίσταν καὶ μεγί-	νοχέναι ἅμ' α[ὑτ]ῇ καλλίστην καὶ μεγί-	she has brought with her that is best and greatest
σταν τὰν εὐταξίαν. πιστεύεν γὰρ χρὴ τῷ	στην τὴν εὐτα[ξί]αν. πιστεύειν δὲ χρὴ τῷ	of all is her good order. And she must
τᾶς ψυχᾶς κάλλει τε καὶ πλούτῳ μᾶλλον	τῆς ψυχῆς κάλλει τε καὶ πλούτῳ μᾶλλον	believe in the beauty and wealth of the soul rather
ἢ τῷ τᾶς ὄψιος καὶ τῶν χρημάτων.	ἢ τῷ τῶν χρημάτων καὶ τῆς ὄψεως.	than in that of money and appearance.
τὰ μὲν γὰρ	τὰ μὲν γὰρ χρήμα[σ]τα καὶ τὰ σώματα χρό-	As for money and looks, time,
φθόνος καὶ νοῦσος παραιρέεται,	νος, φθόνος, νόσος, τύχη παραιρεῖται·	envy, illness and fortune take them away.
τὰ δὲ μέχρι θανά-	ἡ δὲ τῆς ψυχῆς εὐκοσμία μέχρι θανά-	But adornment of soul lasts till
τω πάρεντι ἐκτεταμένα.	του πάρεστι ταῖς κεκτημέναις.	death with women who possess it.

Θεανὼ Εὐβούλῃ [χαίρειν]. Ἀκούω σε	Θεανὼ Εὐβούλῃ χαίρειν. ἀκούω σε	Theano to Euboule, greetings. I hear you
τὰ παιδία τρυφερῶς ἄγειν· ἔστι δὲ	[τὰ παιδία τρυφερῶ]ς τρέφειν· ἔστι δὲ	are bringing up the children indulgently.
ἀγαθῆς μητρὸς οὐχ ἡ πρὸς	[ἀγαθῆς ± 9] μητρὸς οὐχ ἡ πρὸς	But a [good ...] mother's interest is not
ἡδονὴν ἐπιμέλεια τῶν παίδων, ἀλλ' ἡ	[ἡδονὴν ἐπιμέλεια τ]ῶν π[αίδ]ων ἀλλ' ἡ	[concern for the pleasure] of the children but their
πρὸς τὸ σῶφρον ἀγωγή. βλέπε οὖν μὴ	[πρὸς τὸ σῶφρον ἀγωγή. βλέπε οὖ]ν μὴ	[training in moderation. Look] then not ...

Alexander to Cleopatra (New York 1984), p.64, therefore accepts the letters as genuine compositions by women whose names they were. They form 'the only extant body of Greek prose literature attributed to women in the pre-Christian era' (p.61). Waithe (op.cit., pp. 59-74) also argues for the authenticity of the Hellenistic letters attributed to women, but does not treat the case of Melissa. Thesleff proposed to date them as early as the third century BC, Städele as late as the second AD. The dating issue is discussed by Thesleff, W. Burkert and others in K. von Fritz (ed.), *Pseudepigrapha I* (Geneva 1971), pp.23-102.

Although the prominence of women is distinctly greater in the NT (18 women and 72 men are named in connection with Paul), and older women are expressly charged with the instruction of the younger ones (Titus 2.3-5), there is no explicit suggestion of a tradition of women's writing. The 'Acts of Paul and Thecla' (E. Hennecke/W. Schneemelcher, *The New Testament Apocrypha*, London 1965, pp.353-364) and other apocryphal Acts have, however, been claimed as the work of women writers (S.L. Davies, *The Revolt of the Widows: The Social World of the Apocryphal Acts*, Carbondale 1980, pp.95-109). See also P. Wilson-Kastner et al., *A Lost Tradition: Women Writers of the Early Church* (Lanham 1981), for a few known writers of the third to fifth centuries and Antoinette Wire, *The Corinthian Women Prophets* (Minneapolis 1990) for the contribution of women to the first-century church in Corinth.

The composition of works in the name of an authoritative figure was a common practice in antiquity, systematically treated by W. Speyer, *Die literarische Fälschung im heidnischen und christlichen Altertum: Ein Versuch ihrer Deutung* (Munich 1971). Since rhetorical imitation was a skill fundamental to higher education (D.L. Clark, *Rhetoric in Greco-Roman Education* [New York 1957], pp.144-176), the authenticity of works of Graeco-Roman literature is often in doubt. The transmission of philosophical and medical doctrine in the name of the founder of a school is another basic form of pseudepigraphy, e.g. *The Cynic Epistles*, ed. A.J. Malherbe (Missoula 1977). The deutero-Pauline and other NT letters whose authorship is questioned are not, however, easily explained from such classical conventions. The outcome would have had to be much more routine for that to be plausible. For example, one would expect a product of the educational system to be thematic in its approach, as the letter of Melissa is.

The case of the Pastoral Epistles was the subject of three independent studies published in 1986, and treated together by R.J. Karris, *JBL* 107 (1988), pp.558-560. None of them makes use of the pseudo-Pythagorean letters. Lewis R. Donelson, *Pseudepigraphy and Ethical Argument in the Pastoral Epistles* (Tübingen 1986), claims that the Pastorals are indeed pseudepigrapha of the classical type, their complexity being construed as a particularly successful disguise. The purpose was to capture Paul's authority for the more normative ethical compromise of a subsequent generation. Benjamin Fiore, *The Function of Personal Example in the Socratic and Pastoral Epistles* (Rome 1986), also bases his study on classical analogues, defining a category of exhortatory letter that readers would have recognised, approving the artful deception as a means of applying Pauline authority in new circumstances. But David G. Meade, *Pseudonymity and Canon: An Investigation into the Relationship of Authorship and Authority in Jewish & Earliest Christian Tradition* (Tübingen 1986), argues that in Judaism pseudonymity is 'primarily a claim to authoritative tradition, not a statement of literary origins' (p.102). The Pastorals mean to pick up Paul's consciousness of revelation and apply it afresh as he had intended. This is not then to be viewed as literary falsification, but as the 'actualisation' of the Pauline tradition.

C. Why did Melissa need a *koine* paraphrase?

The letter of Melissa and 40 or more other works of the Pythagorean corpus (but not the letters of Theano) were written in Doric. This was the dialect of Tarentum, no doubt used there by Archytas and the revived Pythagorean school of the fourth century BC. It remained in use among Greeks in South Italy well into Roman times. (Dialect forms do not appear in inscriptions after Augustus except in Laconia and Rhodes, though this uniformity need only reflect standardisation at the official level – L. Zgusta in G. Neumann and J. Untermann, eds, *Die Sprachen im römischen Reich der Kaiserzeit* [Cologne 1980], p.124.) But the texts of the Pythagorean corpus show a certain homogeneity which implies a literary convention (so Thesleff in *Pseudepigrapha I*, pp.61-68). For the same reason educated people would have wanted to keep them in that form. Those works composed in the *koine*, however, may be assumed to stem from Alexandria, also a centre of Pythagorean studies. Pomeroy (*op.cit.*, p.64) then sees the Doric Melissa being turned into the *koine* when the letter was brought to Alexandria.

Paraphrasing was an exercise taught in school. *PSI* XII 1276 gives *Iliad* II 617-670 with interlinear paraphrasing (I BC). A wooden tablet in Oxford has on the front *Iliad* IV 349-363 written out in prose (II/III AD), and on the back lines 364-373 in the original, with a list of the archaic words and their contemporary equivalents (G. Nachtergael, *Dans les classes d'Egypte d'après les papyrus scolaires grecs* [Brussels 1980], p.23). In all 22 paraphrases are listed amongst the 395 extant Greek school exercises from the hands of students (as judged by the writing and errors) listed by J. Debut, 'Les documents scolaires', *ZPE* 63 (1986), 251-278. Advanced students of rhetoric practised paraphrasing themselves (Quintilian, *Inst. Or.* 10.5.4-11).

But in the case of Melissa we are apparently dealing with the modernisation of the text by an editor, which must surely imply that it would be more effectively communicated in the *koine*. Was this an advantage for women in particular? John Chrysostom once switched from Attic to the *koine* when a woman complained she could only follow the half of what he said (Zgusta, *op.cit.*, p.130). Stoicism was expounded in the *koine*, as the work of Epictetus and Marcus Aurelius shows (*ibid.*, p.129). Similarly the New Testament was by and large retained in the *koine* though the churches were made painfully aware of its stylistic inadequacy.

The *koine* version of the letter of Melissa can be taken as derived from the Doric, and indeed from a better text of the latter than the one presented by Städele. For example, in *l.*10 the papyrus supports the later MSS against his conjecture (αἰσχύνᾳ), where ἀσυχίᾳ should now be restored. In *l.*22 ἔχοις ἄν can be seen to be an ancient re-reading of the pseudo-Doric participle ἔχοισαν following the omission of χρή from *l.*21. Nevertheless Bülow-Jacobsen notes the following evidence for priority of the Doric text: a) the less common πολιοῦσθαι (*l.*8, 'to grow grey') has been read as the more routine τελειοῦσθαι; b) the unusual plural στολαί (*l.*20) has been rendered singular; and c) the misreading of σαμεῖον (*l.*23, 'the sign') as ἄμεινον has led to the restructuring of the sentence and loss of its point.

One may note also otiose amplifications of the phraseology in *ll.*13, 21, 24, 27, 29, 39, 41. A more striking addition is that of *l.*30, which reads like a feminist improvement, making the wife's obedience conditional on the husband's moderation.

E.A. Judge

§3 Women in Public Life

Xanthus, Lycia — Imperial period

Ed.pr. — A. Balland, *Fouilles de Xanthos VII. Inscriptions d'époque impériale du Létôon* (Paris 1981), p.251, no. 81.

Originally a limestone block in a Doric architrave, the text was inscribed side by side with another recording the honouring of Senbreidase with a bronze statue (ibid., no.80). A third inscription from the statue base is also preserved in fragmentary state (ibid., no.82).

Σενβρειδασην Κλέωνος Ξαν-	To Senbreidase the Xanthian, daughter of Cleon.
θίαν Κλέων Κλέωνος τοῦ	Cleon, the Xanthian, son of Cleon, the
Ἀπολλωνίδου Ξάνθιος, πο-	son of Apollonides
λειτευόμενος δὲ καὶ ἐν ταῖς	who takes part in government also in
κατὰ Λυκίαν πόλεσι πάσαις,	all the cities of Lycia, (erected this)
τὴν ἑα<υ>τοῦ μητέρα ἐπιτροπεύ-	to his mother who acted as guardian
σασαν καλῶς καὶ δικαίως καὶ	well and justly and
[τετει]μημένη̣[ν ὑ]πὸ τῆς Ξανθίων πόλε-	was praised by the city of Xanthus
[ως ταῖ]ς δε[υ]τέ- v. ραις τειμαῖς, εὐ-	with double honours
[νοίας καὶ φιλο]σ̣τοργίας ἕνεκεν.	because of her goodwill and affection.

In the above inscription from Xanthus, a son publicly acknowledges his mother, Senbreidase, for acting fairly in her capacity as his guardian (ἐπίτροπος). In his discussion of the text Balland points out (p.256) that use of the word δικαίως indicates that it was not just a question of maternal supervision and protection, but that the mother, most probably as a widow and head of the family during the son's minority, had legal power over his person and property. (A fragmentary papyrus petition of II BC appears to record another fatherless boy under the control of his mother. There the word used is προστάτις rather than ἐπίτροπος. This document is discussed in *New Docs* 4 [1987], p.243.) The two other associated inscriptions honouring Senbreidase were official rather than private and were erected by decree of the city. Balland believes (p.256), that the city may have had some interest in the correct administration of Cleon's inheritance, and that it was perhaps because of the hope of eventually receiving some benefaction from the son, that the city gave him permission to inscribe a personal vote of thanks to his mother and to place it beside the official texts in her honour.

A good example of such expectations fulfilled may be found in an inscription honouring Iunia Theodora, a Lycian woman who was living in Corinth during mid I. When the Federal Assembly of the Lycians honoured her, it included among its reasons for so doing the fact that 'she has shown her desire to please the nation by the will she has drawn up' (D. Pallas et al., *BCH* 83 [1959] p.498, *ll.* 7-8).

Four other inscriptions on the same stone honour Iunia Theodora. Three of them are from individual Lycian cities, Myra, Patara, Telmessos, and the fourth is a second decree of the Lycian *koinon* or federation (Pallas et al., ibid., pp.496-500). The text of the decree of the city of Patara commences in the following terms (Pallas et al., ibid., p.499, *ll.*22-28):

ἔδοξε Παταρέων τῷ δήμῳ. ἐπεὶ	The people of Patara have decreed. Since
Ἰουνία Θεοδώρα Ῥωμαία τῶν κατοι-	Iunia Theodora, a Roman, living
κουσῶν ἐν Κορίνθῳ, γυνὴ τῶν ἐν	at Corinth, a woman of the greatest honour,
πλείστῃ τειμῇ καθεστηκειῶν, ζῶ-	living

σα σωφρόνως καὶ φιλολύκιος οὖσα καὶ ἀνατεθεικυῖα τὸν ἑαυτῆς βίον	modestly, who is a friend of the Lycians and has dedicated her life
εἰς τὴν πάντων Λυκίων εὐχαριστίαν, πολλὰ καὶ πλείστοις τῶν ἡμετέ-	to earning the gratitude of all the Lycians, and has bestowed numerous benefits on
ρων πολειτῶν ἐπ' εὐεργεσίαν παρέσχηται καὶ τὸ ἑαυτῆς μεγαλοπρε-	large numbers of our citizens; and, revealing the generosity of her
πὲς τῆς ψυχῆς ἐνδεικνυμένη ἐξ εὐνοίας οὐ διαλείπει ξένην τε ἑαυ-	nature, she doesn't cease, because of her goodwill, both from offering herself as host
τὴν πᾶσιν Λυκίοις παρεχομένη καὶ τῇ οἰκίᾳ δεχομένη ...	to every Lycian and receiving (them) in her house ...

And in the decree of Telmessos Iunia's actions are summed up in the following way: τοὺς παρεπιδημοῦντας Λυκίων καὶ τῶν πολ[ειτῶν ἡμῶν ... c.7 δέχε]ται τῇ οἰκίᾳ παρεχομένη αὐτοῖ[ς πάν]τα [c.23] τῶν παραγεινομένων προστασίαν [ἐν]δ[εικνυμένη] (Pallas et al., ibid., p.500, *ll*.76-77) – 'she welcomes in her own house Lycian travellers and our citizens... supplying them with everything ... displaying her patronage of those who are present'.

Such circumstances appear to parallel the instances recorded in Acts and the epistles of the NT where Paul and his friends are given hospitality or protection by certain women. Among these may be singled out Phoibe who is described in similar terms to Iunia Theodora since she is called the προστάτις of the church at Kenchreai (R.A. Kearsley, *Ancient Society: Resources for Teachers* 15 [1985], pp.124-37; M. Zappella, 'A proposito di Febe ΠΡΟΣΤΑΤΙΣ (Rm 16,2)', *Rivista Biblica Italiana* 37 [1989] pp.161-71 and also G.H.R. Horsley, 'Sophia, "the second Phoibe"', *New Docs* 4 [1987], pp.239-44).

Elsewhere on the stone, in the second decree of the Lycian Federal Assembly, other activities of Iunia Theodora are described, actions which extend beyond domestic patronage into the official sphere because (Pallas et al., ibid., p.499, *ll*.48-53):

> διὰ παν[τὸ]ς ἐνδέδεικται τὴν ὑπὲρ τοῦ ἔθνους σπουδὴν καὶ φιλοτειμίαν πᾶ[σι] τοῖς παρεπιδημήσασιν ἰδιώταις τε καὶ [πρ]έσβεσιν τοῖς ἀ[πο]στελλομ[έν]οις ὑπό τε τοῦ ἔθνους καὶ ἰδίᾳ κατὰ πόλιν συ[μ]παθῶς διακειμ[ένη ἠρέ]σκευται πᾶσιν συνκατασκευάζουσα τοὺς ἡγ[ε]μόνα[ς ε]ὐνο[υστάτο]υς ἡμεῖν γείνεσθαι ἀρεσκευομένη τούτοις κατὰ πάντα τρόπον
> **(she) has continuously shown her zeal for the nation and love of honour to all travellers whether private individuals or ambassadors sent by the nation or privately by various cities; and being sympathetically disposed, has procured the gratitude of all of us by assuring the great favour of the authorities which she seeks to win by every means.**

Iunia Theodora's influence among members of the Roman provincial government (see Pallas et al., ibid., p.507 on the interpretation of ἡγεμόνες as Roman officials) does not appear to be based on any formal authority. However, inscriptions such as that below, indicate that other women did sometimes undertake the regular magistracies and liturgies within Greek cities in the hellenistic and imperial periods:

Ed.pr. — *I.Eph.* IV, 1017 = Knibbe, *Forschungen in Ephesos* IX/1/1 (Vienna, 1981), B17, dated AD 93/4-104.

Ἐπὶ πρυτάνεως Οὐηδίας Πο[πλίου]	In the *prytany* of Vedia Marcia,
θυγατρὸς Μαρκίας ἱερῆς καὶ ἀ[ρχιερεί]-	the daughter of Publius, priestess and high-priestess

ας τῆς Ἀσίας · κουρῆτες εὐσεβε[ῖς φιλο]-	of Asia, the pious emperor-loving *kouretes*
σέβαστοι· Γ. Γεμίνιος Παῦλος, Λ.[----	were G. Geminius Paulus. L. [----] etc.

In this Ephesian inscription Vedia Marcia is described by three titles: *prytanis*, priestess and high-priestess of Asia. The *prytanis* had particularly strong religious affiliations because of the office-bearer's duty to maintain the sacred fire of Hestia. In addition, however, the *prytanis* was one of the chief magistrates of the city by whom official documents of the city were dated (cf. *I.Eph.* II, 508 for a *prytanis* as the official by whose term the erection of a statue in a public place is dated). It is clear from the surviving evidence that the *prytany* could equally well be undertaken by men or women. One Ephesian inscription even reveals that a mother undertook the office on behalf of her son, who may have been a minor or was, perhaps, dead (*I.Eph.* III, 650). Epigraphic evidence for women carrying civic burdens other than as *prytanis*, for example, as gymnasiarch, agonothete and, much more rarely, *grammateus* or secretary, is also to be found. The inscriptions (of the first half of II AD) relating to a member of a leading family in Lycian Perge, Plancia Magna, refer to the civic positions of δημιουργὸς and γυμνασίαρχος, for example (R.Merkelbach – S. Sahin, *EA*, 11 [1988], pp.120-23, nos. 29-37; for a survey of female gymnasiarchs in particular, see L. Casarico, 'Donne ginnasiarco', *ZPE* 48 [1982], pp.117-23).

The positions in which women are most commonly to be found, however, are priesthoods. The second title borne by Vedia Marcia, for example, probably refers to the priesthood of Artemis for which many other women's names are known from the inscriptions of Ephesus. Her third title, *archiereia* (high-priestess) of Asia is less common. *Archiereia* of Asia is the feminine form of *archiereus* of Asia which, by analogy with comparable cases, should suggest that the high-priesthood of Asia could also be held by either male or female. However, because many of the women described as *archiereiai* of Asia in inscriptions are known also to have been wives of men bearing the title *archiereus* of Asia or asiarch (which is thought by some to be a different term for the same title – for a summary of the state of recent scholarship on this question, see *New Docs* 4 [1987], pp.53-5), it has generally been argued in the past that women bore the title in an honorary capacity only. Such an interpretation was disputed on the basis of the epigraphic evidence for provincial high-priestesses at Ephesus some years ago (R.A. Kearsley, *GRBS* 26 [1986], pp.183-92). More recently an inscription from Amorium in Phrygia, published by R.M. Harrison (*Anat.St.* 38 [1988] p.181; pl.XXIII), also leads to the conclusion that high-priestesses of Asia held office in their own right. The inscription appears to record the praise of the federation of Asia for the high-priestess, Aelia Ammia, as *archiereia* of Asia during her term of office and her husband's name bears no title:

Ἡ βουλὴ καὶ ὁ δῆμος	The council and the people
ἐτείμησεν Αἰλίαν Ἀλε-	honoured Aelia Ammia,
ξάνδρου θυγατέρα Ἀμ-	the daughter of Alexander,
μίαν, γυναῖκα Μαρ · Ι · Δα-	wife of Mar(cus) I(ulius) Damianus
μιανοῦ καὶ μητέρα	and mother of
Μαρ · Ι · Ἀκύλα τοῦ ἀσιάρ-	Mar(cus) I(ulius) Aquila the asiarch,
χου, θυγατέρα δὲ τῆς πό-	daughter of the city,
λεως, σεμνότητι καὶ ἐπιει-	superior in holiness and seemliness
κείᾳ τρόπου διαφέρου-	of character
σαν πασῶν τῶν ἐν τῷ ἔ-	to all the women of her
θνει γύναικῶν, ἥ ὑπερβε-	nation, who excelled
βληκεν{αι} σωφροσύνῃ τε	in good sense and

καὶ φιλανδρίᾳ καὶ οἱ ἐπὶ τῆς Ἀ-
σίας Ἕλληνες ἀρχιερατεύου-
σ<α>ν τῶν μεγίστων ἐν Ἐφέσῳ
ναῶν ἐμαρτύρησαν.

in love for her husband, and the Greeks in Asia testified that she is high priestess of the greatest temples in Ephesus.

(A detailed discussion of this inscription appears in R.A. Kearsley, *EA* 16 [1990], pp.69-80.)

In noting the fact that certain women played a notable and individual role in a variety of fields within the Greek cities of the early imperial period, the lack of evidence that women of all strata of society could or did attain such independence from their domestic context must be emphasised. It was only by virtue of their wealth and their family connections that some women stepped beyond the conventions of social anonymity and domestic fidelity, so clearly defined in the literary sources of the time such as Plutarch's *Praecepta conjugalia* (*Moralia* 142C-D). Recent treatments of the dual values evident in the expectations placed on women in the Greek East include R. MacMullen, 'Women in Public in the Roman Empire', *Historia* 29 (1980), pp.208-218; R. Van Bremen, 'Women and Wealth' in *Images of Women in Antiquity*, A. Cameron & A. Kührt edd. (1983), pp.223-42; *New Docs* 4 (1987), pp.10-17.

R.A. Kearsley

§4 The Allotment after Death and Paul's Metaphor of Inheritance

Dionysias 24 July AD 48

Ed.pr. — B. Frid, *P. Ups.Frid* 1 (Bonn 1981), pp.1-20.

The papyrus sheet measuring 21.9 x 39.8 cm is badly preserved. Bottom, right and left edges are either broken or cut off, or badly damaged. However, the ending of the document can be conjectured from the formal structure of similar deeds.[34] The editor surmises that it consisted of the donor's subscription, the signatures of six witnesses and a docket of registration. Abrasions and holes affect the reading of other portions of the text. Restoration here is facilitated by context and the use of formulaic expressions. The editor's restorations, which are found in his commentary, have been added to the text.

[ἔτους ὀγδόου Τιβερίου Κλαυδί]ο̣υ
Κ̣[αί]σ̣α̣ρος [Σε]βαστ̣⸢ο⸣ῦ Γερμ̣ανι̣κοῦ
Αὐτοκράτορος μηνὸς Γορπιαίου
τριακάδι σεβαστῇ Ἐπεὶφ τριακάδι
σεβαστῇ ἐν Διονυσιάδ̣[ι] τῇ πρὸς
τ⸢ο⸣ῖ[ς]

[In the eighth year of Tiberius Claudius Caesar Augustus Germanicus Imperator, in the month of Gorpiaios, on the thirtieth *dies augusta*, Epeiph, on the thirtieth *dies augusta* in Dionysias at [the]

34 According to B. Frid, ibid., p.3, the deed consisted of five parts:
- **i.** Date and place (*ll.* 1-2)
- **ii.** The parties and the objects (*ll.* 2-7)
  - (a) The parties (*ll.* 2-6)
  - (b) The objects or possessions (*ll.* 6-7)
- **iii.** The division (*ll.* 7-20)
- **iv.** [Subscription (*ll.* 21-?)
- **v.** Witnesses]

As a control clause (see below) is usually included in these deeds, it may be relevant to note the fact by inserting another subdivision between elements iii. and iv.

[χαλκωρυχίοις τῆ]ς Θεμίσ̣[του]
μ[ερίδος το]ῦ [᾿Αρ]σ̣ι̣ν̣οείτου νομοῦ.
῾Ομ[ο]λογεῖ Σωτήριχος ᾿Απολ[λ]ωνίου
ὡς ἐτῶν ἑξήκο̣ντα πέν̣[τε ο]ὐλὴ
πήχει ἀριστερ[ῶι τ]ο̣ῖς ἑαυτοῦ
[τέκνοις ᾿Απολλ]ωνίωι ὡς ἐτῶν̣
[τ]ρ̣ιάκοντα οὐλὴ μήλωι ἀριστερῶι
καὶ ᾿Ισαροῦτι ὡς ἐτῶν τριάκοντα
πέντε οὐλὴ παρ᾿ ὦς ἀρισ[τ]ερὸν καὶ
᾿Εσ̣ερ̣σ̣ύ̣[θε]ι̣ ὡ̣[ς ἐτῶν εἴ-]
[κοσι πέντε οὐλὴ] ποδὶ δ̣ε̣[ξι]ῷ̣ι μ̣[ε]τ̣ὰ̣
κυρ[ί]ων τῶν γυναιῶν, ἑκατέρας τοῦ
ἑαυτῆς ἀνδρὸς τῆ̣ς μ̣ὲ̣ν ᾿Ισαροῦτος
῾Ηρακλείδου τοῦ Βίθυος ὡς̣ ἐτ̣[ῶν]
τ̣ε̣σ̣σ̣[αρά]κ̣ο̣ν̣[τα οὐ-]
[λὴ γαστροκνημί]ωι ἀριστ̣[ερῶ]ι̣ τῆ̣ς̣ δὲ
᾿Εσερ[σ]ύθιος ῾Εριεῦτος τοῦ
Μεν̣χήους ὡς ἐτῶν τριάκοντ[α]
οὐλὴ δακτύλω πρώτωι χειρὸς
ἀριστερᾶ[ς γεγο]νόσ[ι] αὐ̣[τ]ῷ̣ι ἐκ
[τῆς]
[συνούσης ἑαυτοῦ] γυναικὸ[ς
Τ]α̣υσίριος μ[εμ]ερικέναι αὐτοῖς
μετ̣[ὰ] τὴν ἑαυτοῦ τελευτὴν τὰ
ὑπάρχοντα αὐτῶι ἐν τῆ
προγεγραμμέν[η] Διονυσ̣[ι]άδι [καὶ
τ]ὰ̣ ὑ̣π̣[άρχον-]
[τα αὐτῶι ἐν τόπωι N (± 3)]
λ̣εγομ[ένωι] ο̣ἰ̣κόπεδα [ἅπε]ρ ἐστὶν
οἰ[κ]ία τρίστεγ[ος] κ̣αὶ π̣έμπ̣τον
μέρ[ο]ς {ο} ἑ[τ]έρ[α]ς ο̣ἰ̣κ̣ί̣ας κα̣[ὶ
αὐλῆ]ς κ[α]ὶ τ[ὰ συ]ν̣κ̣ύρ[ο]ν̣[τα
πάν]τα. τ̣[ὸν αὐτὸν]
[Σωτήρι]χ̣[ον μεμερικέναι τῶι
᾿Απολλων]ίωι μέρη [δύο] ἀ̣π̣ὸ̣ μ̣ε[ρῶ]ν̣
τεσσάρων [κα]ὶ̣ τῆ ᾿Ισαροῦτι καὶ τῆ
᾿Εσσε[ρ]σ̣ύθει τὰ λο̣ι̣πὰ [μ]έρη δύο̣
ἑκάστη̣ αὐτῶ[ν] μέρος [ἕ]ν̣, πᾶσ̣ι̣ δ[ὲ
τὸν] λ̣άκκ̣[ον]
[± 21 καὶ τὸν Σω]τ̣ή̣[ριχ]ο̣ν ὁμ̣ο̣ί̣ω[ς
μεμ]ε̣ρικέναι με[τ]ὰ τὴν ἑαυτοῦ
τελευτὴν τ̣ῷ̣ι προγεγραμμένωι
αὐτοῦ υἱῶι ᾿Απολλωνίωι μόνω̣ι̣ . . . . .
. . [. . .]

[coppermine in th]e d[istrict of] Themis
of the Arsinoite nome.
Soterichos, son of Apollonios,
about sixty-five years of age, scar
to left forearm, acknowledges to his
[children, Apoll]onios, about thirty years
of age, scar to left cheek,
and Isarous, about thirty-five years of
age, scar beside left ear, and Esersythis,
a[bout twenty-five years of age],
[scar] to right foot, with
the women's guardians, their
respective husbands – of Isarous,
Heracleides, son of Bithys, about forty
years of age, [scar]
to left [calf]; of
Esersythis, Herieus, son of
Menches, about thirty years of age,
scar to first finger of left hand –
born to him by
[his cohabiting] wife,
Tausiris, that he has allotted to them
after his death the
property belonging to him in the
aforementioned Dionysias [and
the property belonging]
[to him in the place] called [N],
real estate consisting of a
three-storey house and a fifth
part of another house and
a courtyard and all appurtenances.
[(And further) that the same]
[Soterichos has allotted to
Apollonios two] parts of
the four parts and to Isarous and to
Esersythis the remaining two parts,
to each of them one part; and to all (of
them) the la[ke]
[... and that Soterichos] likewise
has allotted after his
death to his aforementioned
son, Apollonios, alone ...

[ὑπάρ]χοντα [± 16].ου. [..]. εν.. .ε[..]. καὶ ὃν ἐὰ[ν] καταλίπῃ [ὁ αὐ]τὸς Σωτή]ριχος χόρτον καὶ πυρὸν καὶ γενή[μ]ατα λαχάνων τὰ εκ..[± 5]

[ἐὰν σ]υμβῇ τὸν [Σωτήρικον τελ]ευτῆσαι τ[ῶι ἐνεστῶτι] ὀγδόωι ἔ[τε]ι Τιβερίου [Κλα]υδίου Καί[σα]ρος Σεβασ[τοῦ Γερμανικοῦ Αὐτοκρά[τ]ορος....ε.ε.θ..[± 8 τὸν]

['Απ]ολλώνιον τῆς ἐγλήμψεως τοῦ ἐ[πι]β[άλλο]ντ[ος τῶι Σ]ωτηρίχω[ι] μέρους [δραγ]ματηγείας καὶ σακκ[ηγε]ίας κωμῶν Φιλωτ[ε]ρίδος καὶ Κανωπι[άδος] τῆς Θε-

[μίσ]του μερίδ[ος] γενή[ματο]ς τοῦ ἐνε[σ]τ[ῶ]τος ὀ[γδόου ἔ]τους Τιβ[ερ]ίου Κλα[υδίου] Καίσαρος [Σ]εβαστοῦ Γερ[μα]νικοῦ Αὐτοκράτορο[ς κ]αὶ ἀποδῶναι τὸν 'Απο[λλ]ώνιον

[± 15 καὶ] τῶ[ι 'Απολλ]ωνί[ω]ι μ[ὲ]ν [ὁμ]οίως [μεμερικ]έναι τὸν Σ[ω]τήριχο[ν καὶ] τὸ δίμοι[ρο]ν μέρος [ὧν] ἐὰν κατ[αλ]ίπῃ ὁ Σωτ[ή]ριχος ἐπιπλόων καὶ σκευῶν καὶ]

[ἐνδομενεία]ς τῇ [δ]ὲ γυναικὶ αὐ[τοῦ Τ]αυ[σίρε]ι τ[ὸ] λοιπ[ὸ]ν τρί]τον μέρος τῶν ἐπιπ[λό]ων καὶ σκευῶν καὶ ἐνδομενε[ί]ας καὶ οἴκ[ησιν καὶ χρῆσιν ἐφ' ὃν]

[περίεστι χρό]νον ἄνευ ἐνοικίου ἐν [ο]ἰ[κ]ωι ἑνὶ] ἐπιπέδωι τῆς προκιμένης οἰκίας· ἐπάναγκον δὲ τὸν 'Απολλώνιον δώ[σ]ειν με[τὰ τὴν τελευτὴν τῆς]

[Ταυσίριος ἐν] ἡμέρα[ι]ς [τρ]ιάκοντα τ]αῖς ἀδελφαῖς τῇ] μὲν 'Ισαροῦ[τ]ι εἰς προοῖκα ἀργυρίου δραχμὰς διακοσίας τεσσαράκοντα καὶ τ[ῇ] 'Εσερσύθει ὁμοίως εἰς]

property ...

... and whatever fodder, wheat and vegetable produce the same Soterichos may leave behind [...]

[If it] happens that [Soterichos dies] in [the present] eighth year of Tiberius Claudius Caesar Augustus Germanicus Imperator, ... [... (it is necessary?) that]

Apollonios (undertake?) the collecting of the part imposed on Soterichos of the conveyance and transport charge for the villages of Philoteris and Kanopias in the

district of Themis for produce of the present [eighth] year of Tiberius Claudius Caesar Augustus Germanicus Imperator and that Apollonios pay

[...] and that [to Apollonios likewise] Soterichos has [allotted] also a two-thirds part of whatever [movable property, utensils and]

[furniture] Soterichos may leave behind and to his wife Tausiris the remaining third part of the movable property, utensils and furniture, and residence [and use while]

[she lives] without rent in one room on the ground floor of the aforementioned house. (It is) necessary for Apollonios to give [after the death of]

[Tausiris within] thirty days [to his sisters], to Isarous for a dowry two hundred and forty silver drachmae and [to Esersythis likewise for]

[προοῖκα ἀργ]υ̣ρίου δρ[α]χμ̣[ὰς
διακ]ο̣[σ]ία[ς ἐκ τῶν κοιν]ῶ̣ν
ἀνυπερθ[έ]τ̣ως καὶ ἑ̣κά‹σ›τ̣ῃ αὐτῶ̣ν
[τ]ε̣λεῖν μ[ε]ρ̣[ιτ]είαν· τὸν δὲ αὐτὸν
'Απολλώ̣ν̣[ιον ± 21]
[. . .]. η [. .]σειν τὰ τῆς Τ̣[αυσίριος ±
24 ἐφ' ὃν δὲ χ]ρόνον περ[ίε]σ̣τιν
ὁ Σω̣[τήριχος ἔχειν αὐτὸν τὴν
κατ]ὰ̣ τ̣ῶ̣ν [ἑα]υτο̣[ῦ ὑπαρχόντων
ὁλοσχερῆ ἐξουσίαν]
[πωλ]ε̣ῖν ὑποτίθ[εσ]θ[αι μεταδιατίθεσθαι
οἰκονομεῖν περὶ αὐτῶν] τ̣ρόπω[ι ὧ̣ι
ἐὰν αἱρῆται ± 12] . . . . .[. .] . . .
[± 27]
[± 5]. νοσω.ε[± 40]βωντ̣ω̣ [± 23
]. . . . [. .]. . . . [± 27]
Faint traces of letters on the remaining strips (4 lines)

[a dowry] two hundred silver drachmae
[from the common property]
without delay and to execute the
allotment for each of them; and (that) the
same Apollonios [to ...
[...] those of Tausiris [...]
but while Soterichos lives
[he has complete authority over] his
[property]

to [sell, to] mortgage, [to alter the
disposition, to manage them] in
[whatever] manner [he may choose ...]

....

2 'Αρσινοίτου 4 γυναικῶν 5 Μεγχήους, δακτύλωι 7 συγκύροντα 8 Ἐσερσύθει
12 ἐκλήψεως, δραγματηγίας, σακκηγίας 13 ἀποδοῦναι 14, 15 ἐπιπλῶν 15 ἐνδομενίας
16 προκειμένης 17 προῖκα

The ages of persons named in *P. Ups.Frid* 1 are all given as multiples of five, i.e. Soterichos 65, Apollonios 30, Isarous 35, Esersythis 25 (?), Heracleides 40 and Herieus 30. This method of approximating ages[35] is frequent in antiquity. R.P. Duncan-Jones, 'Age-rounding, Illiteracy and Social Differentiation in the Roman Empire', *Chiron* 7 (1977), pp.333-53 and 'Age-rounding in Greco-Roman Egypt', *ZPE* 33 (1979), pp.169-77, discusses several variables which appear to have influenced the incidence of age-rounding. They are:

1. *class* – persons belonging to lower social classes are more likely to round their age;
2. *sex* – the age of a female is more likely to be rounded;
3. *geographical location and regional considerations* – e.g. the distance from a cultural centre increases the tendency to round one's age;
4. *age* – older persons are more likely to round their age.

A person's level of literacy appears to have been a significant factor across most variables. For example, members of the lower classes and women were less educated and thus more likely to be illiterate. They also show an increased tendency to round their ages. However, age-rounding must be seen as but one part of a more general inability of individuals to give an accurate statement of their age. Or were they merely careless? For example, Aurelius Isidorus (*P. Cair. Isidor.* 4, 5) records his age as 45 years before June AD 309 but as 40 years of age after that

---

[35] Rounding by fives is not confined to age alone, e.g. John 6.19 – 'having rowed about 25 or 30 stadia'. See also E.A. Judge, 'Veni. Vidi. Vici, and the Inscription of Cornelius Gallus', *Akten des VI. Int. Kongresses für griechische und lateinische Epigraphik* (Munich 1973), pp.571-3, for the Roman practice of rounding to multiples of five when citing the number of days from sighting the enemy to victory.

date (see Duncan-Jones, op.cit., p.334). Table 4.1 contains two further examples (see Duncan-Jones, op.cit., p.347):

Table 4.1: Age Differences for Two Individuals

Age	Date	Age	Date
36	25 Oct. 107 BC	45	27 Feb. AD 310
30	16 Aug. 104 BC	50	3 Apr. AD 317
35	12 Apr. 101 BC	58	Jun. AD 327
40	18 Oct. 99 BC	58	Oct. AD 328

The question of age-rounding is relevant to attempts[36] to date the birth of Jesus from his age at the commencement of his ministry. John commenced his baptism in the 15th year of Tiberius (i.e. AD 27-28) and Jesus his ministry (after his baptism) at the age of about 30 years – ὡσεὶ ἐτῶν τριάκοντα (Luke 3.1, 23). It is argued that this dating is inconsistent with the dating of Jesus' birth by the census taken by Quirinius (AD 6/7). However, the argument assumes a degree of accuracy which may not be warranted by the evidence from antiquity.

The Allotment after Death

P. Ups.Frid 1 is a deed of gift with effect after the donor's death. The beneficiaries of such allotments after death were invariably the donor's children. Where the children were still minors, the deed might appoint guardians for the duration of their minority, e.g. *BGU* I 86, *P. Vindob. Tandem* 27 (?) and *P. Diog.* 11-12. *P. Fam. Tebt.* 7 and 10 are receipts issued by two brothers, now no longer minors, to their guardian (a maternal uncle) for the allotments made to them by their maternal grandmother. In cases where the donor was male a right of usufruct to certain property (e.g. a dwelling and its utensils) might be granted to his surviving wife or other provisions made for her, e.g. *BGU* I 86 and *SB* VIII 9642 (4).[37] This right was usually conditional on the wife's remaining unmarried. Obligations and charges could also be imposed on the beneficiaries. For example, in *P. Ups.Frid* 1 Soterichos charged his son Apollonios to collect the conveyance and transport duties of the villages of Philoteris and Kanopias (*ll.*11-13) and to pay the dowries of his sisters (*ll.*16-18),[38] cf. also the charges imposed in *SB* VI 9377 *ll.*7-11, VIII 9642 (1) *ll.*12-14 and *P. Kron.* 50. A more general charge to pay the donor's debts might also be imposed on the beneficiaries, e.g. *SB* VI 9377, XII 10888, *P. Tebt.* II 381 and *P. Kron.* 50. Another duty which was frequently imposed by deeds of allotment was the burial of the donor, e.g. *SB* VI 9377, VIII 9642 (1), (3), (4) and (5), *SB* XII 10888, *P. Tebt.* II 381, *P. Kron.* 50 and *P. Diog.* 11-12.

---

36 The issue of back-dating the birth arises because of the conflicting dates given elsewhere, i.e. in the reign of Herod (= in or before 4 BC) and at the census of Quirinius (= AD 6/7).

37 For the provision made for a surviving wife in Jewish law see *m. Ket.* 4.12. In the case of remarriage the Jewish widow also ceded the right to maintenance from her husband's estate. She took her *kethubah* and whatever other property she owned and left (*m. 'Ed.* 1.12).

38 *P. Ups.Frid* 1 raises some points of interest for the discussion of the dowry in *New Docs* 6 (1992) §1. Why were the dowries of the two daughters, who were already married at the time of the making of this deed, to be paid on the death of their mother? The clue may lie in the use of the term προίξ in *ll.*17-18. It is probable that each daughter brought a φερνή into her marriage. The προίξ is separate from this, however, and represents a monetary payment to a daughter from her mother's estate (i.e. the property which the mother had brought into her marriage). It was usual on the death of a mother for her dowry to go to her children. Moreover, the division could be formalised by a deed of allotment after death when the marriage itself was formalised (see H.-A. Rupprecht, 'Ehevertrag und Erbrecht', *Miscellània Papirològica Ramon Roca-Puig* [Barcelona 1987], pp.307-11). However, this does not explain the following: a) why one sister received more than the other; b) why Apollonios received nothing; and c) why it was a charge made by the father in his deed of allotment after death.

The deed of allotment after death was in the form of a ὁμολογία. On this form of document see H.F. von Soden, *Untersuchungen zur Homologie in den griechischen Papyri Ägyptens bis Diokletian* (Köln 1973). Essentially the ὁμολογία was an acknowledgement of an underlying arrangement, be it of marriage, lease, sale, *paramone* etc. This is particularly visible in those documents which use a perfect infinitive to express the arrangement. For example, *P. Ups.Frid* 1 reads: ὁμολογεῖ Σωτήριχος ... μεμερικέναι – 'Soterichos acknowledges that he has allotted' (*ll.*2,6). Von Soden, ibid., p.26, observes: 'In all these documents the subject-matter of the ὁμολογεῖν is a completed action. It is confirmed in the document through ὁμολογεῖν, so that also in these cases the meaning of ὁμολογεῖν lies in the acknowledgement of the action in question' (my translation). H.J. Wolff, 'Consensual Contracts in the Papyri?', *JJP* 1 (1946), p.76, also comments on the ὁμολογία: 'Much rather this style seems to indicate that the contractants considered the performance of the recorded act itself as an element which, as its natural consequence, gave rise to such obligations as were intended by them'. The constitutive element of the ὁμολογία was an underlying act or *res*. In other words, the allotment after death must be considered to have been more than a mere expression of the donor's wishes regarding the division of his estate. It was an acknowledgement of a bilateral arrangement between the donor and the beneficiary. The conjunction of deeds of allotment and marriage (see H.-A. Rupprecht, 'Ehevertrag und Erbrecht', *Miscellànea Papirològica Ramon Roca-Puig* [Barcelona 1987], pp.307-11) further confirms the bilateral nature of the arrangement (see below).

Was the allotment after death revocable or irrevocable? Once the donor had allotted his property, could he change his mind? Opinions differ.[39] The reasons for this can be variously assigned. One can note the ambiguity of the expression ὁμολογεῖ ... μεμερικέναι ... μετὰ τὴν τελευτήν, i.e. its 'now and not yet' nature. The verb and its object infinitive imply a present state of affairs, i.e. X acknowledges to have allotted to Y. The prepositional phrase, however, anticipates a future event, i.e. the donor's death.[40] The Jewish law of gifts (see

---

39 I have been unable to consult H. Kreller, *Erbrechtliche Untersuchungen auf Grund der gräco-ägyptischen Papyrusurkunden* (Leipzig 1919), p.244, on this point. Mitteis, *Chrest.* II 1, pp.244-6, distinguish between allotments after death in which the donor retains the right to dispose of the property whilst he lives and other donatives, like *BGU* III 993, in which possession passed to the beneficiary. The question of irrevocabilty is only raised for inheritance agreements (Mitteis, *Chrest.* II 1, pp.242-4). Here it is important to determine whether the beneficiary assists in the drawing up of the agreement and whether and to what extent possession or κατοχή had passed to him. From a discussion of the revocability of gifts in a deed of the fourth century AD, A.G. Roos, *P. Gron.* 10 (Amsterdam 1933), pp.26-7, considers the right to revoke as optional. The deed concerns primarily a one-half-share gift to the donor's wife and a one-half-share gift to the church. On the wife's death her share was to revert to the church, i.e. she had the right of usufruct for the duration of her life. The question asked by Roos is why the deed is in the form of a gift rather than testament. He surmises that the desire to make the gift irrevocable (μηδενὸς ἑτέρου σκοποῦ ἢ ἑτέρου ἐγγράφου τὴν παροῦσαν γνώμην ἀνατρέπειν δυνησομένου *ll.*13f.) may lie behind the choice of form. A testament could be revoked whereas a gift could be made irrevocable by the donor's depriving himself of his right to revoke. In support he cites *P. Monac.* 8 *ll.*28ff. and *P. Cair. Preis.* 42 *l.*3. However, the late date of *P. Gron.* 10 and the possibility of an influence of Roman law makes any inference concerning the revocability of gifts in the earlier period problematic. H.J. Wolff, *Written and Unwritten Marriages in Hellenistic and Postclassical Roman Law* (Haverford 1939), pp.53, also discusses briefly the irrevocability of allotments. He is of the opinion that revocability 'meant only the right to make another distribution, but did not prejudice the protection which the *katoche* procured for the descendants against alienation *inter vivos*'. O. Montevecchi, *La Papirologia* (Turin 1973), p.207, maintains that the majority of allotments were only effective after the death of the donor. H.-A. Rupprecht, 'Ehevertrag und Erbrecht', *Miscellànea Papirològica Ramon Roca-Puig* (Barcelona 1987), p.310, recognises the uncertainty surrounding the question of revocability and adds that his present study of newly published documents offers no general solution. However, in view of the partial alterations made by the donor in the allotments after death, *BGU* I 251 + *BGU* III 719 (AD 81) and *BGU* I 183 (AD 85), Rupprecht argues that there is a *prima facie* case for revocability. Most recently P. Schubert, *P. Diog.* 11-12 (p.102) has stated that such deeds were revocable.

40 The phrases ὃν ἐὰν καταλίπῃ (*l.*10) and ὧν ἐὰν καταλίπῃ (*l.*14) in *P. Ups.Frid* 1 also seem to imply a future allotment. However, the mood of the verbs in these case is misleading. It is important to note that the

below) was influenced by Hellenistic practice and shows a similar ambiguity in the expression 'from today and after death' (מהיום ולאחר מיתה). The gift had been made (i.e. 'from today') and was as such irrevocable (*m. B. Bat.* 8.7). The expression 'and after death' seems to indicate a desire to safeguard the gift against possible future claims which might arise from the donor's continued right of usufruct. Was this also the intention of the expression μετὰ τὴν τελευτήν in the Greek documents? The various influences which bear on the evolution of the Greek allotment after death also complicate its interpretation. For example, its development was influenced by forces both internal (e.g. assimilation to the will) and external to the Greek legal system (e.g. Egyptian and Roman laws). The allotment after death needs, therefore, to be considered as an evolving and changing legal instrument. To ask the question whether it was irrevocable or not seems to ignore the possibility of a difference in deeds of allotment themselves. Clauses which reserve the right of control (i.e. control clauses) are relevant to this point. Indeed, the bilateral nature of the deed of allotment suggests that it could not be revoked unilaterally by the donor, unless that right had been expressly provided for in the deed itself.

Did the right of control imply the right to revoke the allotment as Taubenschlag, *Law*, pp.205-6, believed? The distinction between possession and ownership[41] also poses a difficulty. Did the donor's right of control give him possession without ownership? In other words, had ownership already passed to the beneficiary? If so, it follows that the deed could not be revoked unilaterally by the donor. In *BGU* III 993 (columns II and III dated 127 BC) Psenthotes, a priest of Isis, made an allotment of property (i.e. ἀπομεμερικέναι μετὰ τὴν ἑαυτοῦ τελευτήν), also called an agreement of gift (i.e. συγγραφὴ δόσεως), to his daughter, Tasesis, and wife, Tsennesis. Two aspects of the deed attract attention. First, no right of control is reserved by the donor. Indeed, the donor stipulates: κυριευέτωσαν δ' ἑκάστη κατὰ τὴν σημαινομένην διαστολήν. Second, the papyrus records in a fourth hand that the transfer duty on the gift had been paid (see column IV). Mitteis, *Chrest.* II 1, p.245, observes that the transfer duty was paid at the same time (*gleichzeitig*) as the allotment and conclude from this that ownership had already passed to the women – so also R. Yaron, *Gifts in Contemplation of Death* (Oxford 1960), p.46, who cites discussions by V. Arangio-Ruiz and H. Kreller. In fact the payment of the duty is dated some eight months after the date of the deed itself. The interpretation of the papyrus thus appears to rest on three assumptions: a) the issuing of a receipt for payment of the transfer duty implies that the transfer had actually occurred; b) an eight-month delay before payment of the transfer duty was not exceptional; and c) the donor had not died between the making of the deed and the payment of the transfer duty, i.e. 9 January and 17 September 127 BC respectively. All three assumptions can be questioned. In provisional sales (e.g. *BGU* III 994) a receipt for the transfer duty might be issued before the actual transfer (see P.W. Pestman, *P. L. Bat.* XXIII, 'Agoranomoi et actes agoranomiques', pp.37-9, and 'Ventes provisoires de biens pour sûreté de dettes', pp.45-59). Pestman (p.38) also estimates that after a deed was made, payment of the transfer duty usually occurred within 30 days. The last assumption can also be questioned. There is no evidence to suggest that Psenthotes was still alive when the transfer duty was paid. Indeed, Pestman (p.30) holds that the gift took effect only after the donor's death. It was then, we may assume, that the transfer duty was paid.

P. Oxy. II 237 col.VIII *ll.*27-43 cites an edict of M. Mettius Rufus (AD 89) issued because of an official failure to maintain an adequate record of property transactions at Oxyrhynchus. The edict called for all owners of property as well as others having a claim over property to register the fact. In the latter group were included creditors holding mortgages over property, wives who had secured their alimentation capital by a pledge over their husbands'

---

items referred to either are unrealised or consist of movables. As such they may be subject to a present act of allotment but in an unrealised form – hence the use of the subjunctive mood.

41 The distinction needs to be maintained in other areas of Greek law as well, e.g. marital property (see the discussion in *New Docs* 6 [1992] §1) and leases (see Wolff, op.cit., pp.62-3).

property[42] and children who were beneficiaries of an allotment, i.e. those who had possession (κτῆσις) after their parents' death but where usufruct (χρῆσις) had been retained by the parents. The edict sought thereby to protect any third party who might enter into an agreement over the property from being defrauded by ignorance – ἵνα οἱ συναλλάσσοντες μὴ κατ' ἄγνοιαν ἐνεδρεύονται. The document seems to imply that the beneficiary, like a wife under Egyptian law, had some claim over the property which needed to be recognised in any dealings involving it. P.W. Pestman, *Marriage and Matrimonial Property in Ancient Egypt* (Leiden 1961), pp.136-142, recognises this as a 'right of succession'. According to his view, ownership remains with the donor but he 'needs a statement-of-no-title from his heirs if he wants to alienate a piece of property' (p.137). Without obtaining such a statement the buyer ran the risk of having the purchase declared null and void by any one of those holding the right of succession. *P. Oxy.* IV 713 (AD 97) is of further interest on this point. In this papyrus Leonides writes to the keepers of the records to register his claim (κατοχή) to the remaining one third of his mother's property. His father had already died with his property devolving to the three children. His mother, however, was still alive but in the marriage agreement of Leonides' brother and sister she had already made an allotment of two thirds of her property. Leonides' claim, however, is based on the property settlement agreed to in his parents' marriage agreement which remained in force (ἔνθεσμος) and uncancelled (ἀπερίλυτος) and which itself assured the children of secure (βεβαίως) and irrevocable (ἀναφαιρέτως) ownership. Again deeds in which children resign their claim to a parent's estate (ὁμολογεῖ NN ἐξίστασθαι τῷ NN τῶν καταλειφθησομένων ὑπαρχόντων) are of interest with respect to the notion of κατοχή. *BGU* XV 2476 is such a deed. An allotment of property (μεριτεία) had been agreed upon in his parents' maintenance agreement (συγγραφὴ τροφῖτις). However, Papontos resigns from his allotment consisting of a house and courtyard in return for a sum of 400 silver drachmae which is now paid to him by his father. The other provisions of the allotment remain valid and Papontos agrees not to make any further claims against his father's estate. The issuing of such a deed confirms the fact that an allotment gave the beneficiary a claim to certain property.

The text of *P. Cairo Preis.* 42, though very fragmentary and late (third to fourth century AD), implies that the allotment was irrevocable – ἀναφαιρέτως καὶ ἀμετανοήτως συγκεχωρη[έναι ... μετ]' ἐμὴν τελευτήν; so also *P. Gron.* 10 which is also late (fourth century AD) and formally quite distinct from other deeds of allotment. *P. Mich.* V 321 (AD 42) is of further interest again. The donor Orseus acknowledges that he has allotted after his death to his children certain property consisting of catoecic land, building sites, utensils and furniture. At the same time he forgoes the right of control, i.e. to sell, to mortgage, to alienate or to allot the property to other children, the present allotment excepted. Clearly, the allotment is irrevocable and possession has passed to the beneficiaries. In return the donor receives a maintenance allowance in wheat and money. *P. Mich.* V 321 may be compared to another deed in which a somewhat similar arrangement is met but where the allotment is to take effect from today. In *P. Mich.* V 322a (AD 46) Psuphis and his wife Tetosiris make an allotment of property to their children. They also forgo the right to sell, to mortgage, to alienate, to leave it to others and to dispose of it otherwise. At the same time they acknowledge that their children are κύριοι, having the right to sell, to mortgage, to alienate and to lease the property. In return the parents are to receive a maintenance allowance in wheat, oil and money. The allotment is irrevocable and possession has passed to the beneficiaries. Indeed, the fact is acknowledged in the wording of the allotment itself: ὁμολογεῖ ... μεμερικέναι ἀπὸ τοῦ νῦν. The fragmentary condition of *SB* XVI 12334 (late second century AD) is to be regretted but here also an allotment is made – ἡ δ' αὐτὴ Ταμαρρῆς ὁμοίως συνχωρῖ μετὰ [τὴν ἑαυτῆς τελευτήν] –

42 See *New Docs* 6 [1992] §1 and P.W. Pestman, *Marriage and Matrimonial Property in Ancient Egypt* (Leiden 1961), pp.133-6. Other relevant papyri are *P. Tebt.* III 776 and *P. BM* 10591 recto X *ll.*7-9 (cited Pestman, op.cit., pp.44 and 133).

part of which at least appears to be effective immediately, cf. ἀπὸ δὲ τοῦ νῦν (*l.*14) and the provision for Tamarres' maintenance and her right to take action for recovery (*ll.*21-22).[43]

The question of revocability remains perplexing in view of other deeds of allotment in which the donor reserves the right of control. In *SB* V 7559 *ll.*13ff. (AD 99) Thaisas reserved the right to manage her property.[44]

> ἐφ' ὃν δὲ χρόνον περίεστιν ἡ Θαισᾶς ἔχιν αὐτὴν τὴν τọ[ύ]του ẹ̓ξουσίαν οἰκονομῖν περὶ αὐτοῦ ὡς ἐὰν ἐρῆται.
> **that whilst Thaisas lives she has authority over this to manage it however she chooses.**

In *BGU* I 86 *ll.*23-5 (AD 155), however, the right of the donor is made more explicit.

> ἐφ' ὃν δὲ χρόνον πε[ρίεστιν ὁ ὁμολογῶν, ἔχειν αὐτὸν τὴν ...] ... τῶν ἰδίων π̣ά̣ν̣[των] ὁλοσχερῆ ἐξουσίαν πωλεῖν, ὑποτίθεσθαι, ἑτέροις παρασ[υ]νχωρεῖν[45] τω[...
> **that whilst [the acknowledger lives he has ...]... complete authority over all that is his to sell, to mortgage, to make another agreement (συγχώρημα) with different people ...**

P. Ups.Frid 1 also appears to have a similar clause (*l.*20). Von Soden, op.cit., pp.76-7, assimilates the allotment after death to other types of gifts and in conformity with his understanding of the ὁμολογία considers that the transfer of property had actually occurred. In other words, the beneficiary was now the owner of the property but a right of control was reserved by the donor. The one exception, in von Soden's view, was *BGU* I 86. In this deed the transfer, like the testamentary provisions of the will, was to occur after the donor's death. He appears to base his argument on the use of the term παρασυγχωρεῖν (*Nebenabrede treffen* – F. Preisigke, *Wörterbuch*) in a deed which was itself a συγχώρημα. In other words, the donor retained the right to make other concessions or allotments concerning the property. One might ask, however, whether the deed's writer intended any such association between the terms. Indeed, LSJ citing *BGU* I 86 as the only reference understands παρασυγχωρεῖν to mean 'sublet property by agreement'.[46] Be that as it may, other deeds show that the allotment could be changed. In *SB* VIII 9642 (4) the donor reserves the right to sell, to mortgage and to change the disposition (μεταδιατίθεσθαι) – see also *BGU* I 183 for a similar control clause. Further confirmation of the donor's right to alter the allotment is found, as observed by H.-A. Rupprecht, 'Ehevertrag und Erbrecht', p.310, in the alterations made between the allotments by Satabous which occasioned the recording of the marriages of her children Stotoetis (to Tanephremmis) and Horos (to his sister Erieus), i.e. *BGU* I 251 + *BGU* III 719 (AD 81) and *BGU* I 183 (AD 85) respectively. Though a strict comparison is made difficult by the fragmentary nature of the earlier document, it is clear that an alteration occurred regarding the

---

43 It may also be of interest to note that even in a deed of loan (*P.Lond.* II 311 of AD 149) the borrower forgoes the right to sell, to mortgage and to repay others from the property with which she has secured the loan. Cf. the edict of Mettius Rufus (cited above) which mentions creditors, wives according to Egyptian laws and beneficiaries of allotments as needing to register their claim to property.

44 See also *SB* VI 9377, VIII 9642 (1), (4), (5) and *P.Kron.* 50. No control clause at all is found in *BGU* III 993, *P.Diog.* 11-12 and possibly *P.Vindob. Tandem* 27.

45 It is to be observed that von Soden accepts the reading of *MChr* 306 (= *BGU* I 86) at this point rather than that of the ed.pr. who gave ἑτέροις παρασ[υ]νχωρούντω[ν . .] . α . ν τῶνδε ἐπὶ τῆς ἀρχῆς μαρτυρούντων καὶ συνσφραγισά[ντων] | τοῦτο τῷ συνχωρήματι (*ll.*25-6). In this reading the term in question is not related to the preceding infinitives of the control clause but to the participles which follow. However, in view of the use of the expression παρόντων δὲ ἐπὶ τῆς ἀρχῆς at the beginning of a new sentence (e.g. *P.Vindob. Tandem* 27, *BGU* I 183 and 251), the reading of *MChr* 306 (i.e. ἑτέροις παρασ[υ]νχωρεῖν τω[. π]αρόντων δὲ ἐπὶ τῆς ἀρχῆς ...) is to be preferred.

46 The only other use of παρασυγχωρεῖν that I can find is *CPR* VII 20. Though the document is fragmentary, the editor translates π(αρα)συνχωρήσῃς ἡμῖν as 'you allow us' – *[daß] du es uns erlaubst.*

allotment to the children of her deceased son Tesenouphis. Whilst in AD 81 (*BGU* I 251) they received a share in property, in AD 85 (*BGU* I 183) they only receive a payment of eight drachmae, a feigned donation made purely to save their honour according to Mitteis, *Chrest.* II 2, p.359. This change in the second allotment together with the fact that not all beneficiaries took part in the making of the deed itself further leads Mitteis to hold that such deeds were revocable. *BGU* I 183 is interesting in another respect also. According to Mitteis, *Chrest.* II 2, p.359, the control clause of *BGU* I 183 does not imply that the deed was revocable because τὰ ἴδια πάντα (cf. also *BGU* I 86 above) could refer to the donor's other property which had not been allotted. There are difficulties with this suggestion. First, the clause, if it refers to other property, is superfluous. It goes without saying that if she had retained property, it was under her control. Second, the use of πάντα rather than λοιπά (or similar) implies that the expression is inclusive. The use strikes one as linguistically odd, if the expression were to refer only to remaining property. Third, similar control clauses used in both wills (e.g. *P. Oxy.* III 491 and 494) and allotments refer to the property which was subject to disposition at the time. One expects the clause to have the same reference in *BGU* I 183. If so, the choice of the expression τὰ ἴδια πάντα to describe the allotted property is itself informative. It suggests that the donor continued to hold proprietorial rights.

A similar conclusion regarding revocability of deeds of allotment seems to follow from the donor's right to sell or to mortgage the property, e.g. *BGU* I 86, *P. Ups.Frid* 1, *P. München.* III 80 and *SB* VIII 9642 (4). If the donor could alienate property which was subject to an allotment, then he or she could clearly change the allotment. It might be objected that rabbinic law (*m. B.Bat.* 8.7) also envisaged the situation where a donor, who retained usufruct, sold the gift to a third party. It ruled, however, that the gift was only sold until the donor died and thereafter the property reverted to the beneficiary.[47] The edict of Mettius Rufus (see above), which in part sought to protect any third party entering into an agreement over property from being defrauded by ignorance of a κατοχή, suggests that a somewhat similar situation may also have applied in Egypt. However, if the control clause reserving a right to sell or to mortgage was to be meaningful, then it will have limited at the same time the right and claim of any beneficiary. In other words, the donor and beneficiaries were bound by the acknowledged arrangement, which might give the donor the right to sell, to mortgage, to alter or even to annul the allotment. The wording of the acknowledgement would thus determine the conditions which applied in each particular allotment.

Jewish Gifts in Contemplation of Death

The development of the allotment after death and the question over its revocability are relevant to the rabbinic law of inheritance. R. Yaron, *Gifts in Contemplation of Death* (Oxford 1960), discusses the Jewish practice of gifts in contemplation of death and argues for its having been influenced by Greek legal practice. The Pentateuchal law of succession rigidly defined one's heirs and their proportional share in the estate. However, there were factors which in time came to weigh against its continued application in all matters of succession. These were a growth in wealth (ibid., p.18), a change in the notion of wealth from being familial to being personal[48] (ibid., pp.18, 32) and a growing recognition of the individual's dispositional freedom (ibid., p.52). Yaron (ibid., p.18) argues that the Greek instrument of allotment after death was adopted by Jewish law about 100 BC as a way around the law's rigidity. Since the Pentateuchal law could not be annulled, the innovation depended on the property being called a

47 The sale of such property by the donor appears to be a concession applicable only in unusual circumstances, for *m. B.Bat.* 8.7 also states expressly that the father (= donor) cannot sell it – האב אינו יכול למכור.

48 A similar change (i.e. familial to personal initiative) also appears to have taken place in the notion of marriage. See *New Docs* 6 (1992) §1.

gift – the term 'inheritance' was avoided for fear that it might invalidate the gift (*m. B.Bat.* 8.5 and Yaron, ibid., pp.124-7). The Greek allotment after death thus became the disposition of a healthy person or *matenath bari* (מתנת בריא). It was a bilateral agreement – there had to be an act of acquisition by, or delivery to, the beneficiary (ibid., pp.32, 65, 135-6), though this could also be effected through a third person (ibid., pp.32-3, 127-9). Ownership was thereby transferred to the beneficiary but usufruct was reserved until the donor's death. As such, the *matenath bari* was irrevocable (at least until the Middle Ages – see ibid., pp.46-7, 50-3). On the other hand, the Greek διαθήκη was adopted by Jewish law at a later stage (i.e. in the Tannaitic period = first to second century AD). The *diathiqi* (דייתיקי = διαθήκη) was the disposition of a dying person or *matenath shekhiv mera* (מתנת שכיב מרע). Unlike the *matenath bari*, it could be revoked if the donor recovered from his illness (ibid., pp.64-77, 81-9); however, there were exceptions. For example, the gift of manumission could not be revoked when the donor recovered 'because he (i.e. the slave) has (already) acquired the name of a free man' (*b. Giṭ.*9a; see ibid., pp.170-1).

The use of the *matenath bari* arises as a possibility in three NT contexts. The first is Gal. 3.15. The relevance of the *matenath bari* to an understanding of this verse is discussed fully in *New Docs* 6 (1992) §5. The second is found in the parable of the wicked tenants (Mark 11.1-9 et par.). An apparent illogicality in the parable is the tenants' assumption that they might acquire the vineyard (inheritance v.7) by killing the owner's son. E. Bammel, 'Das Gleichnis von den bösen Winzern (Mark 12, 1-9) und das jüdische Erbrecht', *RIDA* 6 (1959), pp.11-17, argues that the assumption becomes meaningful if the son had received the property by a *matenath bari.*[49] By killing the son the property would be left ownerless – the tenants assumed that the father who was still absent would make no claim to the property – and they would then be able to acquire it by the law of *ḥazaqah* (usucaption). The third possibility concerns the parable of the prodigal son (Luke 15.11-32) and how the father might divide the property so as to exclude the younger son from inheriting in the future (i.e. when the father died) a share of the remaining property. Both Yaron, op.cit., pp.42-5, and D. Daube, 'Inheritance in Two Lukan Pericopes', *ZSS* 72 (1955), pp.326-34, argue that the parable assumes the use of dismission whereby the younger son was 'given certain property so as to have no further claims to the inheritance' (Yaron, op.cit., p.42). No simultaneous division or allotment to the elder brother was necessary. However, this possible legal reconstruction requires one to read Luke 15.11 and 31 loosely. This is indeed possible as one is dealing with a parable and not a legal text. However, that is not to say that the attempt to understand the parable at face value should not be made. In v.11 it is stated that the father divided his property between them (plural). The elder brother is assumed to have been a party to the division. In v.31 the father says to the elder son, 'all that is mine is yours'. Both verses support J.D.M. Derrett's suggestion ('The Parable of the Prodigal

---

49 There are difficulties with Bammel's suggestion. Why would the tenants, or for that matter the hearers of the parable, assume that the son was now the vineyard's owner by a *matenath bari*? The parable provides no tangible marker. It is also improbable that the term κληρονόμος was used in a strictly legal sense. In everyday discourse a son qua son is heir. Even if the term had a strictly legal sense, problems arise. The first concerns the use of the term κληρονομία (Mark 12.7 et par.) to refer to the vineyard. Any term referring to inheritance was to be avoided in a *matenath bari* (see above). If one permits a degree of flexibility in understanding the tenants' words at this point (they were not jurists), a residual problem persists. The hearers, who were likewise not jurists, are supposed by Bammel to have understood the parable's legal context. However, the use of the term 'inheritance' would not have assisted them to infer that a disposition by *matenath bari* had occurred. Second, no mention is made of the donor's right of usufruct. The retention of this right presupposed a continued interest in the vineyard. Thus one might reasonably assume that the donor, whether absent or not, would act to claim his son's estate. Would this also have escaped the attention of both the tenants and hearers of the parable? At this point one enters upon the psychological dimension of the parable, on which see the comment in *New Docs* 6 (1992) §13. J.D.M. Derrett, 'The Parable of the Wicked Vinedressers', *Law in the New Testament* (London 1970), p.303 n.1, suggests a different legal context again. He argues that the owner had perhaps only transferred a one-tenth share to his son so that he might be enabled to initiate a legal action against the tenants.

Son', *Law in the New Testament* [London 1970], pp.108-9 and 114-5) that the father divided his property between both his sons. The allotment to the younger son had immediate effect. However, the allotment to the elder son was probably by *matenath bari* with the father retaining the right of usufruct whilst he lived. By so acting the father had effectively excluded the younger son from any future claim to an inheritance for what property remained had been allotted by *matenath bari* to his elder son.

Allotments after Death and Wills

The allotment after death, though a testamentary instrument, should be distinguished from the Greek will or διαθήκη. The distinction is not made clear to readers by C.K. Barrett, *The New Testament Background: Selected Documents* (London 1987), p.42, when he describes *P. Tebt.* II 381, a deed of allotment, as a will. One way in which they differed was in the forms each deed took. The allotment after death was usually written as a *homologia* – ὁμολογεῖ ... μεμερικέναι μετὰ τὴν τελευτήν.[50] As such, it was an acknowledgement of an underlying arrangement of allotment (μεμερικέναι) between the donor and beneficiaries. The διαθήκη used instead the expression τάδε διετίθετο νοῶν καὶ φρονῶν (or similar) and was a unilateral disposition by the testator (Mitteis, *Chrest.* II 1, p.238-9) which required no underlying arrangement. Furthermore, it only became effective on the testator's death and thus might be revoked by him at any time.[51] The Greek will also differed from the Roman will. In a Roman will the aim was the appointment of an heir or heirs in place of the deceased testator and they were in consequence heirs to the whole estate, assets and liabilities.[52] The Greek will, on the

50 So also *P. Mich.* V 321. Other expressions were also possible, e.g. ὁμολογεῖ συνκεχωρηκέναι (plus possibly διατεταχέναι) μετὰ τὴν τελευτήν (e.g. *P. Tebt.* II 381, *P. Kron.* 50, *P. Mert.* III 105, *SB* VI 9373?, VIII 9642, X 10572, XII 10888) or ὁμολογεῖ ἀπομεμερικέναι μετὰ τὴν τελευτήν (e.g. *BGU* III 993) and συνχωρῶ ... συνχωρῖ ὁ ὁμολογῶν μετὰ τὴν ἑαυτοῦ τελευτήν (e.g. *BGU* I 86). The form of *P. Diog.* 11-12 is exceptional being written as an informal μεσιτία (μεριτεία?). The ed. pr. surmises that Isidora, the donor, probably had it hastily drawn up 'knowing that she will not pass the night'. When the expression occurs in deeds associated with marriage agreements, it usually lacks the verb of acknowledgement, e.g. συνχωρεῖ, συνχωροῦσι, π[ροσ]υνχωροῦσι or προσμερίζει (see *BGU* I 183, 251, 252, IV 1098, *P. Oxy.* II 265, XLIX 3491, *CPR* 28 [= *MChr* 312] and *SB* XVI 12334). The bridegroom and/or his parents make an acknowledgement in relation to the dowry's receipt. However, cf. the *hypographe* of *BGU* I 183 and III 719 (ὁμολογῶ συνκεχωρηκέναι) and the Greek abstract of an Egyptian συγγραφὴ τροφῖτις *P. Mich.* II 121 recto II ii (ἐξομολογοῦμεν ἀπομεμερικέναι).

51 This is not to say that assimilation between wills and allotments after death did not occur. For example, it has already been noted that the use of six witnesses in deeds of allotment may have been an assimilation to the form of the Greek διαθήκη.

52 The essential part of the testament in Roman law was the *institutio heredis*. A testament was not a testament without the naming of an heir who then became the *successor in locum defuncti*. It is important to note that the legal concept of heir is peculiarly Roman. For example, by the *ius civile* the *heres* as the successor in place of the deceased inherited not only the assets of the deceased but also his liabilities. If the testator's liabilities were greater than his assets, then the loss fell to the heir, i.e. his liability was not limited to the inherited assets. The harshness of the *ius civile* at this point was mitigated in time by the *ius praetorium* which allowed the heir to refuse his inheritance (*beneficium abstinendi* - see the discussion of Pliny, *Epist.* 2.4 in J.W. Tellegen, *The Roman Law of Succession in the Letters of Pliny the Younger* [Zutphen 1982], pp.18-29). Also in the case of a plurality of heirs particular assets of the testator could not be left to one heir but instead a fraction of the whole estate had to be left to each heir. The *donatio mortis causa* provided a way round both the above peculiarities of the Roman law of inheritance. It was a gift agreed on by both donor and beneficiary but only became fully effective on the donor's death. The donor agreed to give the named persons particular assets of his estate but they were not thereby subject to the donor's liabilities. Two other aspects of the *donatio mortis causa* are of interest. First, it could involve a charge, i.e. *fideicommissum*, or an obligation, i.e. *modus*, on the beneficiary. Second, as an agreement it could not be revoked unilaterally by the donor (see F. Schulz, *Classical Roman Law* [Oxford 1969], p.332; Schulz maintains that evidence to the contrary is either spurious or able to be interpreted differently). However, the irrevocability of the *donatio mortis causa*, like that of the allotment after death, is

other hand, was a disposition of property only. This can be seen in the use of the phrase καταλείπω τὰ ὑπάρχοντά μου or later and perhaps under Roman influence (Mitteis, *Chrest.* II 1, p.236) in the phrase καταλείπω κληρονόμον τῶν ὑπαρχόντων. See further Taubenschlag, *Law*, pp.190-200.

The Greek will developed its own formal particularities over the period extending from the Ptolemies to the Constitutio Antoniniana. As a result various groupings of them can be made (see D. Klamp, 'Das Testament der Taharpaesis', *ZPE* 2 [1968], p.83 for references). However, as an example of one type Klamp's analysis of the Oxyrhynchite will (p.85) may be cited:

1.	Date and place of the will	ἔτους ... ἐν 'Οξυρύγχων πόλει τῆς Θηβαΐδος, ἀγαθῇ τύχῃ
2.	Introductory formula	τάδε διέθετο νοῶν καὶ φρονῶν
3.	Clause reserving the testator's right to change the will	ἐφ' ὃν μὲν περίειμι χρόνον τῶν ἰδίων κύριον εἶναι καὶ χρᾶσθαι καὶ οἰκονομεῖν περὶ αὐτῶν καὶ μεταδιατίθεσθαι καθ' ὃν ἐὰν αἱρῶμαι τρόπον ... (or similar)
4.	Appointment of heir and division of property	ἐὰν δὲ ἐπὶ ταύτῃ τῇ διαθήκῃ τελευτήσω ... καταλείπω κληρονόμους
5.	Breach and penalty clause	μηδενὶ ἐξεῖναι παραβαίνειν ...
6.	Conclusion	ἡ διαθήκη κυρία
7.	Subscription of testator with repetition of the property division	πεποίημαι τὴν διαθήκην καὶ καταλείπω κτλ
8.	Subscription of witnesses	μαρτυρῶ τῇ διαθήκῃ ...
9.	Registration of the authorities and title.	διαθήκη τοῦ δεῖνος

Various conditions and procedures surrounded the making of wills of the Oxyrhynchite type in the Roman period.

a. The will had to be written.

b. It had to be public, i.e. written before the notaries. See *Gnomon of the Idios Logos* §7 (*BGU* V 1210): Διαθῆκαι ὅσαι μὴ κατὰ δημοσίους χρηματισμοὺς γείνωνται ἄκυροί εἰσι – 'wills which are not made by public document are void'.

c. The will had to be witnessed by six signatories.

d. The deed was sealed and lodged with the authorities in the *agoranomion*.

e. The testator received an official draft (ἐκδόσιμον) of the deed for later use, i.e. in the procedure of the will's delivery and opening.

Inheritance and the NT

In the NT the terms 'inheritance', 'heir' and 'to inherit' are mostly used metaphorically or employed to construct a metaphor, e.g. Gal.4.1. Exceptions are found at the literal level of the parable of the wicked tenants (Matt.21.33-46, Mark 12.1-12 and Luke 20.9-19 – see above) and at Luke 12.13, where Jesus is asked to resolve a dispute over inheritance.

F. Lyall, *Slaves, Citizens, Sons* (Grand Rapids 1984), pp.101-117, argues for the use of Roman law rather than either Jewish or Greek laws to explain Paul's use of the metaphor of inheritance. He justifies the appeal to Roman law by the use of three premises:

1. The meanings of the metaphors are fuller when interpreted in terms of Roman law.
2. The recipients of the letters would have known Roman law (Rome; Corinth and Philippi as colonies; Ephesus as a provincial centre where Roman law was dispensed). Even people who were not Roman citizens took an interest in Roman law as the law of the ruling class.
3. Paul would have known the law of his citizenship. His knowledge would have been facilitated by his training in the Jewish legal system.

---

disputed. On the types of the Roman testament see M. Amelotti, *Il testamento romano attraverso la prassi documentale* (Florence 1966).

The major point of departure for Lyall's argument concerning Paul's use of the metaphor of inheritance is the observation that the concept of 'heir of God' suits Roman law (the discussion is confined to intestate succession) better than either Greek or Jewish law. In the latter legal systems one became an heir on the death of the ancestor but in the Roman legal system the *sui heredes* were so whilst the *paterfamilias* lived. The perceived problem is that the use of the term 'heir of God' under other legal systems entails the death of God. Accordingly, Lyall argues that Roman law offers a better context for the interpretation of the metaphor. The argument, however, seems to overwork the metaphor in order to find a point of conflict between it and Jewish and Greek laws. An indication of this is to be found in the observation that, though under the English legal system *nemo est heres viventis*, the expression 'heir of God' in no way implies to our minds the death of God. The meaning of the expression 'heir of God' results from the cognitive interplay of the vehicle of the metaphor (i.e. heir) and its topic (i.e. the believer's relationship to God) and their respective semantic fields. To assume that every connotation or association of the metaphor's vehicle is retained in the metaphor itself is to overwork the metaphor. The argument also fails to distinguish between a use of the term 'heir' in the legal register and its use in everyday discourse. In the latter context a child can quite naturally and without any implication of its father's death be called an heir. The question is then whether Paul used the term in a strictly legal sense. If not, the metaphor would make as much sense to the Greek or Jewish hearer as it would to the Roman. Thus Lyall's description (p.108) of the metaphor as 'precise' when interpreted in terms of Roman law but 'vague' when interpreted in terms of other legal systems is prejudicial and fails to recognise the nature of language itself. It also ignores the fact that the metaphor's use is not confined to Paul but is found in the synoptic gospels, Hebrews and the OT (e.g. Jer.3.19) as well. Clearly, not all uses of the metaphor should be interpreted by Roman law. Why then seek in Roman law the referent of what was otherwise a traditional metaphor?

Lyall finds a second point of contact between Roman law and Paul's use of the metaphor of inheritance. He sees a parallel between the function of the Holy Spirit (p.111) and the continuity of personality between the *paterfamilias* and his heir. As we have discussed above, under the *ius civile* the heir was *successor in locum defuncti*. Such an argument, however, seems to raise legal abstraction to the status of the contemporary heir's consciousness regarding his own *persona*. Did Paul's Roman contemporaries understand *persona* as *per sonare*? Did they still hold that an heir had the religious function of maintaining the family's *sacra*? Lyall's argument also highlights the danger of placing an uneven emphasis on the *ius civile* at the expense of the *ius praetorium* which must properly reflect the contemporary view of the law. In this regard it is also worth observing that in Lyall's argument many of the parallels between the Pauline metaphors and Roman law arise from the concept of the *paterfamilias*. However, a similar concept had existed in most tribal societies, for the exercise of authority lay in the hands of the head of the clan or family. With the demise of the tribal system and the growth of the state the exercise of power by the *paterfamilias* was curtailed. For example, the patriarchs of the OT exercised the authority of a *paterfamilias*. In time, however, the authority was gradually diminished by the process of settlement, by the imposition of the law and by the institution of the monarch. Thus if Paul shows an awareness of the concept of *paterfamilias*, it does not follow that he derived it from his acquaintance with Roman legal custom. He may well have gained it from his own Jewish tradition which had its origins in patriarchal religion.

Other points of contact between Roman law and Paul's metaphor of inheritance are suggested by Lyall, i.e. co-ownership of estate by the *sui heredes* whilst the *paterfamilias* is still alive (pp.111-2), guardianship (pp.112-4) and extension of inheritance (pp.114-7). These will not be discussed here but that is not to say that they do not need to be subjected to a careful analysis. Before finishing, however, a few observations of a more general nature can be made. First, Lyall's premises, particularly **2** and **3**, must be seen as generalisations based on conjecture rather than on evidence. A more careful justification of them is called for. Second, it is not altogether certain that Paul was a Roman citizen. He makes no claim to it in any of his letters – see further the discussion in *New Docs* 6 (1992) **§20**. Third, it seems to me rather peculiar that Paul's legal metaphors should rely so substantially on Roman law but not so his practical advice on Christian conduct. I am not saying that this is impossible. However, some explanation for the difference between Paul's legal concepts and his ethics would need to be offered.

S.R.L.

§5 The Revocation of Wills and Gal.3.15

Oxyrhynchus AD 161-9

Ed.pr. — V.B. Schuman, *P. Wash.Univ.* 13 (Chico 1980), pp.25-27.

Only the right half of the papyrus sheet (measuring 8 x 22.7 cm) survives. Four hands can be identified in the document. It is identified as a revocation of will by the characteristic expression ἣν ἔθετο διὰ τοῦ ... ἀγορανομίου and the mention of the drawing up of a second will.

	[ἔτους .. Αὐτοκράτορος Καίσαρος	[In year X of Imperator Caesar
	Μάρκου Αὐρηλίου 'Αντωνίνου	Marcus Aurelius Antoninus
	Σεβαστοῦ καὶ Αὐ]τοκράτο[ρο]ς	Augustus and Im]perator
	Κα[ί]σαρο[ς Λο]υκίου Αὐρηλίου	Caesar Lucius Aurelius
	Οὐήρου Σεβαστοῦ 'Επεὶφ ἐ[ν	Verus Augustus, in (the month of)
	'Ο]ξυρ[ύ]γχων π[ό]λει.	Epeiph in the city of Oxyrhynchus.
2	[μαρτυρεῖ ± 35 ἀπὸ τῆς αὐτῆς]	[N, from the same] city
	'Οξυρύγχων πόλεως ἐν ἀγυιᾷ	of Oxyrhynchus, [testifies] in the street
	ἀκολούθως τοῖς κελευθεῖσι ὑπὸ τοῦ	in accord with the instructions of
	θεοῦ Αἰλίου 'Αντωνίνου ὅτι δευτέ-	*divus* Aelius Antoninus that
	[ραν τιθέμενος διαθήκην ἠκύρωσε τὴν	[in making a second will he has annulled
	προτέραν διαθήκη]ν ἣν ἔθετο διὰ	the former will] which he drew up
	τοῦ ἐν τῇ αὐτῇ πόλει ἀγορανομίου	through the *agoronomion* in the same
	τῷ Φαμενὼθ τοῦ πέμπτου ἔτους	city in (the month of) Phamenoth of the
	θεοῦ Αἰλίου 'Αντωνίνου. πρọσ̣έθ̣-	fifth year of *divus* Aelius Antoninus.
4	[ηκε] (m. 2) . . τος μητρὸς	He [has] made additions (m. 2) ... mother
	. . . . . [.] μου τοῦ 'Ερμήνου δευτέραν	[...], son of Hermenos, in making a
	τιθέμενος διαθήκην οὐκ ἠδυνήθην	second will I was unable
	διὰ	because (?)
	[ ] . . . [ ] . . [ ] . .	[...]
	[ ] . . . [ ] . (m. 3) . . . . . καί εἰμι	(m. 3) ... and I am
	[ἐτῶν .. οὐλ]ὴ ὀφρύι δεξιᾷ καί	[age X, sca]r to right brow and
	ἐστίν μου ἡ σφραγὶς	my seal is
6	[Traces of letters between large lacunae]	[...]
	(m. 4) . . τῷ καθ' ἓν αὐτὸν γράφειν	(m. 4) by his writing (them) item by item
	[Traces of letters]	[...]

P. Wash.Univ. 13 is one of several papyri which show that the Greek will, like its Roman counterpart, could be revoked by the testator.[53] In this regard the Greek will appears to have differed from the majority of deeds of allotment after death (see *New Docs* 6 [1992] §4). The papyri show that the will could be revoked in three different ways (see Taubenschlag, *Law*, p.204): a) by the insertion in the new will of a special clause revoking the former will; b) by a special legal act; or c) by the withdrawal of the will from the *agoranomion*. The preparation of a new will did not of itself revoke a former will. Indeed, insofar as there was no contradiction, both wills were allowed to stand. Nor does it seem that individuals were always free to choose between all three different ways of revocation. On the basis of *P. Bibl.Univ.Giss. inv.* 311 P.J. Sijpesteijn, 'New Light on the Revocation of Wills', *CE* XLII 83 (1967), pp.360-68, argues for a possible limitation on revocation in the reign of Antoninus Pius. Since the testator Arius was unable to withdraw his will from the *agoranomion* to annul it, Sijpesteijn suggests that the *strategos* of Oxyrhynchus had decreed that all wills were to be revoked by the sole method of withdrawal from the *agoranomion*. N. Lewis, '*P. Bibl.Univ.Giss. inv.* 311', *CE* XLIII 85 (1968), pp.375-8, interprets the papyrus differently, arguing that it 'is a form of b) attesting that c) is impossible'. A.H.S. El-Mosallamy[54], 'Revocation of Wills in Roman Egypt', *Aegyptus* 50 (1970), pp.63-4, recognises the following steps in the process of revocation:

a. an application to the nome *strategos* asking for revocation;
b. the permission and order for an annulment by the *strategos*;
c. the delivery of the will to the testator by an official of the *agoranomion*;
d. the acknowledgement by the testator that he received the will under seals, i.e. the witnesses' seals were intact;
e. the notification of the *agoranomoi* by the official that the will had been delivered in accord with the *strategos*.

He argues (pp.64-7) that a legal impediment had prevented Arius from withdrawing his will. The debate over *P. Bibl.Univ.Giss. inv.* 311 with its focus on revocation may prove relevant to an understanding of *P. Wash.Univ.* 13, for the testator here (*l*.4) indicates that there was an impediment at the time of his making a second will. Clearly, he believes, if the restoration of *l*.3 is correct, that the former will had already been annulled by the writing of a second will. Was he then unable to withdraw his former will from the *agoranomion* and thereby effect an official registration of its annulment? Unfortunately, the fragmentary condition of the papyrus does not permit a determination on this point.

In special cases the annulment of a will could even occur after the death of the testator. Legal intervention could take place for various reasons. Plato, *Leg*. 922, recognised the problem with granting absolute validity to a man's διαθήκη as it might oppose the law, customs or even the true wishes of the testator himself – he may not have been of a sound mind when he made it or it may have been made under duress or undue influence. Thus Thrasylochos' half-sister sought to have his will annulled (Isocrates, *Aegin*.12, 15) and Caligula likewise the will of Tiberius (Dio Cassius, *Hist*.59.1). In Roman law a near relative could institute proceedings where he/she had either been disinherited without just cause or been passed over by a testator. On the subject of the *querela inofficiosi testamenti* see the discussion of Pliny, *Epist*., 5.1 and 6.33 in J.W. Tellegen, *The Roman Law of Succession in the Letters of Pliny the Younger* (Zutphen 1982), pp.80-94 and 108-18. Also the conditions of a will might be against the interests of the governing powers and thus subject to their veto. Thus Herod the Great submitted his will to Augustus for validation (Josephus, *BJ* 1.669, *AJ* 17.195, 202).

At Gal.3.15 Paul uses an example from everyday life to illustrate the point that a former διαθήκη cannot be annulled – Ἀδελφοί, κατὰ ἄνθρωπον λέγω· ὅμως ἀνθρώπου κεκυρωμένην διαθήκην οὐδεὶς ἀθετεῖ ἢ ἐπιδιατάσσεται. That a will is implied by the

---

[53] Examples of other documents dealing with the revocation of wills are *P. Oxy*. I 106-7, 178, III 601, XXXVI 2759 and *P. Bibl.Univ.Giss. inv.* 311 (*CE* XLII 83 [1967], p.361).

[54] See also A.E. Samuel, 'Six Papyri from Hamilton College', *JJP* 13 (1961), especially pp.39-42.

term διαθήκη is indicated by the reference to inheritance at v.18 and the use of legal language in the verse itself (e.g. κεκυρωμένην, ἀθετεῖ, ἐπιδιατάσσεται). Further confirmation is found in the use of the expression κατὰ ἄνθρωπον λέγω, for the making of wills was extensively enough practised in antiquity to allow its use here. Does Paul at Gal.3.15 then refer to the Greek or Roman testamentary practice? The possibility has traditionally been seen to involve two problems.[55] First, Greek and Roman wills could be revoked. *P. Wash.Univ.* 13 and the papyri more generally only confirm the possibility of annulment. The illustration would then appear to be either vacuous or lame if its referent was the Greek or Roman will. The second difficulty is one of unwelcome association. The Greek or Roman will only took effect on the death of the testator. The illustration, insofar as it portrays God as a testator, permits the hearer to draw the inference that God's promise also will only be effective on his demise. In my opinion, this second area of difficulty is more imaginary than real, for it can only be sustained by overworking the illustration itself (see further the discussion on the metaphor of inheritance in *New Docs* 6 [1992] §4). Be that as it may, in view of these areas of perceived difficulty various attempts have been made to find an appropriate referent for the illustration.

W. Selb, 'Διαθήκη im Neuen Testament', *JJS* 25 (1974), pp.183-196, discusses the several meanings which the term διαθήκη can take in both the LXX and NT. It can mean the following: a) a contract or agreement between two parties; b) a will or testament; or c) an order, decree or law. The Jewish legal instrument of *diathiqi* (דיאתיקי = διαθήκη; see below for further discussion), it is argued, may have lain behind the LXX translators' decision to use the term διαθήκη. In other words, the instrument, though only attested in rabbinic literature, may well have had its origins in the earlier period and could therefore have been the legal practice alluded to by the LXX's choice of the term διαθήκη. The legal practice of *diathiqi*, it is alleged in support of this supposition, covers all three meanings of the term διαθήκη:

a. in form it was an agreement (i.e. bilateral) and as such not unilaterally revocable;
b. in function it was a will effective on death;
c. in content it was a disposition or order made by the donor (i.e. unilateral).

Selb thus resolves the ambiguity caused by the term's usage by placing it within a form, content and function analysis of a postulated legal instrument. A similar analysis of the term's usage in Gal.3.15-19 is offered : 'The διαθήκη is a two-sided agreement, which gains its irrevocability from just this *formal* two-sidedness, and yet it is *functionally* a testamentary enactment in which in terms of *content* God unilaterally and supremely defines the promise of salvation history' (p.192 – my translation).

E. Bammel, 'Gottes ΔΙΑΘΗΚΗ (Gal.3.15-17) und das jüdische Rechtsdenken', *NTS* 6 (1960), pp.313-9, had earlier argued that the source of the illustration was to be found in Jewish rather than either Greek or Roman legal practice. He postulated that the διαθήκη of Gal.3.15 referred to the *matenath bari* (מתנת בריא) and considered three aspects of it as particularly important: a) by the *matenath bari* the donor bequeathed immediate possession to the beneficiary only preserving the right of usufruct whilst he lived; b) the bequest could not be revoked; and c) the bequest was not made with a view to the donor's death (i.e. it was made by those who were healthy). Bammel also argued for the currency of the *matenath bari* in the NT period. A brief description of the *matenath bari* has already be given in *New Docs* 6 [1992] §4. The instrument of *matenath bari* was used to pre-empt the strict laws of hereditary succession as laid down in the OT (Num.27.8-11 and Deut.21.16-17) and by the rabbis (*m. B. Bat.* 8-9) by making a gift of the property to a beneficiary but retaining its usufruct until death. The act of giving is said to take effect 'from today' and as such presented itself as a *fait accompli*. In other words, it could not be revoked once made. In this respect it differed from Greek and Roman

55 Another perceived complication at Gal.3.15 has been the interpretation of ὅμως; however, in view of 1Cor.14.7-9 (see the use of ὅμως – οὕτως) it appears that Paul can use the term to mark his use of an illustration.

wills which since they only took effect on the death of the testator, were able to be annulled or altered by the testator whilst living. According to Bammel then, Paul's illustration is anything but vacuous or lame, for by it he was able to reconcile the problem caused by the two acts (i.e. promise and law) of the one God without allowing the latter to supersede or to replace the former.

The assumption that Paul refers to the *matenath bari* is not without its own difficulties. First, if the testator's death poses a problem for the illustration under Greek and Roman law, it remains as much a problem under the Jewish legal practice also. In the *matenath bari* ownership, not possession, was granted to the beneficiary. The beneficiary's enjoyment of the gift/promise likewise was only effective after the death of the donor. Second, it may be observed that the illustration does not permit an adequate explanation for Paul's introduction of it. There Paul says that he speaks κατὰ ἄνθρωπον. C.K. Barrett, *A Commentary on the First Epistle to the Corinthians* (London 1971), p.365, notes that the expression 'may draw attention to a human turn of speech or experience, used in order to illustrate theological truth ...'. If so, there is no indication at Gal.3.15 that the illustration refers to a particular legal practice (i.e. the *matenath bari*). It is true that the expression can possess a negative association elsewhere in the Pauline epistles.[56] However, a study of its use in Greek literature[57] indicates that this was not

---

56 Apart from Gal.3.15 the expression is used five times by Paul (Rom.3.5, 1Cor.3.3, 9.8, 15.32, Gal.1.11). Though the expression is not the same, one might note also Rom.6.8. Usage is distinguished according to whether it refers to a verb of speaking or not. At 1Cor.3.3 Paul asks: 'For where there is envy and strife among you, are you not worldly (σαρκικοί) and do you (not) walk κατὰ ἄνθρωπον?' In equivalent expressions at Rom.8.4 and 1Cor.10.2-3 Paul uses κατὰ σάρκα. At Gal.1.11 Paul seeks to inform his hearers that his gospel is not κατὰ ἄνθρωπον. Paul goes on to explain what is meant in the subsequent verse: 'for neither did I receive it from man (παρὰ ἀνθρώπου), nor was I taught it but by a revelation of Jesus Christ'. At Rom.3.5 Paul asks the question whether God is not unjust in bringing his anger against the unrighteous. Though the question expects a negative answer (see μή), Paul feels the need to qualify his rather 'blasphemous' words by stating that he is speaking κατὰ ἄνθρωπον. At 1Cor.9.8 Paul draws on everyday examples of pay for service to argue that he is entitled to support in his ministry. He asks whether he has spoken κατὰ ἄνθρωπον (the negative μή expecting the answer no) or whether in accord with God's law (the negative οὐ expecting the answer yes). The meaning of the expression at 1Cor.15.32 is complicated by the fact that it is debated whether ἐθηριομάχησα should be understood literally or figuratively. If the verb is figurative, then the prepositional phrase can be construed as a parenthetic indicator of this, i.e. ὡς κατὰ ἄνθρωπον εἰπεῖν or κατὰ ἄνθρωπον λέγω. If the verb is to be interpreted literally, then the prepositional phrase indicates the human (as opposed to divine) nature of the struggle. Paul's use of the prepositional phrase with verbs of speaking (explicit or implied) at 1Cor.9.8, 15.32 and Gal.3.15 agrees with Barrett's analysis of it. However, at Rom.3.5 one senses a pronounced negative association in conformity with Paul's usage at 1Cor.3.3. Usage is therefore not uniform across the Pauline corpus.

57 The prepositional phrase κατὰ ἄνθρωπον is used by various philosophical, theological, medical and historical authors. Three formally distinct uses are found:

a) An adjectival use:

The predominant use is attributive with the meaning 'human', e.g. τὴν κατὰ ἄνθρωπον δόξαν – 'human glory' (Athanasius, *Contra Sab*. 28.112); περὶ τῶν τόπων τῶν κατὰ ἄνθρωπον – 'on the human parts' (Hippocrates); τὴν κατὰ ἄνθρωπον γέννησιν – 'the human genealogy' (various theological authors – cf. ἐκ σπέρματος Δαυὶδ κατὰ σάρκα Rom.1.3, τὸν προπάτορα ἡμῶν κατὰ σάρκα Rom.4.1 and ὁ κατὰ σάρκα γεννηθείς Gal.4.23). The adjective can also function as a substantive: τὰ κατὰ ἄνθρωπον – 'the human lot', e.g. poverty and disgrace (anon., *In ethica Nicomachea* 54). A predicative use like that at Gal.1.11 is rare and largely confined to allusions to or quotations of it (e.g. Eusebius, Marcellus, *De incarn*. 1013)

b) After a comparative adjective/adverb:

It is used to indicate an extraordinary or almost divine quality of some deed, event, person etc., e.g. καὶ ἔτυχε σεμνοτέρας ἢ κατὰ ἄνθρωπον ταφῆς – 'and he received a burial more solemn than κατὰ ἄνθρωπον' (Xenophon, *Hell*. 3.3.1); τὸ ... μεγαλεῖον τῆς φύσεως αὐτοῦ καταπληττόμενοι τελειοτέρας οὔσης ἢ κατὰ ἄνθρωπον – 'amazed at the magnificence of his nature which was more complete than κατὰ ἄνθρωπον' (Philo, *Virt*. 217); ἐκτελέσαι δὲ κρεῖττον ἢ κατὰ ἄνθρωπον – 'to accomplish more than κατὰ ἄνθρωπον' (Aelius Aristides, *Pan. in Kyz*. 240); προσελθόντος αὐτῷ μείζονός τινος ἢ κατὰ ἄνθρωπον – 'something greater than κατὰ ἄνθρωπον meeting him' (Dio Cassius, *Hist.Rom*. 68.25.5); τὸ μὲν γὰρ μηδέποτε

generally the case. Moreover, it is difficult to see how κατὰ ἄνθρωπον can be construed to have a negative association at Gal.3.15. Third, how can Paul be sure that his readers will understand the use of an illustration relying on a knowledge of Jewish legal practice? Two answers are possible:

i. Practices similar to the *matenath bari* were in use in Greek law and it is to these that Paul alludes (see H.D. Betz, *Galatians* [Philadelphia 1979], p.155 n.23, quoting R. Yaron, suggests a wider usage of legal practices similar to *matenath bari*). Two points need to be made concerning this. First, the proposition will need to be balanced against Bammel's (op.cit., p.315) assessment that such practices were in sharp decline elsewhere (i.e. Babylon and Egypt). However, against Bammel's assessment it needs to be stated that the practice was not in sharp decline in Graeco-Egyptian law (see discussion of the allotment after death in *New Docs* 6 [1992] §4). Second and more importantly, if Paul were indeed referring to a more widespread practice in Greek law, then a reference failure seems to result from his use of the term διαθήκη. Not being privy to the contents of Yaron's letter to Betz, one must rely on Yaron's discussion in *Gifts in Contemplation of Death* (Oxford 1960). Since there he argues that the *matenath bari* arose as an adaptation of the Graeco-Egyptian allotment after death, one assumes that this was the more widespread legal practice to which Paul alluded. However, as argued in *New Docs* 6 (1992) §4, the allotment after death was legally and formally distinct from the διαθήκη and to call it a διαθήκη results in an apparent reference failure.

ii. The illustration might have been understood by Paul's readers because they were Jewish or persons closely associated with the synagogue.[58] However, again the same problem of reference failure needs to be addressed. In using διαθήκη the audience would infer that Paul was referring not to the *matenath bari* but to the legally distinct *diathiqi* (later in Amoraic period called *matenath shekhiv mera* – מתנת שכיב מרע). To illustrate the possible confusion, consider the argument adduced by R.Simeon b.Yohai,[59] a fourth generation (AD 140-165)

ἁμαρτάναι μεῖζον ἢ κατὰ ἄνθρωπον – 'for never to make a mistake is more than κατὰ ἄνθρωπον' (Galen, *In Hipp*. 18b.315).
c) An adverbial use:
It is this use which predominates in Paul (Rom.5.3, 1Cor.3.3, 9.8, 15.32, Gal.3.15). However, it is less frequent than the other uses outlined above, e.g. φαίνεσθέ μοι οὐ κατὰ ἄνθρωπον ζῶντες – 'you appear not to live κατὰ ἄνθρωπον' (Ignatius, *Epist*. 3.2.1 – cf. τοῦ κατὰ σάρκα ζῆν Rom.8.12); τοῦτο μὲν οὖν κατὰ ἄνθρωπόν ἐστι λελογισμένον, μὴ ὁλοσχερῶς μηδὲ ὠστικῶς μηδὲ ὑπερηφάνως πρὸς τὸν θάνατον ἔχειν – 'this, however, is reasoned κατὰ ἄνθρωπον, to be neither rash nor impetuous nor disdainful towards death' (M. Aurelius, *Med*. 9.3.1). The use by Marcus Aurelius is interesting in that it affirms reasoning κατὰ ἄνθρωπον as a positive quality.

58 The hypothesis that Paul's audience was Jewish or composed of persons closely associated with the synagogue might be supported by the epistle's use of rabbinic-style arguments and theological constructs. For example, see Paul's use of 'seed' in Gal.3.16 and M. Wilcox's discussion 'The Promise of the "Seed" in the New Testament and the Targumim', *JSNT* 5 (1979), pp.2-20.

59 The passage is cited in full below using the reconstruction argued by E. Bammel, 'Any deyathiqi partially cancelled is completely cancelled', *Judaica* (Tübingen 1986), pp.129-133. The Jerusalem Talmud uses the illustration of the will to argue that the *torah* cannot be altered in the smallest detail (i.e. the yod) without dire consequences for the *torah* as a whole. The rabbinic comparison of the *torah* // *diathiqi* is relevant to Paul's comparison of God's promise (rather than the *torah*) // διαθήκη.

תני ר´ש בן יוחי
עלה ספר משנה תורה ונשתטח לפני הקב´ה
אמר לפניו רבון העולם כתבת בה תורתך כל
דייתיקי שבטלה מקצת בטלה כולה והרי שלמה
מבקש לעקור יו´ד ממני א´ל הקב´ה שלמה ואלף
כיוצא בו בטילין ודבר ממך אינו בטל

Tannaitic teacher: 'every *diathiqi* which is void in part is void in full' (*y. Sanh.*2.6) or R. Dimi, a fourth century AD Amoraic teacher: 'a (later) *diathiqi* annuls a (former) *diathiqi*' (*b. B. Bat.* 135b). Another interesting rabbinic parallel is found at *y. Ber.* 5.2:

בדייתיקי נתתיו לאברהם? במתנה נתתיו לו

Did I give it (i.e. the dew = symbol of life) to Abraham by *diathiqi* (i.e. revocable)? I gave it to him by *matanah* (i.e. irrevocable).

Note that the distinction between the *diathiqi* and *matenath bari* is used here also in connection with God's dealings with Abraham. However, at *y. Ber.* 5.2 the gift is not by *diathiqi* for it cannot be revoked. The problem for Gal.3.15 is this. Might not Paul's Jewish audience have reasonably assumed that the term διαθήκη referred to the *diathiqi* which like the Greek διαθήκη could be revoked?

Conversely, the expression κατὰ ἄνθρωπον and the use of Greek legal vocabulary (see above) seem to indicate that the illustration refers to a Greek legal practice. There is no indication in the text itself which points to any other legal context.

The above discussion has centred on the problematic nature of Gal.3.15. What does Paul mean when he says that no one revokes or adds to a validated διαθήκη? The Roman and Greek will could be revoked. In the face of this difficulty Bammel suggested that Paul was referring to a Jewish legal procedure. Though attractive in many respects, his suggestion is not without difficulties. If so, must we then conclude that Paul's legal illustration is lame? Another suggested solution is that Paul's use of οὐδεὶς (Gal.3.15) referred not to the testator himself but to all those others who did not have the legal capacity to annul the will. The problem with this suggestion is that the illustration remains problematic, for surely its point is to show that the law does not annul the promise. However, both the law and the promise are the dispositions of the same God. The law is not a subsequent attempt (even though mediated through angels) by a second person to annul the promise made by God.

There is another solution to the problem posed by Gal.3.15. The solution is that in Greek-speaking Jewish communities there was a transaction comparable to the *matenath bari* which was irrevocable and denoted by the term διαθήκη.[60] Tentative support for this solution is found in the Babatha archive. *P. Yadin* 19 (AD 128), = N. Lewis, Y. Yadin and C. Greenfield, *The Documents from the Bar Kokhba Period in the Cave of Letters* (Jerusalem 1989), is a deed of gift in Greek from Palestine which like most other documents in the archive was witnessed in Aramaic. In the deed Judah, son of Elazar Khthousin, gave to his daughter Shelamzious half of his property 'from today and the other half after his death' (ἀ[πὸ τῆς σήμερον καὶ τὸ] ἄλλο ἥμ[ι]συ μετὰ τὲ τελ[ευ]τῆσαι *ll.*22-23; cf. also Tobit 8.21 and 10.10 where a similar gift is made to Tobias by Raguel, his father-in-law). As such the gifts are distinct from the *matenath bari* described above, i.e. the gift is not 'from today and after my death' but half is given today and the other half after death; also Judah cedes the right of usufruct over both halves (*ll.*24-25). The disposition must be irrevocable. What is of further interest is that both acts of disposition are expressed by the verb διέθετο (see [δι]έθετ[ο *l.*11 and διέθετο *ll.*15-6; cf. the introductory formula of the Greek will, i.e. τάδε διέθετο νοῶν καὶ φρονῶν) and the donor denoted by ὁ

R.Simeon b.Yohai taught:
The book of Deuteronomy went up and prostrated itself before the Holy One, blessed be He,
saying to him, 'Lord of All, you wrote your *torah* with it (i.e. using the letter yod). Every
diathiqi which is void in part is void in full. Behold, Solomon
seeks to up-root (one) yod from me'. The Holy One, blessed be He, said, 'Solomon and a thousand
like him are void but your word is not void'.

60 It may be the case that the use of διαθήκη to refer to such a gift was not confined only to the Greek-speaking Jewish communities. If so, Paul's metaphor may have been drawn from a more general social milieu. That, however, remains to be argued. The question concerning the racial composition of Paul's audience in Galatia is also relevant to this matter.

διεθετῶν *l*.18. The deed also appears to be subject to public registration (*ll*.25-27; cf. Paul's use of the terms κεκυρωμένην, ἀθετεῖ and ἐπιδιατάσσεται at Gal.3.15). Further support can also be found for the hypothesis that Greek-speaking Jewish communities may have called the deed of gift a διαθήκη. For example, Rabban Simon b. Gamaliel (*t. B. Bat*. 9.14) states:

הכותב דיותימין בלעז הרי זו מתנה

He who writes διεθέμην in Greek, behold this is a gift.

It seems to be a reasonable assumption then that in the second century AD the Jewish deed of gift when made in Greek used the expression διεθέμην or διέθετο and could thus have been called a διαθήκη. If the same practice and terminology can be assumed to have been in use in the first century, then it is to such an instrument that Paul, a Greek-speaking Jew, referred at Gal. 3.15. In other words, Paul's illustration is neither drawn from Greek nor Roman legal procedures but from a Jewish legal procedure which evolved in the Greek-speaking communities of Palestine and the diaspora. If this is indeed the case, it can be seen that the problem of reference failure disappears, for the term διαθήκη could designate both a will and a gift. Another advantage is also apparent. Paul did not require his readers to cross a linguistic barrier and understand διαθήκη as *matenath bari*. The illustration and its understanding remains confined within the Greek linguistic medium. **S.R.L.**

SLAVES AND MASTERS

§6 The Sale of a Slave-Girl: The New Testament's Attitude to Slavery

Side in Pamphylia — AD 142

Ed.pr. — D. Hagedorn, *P. Turner* 22 (London 1981), pp.107-113 (= *P. Colon. inv.* 6211).

The left and lower portions of the papyrus (18.5 x 21 cm) are incomplete. The document is in the form of the διπλώματα, i.e. it is written on the recto of the papyrus roll but across its long axis and fibres. The above text can be substantially reconstructed both by the comparison of *ll*.1-12 with *ll*.13-25 and by the use of *BGU* III 887.

[Λ. Κουσπίῳ Ῥουφίνῳ καὶ Λ. Στατίῳ
Κοδράτῳ ὑπάτοις ἐν Σίδῃ
ἐπὶ δημιουργοῦ ἱερέως θεᾶς]
Ῥώμης Λ. Κλ. Αὐσπικάτου
μη(νὸς)
[Λῴου ς̄κ̄. Πάμφιλος ὁ καὶ
Κάνωπος Αἰγύπτου
Ἀλεξανδρεὺς ἐπρίατο ἐν ἀγορᾷ
παρὰ Ἀρ]τεμ̣ι̣δ(ώρου)
Ἀριστοκλέου̣ς̣ κορ̣ά̣σιο̣ν̣
[Ἀβασκαντίδα γένει Γαλάτιν ὡς
(ἐτῶν) ῑ τιμῆς ἀργυρίου ✻ σ̄π̄
βεβαιοῦντος καὶ τῇ ἰδίᾳ] π̣ίστει
κ̣ελεύο̣ντος Μάρκου Αἰ-
[λίου Γαουιανοῦ ὑγιῆ ἐκ
διατάγματος . . . . ἀνέπαφον
πρὸς πάντων καὶ μήτε ῥέ]μ̣[βο]ν̣
μ̣ή̣τ̣ε δραπετικὸ̣ν̣ ἱ̣ε̣ρᾶ̣ς̣
[τε νόσου ἐκτός. ἐὰν δέ τι τούτων ᾖ
ἢ μὴ ᾖ ὑγιὴς ἢ ἐπαφὴ αὐτοῦ ἢ ἐκ
μέρους γέν]ηται καὶ ἐγνεικηθῇ,
τότε δι-
[πλῆν τὴν τιμὴν χωρὶς παραγγελίας
καλῶς δοθῆναι πίστει ἐπερώτη]σεν
Π̣ά̣μ̣φ̣ι̣λ̣ο̣‹ς› ὁ καὶ Κ̣ά̣ν̣ω̣π̣ο̣[ς],
[πίστει δοῦναι ὡμολόγησεν
Ἀρτεμίδωρος καὶ τὴν τιμὴν
κεκομίσθαι, καὶ ταῦτα ὑ]πὲρ αὐτοῦ
τῇ ἰδίᾳ πίστει κ̣α̣ὶ̣
[βεβαιώσει εἶναι ἐκέλευσεν Μᾶρ]κ̣[ο]ς̣
Αἴλιος Γαο[υ]ι̣ανὸς κ̣ ̣ ̣ [. . . .] ̣ ̣
(m. 2) [Ἀρτεμίδωρος Ἀριστοκλέους
πέ]πρακα τὸ κοράσ̣ᾳ̣ιον δ̣η̣[ναρί]ων
διακοσαίων ὀγδο-

[In the consulship of L.Cuspius Rufinus
and L.Statius Quadratus, in Side,]
L.Claudius Auspicatus, [being
demiourgos and priest of *dea*] *Roma*, in
the month
[of Loos 26. Pamphilos, also called
Kanopos, son of Aegyptos, an
Alexandrian, has bought in the market-
place from] Artemidoros, son of
Aristocles, a slave-girl,
[Abaskantis, a Galatian by descent, about
10 years of age for the sum of 280 silver
denarii,] with Marcus Aelius [Gavianus
acting as guarantor and] declaring [by
personal] warrant [that (the slave-girl is)
healthy in accord with the edict ... not
liable to seizure by anyone and likely
neither to roam about] nor run away
[and without epilepsy. If any of these
apply or she is not healthy or a claim to
seizure arises against her or part thereof]
and is won, then
Pamphilos, also called Kanopos, [has
asked in good faith that the double sum
be rightfully paid without summons;]
[Artemidoros has agreed to pay (it) in good
faith and that he has received the sum;
and] on his behalf
by personal warrant and
[guarantee Marcus] Aelius Gavianus [has
declared these things are so.]
(m. 2) [I, Artemidoros, son of Aristocles,]
have sold the slave-girl for two hundred
and eighty denarii

[ἥκοντα καὶ τὴν τιμὴν κ]ẹκόμạιμαι ὡς προγάγρ[α]π̣τ̣α̣ι̣. (vac.)	[and] have received [the sum] as written above.
(m. 3) [Μ. Αἴλιος Γαουιανὸς βεβαιῶ τὸ] κοράσιον καὶ τῇ ẹμ̣ῇ π̣ί̣σ̣τ̣ẹι̣ κ̣ẹλ̣[εύω ὡς] προγέγραπται ἣν̣ δ̣έχο̣μ̣α̣[ι]	(m. 3) [I, M.Aelius Gavianus, guarantee the] slave-girl and declare by personal warrant, [as] written above, which I receive ...
[ ]. . . . . .ς	[...] ...
δημόσιος διὰ τὸ λέγειν αὐτὸν γράμματα μὴ εἰδέναι.	public (scribe) because he says that he is illiterate.

(m. 4) [Λουκίῳ Κουσπίῳ Ῥουφίνῳ κ]α̣ὶ Λουκίῳ Στατίῳ Κοδράτῳ ὑπάτοις ἐν Σίδῃ ἐπὶ δημ̣[ι-]
[ουργοῦ ἱερέως θεᾶς Ῥώμ]ης Λουκίου Κλαυδίου Αὐσπικάτου μηνὸς Λῴου ς̄κ̄.
[Πάμφιλος ὁ καὶ Κάν]ωπος Α̣ἰγύ̣πτου Ἀλεξανδρεὺς ἐπρίατο ἐν ἀγ[ο]ρᾷ̣ π̣[α]ρ̣ὰ̣
[Ἀρτεμιδώρου Ἀριστοκλέου]ς̣ κοράσιον Ἀβασκαντίδα ἢ εἴ τινι ἑτέρῳ̣
[ὀνόματι καλεῖται γ]ένει Γαλάτιν ὡς ἐτῶν δέκα τειμῆς ἀργυρίου
[δηναρίων διακοσί]ων ὀγδοήκοντα (vac.)
[βεβαιοῦντος καὶ τῇ ἰδίᾳ] π[ί]στει κελεύοντος Μάρκου Αἰλίου Γαουιανοῦ ὑγιῆ ἐκ διατά-
[γματος . . . . ἀ]νέπαφον πρὸς πάντων καὶ μήτε ῥέμβον μήτε δρα-
[πετικὸν ἱερᾶς τε ν]όσου ἐκτός. ἐὰν δέ τι τούτων ᾖ ἢ μὴ ᾖ ὑγιὴ‹ς› ἢ ἐπαφὴ αὐ̣τ̣[οῦ]
[ἢ ἐκ μέρους γένη]τ̣α̣ι̣ καὶ ἐκνεικηθῇ, τότε διπλῆν τὴν̣ τ̣ε̣[ι]μ̣ὴ[ν] χ̣ω̣ρ̣ὶ̣[ς] π̣α̣-
[ραγγελίας καλῶς δο]θ̣ῆναι πίστει ἐπερώτη[σεν] Π̣ά̣μ̣φ̣ιλο̣[ς ὁ] κ̣α̣[ὶ] Κ̣ά̣ν̣ω̣[π]ο̣ς
[Αἰγύπτου, πίστει δοῦ]ν̣αι ὡμολόγησεν Ἀ[ρ]τ̣ε̣[μίδωρ]ο̣ς Ἀριστο[κ]λ̣έ̣ους καὶ τὴν̣
[τιμὴν κεκομίσ]θ̣α̣ι̣ καὶ ταῦτα [ὑπὲρ αὐτοῦ τῇ ἰδίᾳ] πίστει καὶ βεβαιώσει
....

5 ἐκνικηθῇ 9 κοράσιον, διακοσίων 10 κεκόμισμαι, προγέγραπται 17 τιμῆς 22 ἐκνικηθῇ, τιμήν

The sale contract for the slave-girl Abaskantis was originally written at the point of sale, Side in Pamphylia (see also *BGU* III 887 which concerns the sale of a slave-girl at Side dated AD 152; it shows similar formulae and script style). The document is of interest as it is one of a relatively few surviving papyri written outside Egypt. Although it is not known where the papyrus was found, one may be fairly certain that it owes its survival to the fact that the purchaser, probably a slave merchant, brought the papyrus with him to Egypt (see *l.*2 = 15 where Pamphilos is described as an Alexandrian). On resale the papyrus was then handed over as proof of ownership to the new purchaser. The document and its history, as the editor notes, confirm the role played by Side and Alexandria in the slave trade of antiquity.

On *l.*4 (= *l.*20) Hagedorn suggests that the scribe had understood the forms ἀνέπαφον, δραπετικόν, ὑγιή‹ς› and αὐτοῦ in the masculine sense rather than in the neuter sense in agreement with κοράσιον or in the feminine sense in agreement with the slave's sex. He concludes that the scribe had copied an *exemplum* in the masculine without regard to the slave's actual sex. If this is indeed so, then we have an interesting case of interference between the use of an *exemplum* and the production of a new document. However, as K.L. McKay (per litt.) points out to me, the suggestion is problematic in that it depends on the rather doubtful reading of δραπετικὸ̣ν̣ in *l.*4 – ἀνέπαφον and ῥέμβον have no separate feminine form. McKay writes:

'All clear evidence of masculine forms has been inserted by the editor and is therefore no evidence at all'. The same, however, cannot be said for *BGU* III 887, a similar document concerning the sale of the slave-girl Sambatis at Side. Here ὑγιῆ, δραπετικόν and αὐτοῦ (i.e. ἐπαφ]ῇ αὐτοῦ) are clearly legible (*ll.*4-6). More generally, H.J. Wolff, *Das Recht der griechischen Papyri Ägyptens* (Munich 1978), p.6, observes the frequency with which such phenomena (e.g. the masculine form for a female and the singular form for a plural) occur within the papyri and postulates the widespread use of *Formularbücher* in the Greek-speaking world. For similar instances of interference (singular for plural) in Latin documents see *P. Ital.* II 30 (l.50), 37 (l.5) and the editor's note on p.5. Alleged cases of interference have also been used in the synoptic debate as directional indicators in an attempt to establish the chronological priority of one gospel (the *exemplum*) over the other gospels (the copies). One example is that of Matthew's and Mark's handling of the request by the sons of Zebedee (see Matt.20.20-28 and Mark 10.35-45). In Mark's version the two sons approach Jesus and ask to sit on his right and left hand. Jesus' reply is directed to them: οὐκ οἴδατε τί αἰτεῖσθε· δύνασθε κτλ. In Matthew's version the mother of the two brothers approaches Jesus to make the request; however, Jesus' reply is the same as that in Mark, i.e. the reply is to the brothers (plural) and not the mother (singular). It is alleged that Matthew at this point has lapsed into the wording of his *exemplum*. The decision here, however, is more complicated than is the case with the documentary examples, for clearly concerns of discourse and narrative need to be taken into account. For example, it is not impossible that the events actually unfolded as Matthew relates them. Alternatively, Matthew may have had his reasons telling the story the way he did.

The above contract calls for some comment, albeit brief, on the slave's lot in antiquity. The slave-girl Abaskantis was the property of her master. She had no legal rights (e.g. to own property, to enter into contracts or to marry). Any benefits which might be extended to her were at the complete discretion of her master and could be withdrawn at any moment, e.g. the permission to keep a *peculium*, the promise of manumission, the permission to have a family etc. If she were to bear a child, then it also was a slave and the property of her master. The child could be sold and separated from Abaskantis. Family and personal relationships could be ended at any time by the master. For example, though we do not know how she came to be a slave (war, piracy, house-born etc.), it seems reasonable to conjecture that Abaskantis had been separated from her mother by the act of sale attested here.[61] As a slave she had to do what her master told her and go wherever he commanded. For non-compliance or for any reason whatsoever her master could discipline and punish her as he saw fit. On the other hand, her master had to provide the basic necessities of food and clothing. However, in practice a slave's productivity depended on a system of reward and punishment, the carrot and the stick. For example, in time Abaskantis may have been allowed both to own property and to form personal relationships. But if so, her master's actions need not have been motived by altruism. By permitting her to save for manumission he not only increased her productivity, but also received the purchase price of a new slave who would serve in her place. Indeed, if she were already old at the time of manumission, a younger and more productive slave could always be bought to replace her. It should also be borne in mind that rewards were at the discretion of the master and acted as yet another form of coercion. One can well imagine the coercive force exerted on slaves who were permitted to form families.

The notion of the slave as the chattel possession of the master and subject to his authority and will is forcibly expressed in *SB* XIV 11277 (20 Jan. AD 225): [... Κυριεύειν οὖν] καὶ ἐγ[κρ]ατεῖν καὶ [διοικεῖν αὐτῆς τὸν Ἀπίωνα] καὶ ἐπιτελεῖν περὶ αὐτῆς ὃν ἐὰ[ν

[61] In Egypt it seems that an *anakrisis* was conducted by officials before the first sale of a slave. The procedure determined the identity and servile status of the person to be sold. See *P. Oxy*. XII 1463 (AD 215) and XLIX 3477 (AD 270). It is unclear whether an *anakrisis* at Side had preceded the sale of Abaskantis or indeed whether the deed represents the first sale.

αἱρῆται τρόπον] – '(Kephalon agrees) that [Apion therefore is master] and has possession of and [controls her] and can deal with her in whatever [manner he chooses]'. The document concerns the sale of a slave-girl Soteris, aged nine years, to Apion by Kephalon. It is true that from the first century AD, legislation which had the effect of ameliorating the slave's situation began to be passed. However, the reasons for the legislation remain unclear. In some measure it can be ascribed to a humanitarian concern, perhaps under Stoic influence. For example, Claudius legislated that a master who had forsaken a sick slave could not seize him/her if he/she should become well again. However, other pieces of legislation may be interpreted differently and their humanitarian concern questioned. For example, A.J.B. Sirks, 'Informal Manumission and the Lex Junia', *RIDA* 28 (1981), pp.247-76, argues that the *lex Junia* (17 BC) was introduced from an economic concern to secure the right of the manumitter to the property of his deceased freedman. The examples highlight the need to set each piece of legislation within the context of the evolving political, social and economic conditions. On the one hand, the principate sought to extend its control over matters which had formerly been the preserve of the citizens. At points this involved legislation affecting the master-slave relationship. On the other hand, as the labour cost of slavery rose, new sources of labour needed to be found. This was achieved through the impressing of the free labourer, i.e. a person who was bonded to the land or a village (= a serf) rather than to a person (= a slave) – see G.E.M. de Ste Croix, *The Class Struggle in the Ancient Greek World* (London 1981), pp.249-59, on the colonate. The effect was a blurring of distinctions between the lower strata of the society and a movement towards an economy based on a type of serfdom. To what extent did these forces of politicial, social and economic change – rather than a purely humanitarian concern – influence and affect the legislative process governing slavery?

The above description of a slave's lot may be considered as too negative by some. Pointing to funerary and other inscriptions dedicated to or by slaves they could argue for a more positive assessment of the master-slave relationship. D.B. Martin, *Slavery as Salvation: The Metaphor of Slavery in Pauline Christianity* (Yale 1990), pp.2-11, has recently taken up this line of argument, finding in the management/agent slave of antiquity the appropriate vehicle for the slave metaphor of 1Cor.9. However, several factors will need to be taken into account before any affirmation can be given to this suggestion. First, much of the surviving evidence, as Martin himself acknowledges, is biased by considerations of wealth and status. For example, slaves and freedmen possessing wealth and social standing (i.e. those who had done well despite their slavery) were more likely to be recorded in epigrams. The evidence is thus highly skewed. Second, the public nature and occasion of such inscriptions precluded any opportunity for criticising the system. This last consideration is associated with a third. Many inscriptions were either erected or approved by the slave's master[62] and as such were written from his perspective and function as much to cultivate his own image as to commemorate the deceased. For example, some epitaphs even state that the master-slave relationship extends beyond death: 'I am yours, master, even in Hades'; and again: 'to you even now under the earth, yes master, I remain faithful as before'. See further the discussion and references in *New Docs* 2 (1982), pp.52-4. Consequently, one needs to find other evidence to correct the bias of the inscriptional evidence. This might be sought in the literary stereotypes of slaves as lazy, conniving and apt to talk behind their masters' backs (expressions of non-compliance), in the promulgation of laws governing slaves and freedmen and in any other extant document which provides relevant information. For example, *P. Turner* 41 (see *New Docs* 6 [1992] §7) instances the underlying

---

62 It should be noted that a slave's burial arrangements were not always in the hands of his master alone. According to the *Lex collegii funeraticii Lanuvini* II 3-4 (*FIRA* III p.103) a slave could be a member of a *collegium funeraticium* and as such was entitled to be buried at the corporation's expense. See further the discussion by J.W. Tellegen, *The Roman Law of Succession in the Letters of Pliny the Younger* (Zutphen 1982), pp.147-150.

discontent of a management slave (a counter-example to Martin's hypothesis) as well as the difference of perception which might exist between the slave and his master. It goes without saying that such discontent would be concealed in any inscription. Other evidence might be sought in the NT. For example, the fact that manumission and the slave's attitude to and behaviour towards his/her master were live issues for the writers of the NT indicates the existence of some tension between the perceptions of masters and their slaves. One catalyst, no doubt, was the gospel itself and its message that οὐκ ἔνι 'Ιουδαῖος οὐδὲ Ἕλλην, οὐκ ἔνι δοῦλος οὐδὲ ἐλεύθερος, οὐκ ἔνι ἄρσεν καὶ θῆλυ· πάντες γὰρ ὑμεῖς εἷς ἐστε ἐν Χριστῷ 'Ιησοῦ (Gal.3.28).

A. Rom.7.13-25: πεπραμένος ὑπὸ τὴν ἁμαρτίαν (v.14)

The traditional focus of debate over Rom.7.13-25 has centred on the intended referent of 'I' and the use of the present tense. Is Paul referring to himself or humanity generally? If he is referring to himself, is it to the pre-conversion or post-conversion Paul? See A. Nygren, *Der Römerbrief* (Göttingen 1965), pp.208-22, for a discussion of the debate. K. Stendahl, 'Paul and the introspective conscience of the West', *Harv.Theo.Rev.* 56 (1963), pp.199-215, and *Paul among Jews and Gentiles* (Philadelphia 1978), pp.78-96, has attempted to refocus the debate away from its concentration on the 'I' to the Jew/Gentile question in the early church and the meaning of the Law. The debate as a whole, however, continues to pay insufficient attention to the metaphor upon which the passage is built.

The prevailing metaphor is that of slavery. Four pieces of evidence can be adduced to support the suggestion:

1. The passage is headed by the expression 'sold under sin' (Rom.7.14), an allusion to slavery. Though E. Käsemann, *An die Römer* (Tübingen 1980), pp.190-204, cf. *Commentary on Romans* (Grand Rapids 1980), pp.198-212, places the passage under the heading 'sold under sin', the choice appears to have been determined not by a cognizance of the prevailing metaphor but with a view to his interpretation of the 'I'.
2. The passage ends with a direct reference to slavery, 'So then, I myself in my mind am a slave to God's law, but in the flesh a slave to the law of sin' (Rom.7.25). The metaphor of slavery thus acts as an *inclusio* to the passage.
3. Within the immediate context of Romans (see especially chapter 6 but also 8.15) the metaphor of slavery is prominent. Paul constructs an opposition between a slavery to sin and a slavery to righteousness.
4. Rom.7.13-25 is concerned with the tension and struggle between what one wants to do and what one actually does. The slave knew too well a similar struggle, for he was subject to his master's will and thus not free to do as he pleased. Manumission entailed release and the newly obtained freedom could be expressed thus: ποιῶν ὅ κα θέλῃ καὶ ἀποτρέχων οἷς κα θέλῃ – 'doing whatever he wishes and going wherever he wishes' (see the Delphic manumission inscriptions in H. Collitz, J. Baunack et al., *Sammlung der griechischen Dialect-Inschriften* II [Göttingen 1899 – reprinted Nendeln 1973/78]).

Paul, it seems, drew on a topic of conversation which was current at the time of writing to fashion his metaphor.[63] The topic arose in Stoic circles in particular and concerned the tension between a growing recognition of the slave's humanity (i.e. the slave possessed a mind like any free person and as such was not a morally neutral object) and the legal fact that the slave was the property of another and therefore not free to choose his fate or actions. Seneca uses the classical distinction between the mind and body to describe the tension. He argues that the slave's servitude is of the body but he is free in mind.

> Errat, si quis existimat servitutem in totum hominem descendere. Pars melior eius excepta est: corpora obnoxia sunt et adscripta dominis, mens quidem sui iuris, quae adeo libera et vaga est, ut ne ab hoc quidem

63 Paul's use of a subsidiary metaphor (i.e. prisoner of war at v.23) is not inconsistent with the primary metaphor of slavery. Indeed, because war was traditionally a major source of slaves, the subsidiary metaphor may have even been suggested by the primary metaphor of slavery. Moreover, we note below that Seneca describes the slave's mind as imprisoned in the body.

carcere, in quo inclusa est, teneri queat, quominus inpetu suo utatur et ingentia agitet et in infinitum comes caelestibus exeat. Corpus itaque est, quod domino fortuna tradidit; hoc emit, hoc vendit; interior illa pars mancipio dari non potest. Ab hac quidquid venit, liberum est; nec enim aut nos omnia iubere possumus aut in omnia servi parere coguntur: contra rem publicam inperata non facient, nulli sceleri manus commodabunt.

It is an error to think that slavery penetrates to the whole person. The better part is excluded: the body is subject to and at the disposition of its master; the mind, however, is its own master and is so free and able to move that it cannot even be restrained by this prison, in which it is confined, from following its own impulse, setting in motion great ideas and passing over to infinity as a comrade to the gods. And so it is the body that fate surrenders to the master; he buys this, he sells this; that inner part cannot be given by purchase. Whatever issues from this is free. For neither can we command everything nor are slaves compelled to obey in everything. They will not act on orders against the public interest; they will not lend a hand to any crime. (Seneca, *De beneficiis* 3.20)

Of course, Paul adapts the topic of conversion but the gist of it remains.[64] The body (*corpus* – σάρξ) has been sold under sin but the mind (*mens* – ὁ νοῦς) or the inner man (*interior pars* – ὁ ἔσω ἄνθρωπος) serves the Law of God. Lacking the terminology of psychology, Paul availed himself of a metaphor to extend the descriptive capacity of his language. In the words of E.F. Kittay, *Metaphor, Its Cognitive Force and Linguistic Structure* (Oxford 1987), p.125, 'We use metaphor when the resources of literal language are inadequate to articulate significant distinctions or unities'. We might therefore paraphrase Rom.7.13-25 in these words:

I have been sold as a slave to sin. But as the slave is subject to his master in his body, so also am I only a slave to sin with my body. My mind is free and with it I give assent to the law of God.

The last lines of Seneca's passage draw attention to a moral dilemma facing slaves. If the slave was free in mind, how responsible was he for the actions taken at the behest of his master? Here the state is seen to intervene to limit the master's right to command. The tension can also be seen in the advice of 1Pet.2.18-20 to slaves. The slave was to suffer for doing right. In other words, the slave was seen as a moral agent responsible for his actions and as such may have to suffer at the hands of an unjust master. Paul's metaphor at Rom.7.13-25 also raises, though this time indirectly, the moral dilemma posed by slavery. When slavery is used as a metaphor to describe the bondage to sin (i.e. where the individual cannot do what he knows to be right), it follows that slavery itself poses a problem for the just slave of an unjust master.

B. The NT Attitude to Slavery

The NT writers shared in the ethos of their time with respect to the institution of slavery. Slaves were to remain in their slavery (1Cor.7.20). Slaves were to obey their masters with fear and trembling as if obeying the Lord (Eph.6.5). Slaves were to remain obedient to unjust masters (1Pet.2.18-20). When confronted by the modern abhorrence of slavery, the stance of the NT poses a dilemma.

64 Both Seneca and Paul are drawing on a common topic of conversation. Therefore, whilst noting the parallels between Paul and Seneca I do not intend to assert that there are not important differences between them. For example, one may note a functional difference. Seneca treats the topic of slavery itself whereas Paul uses slavery as a theological metaphor for the human condition. Again, K.L. McKay writes to me: 'Seneca is concerned with the mind's ability to rise above the problems of the body, but Paul is concerned with control, and the conflict between will and natural inclination (cf. Rom.6.12ff., 1Cor.6.13-20, 9.27, 2Cor.4.10ff., Phil.1.20, 1Thess.4.4) and the effect Christ's redemption has on the body as well as the mind'. Clearly, Paul in fashioning a metaphor made it function within his own theological context.

W.L. Westermann, *The Slave Systems of Greek and Roman Antiquity* (Philadelphia 1955), p.151, argues that the fires of persecution during the first three centuries blurred for the early church the distinction between free and slave. K.R. Bradley, *Slaves and Masters in the Roman Empire* (Brussels 1984), p.38, who portrays the forces of coercion used by the masters to ensure the compliance of slaves, likens the NT attitude to a victim's internalisation of the structures which oppress him. He assumes that the early church was composed predominantly of the lower social strata. Other authors offer mitigating arguments either in the form of a more positive description of the slave's lot (e.g. D. Tidball, *The Social Context of the New Testament* [Grand Rapids 1984], p.115), or by placing the social considerations of the NT under the imperative of eschatology. J.M.G. Barclay, 'Paul, Philemon and the Dilemma of Christian Slave-Ownership', *NTS* 37 (1991), pp.161-86, focuses on the vagueness of Paul's request to Philemon and concludes that Paul was himself struggling with the tension between the realities of slavery and the demands of Christian brotherhood. Paul did not know what to recommend and left the decision to Philemon. De Ste Croix, op.cit., pp.418-52, offers a critique of the church's stance on slavery and property. His basic thesis is that Christianity's concentration on moral (man to man) and spiritual (man to God) issues to the exclusion of institutional (men to men) factors made it an instrument which both maintained and justified the *status quo*. H. Bellen, *Studien zur Sklavenflucht im römischen Kaiserreich* (Wiesbaden 1971), pp.78-81, interprets Paul's decision to return Onesimus (*contra* Deut.23.15-16) as an attempt to protect Christianity from the charge of kidnapping which would have adversely affected his missionary activity. Paul sought to stop slaves from using Christianity and its call to 'forsake everything' as a way of avoiding slavery. The lack of distinction in Christ between slave and free had for Paul and other NT writers, it is argued, no direct implication for social structures. In a similar fashion J.D.M. Derrett, 'The Function of the Epistle to Philemon', *ZNTW* 79 (1988), pp.63-91, argues that epistle was a public manifesto to absolve the church of the suspicion that it acted as an asylum for slaves. For Paul the church's mission took precedence over the question of a slave's 'civil right'. For J. Gnilka, *Der Philemonbrief* (Freiburg 1982), pp.71-81, such a concern is only evident in the advice to slaves in the Pastoral Epistles. There the concern for the church's order and image[65] provoked a one-sided teaching to the slaves to obey and to submit to their masters. As such the writer's interest is merely in outward and external compliance. For Gnilka, Paul himself shows a different concern in his treatment of slavery. The equality affirmed at 1Cor.12.13 and Gal.3.27-28 refers only to the body of Christ, the church; it does not extend to cover social structures generally. As a practical outworking of this theological stance, Onesimus is returned to his master. Nothing on the political or legal level is said, but Philemon should receive Onesimus as a brother in Christ. In one important respect the teaching of Colossians and Ephesians is seen by Gnilka to be quite different from that of Paul elsewhere; in these two letters equality is perceived not in terms of the body of Christ but rather in terms of the final judgement where all will stand answerable to the same impartial judge. The teaching of 1 Peter is seen to be different yet again. Here attack and persecution fall on slave and free alike and both are called to follow the example of the suffering Christ. The important difference here, however, is that the problem faced by Christian slaves living in heathen households is now an issue. This presented a dilemma, for the church recognised the moral responsibility of the slave, though the civil law did not. The slave should suffer for doing right rather than for doing wrong, i.e. the principle of a slave's moral responsibility is recognised.

H. Gülzow, *Christentum und Sklaverei in den ersten drei Jahrhunderten* (Bonn 1969), places the NT discussion of slavery within three periods. Thereby one must properly speak of a changing context to the NT discussion. The discussion of the first period, to which the letters to

---

[65] Gnilka suggests that the threat to the church's order and image was a heresy (gnostic?) which promoted the aspirations of slaves.

Philemon, the Corinthians and Romans belong, is made under the expectation of the imminent parousia. For Gülzow the majority of believing slaves in the period had come to their faith through the conversion of their masters and therefore belonged to Christian households. Therefore, the issue is whether the believing slave of the Christian master should be manumitted. Paul's advice is that each person, whether uncircumcised, unmarried or in slavery, should remain in the state in which he was called. Paul's failure to address the question of social distinction, no doubt, arises from a prevailing eschatological expectation. The discussion of the second period, to which Colossians and Ephesians belong, is made under the receding expectation of the parousia and the attempt to regulate the moral life of Christian households. Here the church's advice to the slave and his master is placed within its baptismal teaching. Although the church made no distinction between slave and master before the Lord, the believing slave should not infer from this equality that he owed no service to his master. Rather, the slave should serve his master as if serving the Lord. Particular attention is focused on the motivation behind the slave's obedience. As in his discussion of the first period Gülzow places the majority of slaves within Christian households; he also reinterprets the harsh sounding expression μετὰ φόβου καὶ τρόμου (Eph.6.5) – 'with fear and trembling' – to mean 'with earnestness and concern' (*mit Ernst und Sorge*, p.65). The third period arises from events which were cataclysmic for the church, i.e. the break with Judaism, the destruction of the mother church in Jerusalem, the death of the Apostles and the rise of persecution. The Gentile mission led to an increase in the number of Christian slaves of unbelieving masters. Accordingly, 1Peter and 1Timothy address their advice to the slave alone, i.e. there is no corresponding advice to the master. Slavery is a duty placed on the slave by God and its associated suffering can be likened to the suffering of Christ. As martyrs of Christ the slave should hope to win his master for Christ. At the same time the slave's vulnerability to persecution became a growing concern for the church as evidenced by 1 Clement, Ignatius, Hermas and the Apostolic Constitutions.

Gülzow argues that the oppressive nature of slavery was not apparent to the first-century church because most Christian slaves belonged to Christian masters. In the second century, however, persecution and the rise in the number of Christian slaves in non-believing households brought the issue of slavery to a head. Does this adequately account for the NT attitude to a slave's situation? An affirmative answer to the question assumes a positive assessment of the Christian slave's lot in the Christian household. At the same time it seems to disregard the slave's own perception of his fate and aspiration for freedom.

S.R.L.

§7 A Petition Concerning a Runaway: Paul's Letter to Philemon

Oxyrhynchus — Third century AD

Ed.pr. — U. Hagedorn, *P. Turner* 41 (London 1981), pp.167-172 (= *P. Colon. inv.* 7921).

The papyrus (11 x 14 cm) is complete except for the bottom portion. The editor estimates that perhaps as much as half the document has not been preserved. See *New Docs* 6 (1992) §18 for the petition's form. The present fragment contains only the opening and part of the background.

Αὐρηλίῳ Π̣[ρω]τ̣άρχ[ῳ] τῷ καὶ Ἥρωνι στρα(τηγῷ) Ὀξυ(ρυγχίτου)	To Aurelius Protarchos, also called Heron, *strategos* of the Oxyrhynchite (nome)
παρὰ Αὐ[ρ]ηλ[ίας] Σ̣α̣ρ̣α̣π̣ιάδος τῆς καὶ Διονυ-	from Aurelia Sarapias, also called Dionysarion,
σαρίου θυ[γα]τρὸς Ἀπολλοφάνους τοῦ καὶ Σαρα-	daughter of Apollophanes, also called Sarapammon,

πάμμων̣ο̣ς ἐξηγητεύσαντος τῆς Ἀντιν̣ο̣έω̣(ν)	former *exegetes* of Antinoopolis,
πόλεως [χω]ρὶς κ̣υ̣[[ρ]]ρίου χρηματιζούσης	acting without guardian
δικαίῳ τέκ̣νων. ἔχουσα πρότερον	according to the *ius trium liberorum*. I have a slave, who formerly
τοῦ πατρός μου δοῦλον ὀνόματι Σαραπίωνα	belonged to my father, by the name of Sarapion,
καὶ τοῦτον νομίσασα μηδὲν φαῦλόν τι δια-	and I considered that he had done no base deed whatsoever
πρά[ξ]ασθαι τῷ εἶναί μου πατρικὸν καὶ πε-	as he was part of my inheritance and
πιστεῦσθαι ὑπ' ἐμοῦ τὰ ἡμέτερα, οὗτος	had been entrusted by me with our household. (Nevertheless) he,
οὐκ οἶθ' ὅπως ἐξ ἐπιτριβῆς τινων ἀλλό-	I know not how, at the instigation of certain folk,
τρια φρονήσας τῆς παρεχομένης αὐτῷ	disdaining the honour afforded him
ὑπ' ἐμοῦ τειμῆς καὶ χορηγίας τῶν ἀναγ-	by me and the provision of the necessities
καίων πρὸς δίαιταν ὑφελόμενός τινα	for life, (and) purloining some items of clothing
ἀπὸ τῶν ἡμετέρων μεθ' ὧν αὐτῷ	from our household with which
κατεσκεύασα ἱματίων καὶ ἄλλων καὶ ὧν	I had provided him and even other items which
καὶ αὐτὸς ἑαυτῷ περιεποιήσατο ἐκ τῶν	he also took possession of for himself from
ἡμετέρων λάθρᾳ ἀπέδρα. περιηχηθεῖ-	our household has secretly run away. Having heard
σα δὲ εἶναι τοῦτον ἐν τῷ Νόμου ἐποικ̣[ίῳ]	that he resides in the hamlet of the Nome
[π]αρὰ Χαιρήμονι ἠξίωσα παρὰ τῷ δια̣κ̣[. . . . .]	with Chairemon, I asked ...
[. . .] ( ) [τ]οῦ νομοῦ εἰρην[αρ]χ ( ) Αὐρηλι[	
[. . . . .] . γι . [ ] . . . . . . [.] .[	
] . υδρ . [	
] . . [	

....

13 τιμῆς

The fragmentary state of the papyrus makes its interpretation difficult. What was the petition actually requesting? Was Sarapias seeking the help of the *strategos* (administrator of the Nome or district) only to apprehend the slave or also to prosecute those who had assisted the runaway (e.g., as in *P. Oxy*. XIV 1643)? The law forbade the encouragement of a slave to run away (*Dig*. 48.15.6.2 and *Dig*. 11.3.1.5). It was also illegal to harbour a runaway.

The editor leaves undecided the question whether the expression ἐξ ἐπιτριβῆς τινων implied a knowledge of these laws, preferring to understand it as an expression of the mistress' perplexity over the event.[66] The editor infers this from Sarapias' statements concerning the provision of necessities and the honour afforded the slave. In her opinion there were no grounds for flight. The same can also be inferred from the use of the expression ἀλλότρια φρονήσας by spouses in complaints against a partner's infidelity (*P. Oxy.* II 282, *P. Bon.*21 and *P. Heidelberg* (n.f.) III 13). Other features of the text might also be considered in arguing the mistress' state of mind, e.g. the use and position of the parenthetic expression 'I know not how', the emphasis on the slave's being inherited from her father and the search for some reason to account for the flight (i.e. under the influence of others). The picture that the petition gives is of a mistress' perplexity resulting from the slave's unexplained disloyalty. However, one needs to bear in mind that we possess only one side of the story.

The papyrus further raises the issue of the relation between the roles of masters and the authorities in the apprehension of runaways. The Roman law which involved administrative officials in the arrest and return of runaways was extended in the time of Antoninus Pius to cover the empire. However, as the editor notes, the papyri cast doubt on its actual effectiveness. For example, *P. Turner* 41 implies that the mistress had discovered the slave's location for herself. Further, since the document does not appear to be the first petition (see *ll.*19-20 especially the aorist ἠξίωσα), it could be concluded that the former petition had been unsuccessful, with the slave surprisingly still residing in the Oxyrhynchite nome. The editor, though not ruling out the possible assistance of officials, further notes the continued use of privately contracted persons authorised to apprehend and deal with the runaways (see also *P. Oxy.* XII 1423 and XIV 1643).

A slave was usually a master's largest investment apart from his investment in land. If the runaway slave was not recovered, the master's loss might be substantial. Even if recovered, the loss might not be inconsiderable. Not only did the owner face a reduced resale value (contracts of sale included clauses concerning the slave's propensity to run away – see *P. Turner* 22 above) but he may also have incurred costs associated with the finding and apprehension of the runaway (see *P. Cair. Zen.* I 59015 verso *l.*5 and comments in *New Docs* 6 [1992] §13). There is another aspect of flight from slavery which might profitably be considered. The non-compliance of slaves manifested itself in several ways, from the most drastic, like slave rebellion and murdering one's master,[67] to the more subtle, like careless workmanship and

---

[66] A question arises as to whether the mistress' state of mind should be construed as genuine or as a routine pose used to blacken the slave and thereby to remove any blame from herself. One needs to recognise that poses were frequently used by petitioners in their attempt to gain the compliance of the authorities. In the present petition, however, a decision as to the genuineness of the mistress' state of mind will depend on two factors: a) how frequently one might expect such perplexity/confusion in the master. Here one needs to bear in mind the nature of the master/slave relationship, e.g. the importance of the slave's role in the household and the degree of his intimacy with the family; and b) the interpretative value of other evidence (see below) for the master's state of mind in the present petition. Whether or not the mistress' state of mind is judged as genuine in this particular case, it appears that perplexity was at least considered by the petitioner to be a plausible response to the event. In turn, this gives credence to the proposition that such a state of mind was not unexpected in masters.

[67] The great slave rebellions in Sicily and Italy occurred in 135-132, 104-101 and 73-71 BC. They resulted from a number of concomitant factors such as the slaves' origins and training and the opportunities afforded by the nature and conditions of their servitude. See W.L. Westermann, *The Slave Systems of Greek and Roman Antiquity* (Philadelphia 1955), p.75. J. Vogt, *Ancient Slavery and the Ideal of Man* [Oxford 1974], p.46, states: 'It was this combination of violence and weakness, authority and lawlessness, that created a revolutionary atmosphere'. Literary and documentary evidence witnesses also to the murder of masters by their slaves. Seneca, *De clem.* 1.26.1, observes that slaves have been known to kill their masters to avenge the cruelty shown them. In the reign of Nero the senate renewed the decree that if a master was murdered by one of his slave, all slaves in his household were to be put to death (Tacitus, *Ann.*, 13.32.1); the reason was presumably that they either were involved in or knew of the plot. The decree was applied against popular protest when the prefect Pedanius Secundus was murdered by one of his slaves (Tacitus, *Ann.* 14.42-45). See also J.& L. Robert, *Fouilles*

tardiness. No doubt the frequency and type of non-compliance were correlated; it is reasonable to assume that the more drastic the non-compliance the rarer its occurrence and the more subtle the non-compliance the more frequent its occurrence. However, of all the forms of non-compliance, the one which was both drastic and frequent enough to manifest a clear breakdown in the institution itself was flight from slavery. In a similar fashion, H. Bellen, *Studien zur Sklavenflucht im römischen Kaiserreich* (Wiesbaden 1971), pp.155, 158, describes flight as a structural failure of the slave system arising from its basic inhumanity (particularly its *saevitia* and *avaritia*). Lacking any effective legal redress against a harsh and oppressive master, the slave had little alternative but to turn to flight (see J. Gnilka, *Der Philemonbrief* [Freiburg 1982], pp.59, 68-71). In doing so, he might hope to be lost in the subculture of a large city, for example, or to find work in another region or he might resort to brigandage. Alternatively, he might seek the assistance of a person of social standing to advocate his cause or seek asylum in an appropriate temple (and later in a church or monastery) and have its priests decide his fate.

It is important to differentiate between the origins and conditions of servitude. For example, there were house-born slaves and slaves taken in distant wars; there were slaves who developed close relationships within their master's family (e.g. nurses, tutors and doctors; see Vogt, op.cit., pp.103-121) and those who worked on large capital-intensive estates (i.e. on estates with a large number of slaves – slaves were a form of capital investment) and who never knew their masters. The flight of the latter type of slave, we can guess, was perceived by the owner as an economic loss. However, the flight of a house-born slave or a slave with a close association with the family and entrusted with a degree of responsibility within the household was viewed quite differently. It provided the clearest indication of the failure of the master/slave relationship and was bound to lead to considerable anxiety in the master. Two aspects of the above papyrus are directly relevant at this point; they are the mistress' apparent perplexity over the slave's conduct and her subsequent attempt to explain the event. The same features are present in Cicero's letter to P. Sulpicius Rufus (*Ad fam.* 13.77.3) written in part to request the latter's assistance in the apprehension of a runaway slave. The alleged reason for the slave's action is his fear of being discovered (he had stolen some books). Cicero concludes that though the slave's running away was only a small matter, it had caused him much distress: *res ipsa parva, sed animi mei dolor magnus est.* See also Seneca, *Epist.* 107.1 where Seneca questions a master's anxiety over so small a matter as a slave's flight: *iam pusilla te res angit ?*

The above observations concerning a master's anxiety at the flight of slaves may also inform the interpretation of a papyrus letter written about 500 years earlier. *P. Mich. Zen.*18 was the second of two letters. The first letter, *P. Lond.*VII 1951, had been written informing Zenon of the apprehension of two slaves. The second letter, *P. Mich. Zen.* 18, was then written on the same or following day to inform Zenon of the apprehension of the third runaway. It was written with the express purpose of allaying his anxiety. As Apollonios' steward (and freedman) Zenon was responsible for all the affairs of his estate in the Fayum.

Alexandria received (at Arsinoe) 21 July 257 BC
Ed. – W.J. Tait, *P. Lugd.Bat.* XX 36 (Leiden 1980), pp.152-154 (= *P. Mich. Zen.* 18).

Μένης Ζήνωνι χ[α]ί̣ρ̣ε̣ι̣ν̣. [μετὰ τὸ	Menes to Zenon, greeting. [After
ἀποστεῖλαι τὴν πρότερον	sending the previously]
γ]ραφεῖσαν ἐπιστολήν,	written letter

---

d'Amyzon en Carie (Paris 1983), pp.259-66. This second-century BC poetic epitaph is dedicated to Demetrios who was killed whilst asleep by one of his slaves. The slave then set fire to the house presumably in an attempt to cover his crime. See also Pliny, *Epist.* 8.14, where the possibility of the slaves' involvement in their master's death is entertained.

2	μικρῶι ὕστερον συνέλαβον Στάχ[υν τὸν παρὰ Ζηνοδώρου παῖδα καὶ] ἀπαγαγὼν εἰς τὰ Ἀμύντου παρέδωκα μετὰ τῷ[ν ἄλλων παιδαρίων. καὶ τήνδε νῦν] γεγράφαμέν σοι	a little later I apprehended Stachys, [the slave of Zenodoros, and] taking (him) off to Amyntas' house I handed (him) over with the [other slaves. And this (letter) now] we have written to you
4	ἵνα εἰδῶς μὴ ἀγωνιαῖς	that you may know and not be troubled.
	[ἔρρωσο. L κ̅θ̅ Δαισίου κ̅α̅]	[Farewell. Year 29, Daisios 21]
6	(Back) Ζήνωνι.	To Zenon.
	Μένης περὶ Στάχυος.	Menes concerning Stachys.
8	L κ̅θ̅ Δαισίου κ̅α̅,	Year 29, Daisios 21,
	ἐν Ἀρσινόηι.	in Arsinoe.

In his epistle to Philemon Paul deals with the situation of the runaway slave Onesimus. It presents the reader with an insight into the practical out-working of Paul's theology. Like Sarapion, the slave in *P. Turner* 41, Onesimus had run away from his master and stood accused of taking certain property (see Phlm.18-19).

H. Gülzow, *Christentum und Sklaverei in den ersten drei Jahrhunderten* (Bonn 1969), p.31, surmises that Onesimus may have administered his master's finances and had his hand in the till, so to speak. Onesimus' flight is thus prompted by a fear of discovery (see Cicero above). If so, he held a position of trust similar to Sarapion who, as we have seen, was entrusted with the running of the household. The events and motives behind the letter to Philemon must remain a matter of conjecture. If fear of discovery had prompted the flight, then Onesimus may well have sought Paul's assistance to intercede as an *amicus domini* on his behalf (see B.M. Rapske, 'The Prisoner Paul in the Eyes of Onesimus', *NTS* 37 [1991], pp.187-203). However, it remains unclear whether theft was the actual cause which prompted Onesimus' action in the first place. For example, if Onesimus' theft like that of Sarapion only comprised the necessary provisions for flight, then it could not have prompted his action. Be that as it may, Onesimus encountered Paul (probably in Ephesus) and was converted to Christianity. Thereafter, he returned to his master carrying Paul's letter and request that he be accepted no longer as a slave but as a brother. In returning Onesimus and offering to make good any losses, Paul recognised the legal and financial right of a master to decide the fate of his slave. However, P. Stuhlmacher, *Der Brief an Philemon* (Zürich 1975), pp.67-8, argues that for Paul Philemon's decision was essentially limited by the response which was expected of him as a Christian. In this sense 1Cor.12.13 and Gal.3.26-8 were programmatic for Christian behaviour in the world. Either Philemon could retain Onesimus as a slave but pardon and accept him as a brother or he could free him for the Christian mission. Stuhlmacher suggests that Philemon actually decided to free Onesimus (see his argument pp.18-9). J.M.G. Barclay, 'Paul, Philemon and the Dilemma of Christian Slave-Ownership', *NTS* 37 (1991), pp.161-186, takes a different stance and concludes that Paul was himself struggling with the tension between the realities of slavery and the demands of Christian brotherhood. Not knowing what to recommend, Paul left the decision concerning Onesimus' fate to Philemon.

P. Turner 41 offers an insight into the perplexity and anxiety which might be experienced by the owner of a runaway slave. Should these emotions be 'factored in' when assessing the reader response to the epistle to Philemon? Might Paul himself have anticipated these emotions in his readers and responded to them? The questions are difficult to answer as the epistle leaves many background details unclear (see Gülzow, op.cit., pp.29-41). However, two tentative lines of argument suggest themselves. First, it has been noted that the petitioner in *P. Turner* 41 sought some explanation for the slave's action. Perhaps he had run away at the instigation of others. Cicero considered the cause of his slave's flight to have been a theft of books. In each case some weakness in the character of the slave was suggested as the reason for flight – one might profitably compare Pliny, *Epist.*9.21 – and this in turn precluded the raising of broader questions about the nature of slavery itself. Paul also alleges a reason for Onesimus' action; he suggests that it was perhaps part of God's purpose that Onesimus should run away that he might be restored again no longer a slave but a brother (Phlm.15-16). Unlike the above examples, however, Paul does not find the reason for the slave's action in some weakness of character. Did Paul thereby anticipate Philemon's perplexity and the sort of questions that such a person might ask? Indeed, by suggesting the event's cause in some divine purpose, did Paul attempt not only to diffuse Philemon's present anxiety but also to avoid its turning to anger on Onesimus' return?

Second, the letter is addressed not only to Philemon but also to the members of the church which met in his house. How might this be explained? Stuhlmacher, op.cit., p.24, argues that Paul thereby placed Philemon in the position of having to make his decision before the community. In other words, Paul's request and Philemon's response were open to the scrutiny of the community. J.D.M. Derrett, 'The Function of the Epistle to Philemon', *ZNW* 79 (1988), pp.63-91, argues that the epistle had a 'public, archival function'. It was a manifesto directed at pagan scrutineers and synagogue rulers who might otherwise harbour the suspicion that the church acted as an asylum for runaways.[68] As such, the question of the addressees is irrelevant. A more interesting interpretation is that offered by R. Lehmann, *Épître à Philémon* (Geneva 1978), p.30. He suggests that Paul's opening address to the community and the praise of Philemon which follows may be associated. Philemon's character may have been put in doubt by Onesimus' flight (i.e. it might be supposed by the community that Philemon was a cruel master). In other words, Paul wished to rehabilitate Philemon in the eyes of his community. If so, one can further suppose that the whole affair had caused Philemon considerable perplexity and anxiety. Indeed, this was not only confined to the master/slave relationship but extended also to the relationship (patron/client ?) between Philemon and the church which met in his house.

S.R.L.

§8 'He gives authority to his slaves, to each his work ...' Mark.13.34

Provenance unknown — 11 Aug. AD 275

Ed.pr. — B. Frid, *P. Ups.Frid* 7 (Bonn 1981), pp.73-77.

A regularly cut papyrus (10.4 x 10.7 cm) written along the fibres and folded vertically twice. The papyrus is not badly damaged but in places the ink has faded.

Ἰσίδωρος Ἀμμω̣νίλα̣	Isodorus to Ammonilla,
(vac.) χαίρειν.	greeting.
ἐπί τινει χ̣ρ̣όνω̣ ἐ̣γένου μου	Since for some time you have been my
κοράσιν̣ ἐ̣ξου̣σ̣ία̣ν̣ σ̣ο̣ι δίδωμι ἐν-	slave-girl, I give you authority
τκεῦ̣θεν̣ ὧ ἠ̣ὰ̣ν β̣ουλίσοι ἐρθῖν	henceforth to go wherever you wish
μὴ ἐ̣νκαλου̣μένη ὑπ' ἐμοῦ.	without being accused by me.
(ἔτους) ϛ Αὐρηλιανοῦ τοῦ κυρείου	In year 6 of Aurelianus, the lord,
(vac.) Μεσορὴ ιη̄.	Mesore 18.

....

1 Ἀμμωνίλλα̣ 3 ἐπεί τινι (?) 4 κοράσιον 5 οὗ ἐὰν βουλήσῃ ἐλθεῖν 6 ἐγκαλουμένη 7 κυρίου

---

68 On Paul's consciousness of the outsider's view of the church and his desire for church order generally see, for example, H.C. Kee, *Christian Origins in Sociological Perspective* (Philadelphia 1980), pp.94-6.

The editor states quite baldly the difficulty of the papyrus: 'This document appears to be unparalleled, and as to its interpretation I am in serious doubt'. The options envisaged are that the *cheirographon* represents either the manumission of a slave or the release (= ἀπόλυσις) of a person of free status from a labour contract (= παραμονή). Frid observes that: a) both deeds of manumission and deeds of release from labour contract could use the expression 'to go wherever you wish'; b) the term κοράσιον only rarely signifies a female slave; and c) a reference to the woman's new legal status of freedom[69], which might otherwise have been expected in a deed of manumission, is wanting in the case of *P. Ups.Frid* 7. Consequently, he concludes that the *cheirographon* is better understood as a release from labour contract.

B. Adams, *Paramoné und verwandte Texte* (Berlin 1964), deals with labour contracts between persons of free status.[70] In particular he discusses four types of contracts: a) the παραμοναί (pp.10-113); b) teaching contracts (pp.114-145); c) wet-nurse contracts (pp.146-165); and d) artist contracts (pp.166-192). Clearly, the editor of the present papyrus has in mind a release from a type a) labour contract. The essence of such contracts is that one person is obliged to provide a service to the other. W.L. Westermann, 'The Paramone as General Service Contract', *JJP* 2 (1948), pp.9-50, distinguishes the *paramone* contract from other types of labour contracts by virtue of the fact that the services to be rendered were unspecified. This usually required the person supplying the service to παραμένειν or remain with the other, e.g. *BGU* IV 1126, *P. Tebt.* II 384, *P. Flor.* I 44 and *P. Dura* 20. This requirement naturally implied a limitation on the labour-giver's freedom of movement. However, actual co-residence of the parties will have depended on the type of service to be rendered. Central to all four types of labour contracts, as discussed by Adams, is the payment of a sum which, though styled as a loan, is actually a prepayment for services to be rendered. The contracts are thus not consensual but based on this debt.[71] Clearly, a release from or termination of such labour contracts will need to refer to the repayment of the prepaid sum, e.g. *BGU* IV 1153 and 1154, *P. Med.* I 7 and the entries to the *grapheion* registers of *P. Mich.* II 123 XI (*l*.26) and *P. Mich.*V 238 IV (*l*.167).

The difficulties in interpreting the papyrus arise from several factors. First, the papyrus lacks any context which might indicate its function and thus supply a semantic control. For example, similarity of form or an extended text in many other papyri can be used to construct a context. In the present case such possibilities are not available. Second, the question of variant orthography bears on the text's interpretation. Does ἐπί (*l*.3) represent the conjunction ἐπεί or

---

69 It might be noted at this point that a release (ἀπόλυσις) from *paramone* (παραμονή), where the labour contract arises in conditional manumission, can also refer to freedom. For example, a Delphic release from *paramone* (see *GDI* 2327 and re-edited by G.Daux, 'Inscriptions de Delphes inédites ou revues', *BCH* 73 [1949], p.285) states:

ἀπέλυσε τᾶς παραμονᾶς [Νικόβουλος]	[Nikoboulos] has released from *paramone*
Σωσικλῆν, καὶ ἔστ[ω] Σωσικ[λ]ῆς ἀπὸ τού-	Sosikles, and let Sosikles from this
του τοῦ χρόνου ἐ[λεύ]θερος [καὶ ἀνέφα-	time be free [and not liable to seizure]
πτος ἀπὸ πάντ[ων τὸν πάντα χρόνον]	by anyone [always.]

Release from *paramone* was also accompanied by the payment of money. See C.W. Tucker, 'Women in the Manumission Inscriptions at Delphi', *TAPA* 112 (1982), pp.232-3 n.28.

70 Adams does not discuss at any length the other legal instruments involving *paramone*, such as the conditional manumission of a slave or the surety that a person will appear in court or perform a liturgy. On the distinction between *paramone* contracts involving persons of free status and those involving ex-slaves see M.I. Finley, 'The Servile Statuses of Ancient Greece', *RIDA* 7 (1960), pp.180-2.

71 The prepayment of a sum also distinguishes this type of labour contract from the other way of contracting service by μισθός. The loan in a *paramone* contract was without interest and a fixed date of repayment. The labour appears to have been in lieu of interest. However, in teaching contracts wages could be paid in the later stages of the contract.

is it the preposition? If the latter, then the text would need to be punctuated after κοράσιν with asyndeton in the next sentence. Is ῶ (*l*.5) to be understood as ᾧ (to whom) or οὗ (where)? Third, there is an ambiguity about how τινει χρόνῳ and ἐγένου (*l*.3) are to be understood. Frid points out that the dative can be used for duration of time. For examples of this use see N. Turner, *Grammar of New Testament Greek* (Edinburgh 1963), vol. 3, pp.243-4, and *P. Oslo inv*.1518 *ll*.7-8 reproduced at *New Docs* 6 (1992) §**19**. G.H.R. Horsley (per litt.) draws attention to the aorist ἐγένου and notes the importance of verbal aspect. See further S.E. Porter, *Verbal Aspect in the Greek of the New Testament, with Reference to Tense and Mood* (NY 1989), pp.182-8. A good example of the two difficulties can be seen in John 2.20: τεσσαράκοντα καὶ ἓξ ἔτεσιν οἰκοδομήθη ὁ ναὸς οὗτος – 'It has taken forty-six years to build this temple'. In this clause the dative is used for duration of time and the aorist describes an extended action. Therefore, *l*.3 above can be rendered variously: 'at a certain time you became ...' or ' for some time you have been ...' or 'for some time you were'. The translation will largely depend on the constructed context of the *cheirographon* as a whole.

Given the above difficulties, there remain residual difficulties in Frid's interpretation of the *cheirographon* as a release from a labour contract. First, the papyrus neither refers to παραμονή nor to the fact that the prepaid sum has been repaid. The lack of any reference to a prepaid sum (see above references to releases and terminations of παραμοναί) must raise a serious question as to whether this can actually be considered a release. Second, the editor's view that 'κοράσιον is a relatively rare word for a female slave' must be questioned. To the examples cited for and against such a usage by Frid, the following occurrences of the term to designate a slave-girl should be added *P. IFAO* II 24 *l*.6 (31 BC – AD 14), *P. Turner* 22 *ll*.2,9,11,16 (AD 142 – see *New Docs* 6 [1992] §**6**), *P. Oxy*. L 3593 *l*.11 (AD 238 – 244), *BGU* III 913 *l*.7 (third century AD), *P. Ness*. III 89 *l*.21 (sixth to seventh century AD) and a Thessalian manumission inscription (ed.pr. – P. Lazaridis, *Praktika* [1972], p.31 *l*.11). It might also be noted that Ammonilla is a possible slave name, for the slave-mother mentioned in *P. Strassb*. II 122 (AD 161-9) bears that name.[72] Thirdly, the fact that Isodorus gives his authority to Ammonilla does not necessarily entail the notion that she is freed from his service, whether by manumission[73] or by release from a labour contract. The wording may imply that the ceded authority[74] can be revoked at any time. See the reference to Mark 13.34 below where the expression entails this much.

For these various reasons *P. Ups.Frid* 7 may be neither a manumission nor a release from a labour contract but instead an authority to the slave-girl Ammonilla giving her freedom of movement.[75] The difficulty is the scope of freedom allowed her. W.L. Westermann, *The Slave Systems of Greek and Roman Antiquity* (Philadelphia 1955), recognises a divisibility of freedom and notes four types, i.e. legal freedom, freedom of movement, freedom of work and freedom from seizure. M.I. Finley, 'The Servile Statuses of Ancient Greece', *RIDA* 7 (1960), pp.183-8, takes issue with Westermann's distinctions preferring to conceive of status as a

72 F. Preisigke, *Namenbuch* (Heidelberg 1922 – reprinted Amsterdam 1967); D. Foraboschi, *Onomasticon* (Milano) and H. Solin, *Die griechischen Personennamen in Rom* (Berlin 1982) give 16 persons with the name Ammonilla. Of these only one is certainly a slave. The status of the others is either free or uncertain. The disproportion may only indicate the fact that free or freed persons were more likely to have their names recorded, i.e. the slave had limited legal rights and thus did not enter into contracts.

73 It may be worth noting that the expression met in deeds of manumission is ἐξέστω τῷ δεῖνι (e.g. in manumission inscriptions from Thessaly) rather than ἐξουσίαν σοι δίδωμι.

74 That the term ἐξουσία implies a conferred authority is indicated by the use of epithets to qualify the emperor's imperium as ἐξουσία αὐτοτελής (Strabo, *Geogr*. 6.4.2) or αὐτοκρατής ἐξουσία (Philo, *Leg. ad Cai*. 4.26, 8.54) or μόναρχος ἐξουσία (Appian, *Illyr*. 30.88) or αὐτοκράτωρ ἐξουσία (Herodian 1.3.1). See H.J. Mason, *Greek Terms for Roman Institutions* (Toronto 1974), pp.132-4.

75 The ambiguity of ῶ has already been alluded to. I understand it to be οὗ – 'where' since a) a verb of motion (ἐλθεῖν) can be expected to take an accusative with preposition; b) in view of the papyrus' dating and the problem of absenteeism (ἀναχώρησις) a document permitting movement is more plausible.

'bundle' of privileges and rights allocated variously across the community.[76] One such privilege or right was the 'power over a man's labour and movements'. Be that as it may, both conceptions of freedom afford a better understanding of *P. Ups.Frid* 7. The document appears to permit the slave-girl freedom of movement only. One may therefore assume that the slave-girl was employed by her master in work which required freedom of movement. However, comparisons between Ammonilla and the handicraft slaves of Athens, i.e. οἱ χωρὶς οἰκοῦντες, who worked and lived independently of their masters and in return paid to their masters a proportion of their earnings, must remain tentative for there is no evidence for such practice in Ptolemaic or Roman Egypt. An alternative suggestion might be that the master Isodorus had to be absent himself for a period. In his absence he gave a trusted (thus the opening clause 'Since for some time you have been ...' and the discretionary freedom afforded 'wherever she wishes') slave-girl this *cheirographon* allowing her free movement to attend to any matters which might arise. A parallel to this supposed permit is provided in Mark's gospel. In his apocalypse (i.e. Mark 13) Mark emphasises the need for disciples to be awake as the hour of the Lord's return is unknown. He uses the metaphor of the man who travels abroad:

> ὡς ἄνθρωπος ἀπόδημος ἀφεὶς τὴν οἰκίαν αὐτοῦ καὶ δοὺς τοῖς δούλοις αὐτοῦ τὴν ἐξουσίαν, ἑκάστῳ τὸ ἔργον αὐτοῦ, καὶ τῷ θυρωρῷ ἐνετείλατο ἵνα γρηγορῇ. Mark 13.34

S.R.L.

§9 'If you can gain your freedom': Manumission and 1Cor.7.21

Oxyrhynchus 2 Feb. AD 101

Ed. — T.C. Skeat, *P. Turner* 19 (London 1981), pp.93-99 (= E. Boswinkel, *P. Lugd.- Bat.* XIII 24 + *P. Lond. inv.* 2938).

Until joined by T.C. Skeat the deed of manumission existed as the two fragments *P. Lugd.-Bat.* XIII 24 (33 x 22.2 cm) + *P. Lond. inv.*2938 (57 x 20.5 cm). The point of juncture is in *l*.10 with *P. Lugd.-Bat.* XIII 24 breaking off after the name Aristios. The first fragment is badly damaged by worm-holes. I have followed K.L. McKay's suggestion (per litt.) and removed the colon after the name Theon.

[ἔτους τετάρτου Αὐτοκράτορος	[In the fourth year of the Imperator
Καίσα]ρ̣[ος Νέ]ρ̣ο̣υα Τραιανοῦ	Caesar Ne]rva Trajan
Σεβαστοῦ Γερμανικοῦ, Ξανδικοῦ η̣̄	Augustus Germanicus, Xandikos 8,
\`Σεβα(στῇ)´, Μεχεὶρ η̄ \`Σεβα(στῇ)´	*dies Augustus*, Mecheir 8, *dies*
ἐν Ὀξυρύγχων̣ [πό]λ̣ε̣ι̣ τῆς	*Augustus*, in the city of Oxyrhynchus of
Θηβαίδος ἐπ' ἀγορανόμων	the Thebaid; the *agoranomoi* being
[Σα]ραπίωνος καὶ Διονυσίου καὶ	Sarapion, Dionysios,
Δίου καὶ Ἀρτεμιδώρου	Dios, Artemidoros,
[καὶ Ἀριστίου καὶ Ἡρακλείδου καὶ]	[Aristios, Heraclides],
Ἀ̣[λεξ]άνδρου καὶ Θέωνος.	Alexander and Theon
[ἀφεῖκεν ἐλευθέραν ὑπὸ Δία] Γ̣ῆν	[Under Zeus], Earth and [Sun]
[Ἥλι]ο̣ν Σ̣[ι]νθοῶνις Θο̣ώνιος τοῦ	Sinthoönis, daughter of Thoönis, son of
Ἁρθοώνιος μητ̣ρὸς Ταυσοράπιος	Harthoönis, her mother being
τῆς Τα̣ω̣ . . . τῶν ἀπ' Ὀξυρύγχων	Tausorapis, daughter of Tao[...] of the
πόλεως [ἱέ]ρεια Θοήριδος καὶ	city of Oxyrhynchus, priestess of
Ἴσιδος καὶ Σαράπιδος καὶ	Thoëris, Isis, Sarapis and

76 In Finley's opinion, a strict distinction between free and servile status fails to take into account all the grey areas of status which existed between the two, i.e. the 'broad status-spectrum'.

[τῶν συννάων θεῶν μεγίστων
ὡς L] μ̣[. μ]έ̣ση
μελίχ(ρως) μακ[ρ]ο̣π̣(ρόσωπος)
ἄσημ̣ος μετὰ κυρίου τοῦ ἑαυτῆς
γνησίου ἀδελφοῦ Ἁ̣ρ̣θ̣ο̣ώνι̣ο̣ς̣
ἱερέως τῶν αὐτῶν θε[ῶ]ν̣ ὡς L ν̄
μέσου μελίχ(ρωτος)
μακροπ(ροσώπου) οὐλ[ὴ] ῥινὶ
ἐν ἀ[γ]υιᾷ

[the associated gods most great,
about] 4[5 ?] years of age, of medium
height, with honey skin, oval face,
without distinguishing mark, with her
lawful brother, Harthoönis, priest of the
same gods, about 50 years of age, of
medium height, with honey skin, oval
face, scar to the nose, acting as
guardian, [has set free] in the street

[τὴν ὑπάρχουσαν αὐτῇ δούλην
Σινθοῶ]ν̣ι̣ν̣ [ὡς] L ιζ̄ μελίχ(ρωτα)
μακροπ(ρόσωπον) [ο]ὐλ(ὴ) ὑ̣π̣ὲρ
ὀ[φρύ(ν)] δεξι(ὰν) οἰκο̣γεν̣ῆ [ἐκ
δ]ούλης Σι̣[νθ]οώνιος ἀ[ργυρ]ί̣ου
ἐπισήμ̣ο̣υ δραχμῶν δέκα καὶ ὧ[ν]
τέτακται ὑπὲρ αὐτῆς Ἀμμώνιος
ἀπελεύθερος
[. . . . . τῶν ἀπὸ τῆς αὐ]τ̣ῆ̣ς
π]ό̣λ̣εως ὡς L λ̄ μέσος μελ̣ί̣χ(ρως)
μα̣[κ]ρ̣οπ(ρόσωπος) οὐλ(ὴ) σ̣ι̣α̣γ̣ό̣(νι)
δεξι(ᾷ) τῇ προγε̣γ̣[ρ]α̣μμένῃ αὐτῇ̣[ς]
δ̣εσποίνῃ Σινθοώνει λύτρων
ἀ[ργυ]ρίου Σεβαστοῦ νομίσματος
δραχμῶν χιλίων,

[her slave woman, Sinthoö]nis,
[about] 17 years of age, with honey
skin, oval face, scar above
the right eyebrow, home-born of the
slave woman, Sinthoönis, for ten
drachmae of coined silver and for the
ransom of one thousand drachmae of
imperial silver coin which Ammonios,
freedman, [... of the same] city, about
30 years of age, of medium height, with
honey skin, oval face, scar to the right
cheek, has paid for her to her
aforementioned mistress, Sinthoönis,

[οὐκ ἐξόντος τῷ Ἀμμωνίῳ οὐδ' ἄλλῳ
ὑπὲρ αὐ]τ̣[οῦ] ἀπαίτησιν
ποιήσασθα[ι] πα[ρ]ὰ̣ τῆς
ἐλευθε̣ρουμένης οὐ̣δὲ τῶν παρ'
αὐ̣τῆς τῶν̣ λ̣ύ̣τρων οὐδὲ μέρους
τρό̣[π]ῳ̣ οὐδενί. γνωστὴρ τῆς
ἐλευθερώσεως Ἁρθοῶνις
[. . . . .
τῶ]ν̣ ἀπὸ τῆς α̣ὐ̣τ̣ῆ̣ς πόλ̣ε̣ω̣[ς] ὡς L
λ̄ μέσος μ[ε]λ̣ίχ(ρως)
μακροπ(ρόσωπος) οὐλ(ὴ) ὀφρύ(ι)
δεξιᾷ· ἐφ' ᾧ μετὰ τὴ[ν τ]ῆ̣ς
ἐλευθερουμένη[ς Σι]νθοώνιος
{τε}τελευτὴν οὐκ ἐπελεύσεται ἡ
προ-

[it being unlawful for Ammonios or
another acting on his behalf] to make a
formal demand from the
freed woman or her representatives
for the ransom or part thereof in any
manner whatsoever. Guarantor of the
manumission being Harthoönis
[...
of the] same city, about 30 years of age,
of medium height, with honey skin,
oval face, scar to the right eyebrow,
on condition that after the death of the
freed woman, Sinthoönis, neither the
afore[mentioned

[γεγραμμένη Σινθοῶνις οὐδ' ἄλλος
οὐδεὶς ὑπὲ]ρ αὐ̣[τ]ῆ̣[ς] ἐπ̣ὶ̣ μηδ̣ὲ̣ν
τ̣[ῶν] ὑπ̣' [α]ὐ̣τῆς̣ ἀπ̣ο̣λ̣ε̣ι̣φθησομ̣[έν]ω̣ν̣

Sinthoönis nor another acting on] her
behalf will proceed against any property
left by her in any manner whatsoever

καθ' ὁνδηποτοῦν τρ[όπο]ν διὰ τὸ
ἐπὶ τούτοις ἐ[στά]σθαι. ἐν ἀγυιᾷ
τῇ αὐτῇ ἔτους τετάρτου
Αὐτοκράτορος
[Καίσαρος Νέρουα Τραιανοῦ Σεβαστοῦ
Γερμανικοῦ, Μεχεὶρ] . . . (m. 2) δ[ιὰ
Σ]αραπίωνος τ[οῦ σὺν Διον]υσί[ῳ]
καὶ Ἡρ[α]κλείδῃ καὶ . [. . .] Δίῳ καὶ
Ἀλε[ξάν]δ[ρ]ῳ καὶ Θέ[ωνι καὶ]
Ἀρτεμιδώρῳ κ[αὶ] Ἀριστίῳ τ[οῖς
ὁ]μαγορα(νόμοις) κεχρημ(άτισται).
(space)
(m. 3) Θέων ὁ ἀσχολούμενο[ς] τὸ
ἐνκύκλι[ον] τὸ ἐνε(στὸς)
ἔτος Σινθοώνει [[δου]] ἠλευθ(ερωμένῃ)
ὑπὸ τῆς δεσπ(οίνης) αὐ(τῆς)
Σινθο(ώνιος)
Θοώνιος τοῦ Ἁρθοώνιος μητρὸς
Ταυσοράπ[ιος] ἱερείας τῶν
ἀπ' Ὀξ(υρύγχων) πό(λεως) χαίρειν.
ἀπέχω{ι} παρὰ σοῦ τὸ ο . [. .] . . μ( )
ὑπὸ σοῦ
τέλος τῆς προκειμένης
ἐλευθερώσ[ε]ως . . . ο
. . . ν Ὀξ( ) πο( ) . . τῶι ἐνε(στῶτι)
μη(νὶ) Μεχεὶρ [.] . υ τέλους
τὸ ῑ μέ(ρος) διαστελ( ) ἐπ[ὶ] τὴ(ν)
δημ(οσίαν) τράπ(εζαν) τ[.] . . . . . ου
τοῦ ἐνε(στῶτος) L κ(αὶ) ἀναδώσω σοι
τὸ καθ(ῆκον) σύμ(βολον). ἔτους
τετάρτου Αὐτο{υ}κράτορος Καίσαρος
Νέρουα Τραιανοῦ
Σεβαστοῦ Γερμανικοῦ, Μεχεὶρ η̄
Σεβ(αστῇ).
(m. 4) Θέων ἀπέχω τὸ τέλ(ος) ὡς
πρό(κειται). χρό(νος) ὁ αὐ(τός).

because (the manumission) has been
made on these conditions. In the same
street, in the fourth year of the
Imperator
[Caesar Nerva Trajan Augustus
Germanicus, Mecheir] .. (m. 2) (The
manumission) has been executed
through Sarapion with his fellow-
agoranomoi, Dionysios, Heraclides,
.[...] Dios, Alexander, Theon,
Artemidoros and Aristios.

(m. 3) Theon, the contractor for the
enkyklion for the current
year, to Sinthoönis manumitted
by her mistress,
Sinthoönis, daughter of
Thoönis, son of Harthoönis, her mother
being Tausorapis, priestess, of the
city of Oxyrhynchus, greeting.
I receive from you the [...]
by you
tax of the above
manumission [...]
[...] city of Oxyrhynchus [...] in the
current month of Mecheir [...] of the tax
the 1/10th part transmit(?) to the
public bank [...]
of the current year and I will issue you
with the appropriate receipt. In the
fourth year of the Imperator Caesar
Nerva Trajan
Augustus Germanicus, Mecheir 8, *dies
Augustus.*
(m. 4) I, Theon, receive the tax as
above. The same date.

T.C. Skeat took over the restoration αὐτῆς in *l.*7 from *P. Lugd.-Bat.* XIII.24. However, in view of *l.9* and *P. Oxy.* XXXVIII 2843 it is clear that the pronoun refers to Ammonios. The restoration αὐτοῦ is required. The condition, therefore, guarded the manumittee against a future claim over her property made by either Ammonios, as the one who paid the ransom price, or Sinthoönis, as her former mistress.

Sinthoönis, daughter of Sinthoönis, was the house-born slave of a priestess (also called Sinthoönis) of Thoëris, Isis, Sarapis and associated gods.[77] As Sinthoönis, a slave, could not properly enter into a legal contract to effect her manumission, Ammonios acted on her behalf by paying the ransom, presumably with money provided to him from her *peculium*, i.e. the property permitted to a slave at the owner's discretion. In all, three payments are made:

1. the 10 drachmae levy (the *propraktikon*) payable to the authorities;
2. the 10% manumission tax mentioned in the receipt;
3. the ransom of 1000 drachmae. See the discussion at *P. Oxy.* XLV 3241.

T.C. Skeat (p.94) argues that the space between the manumission and tax receipt confirms the administrative process suggested by Taubenschlag, *Law*, pp.97-8. In other words, on payment of the manumission tax, or notification thereof, Theon, the tax-farmer, instructed the *agoranomoi* to proceed with the contract. Accordingly, it appears that the receipt was written by the tax-farmer with sufficient space left for the scripting of the manumission text. In this case more space was allowed than was required, resulting in the indicated space. K.L. McKay (per litt.) disputes this order of procedure in the document. He writes: 'The second hand at *l.*10 suggests that the main body of the document was written first and a gap left for the execution by the *agoranomoi*. The first scribe has written not only the formal description of the transaction but (end of *l.*9) the beginning of the execution section up to the point where the duty *agoranomos* adds his signature (the second hand). In support of this note the participles ἐλευθερουμένης in *ll.*7,8 are imperfective (present) but in the receipt a perfect is used.'

Of interest in the deed of manumission is the addition of the expression 'after the death of the freed woman Sinthoönis', which according to T.C. Skeat is 'an apparently unique condition'. As the expression limits a condition which normally (see *P. Turner* 26 *ll.*10-12) restricted the right of seizure by the former owner, it might be interpreted as extending the owner's right, i.e. nothing is said to exclude any such action during the slave's life-time. However, the absence of any expression in the deed implying that conditions of *paramone* were imposed on the slave makes this interpretation difficult. To account for the unique expression, Skeat suggests that 'possibly the slave possessed some special skills which might enable her to amass a considerable property'. It was usual practice for a manumission to be effected at a ransom amount higher than the market price and with a surcharge for skill. However, if as Skeat argues the amount conforms to the sale price of slaves, then the ransom price is lower than might otherwise have been expected. The ransom price has not been an issue for others who have considered the document. E.Boswinkel, *P. Lugd.-Bat.* XIII 24, reads *l.*7 as referring to Sinthoönis and thus postulates that Ammonios may be redeeming her for marriage. Dunand, op.cit., suggests that Sinthoönis' mistress as a priestess may have possessed several slaves and thus was able to emancipate one of them. One last point is worth noting. The formula 'under Zeus, Earth and Sun', in view of its position within the clause, invokes the deities to protect the freed person. However, the protection offered was not considered sufficient in itself and a guarantor of manumission was called on (*ll.*7-9). The formula itself had a wide currency and is even found in synagogue inscriptions which record manumission (see B. Latyschev, *Inscriptiones Antiquae* II [Petersburg 1890 – reprinted Hildesheim 1965] §54 and §400). Philo,

---

[77] F. Dunand, 'Le statut des hiereiai en Égypte romaine', *Hommages à Maarten J.Vermaseren*, vol.1, ed. M.B. de Boer and T.A. Edridge (Leiden 1978), pp.352-374, in listing the documentary evidence for priestesses in Roman Egypt finds 31 instances of which 21 come from Socnopaiou Nesos. The present document is one of the few exceptions to this provenance. Dunand surmises that the disproportionate representation of one town results from a disparate and unequal distribution of papyri. The appeal to chance is frequently encountered in papyrology to account for various observations about documents and each case must be judged on its own merits. Though the process whereby documents are created, disposed of, preserved through the centuries and then discovered – not to mention the processes whereby the documents find their way to museums, universities and private collections – appears to afford an unbiased sampling method, this is not always the case. The chance find of a large personal library or the preservation and discovery of documents from one section of the village may well skew the data.

De spec. leg. 2.5, allowed oaths made by 'earth, sun, stars, heaven, the whole universe. For these are worthy of highest respect, since they have precedence in time over our place in creation, and also will remain for ever untouched by age according to the purpose of Him Who made them' (Loeb Translation). One may compare Philo's position to that of the NT where oaths by Heaven, Earth, Jerusalem etc. are expressly not allowed (Matt.5.33-37).

The slave Sinthoönis availed herself of the opportunity to gain her freedom through a deed of manumission. As indicated, Ammonios probably acted on her behalf with money paid to him by the slave herself. Sinthoönis initiated her own manumission with money that she was able to save. Paul addressed his Corinthian audience on the same practice – ἀλλ' εἰ καὶ δύνασαι ἐλεύθερος γενέσθαι, μᾶλλον χρῆσαι (1Cor.7.21). However, his intended meaning is unclear and a debate about whether or not he advocated manumission has ensued. For a history of the interpretation of 1Cor.7.21 see S.S. Bartchy, *ΜΑΛΛΟΝ ΧΡΗΣΑΙ: First-Century Slavery and 1 Corinthians 7.21* (Missoula 1973).

The crux of the problem resides in the use of ellipsis in the apodosis of 1Cor.7.21. Did Paul want to say μᾶλλον χρῆσαι τῇ ἐλευθερίᾳ or μᾶλλον χρῆσαι τῇ δουλείᾳ? J.N. Sevenster, *Paul and Seneca* (Leiden 1961), pp.189-190, argues for the latter interpretation. The position of καί (not before ἐλεύθερος γενέσθαι but with εἰ indicating a strong contrastive sense, i.e. 'even though'), the use of μᾶλλον (i.e. a contrastive 'rather') and the tenor of the entire passage[78] suggest to him that Paul is recommending that the slave remain in slavery.

Arguments can be mustered for the other interpretation. For example, F. Lang, *Die Briefe an die Korinther* (Göttingen 1986), p.97, uses three features to argue his case. They are the use of the aorist χρῆσαι, the use of the adversative conjunction ἀλλά and the position of the adverbial καί after εἰ. The last two points require that καί be interpreted without reference to εἰ so that the sentence begins 'But if you (indeed) can ...'. Bartchy, op.cit., p.171, adds a fourth point against Sevenster's (and others') reading of the verse. He observes that since Paul's style of argumentation in 1Cor.7 makes frequent use of exceptions to stated rules or principles, the argument based on the general tenor of the passage is not decisive.

The above arguments in support of the contrasting interpretations of 1Cor.7.21 are inconclusive and will remain so as long as they disregard an analysis of ellipsis in the *koine* Greek of the NT. According to M.A.K. Halliday, *An Introduction to Functional Grammar* (London 1985), p.302, ellipsis in English is a form of anaphoric cohesion, the referring function of which 'is largely limited to the immediately preceding clause'. In other words, what is omitted in ellipsis should be inferred from the immediately preceding clause. Consider the sentence: 'If you are able to fix the problem easily, then do!'. Ellipsis occurs because the repetition of the phrase 'then do fix it' can be inferred from the preceding clause 'If you are able to fix the problem easily' and is thus redundant.[79] Does the same general rule apply to the use

78 The argument places the verse within the larger context of 1Cor.7 with its advice that a believer should remain in the state in which he/she was called. Whether married or unmarried, circumcised or uncircumcised, free or slave, each is advised to remain in that state. H. Gülzow, *Christentum und Sklaverei in den ersten drei Jahrhunderten* (Bonn 1969), pp.177-181, places the saying in a broader context again. He suggests that the Corinthians in their enthusiasm (see 1Cor.4.8ff) may have attempted to apply their new found religious equality to the social sphere but Paul, believing slavery to be neither a disgrace nor irreconcilable with Christianity, advised them against this. For Gülzow the majority of Christian slaves in Corinth belonged to Christian households and Paul's advice is to be understood within this particular context only.

79 In cases where the general rule is not followed, there should be some marker to permit a correct reference. For example, take the translation of John 15.4: 'Just as the branch cannot bear fruit by itself unless it abides in the vine, so neither can you unless you abide in me'. The ellipsis, i.e. 'can bear fruit by yourself', is inferred from the penultimate clause. However, certain markers, i.e. the use of a simile marked by 'just as ... so' and the repetition of the 'unless' clause, facilitate the correct reference. The repetition in particular removes the possibility of incorrect reference. If markers are absent and ellipsis refers to a more distant clause than the one which immediately precedes it, confusion and ambiguity arise. For this reason it is avoided.

of ellipsis in koine Greek? BDF §479 gives no ruling on this, though the examples used suggest that it is indeed the case.

An analysis of ellipsis in conditional sentences[80] in the NT shows that what is omitted should be inferred from the immediately preceding clause. The cases of ellipsis are of several types.

A. Thirteen cases of the ellipsis of a verb (and where applicable its subject or object):

1. Matt.6.30: εἰ δὲ τὸν χόρτον τοῦ ἀγροῦ σήμερον ὄντα καὶ αὔριον εἰς κλίβανον βαλλόμενον ὁ θεὸς οὕτως ἀμφιέννυσιν, οὐ πολλῷ μᾶλλον ὑμᾶς, ὀλιγόπιστοι;

2. Luke 12.28 (= Matt.6.30):[81] εἰ δὲ ἐν ἀγρῷ τὸν χόρτον ὄντα σήμερον καὶ αὔριον εἰς κλίβανον βαλλόμενον ὁ θεὸς οὕτως ἀμφιέζει, πόσῳ μᾶλλον ὑμᾶς, ὀλιγόπιστοι;

3. Matt.10.25: εἰ τὸν οἰκοδεσπότην Βεελζεβοὺλ ἐπεκάλεσαν, πόσῳ μᾶλλον τοὺς οἰκιακοὺς αὐτοῦ;

4. Mark 14.29: Εἰ καὶ πάντες σκανδαλισθήσονται, ἀλλ' οὐκ ἐγώ.

5. 1Cor.4.15: ἐὰν γὰρ μυρίους παιδαγωγοὺς ἔχητε ἐν Χριστῷ ἀλλ' οὐ πολλοὺς πατέρας·

6. 1Cor.9.12: εἰ ἄλλοι τῆς ὑμῶν ἐξουσίας μετέχουσιν, οὐ μᾶλλον ἡμεῖς;

7-8. 2Cor.5.13: εἴτε γὰρ ἐξέστημεν, θεῷ· εἴτε σωφρονοῦμεν, ὑμῖν.

9. 2Cor.7.12: ἄρα εἰ καὶ ἔγραψα ὑμῖν, οὐχ ἕνεκεν τοῦ ἀδικήσαντος οὐδὲ ἕνεκεν τοῦ ἀδικηθέντος ἀλλ' ἕνεκεν τοῦ φανερωθῆναι τὴν σπουδὴν ὑμῶν τὴν ὑπὲρ ἡμῶν πρὸς ὑμᾶς ἐνώπιον τοῦ θεοῦ.

10. Phil.3.4: εἴ τις δοκεῖ ἄλλος πεποιθέναι ἐν σαρκί, ἐγὼ μᾶλλον·

11. Heb.12.25: εἰ γὰρ ἐκεῖνοι οὐκ ἐξέφυγον ἐπὶ γῆς παραιτησάμενοι τὸν χρηματίζοντα, πολὺ μᾶλλον ἡμεῖς οἱ τὸν ἀπ' οὐρανῶν ἀποστρεφόμενοι ...

12-13. 1Pet.4.11: εἴ τις λαλεῖ, ὡς λόγια θεοῦ· εἴ τις διακονεῖ, ὡς ἐξ ἰσχύος ἧς χορηγεῖ ὁ θεός

B. Five cases of the ellipsis of a predicate or part thereof:

14. Rom.11.12: εἰ δὲ τὸ παράπτωμα αὐτῶν πλοῦτος κόσμου καὶ τὸ ἥττημα αὐτῶν πλοῦτος ἐθνῶν, πόσῳ μᾶλλον τὸ πλήρωμα αὐτῶν;

15-16. Rom.11.16: εἰ δὲ ἡ ἀπαρχὴ ἁγία, καὶ τὸ φύραμα· καὶ εἰ ἡ ῥίζα ἁγία, καὶ οἱ κλάδοι.

17. 1Cor.9.2: εἰ ἄλλοις οὐκ εἰμὶ ἀπόστολος, ἀλλά γε ὑμῖν εἰμι·

18. 2Cor.11.6: εἰ δὲ καὶ ἰδιώτης τῷ λόγῳ, ἀλλ' οὐ τῇ γνώσει, ἀλλ' ἐν παντὶ φανερώσαντες ἐν πᾶσιν εἰς ὑμᾶς.

C. One case of the ellipsis of a verb's object (or its pronoun) and prepositional phrase:

19. 2Cor.5.16: εἰ καὶ ἐγνώκαμεν κατὰ σάρκα Χριστόν, ἀλλὰ νῦν οὐκέτι γινώσκομεν.

D. Two cases of the ellipsis of the subject of a clause:

20. 2Cor.8.12: εἰ γὰρ ἡ προθυμία πρόκειται, καθὸ ἐὰν ἔχῃ εὐπρόσδεκτος, οὐ καθὸ οὐκ ἔχει. (the subject of the apodosis is ἡ προθυμία)

21. Gal.3.18: εἰ γὰρ ἐκ νόμου ἡ κληρονομία, οὐκέτι ἐξ ἐπαγγελίας·

In all twenty one cases the ellipsis in the apodosis is inferred from the immediately preceding clause, i.e. its protasis.[82] 1Cor.7.21 may be classed as an ellipsis of type C.

---

80 All NT conditional sentences using εἰ were read and every case of ellipsis noted. An analysis of ellipsis more generally lies beyond the immediate scope of this entry.

81 The counting of ellipsis in the two parallel sayings should be permitted as both occurrences are tokens of the same type repeated by different evangelists who were not averse to changing their traditions.

82 1Tim.3.15 appears to be the only exception. However, closer examination shows that sentence structure must be considered. 1Tim.3.14-15 is structurally (though not semantically) complicated. For this reason it is difficult to construct from it any hypothesis about ellipsis. Nevertheless, it can be argued that 1Tim.3.14-15 contains no ellipsis. The author wants to say that he is writing in case he is delayed in coming. For this reason the insertion of the semi-colon is unnecessarily awkward and should be removed. If so, there is no ellipsis. K.L. McKay (per litt.) has accordingly suggested the translation: 'I am writing to you in the hope of coming to you soon, but if I am delayed, to remind you how ...'.

In the present case, an interpretation of 1Cor.7.21 based on the sentence itself must be preferred to one based on its larger linguistic context, namely that the believer should remain in the state in which he was called.[83] The reason is simple. The proposed interpretation does not necessarily contradict the larger linguistic context but can be accommodated by it (see Bartchy above). Therefore, in view of the fact that there is no sentence structure to indicate an exception to the general rule (i.e. to indicate that the ellipsis has a more distant reference), it is apparent that the use of ellipsis at 1Cor.7.21 must imply the pleonastic reading μᾶλλον χρῆσαι τῇ ἐλευθερίᾳ. If Paul had meant to say μᾶλλον χρῆσαι τῇ δουλείᾳ or, as Bartchy, op.cit., p.156-7, has suggested μᾶλλον χρῆσαι ταῖς ἐντολαῖς θεοῦ or τῇ κλήσει, then he would have needed to say so explicitly. Accordingly, Paul advised the believing slave, when presented with the opportunity to acquire freedom, to avail himself of it. But what of the other linguistic arguments against this interpretation?

It is just not the case that εἰ καί always has a strong contrastive sense. Besides two NT counter examples (2Cor.11.15 and Gal.6.1) consider the following pertinent uses:

a. Isocrates, *De pace* 1:
οὐ μὴν ἀλλ' εἰ καὶ περὶ ἄλλων τινῶν πραγμάτων ἥρμοσε τοιαῦτα προειπεῖν, δοκεῖ μοι πρέπειν καὶ περὶ τῶν νῦν παρόντων ἐντεῦθεν ποιήσασθαι τὴν ἀρχήν.
Nevertheless, if it was ever appropriate to preface the discussion of any other subject with such words, it seems to me fitting also to begin with them in speaking upon the subject before us. (Loeb translation)

b. Josephus, *BJ* 7.351:
οὐ μὴν ἀλλ' εἰ καὶ τῆς παρὰ τῶν ἀλλοφύλων δεόμεθα πίστεως, βλέψωμεν εἰς 'Ινδοὺς τοὺς σοφίαν ἀσκεῖν ὑπισχνουμένους.
If, however, we really need an assurance in this matter from alien nations, let us look at those Indians who profess the practice of philosophy. (Loeb translation)

c. *P. Oxy*. VI 904 *l*.4:
οὐ μόνον δὲ τοῦτο, ἀλλ' εἰ καὶ συμβῇ ἀτόπημά τι γενέσθαι, αὐτὸν τὸ ἀζήμιον πληροῖν τοῖς τὴν βλάβην ὑπομένουσιν.
not only this, but that if ever some offence occur, he will pay in full the loss to those suffering the harm.

When εἰ καί carries a strong contrastive sense, it does so because of a semantic contrast between the protasis and apodosis. For example, see 2Cor.4.16 (a contrast between the inner and outer person), Phil.2.17 (a contrast between Paul's sacrifice and rejoicing) and 1Pet.3.14 (a contrast between suffering and blessedness). See also Dio Cassius, *Hist. Rom.* 46.25.2 and 62.4.3 and Isocrates, *Busiris* 48 (contrasts between past and present action); Demosthenes, *In Tim.* 202 (a contrast between having done no wrong and being worthy of destruction); Josephus *BJ* 3.359 (a contrast between one person's forgetfulness and the other's need to take forethought). The relevance of the above study of ellipsis for the interpretation of εἰ καί is now clear. Since the pleonastic reading of the apodosis is μᾶλλον χρῆσαι τῇ ἐλευθερίᾳ, there is no semantic contrast between it and its protasis and consequently there is no need to translate εἰ καί by 'even though' or 'even if'.

There are numerous examples of the construction εἰ ... μᾶλλον in the NT (e.g. Matt.6.30, 7.11, 10.25, Luke 11.13, 12.28, Rom.5.10,15,17, 11.12,24, 1Cor.7.21, 9.12, 2Cor.3.9,11, Phil.3.4). A survey of the examples confirms the conclusion of the previous section. The occurrences of μᾶλλον qualified by πολλῷ or πόσῳ indicate a *qal vaḥomer* (קל חומר – from the lesser to the greater) argument. Since neither πολλῷ nor πόσῳ is present in 1Cor.7.21, these uses are best left to one side. However, two occurrences remain which are particularly relevant to 1Cor.7.21; they are 1Cor.9.12 and Phil.3.4. As these verses are cited

83 E.g. as argued by Gülzow, *op.cit.* (Bonn 1969), pp.177-181, and J. Gnilka, *Der Philemonbrief* (Freigurg 1982), pp.73-4

above they are not repeated again here. However, two points need to be made. First, both verses, like 1Cor.7.21, contain ellipsis. Second, the use of μᾶλλον in both sentences cannot be translated by the contrastive 'rather'. A better translation is 'all the more', i.e. 'But if ever you are able to become free, avail yourself of it all the more.'

It follows from this linguistic study that at 1Cor.7.21 Paul's advice to Christian slaves was that they, if able, should become free. Gülzow, op.cit., argues that when Paul was writing Christian slaves predominantly belonged to Christian masters – see further *New Docs* 6 (1992) §6. If so, further questions follow. How was manumission achieved and what form did it take? Was it by deed as in the present document? Would the manumission have received the divine sanction implied in the expression 'under Zeus, Earth and Sun'? An answer cannot be given. To continue, does Paul's use of δύνασαι imply that a slave was expected to buy freedom from his Christian master? If so, how did the price compare with the usual price for the purchase of manumission? In other words, were Christian masters generous or not? Or does the verb imply that a master's consent may not always be forthcoming? If so, why is there no specific advice to the Christian master in this matter? In his letter to Philemon, Paul left the decision on Onesimos' future to his master. Should Paul's silence here be construed as consistent with his stance on Onesimos' future? Clearly, 1Cor.7.21 continues to raise many questions. **S.R.L.**

§10 The Slave of God (Rom.6.22) and Sacral Manumission

Ptolemais Euergetis AD 193-8

Ed.pr. — N. Lewis, *P. Turner* 26 (London 1981), pp.126-129 (= *P. Yale inv.*1579).

The papyrus measures 8.5 x 13 cm. The editor estimates that about three quarters of the document is lost approximately equally from the left and right hand sides of the papyrus fragment. The text is, therefore, largely reconstructed from known formulaic expressions.

(m. 3) Τῦβι̣ [...]	(m. 3) Tybi [...]
[ἔτους .. Αὐτοκράτορος Καίσαρο]ς Λουκίου Σεπ[τι]μίου Σεουήρ̣[ου Εὐσεβοῦς Περτίνακος Σεβαστοῦ]	[In year X of Imperator Caesar] Lucius Septimius Severus [Pius Pertinax Augustus]
[᾽Αραβικοῦ ᾽Αδιαβηνικοῦ μηνὸς Δ]ύ̣σ̣τρου Τῦβι κ̣̄[̣] ἐν Πτολεμα̣[ίδι Εὐεργέτιδι τοῦ ᾽Αρσινοίτου νομοῦ.]	[Arabicus Adiabenicus, in the month] of Dystros-Tybi 2[.], in Ptolemais [Euergetis of the Arsinoite nome.]
[ὁμολογεῖ ῾Ηρακλοῦς ῾Ωρίωνος τοῦ Ν] ̣ονος τοῦ καὶ Πτολεμαίου μητ̣[ρὸς Ν ἀπὸ]	[Heraklous, daughter of Horion, son of N], also known as Ptolemaios, her mother [being N, from]
[loc. ὡς ἐτῶν ..] ἄσημος μετὰ κυρίου τοῦ υἱοῦ [N.N. ἀπὸ loc.]	[loc., about X years of age], without distinguishing mark, with her son acting as guardian, [N.N., from loc.],
[ὡς ἐτῶν .. οὐλὴ ἀντικνημί]ῳ̣ δεξιῷ̣ τῇ ὑπὸ αὐτῆς ἀφι̣[μένῃ Εὐποροῦτι ὡς ἐτῶν ..]	[about X years of age, scar] to the right [shin, acknowledges] to the woman released by her, [Euporous, about X years of age],
[οὐλὴ] πεποιῆσθαι τὴν ὁμολογοῦσα̣[ν ῾Ηρακλοῦν τὴν ἐλευθέρωσιν ταύτην διὰ]	[... scar ...] that the one who acknowledges, [Heraklous, has effected this manumission through]

[τοῦ ἐν Πτολεμαΐδι Εὐεργέτιδι ἀγορανο]μίου καὶ μνημοṿί̣ου, καὶ ωṿ[ ]	[the *agoranomion* in Ptolemais Euergetis] and record office and [...]
[ ]ọν ἱεροῦ Σούχου θεοῦ μεγάλου [ἀργυρίου δραχμὰς ..]	[...] of the sanctuary of the great god Souchos [for X silver drachmae]
[καὶ πρὸς ταῦτα μηδὲν τὴν ὁμολογοῦσαν] Ἡρακλοῦν ἐνκαλῖν μηδὲ ἐ[νκαλέσιν μηδὲ ἐπελεύσεσθαι περὶ]	[and further that the one who acknowledges], Heraklous, neither makes nor [will make] any claim [nor will she proceed in]
[μηδενὸς τῶν τῇ δουλίᾳ ἀνηκόντων μηδὲ ἐ]πὶ τὴν Εὐπoροῦν μηδ[ὲ ἐπ' ἄλλον μηδένα τῶν παρ' αὐτῆς μηδὲ]	[any matter pertaining to slavery either] against Euporous or [against any other of her representatives or]
[ἐπὶ μηδένα τῶν ἐξ αὐτῆς ἀπὸ τοῦ νῦν ἐσο]μ̣ένων ἐγγόνων μηδ[ὲ ἐπὶ ±10 παρευρέσι μηδεμιᾷ·]	[against any of her future] progeny nor [on ... ... any pretext at all];
[ἐὰν δὲ ἐπέλθῃ ἢ ἐνκαλέσῃ, τὴν μὲν ἔ]φοδον καὶ ἔνκλησιν ἄκυρον ε[ἶναι, ἔτι δὲ ἀποτίσειν τὴν ὁμολογοῦσαν]	[if she proceeds against (her) or makes a claim, that the] suit and claim are invalid [and further that the one who acknowledges,]
[Ἡρακλοῦν τῇ Εὐποροῦτι τὰ βλάβη καὶ τὰ δα]πανήματα διπλᾶ καὶ ἐπίτιμον ἀ[ργυρίου δραχμὰς .. καὶ]	[Heraklous, will pay to Euporous her damages and] expenses twofold and (as) penalty [X silver drachmae and]
[εἰς τὸ δημόσιον τὰς ἴσας, κυρίων μενό]ṇτων καὶ τῶν προγεγραμμέ[νων. γνωστὴρ τ]ῆς ἐλευθερώσεως ὁ τῆς Ἡρακλο[ῦτος υἱὸς N.N. ἀπὸ]	[the same to the public treasury], the aforementioned (conditions) also [remaining valid. Guarantor] of the manumission is the [son of] Heraklous, N.N., from]
[loc. ὡς ἐτῶν .. οὐλὴ ἀντι]κνημίῳ δεξιῷ. (m. 2) Ἡρακλοῦς Ὡρίων[ος μετὰ κυρίου τοῦ υἱοῦ]	[loc., about X years of age, scar] to the right shin. (m. 2) I, Heraklous, daughter of Horion, [with my son acting as guardian,]
[N.N. πεπ̣οίημαι τὴν τῆς Εὐπορο]ῦτο[ς] ἐλευθ̣[έρ]ω̣σ̣ιν καὶ εὐδοκῶ[ ] . [ ]	[N.N., have effected Europous'] manumission and I approve [...]

For the editor, a major interest of the document lies in *ll.*8-9 and the mention of the sanctuary of 'the great god Souchos'. He states: 'This reference to the "great god Souchos" is altogether unprecedented in extant manumissions. As this is the place in the document for specifying the "ransom", or price, paid for emancipation, it looks very much as if we have before us a fragment of a sacral manumission, with the Souchos sanctuary (ἱεροῦ must be the neuter noun, since gods are not characterized as "sacred") serving in a role comparable to that familiar to us from the shrine of Apollo at Delphi ... and attested also for synagogues (e.g.

P. Oxy. IX 1205 and *IGRR* I 881).' Accordingly, the editor suggests the following restoration of the lacuna in *ll.*8-9: καί ὠν[ῆς προφάσει ἀριθμηθῆναι ἑαυτῇ | ὑπὲρ τῆς ἀφιμένης Εὐποροῦτος παρὰ τ]οῦ ἱεροῦ κτλ – 'and [that for the purpose of] sale [she has received for the liberated Euporous from t]he sanctuary etc'.

Delphi — First Century BC

Ed. – J.-F. Bommelaer, 'Quatre notes delphiques', *BCH* 105 (1981), pp.461-3 (= *SEG* [1981] 543).

The inscription consists of the two fragments inv.8127 (*ll.*1-6) and inv.1770 (*ll.* 7-8). Though there is no physical fit between the fragments, Bommelaer argues that they belong to the same inscription. They are both in blue marble (rare at Delphi), have the same appearance and are palaeographically similar. On the basis of inv.1770 he argues that the inscription is probably to be dated to the 14th priesthood at Delphi (i.e. 84/83 to 60/59 BC). As the manumission inscriptions of Delphi are formulaic, the opening 4 lines have been restored to the editor's text.

[ἄρχοντος N.N. μηνὸς]	[When N.N. was archon in the month of]
[... ἀπέδοτο N.N. τῷ Ἀπόλλωνι τῷ Πυθίῳ]	[... N.N. gave up to Pythian Apollo]
[σῶμα ἀνδρεῖον ᾧ ὄνομα Θεοφάνης τὸ γένος ...]	[a male slave by the name of Theophanes, by race ...]
[τιμᾶς ἀργυρίου μνᾶν .. καὶ]	[for the price of X silver minae and]
[τειμὰν ἔχει πᾶσαν, καθῶς ἐπίστευσε Θεοφάν]η̣ς τὰν ὠνὰν τῷ θε̣[ῷ]	[he has the entire price, just as Theophan]es entrusted the sale to the god
[ἐφ' ᾧτε ἐλεύθερος εἶμεν καὶ ἀνέφαπτος ἀπὸ] πάντων τὸν πάντα βίον·	[on condition that he be free and not be seized as a slave by] anyone for the duration of his life.
[βεβαιωτὴρ N.N. εἰ δέ τις ἐφάπτοιτ]ο Θεοφάνεως ἐπὶ καταδουλ̣[ισ]μῷ,	[Guarantor, N.N. If anyone should seize] Theophanes with a view to enslavement,
[βέβαιον παρεχόντω τῷ Θεῷ τὰν ὠνὰν ὅ τε ἀπ]οδόμενος καὶ ὁ βεβαι-	[let the sale to the god be confirmed by the one who] gave (him) up and the guarantor.
[ωτὴρ. ±25 κύριο]ς ἔστω συλέων Θεο-	[... Let him be entitled] to rescue Theophanes
[φάνην ... ἀζάμιος ὢν καὶ ἀνυ]πό[δικο]ς πάσας δίκας καὶ	[... being immune and not liable] to any lawsuit or
[ζαμίας. μάρτυροι οἱ ἱερεῖ]ς τοῦ Ἀπ̣[όλλωνος Αἰα]κ̣ί̣δας, vac.	[penalty. Witnesses are the priests] of Apollo, Aiakidas,
[Ἐμμενίδας καὶ Χαλεεῖς Δάμ]ων, Καλλίμ̣[αχος ±6]ς. vac	[Emmenidas and Chaleans Dam]on, Kallimachos ...

Sacral manumission is best known from the 1000 or so inscriptions which date from 201 BC till approximately AD 100 and which record the sale of slaves to Pythian Apollo at Delphi. As a slave had no legal right, the sanctuary's deity acted as a party to the contract for sale. The deity bought the slave from his/her former owner with money supposedly deposited into the sanctuary's treasury by the slave or someone acting on his/her behalf. The slave became the property of Apollo and thus ἱερός. However, the sale was fictitious, for the god made no use of his property rights and the slave became in effect free. See further F. Bömer, *Untersuchungen über die Religion der Sklaven in Griechenland und Rom*, vol. II (Wiesbaden 1960), p.32. One supposed advantage of sacral manumission over other forms of manumission was the belief that the sale and the oath made in connection with it were sanctioned and guaranteed by the deity and its sanctuary. Why then was an inscription made? Bömer, ibid., p.30, suggests that it was a publically accessible document set up by the freed person in case of future attempts against his/her freedom. However, A. Kränzlein, 'Bemerkungen zu Form und Inhalt der delphischen Freilassungen', *RIDA* 27 (1980), pp.81-91, discounts any interpretation of an inscription which considers its function either to be legal or to proclaim the manumission.[84] Whilst the question over the inscriptions' function remains unanswered, some caution is required when interpreting them. Were all manumissions at Apollo's sanctuary inscribed? If not, do the surviving inscriptions represent an unbiased sample of Delphic manumission?

F. Sokolowski, 'The Real Meaning of Sacral Manumission', *Harv Theol Rev* 47 (1954), pp.173-81, argues that the origin of sacral manumission is to be found in the institution of asylum at sanctuaries and the ensuing need for sacral functionaries to decide the refugee's fate. Other forms of manumission were a later development. Bömer, op.cit., pp.34-5, 46-8, 117-23, 139-41, develops a different hypothesis arguing the priority of secular manumission. Indeed, it was under Eastern influence, he suggests, that sacral manumission developed in Greece receiving wide-spread renown with its adoption at Delphi in the late third century BC. K. Hopkins, *Conquerors and Slaves* (Cambridge 1978), pp.142-6, seems to infer a connection between the decline of civil authority and its ability to guarantee manumission, and the growth of sacral manumission which gave 'religious sanction to the slave's freedom'. If correct, this also suits a later dating for the advent of sacral manumission in Greece.

Hopkins, op.cit., pp.133-171, offers an analysis of the Delphic inscriptions on the basis of data gathered from them. He divides the inscriptions into periods of approximately 50 years (periods coinciding with the priesthoods from 201 – 1 BC) and studies the effect that the variables of date, sex, age (adult or child), birth status (home-born or alien-born slave), and type of manumission (conditional or unconditional release) have on the manumission price. Tables 10.1 and 10.2 below are taken from Hopkins' data contained in the lower sections of his Table III.3 (p.159) and Table III.4 (p.171).[85]

Table 10.1: Sex by age by period for slaves manumitted at Delphi

		Period (BC)			
Sex	Age	201 – 153	153 – 100	100 – 53	53 – 1
Male	Adult	130	83	9	19
	Child	11	19	8	10
Female	Adult	190	128	27	19
	Child	9	18	15	15

Hopkins acknowledges that religious and price factors create a bias in the data and that this in turn affects the drawing of inferences concerning the practice of manumission beyond Delphi (op.cit., p.138). In view of the questions asked above, the caution may also need to be

84 The inscription was not itself the original deed of sale but a rendition of it. Certain factors point to the freedom exercised in its rendition, e.g. the absence of the ἐπίστευσε-clause or the τὰν τιμὰν ἔχει πᾶσαν-clause in some texts (see Kränzlein, op.cit., pp.85-90). The original deed was kept in the temple archive (later the city's archive).

85 It should be noted that totals for the two sets of tables do not tally. This is because not all the inscriptions permit a classification by every category. For example, a lacuna may occur at a point in one text which hinders a decision on the classification by age.

extended to include Delphi itself. Were all sales of slaves to Apollo inscribed? If not, do the inscriptions represent an unbiased sample? What caused one sale to be inscribed and another not? Such questions will need to be borne in mind when drawing any inference from the data.

Table 10.2: Sex by type of manumission by period for slaves at Delphi

		Period (BC)			
Sex	Type	201 – 153	153 – 100	100 – 53	53 – 1
Male	Unconditional	112	72	9	14
	Conditional	34	19	4	11
Female	Unconditional	151	116	23	13
	Conditional	65	25	6	17

From his analysis of the Delphic inscriptions W.L. Westermann, *The Slave Systems of Greek and Roman Antiquity* (Philadelphia 1955), pp.32-33, observed that there was an increase in the proportion of home-born slaves over the period. Hopkins adds further observations on the data:

1. There was a decline in the number of manumissions.
2. Parties to the manumissions became more local.
3. There was an increase in the use of conditional release.[86]
4. The cost of manumission rose for unconditional release but remained fairly static for conditional release.[87]
5. There was an increase in the rate of release of children.

The tables provided by Hopkins do not tell us everything that we might want to know about the data. For example, it would be of interest to know the distribution of manumissions within each period. If manumissions bunch at certain times in each period, this fact will need to be considered in determining the grouping of the data by date. Again, it would also be of interest to know whether the variables of age and type of manumission are independent. In other words, instead of two three dimensional tables, one four dimensional table categorising the data by period, sex, age and type of manumission might produce further interesting results. Also, we do not know to what extent the prices in any period varied from the mean price. Perhaps the higher prices paid in the later periods were the result of a few extraordinarily high and therefore unrepresentative manumission prices. In particular, R.P. Duncan-Jones ('Problems of the Delphic Manumission Payments 220 – 1 BC', *ZPE* 57 [1984], pp.203-9) argues against conclusion 4, i.e. that the cost of manumission rose in the later periods. Replacing the mean by the median and using Calderini's categorical data he observes that 'the main variations in the evidence are synchronic, not diachronic'. The increased mean value in the later periods arises from a fall in sample size and a shift in its social composition. In other words, though fewer slaves were manumitted in the later periods, those that were manumitted tended to be of a more valuable type. Here, it is argued, one needs to bear in mind the variables affecting price, e.g. the slave's original or replacement cost, age, nationality, skill and relationship to the master.

Hopkins' conclusions can be extended by a modelling of the count data contained in Tables 10.1 and 10.2. See Appendix i) for the relevant statistical tables.

---

86 For general information on the *paramone* labour contract see the discussion in *New Docs* 6 (1992) §8. For the use of loans to enable manumission in rabbinic law compare *m. 'Ed.* 1.13.

87 The conditions of the *paramone* clause, it is argued, become more severe. In particular, a defined period of *paramone* was replaced by an indefinite period, i.e. for as long as the manumittor lived. See Hopkins, op.cit., pp.150-1 Table III.2 as well as C.W. Tucker, 'Women in the Manumission Inscriptions at Delphi', *TAPA* 112 (1982), pp.231-2.

6. Sex has no significant effect on the proportions of adults and children released. In other words, the percentage of male children released does not significantly differ from the percentage of female children released, i.e. 16.61% and 13.54% respectively in the relevant marginal table. Similarly, the percentage of male adults released does not significantly differ from the percentage of female adults released.
7. The period of release has a significant effect on the proportions of adults and children released. Adult releases are above expectation in the first period, but below in the third and fourth periods.
8. The period of release has no significant effect on the proportions of males and females released.
9. Sex has no significant effect on the proportions of conditional and unconditional release. In other words, the percentage of male conditional releases does not significantly differ from the percentage of female conditional releases, i.e. 24.73% and 27.16% respectively in the relevant marginal table. Similarly, the percentage of male unconditional releases does not significantly differ from the percentage of female unconditional releases.
10. The period of release has a significant effect on the proportions of conditional and unconditional releases. The effect is significant in the second and fourth periods only. The suggestion by Hopkins, that the data show a tendency towards an increased use of conditional manumission, arises from the fact that conditional releases are significantly below expectation in the second period and significantly above expectation in the last period. But can we safely speak of a tendency here? An increased use of conditional release is only observed for the third and fourth periods, i.e. over two not three periods. Hopkins' suggestion also disregards the decreased use of conditional release in the second period.

Deissmann, *LAE*, pp.319-330, sought to interpret the Pauline concept δοῦλος Χριστοῦ in terms of the practice of sacral manumission. The believer, once a slave to sin and death, had been bought at a price (1Cor.6.20, 7.23) and thereby become a slave of righteousness and God (Rom.6.18, 22). However, as in sacral manumission the slave was ransomed for freedom and ought not to become enslaved again to sin and death (1Cor.7.23, Gal.5.1,13). But his freedom was conditional. As the freedman of the Lord, the believer was now under an obligation of παραμονή to the God (1Cor.7.24, 35).[88] In opposition to Deissmann's hypothesis Bömer, op.cit., pp.133-139, stresses the difference between the Pauline concept and the Delphic practice of sacral manumission. In his view, any similarity between them arises from the fact that both speak of slavery, manumission and freedom. Suggesting that Paul may not have even known of the Delphic practice, Bömer argues that Paul probably obtained a knowledge of manumission from his own cultural milieu.[89] The difficulties with Deissmann's hypothesis (see Bömer's discussion) and the simplicity of Bömer's suggestion argue for the plausibility of the latter. In this connection, one further criticism of Deissmann can be added. It will be noted that Deissmann drew on material from various parts of the Pauline epistles to support his hypothesis. There is no one locus for Paul's use of the metaphor of sacral manumission. This

---

[88] F. Lyall, *Slaves, Citizens, Sons* (Grand Rapids 1984), pp.27-46, and 'Roman Law in the Writings of Paul – the Slave and the Freedman', *NTS* 17 (1971), pp.73-99, in the same fashion as Deissmann seeks to find a particular context for Paul's use of the slave metaphor. He argues that the metaphor has a fuller meaning (with particular reference to the patron-freedman relationship) when interpreted in terms of Roman law and accordingly refers it to this context rather than to the Greek practice of sacral manumission. Lyall's approach is probably too particular in assigning the metaphor's context.

[89] Synagogue inscriptions recording the manumission of slaves seem particularly relevant to this discussion. See B. Latyschev, *Inscriptiones Antiquae* II (Petersburg 1890 – reprinted Hildesheim 1965) §52, 53, 400 and 401.

further suggests, I argue, that Paul did not have any strict parallel usage in mind but loosely used the metaphor and language of manumission to describe the work of Christ in the believer.

S.R.L.

§11 Manumission in Thessaly and at Delphi

Larissa (Thessaly) Early first century BC

Ed.pr. — K.I. Gallis, *AAA* 13 (1980), pp.256-261 (= Museum at Larissa, inv.75/30).

The end of a list of manumissions dated paleographically. The stele is broken above with several chips to its edges and centre (height 1.64m; width 0.42-0.455m; thickness 0.155-0.195m).

Bib. – G.-J. M.-J. Te Riele, 'Nouveaux affranchissements à Larissa', *ZPE* 49 (1982), pp.161-176; *SEG* 31 [1981], pp.135-8.

[. . ἀπηλευθερῶσθ]αι ἀπὸ Ἡροδότου τοῦ[ ]	[... to have been freed] from Herodotos, son of [...]
[. .]ναίου v (9cm) στατῆρας [ιε΄]	[...] for [15] staters
<u>Θύου</u>·	<u>In the month of Thuos</u>:
[Ἑρ]μιόνη Σίμμου, ἡ καλουμένη καὶ Σῶσις,	Hermione of Simmos, also called Sosis,
[ἡ φ]αμένη ἀπηλευθερῶσθαι ἀπὸ Σίμμου τοῦ	[who] has declared herself to have been freed from Simmos, son of
Δ[ι]φίλου στατῆρας vv ιε΄· v Κάλλιππος Ἀμω-	Diphilos, for 15 staters. Kallippos of
[μ]ήτου ὁ φάμενος ἀπηλευθερῶσθαι ἀπὸ Ἀ-	Amometos who has declared himself to have been freed from
[μ]ωμήτου τοῦ Φιλοξενίδου καὶ Θεανοῦ[ς]	Amometos, son of Philoxenides, and Theano,
[τῆ]ς Νικοπόλιδος στατῆρας v ιε΄· vv Νίκαν-	daughter of Nikopolis, for 15 staters. Nikandros
[δρο]ς Πτολεμαίου ὁ φάμενος ἀπηλευ-	of Ptolemaios who has declared himself to have been freed
θερῶσθαι ἀπὸ Πτολεμαίου τοῦ Φιλοκρά-	from Ptolemaios, son of Philokrates,
[τ]ους καὶ Ἀλεξιμ[ε]νείας τῆς Κρατεραίο[υ]	and Aleximeneia, daughter of Krateraios,
[κα]ὶ Κρατεραίου κ̣[αὶ Φ]ιλοκράτους τῶν Π[το]-	and Krateraios and Philokrates, sons of
[λ]ε̣μαίου στατῆρας v ιε΄· vv Σωκράτης Ε. .	Ptolemaios, for 15 staters. Sokrates of E ..
[. .]ου ὁ φάμενος ἀπηλευθερῶσθαι ἀπὸ	[..] who has declared himself to have been freed from
[.]χίου τοῦ Δημητρίου στατῆρας v ιε̣΄.	[...]chios, son of Demetrios, for 15 staters.
<u>Ὁμολῴου</u>·	<u>In the month of Homoloos</u>:
[Ἀφ]ροδίσιος Μικαλίωνος ὁ φάμενος ἀπη̣-	Aphrodisios of Mikalion who has declared himself

[λ]ευθερῶσθαι ἀπ[ὸ] Μ̣[ι]κλίωνος τοῦ Δη[μη]-	to have been freed from Mikalion, son of Demetrios,
τρίου στατῆρ̣[ας ιε΄·] Εὔτοκος κα̣[ὶ . . .]	for 15 staters. Eutokos and [...]
[.]α οἱ Θαυμαρ[έτου οἱ φάμενο]ι ἀπηλ[ευθερ]ῶσ-	[.]a of Thaumaretos [who have declared themselves] to have been freed
[θα]ι ἀπὸ Θαυμ[αρέτου το]ῦ Δ̣άμων[ος στατῆ]-	from Thaumaretos, son of Damon, for
[ρ]ας ν λ΄ ν· Ὀφ[. . . . μ]ω̣νίου ὁ φάμε[νος]	30 staters. Oph[... of ...]onios who has declared himself
[ἀ]πηλευθερῶσ[θαι ἀπὸ . .]μω̣νίου τ[οῦ . . .]	to have been freed [from ..]monios, [son of ...]
[.]άρχου Γυρτ[ωνίου καὶ . .]έωνος [τοῦ . . .]	[.]archos, a Gyrt[onian, and ..]eon, [son of ...]
[.]ίου Λαρισαίο[υ στατῆρ]α̣ς ν ιε΄· [. . . .]	[.]ios, a Larissan, for 15 staters. [.... of]
[Δ]ιονυσίου ὁ φά̣μ̣[ενος ἀπ]ηλευθ[ερῶσθαι]	Dionysios who has declared himself to have been freed
[ἀ]πὸ Διονυσ[ίου τοῦ . . .]ους Η[. .] Ν̣[. .]	from Dionysios, [son of ...]es E[..] N[..]
καθεστακότος [π]ρ[οστά]την Ἀρισ[. .] Ε[. .]	having appointed as guardian Aris[..] E[..],
Ἀπολλωνίου στατ[ῆ]ρ̣ας ν ιε΄. ν Λιβ[. . . . .]	son of Apollonios, for 15 staters. Lib[... of]
Ξένωνος ὁ φάμενος ἀπηλευθερῶσ[θαι ἀπὸ]	Xenon who has declared himself to have been freed [from]
Ξένωνος τοῦ Εὐκρατ̣ίδου στατῆρας [ιε΄.]	Xenon, son of Eukratidos, for [15] staters.
[Νι]κασὼ Δάζο[υ ἡ] φ[α]μένη ἀπηλευθερ[ῶσ-]	Nikaso of Dazos who has declared herself to have been freed
[θαι] ἀπὸ Κρατε[. . τῆ]ς Σελεύκου	from Krate[..., daughter] of Seleukos,
[σ]τα̣ ν τῆρας νν ιε΄.	for 15 staters.
Ἱπποδρομίου·	In the month of Hippodromios:
[Π]ο[λ]έμαρχος Ἀρνίου ἀπὸ Ἀρνίου τοῦ Κλεάρχ[ου] .	Polemarchos of Arnios from Arnios, son of Klearchos.
[. . . .]ος Φιλολάου ἀπὸ Φιλολάου τοῦ Πυρρίνο̣[υ]	[....]os of Philolaos from Philolaos, son of Pyrrhinos,
[καὶ] Ν̣εμέας τῆς Εὐδήμου· νν Σώσυλος ν	[and] Nemea, daughter of Eudemos. Sosylos
[Ὀλ]υμπίχου ἀπὸ Ὀλυμπίχου τοῦ Ὀλυμπίχου· νν	of Olympichos from Olympichos, son of Olympichos.
[Νί]κανδρος Μενεστράτου ἀπὸ Μενεστράτου	Nikandros of Menestratos from Menestratos,
[τ]οῦ ‹του› Πορτίνου.	son of Portinos.

Φυλλικοῦ·
[Ξ]ένετος Σωσιβίου ἀπὸ Σωσιβίου τοῦ Κεφάλου·
Π̣αράμονος ᾿Αγάθωνος ἀπὸ ᾿Αγάθωνος τοῦ ᾿Εργα-
σίωνος· v ᾿Απολλωνία Φιλοκράτους ἀπὸ Φιλοκράτους τοῦ ᾿Αρχελάδου· v Κέρδων v
᾿Αριστοκλέους ἀπὸ ᾿Αριστοκλέους τοῦ vv
᾿Αριστοκλέους· v ᾿Αλέξανδρος ᾿Ανα-
ξίππου ἀπὸ ᾿Αναξίππου τοῦ Νικοστράτου·
Νίκαια Αἰνέτου ἀπὸ Αἰνέτου τοῦ Φρυνίχου
καὶ Πολυξένας τῆς ᾿Αντιλέοντος· vac. 7 cm
Φίλιππος Γοργώπα ἀπὸ ῾Αδίστας τῆς Κλε-
ονίκου.
᾿Ιτωνίου·
Σωσικράτης ᾿Ενπεδίωνος ἀπὸ ᾿Ενπεδίωνος vv
τοῦ ᾿Αφθονήτου· Πελοποννησὶς ᾿Αριστοδήμου
ἀπὸ ᾿Αριστοδήμου τοῦ Νικάρχου καὶ Πραξιβού- v
λας τῆς Νικάρχου καὶ Δυσμέντας τῆς ᾿Αριστο-
δήμου· v Θεόμνηστος Μενεστράτου ἀπὸ Με- v
νεστράτου τοῦ Σωτηρίδου Θεσπίεως· v Σῶσος
καὶ Νικόλαος οἱ Θέρσωνος ἀπὸ Θέρσωνος τοῦ vv
Πανφύλου· v ᾿Ολβία, Εὔκλεια, Τρυφερὰ αἱ Θέρσωνος
ἀπὸ ᾿Αντιγένειας τῆς ᾿Αντιγένους· Νίκη Κρατίνου ἀπὸ Κρατίνου τοῦ Φιλοξένου καὶ Κρατίνου καὶ Φιλοξένου τῶν Κρατίνου. vv

<u>In the month of Phyllikos</u>:
Xenetos of Sosibios from Sosibios, son of Kephalos.
Paramonos of Agathon from Agathon, son of Ergasion.
Apollonia of Philokrates from
Philokrates, son of Archelades. Kerdon
of Aristokles from Aristokles, son of
Aristokles. Alexandros of Anaxippos
from Anaxippos, son of Nikostratos.
Nikaia of Ainetos from Ainetos, son of Phrynichos,
and Polyxena, daughter of Antileon.
Philippos of Gorgopas from Hadista, daughter of
Kleonikos.
<u>In the month of Itonios</u>:
Sosikrates of Enpedion from Enpedion,
son of Aphthonetos. Peloponnesis of Aristodemos
from Aristodemos, son of Nikarchos, and Praxiboula,
daughter of Nikarchos, and Dysmenta, daughter of Aristodemos.
Theomnestos of Menestratos from Menestratos,
son of Soteridos, a Thespian. Sosos
and Nikolaos of Therson from Therson, son of
Panphylos. Olbia, Eukleia, Tryphera of Therson
from Antigeneia, daughter of Antigenes. Nike of Kratinos
from Kratinos, son of Philoxenos, and Kratinos
and Philoxenos, sons of Kratinos.

The Larissa inscription is the published record of civil manumissions over a period of six months. It is part of a more extensive record of manumissions effected by the local government of Larissa in accord with the legislation of the Thessalian federation (see further B. Helly, 'Lois sur les affranchissements dans les inscriptions thessaliennes', *Phoenix* 30 [1976], pp.153-6). The public record of manumission functioned as an authenticating document for the status of the freed slave. The form of each publication is that of declaration by the freed person followed by the price of publication (= 15 staters). *Ll.*1-36 contain a fuller version of the formula and *ll.*37-67 an abbreviated version. The form of manumission records from Thessaly varies with time and administrative practice.

The inscription illustrates the following points of interest concerning slavery:[90]

a. Legally the slave had no father (only the maternal relationship was recognised) but was required on emancipation to assume the patronym of a free citizen. The slave usually took his/her owner's name (exceptions are Νικασῶ Δάζου *l.*34, Φίλιππος Γοργῶπα *l.*54, Ὀλβία, Εὔκλεια, Τρυφερὰ Θέρσωνος *l.* 64). A question arises as to the source of the patronym where it is not the name of the owner. J. Bousquet, 'Affranchissements de Larissa', *BCH* 95 (1971), pp.277-82, suggests that in these cases the slave formed part of an inheritance and that as a consequence he took his patronym from a former owner. If so, one would expect the manumittor and his slave frequently to share the same patronym. However, this does not appear to be the case. A. Babakos, 'La mention du prostate dans les affranchissements thessaliens', *BCH* 86 (1962) 494-503, proposes that the patronym is the name of the slave's patron (see below for the use of patrons in manumissions). Helly, op.cit., p.158, and G.-J. M.-J. Te Riele, 'Un nouvel affranchissement de Larissa', *ZPE* 27 (1977), p.261, question this suggestion. Te Riele believes that it is simply the slave's current name.

b. The inscription also shows that where joint ownership applies, the joint owners are likely to be members of the same family, e.g. the joint owners of Νίκανδρος in *ll.*10-15, Πελοποννησίς in *ll.*58-61 and Νίκη in *ll.*65-67.

c. Though *ll.*28-31 show the use of a patron by a manumittor who was not Larissan, the practice does not appear to be mandatory as *l.*61 above and Larissa inv.75/33 *l.*33 show. The manumittor need not be an individual either. In the case of Larissa inv.74/47 *l.*23 (dated paleographically to early first century AD) the slave Philemon (a state slave ?) is manumitted by the Thessalian federation (τὸ κοινὸν τῶν Θεσσαλῶν).

d. The Thessalian manumission records are extensive enough to allow a partial comparison with the Delphic records. For Delphi the statistics from K. Hopkins, *Conquerors and Slaves* (Cambridge 1978), pp.133-171, have been grouped. For Thessaly a sample of manumission lists which have appeared in recent publications[91] has been taken. The use of manumission lists rather than the more extensive deeds of manumission allows only a comparison on the basis of period (between second and first centuries BC) and sex. The results are given in Table 11.1.

---

90 Interest has tended to focus on officials and manumittors named in the inscriptions in an attempt to reconstruct the ruling families of Thessaly and to date its published records (see J. Pouilloux, 'Actes d'affranchissement thessaliens', *BCH* 79 [1955], pp.442-466, and H. Kramolisch, 'Bemerkungen zu einer Freilassungsurkunde aus Larisa', *ZPE* 9 [1972], pp.22-34).

91 K. Hopkins notes in *Conquerors and Slaves* that there will be a forthcoming work on Thessalian manumissions. As I have been unable to consult this, a sample consisting of all the second and first century BC manumission inscriptions from the following publications has been taken: J. Pouilloux, *BCH* 79 (1955), pp.442-66; J. Bousquet, *BCH* 95 (1971), pp.277-82; G.-J. M.-J. Te Riele, *ZPE* 27 (1977), pp.259-62; *SEG* 30 (1980) 531a,b; *SEG* 31 (1981) 577; G.-J. M.-J. Te Riele, *ZPE* 49 (1982), pp.161-176; and *SEG* 35 (1985) 593, 599 and 600. The sampling method, as far as I am aware, ought not to create any bias in the data.

Table 11.1: Sex of slaves manumitted

Place	Sex	Period II BC	I BC
Delphi	Male	248	46
	Female	362	76
Thessaly	Male	51	53
	Female	51	43

Table 11.1 indicates that there was a sharp decline in the use of sacral manumission at Delphi over the two centuries. J. Vogt, *Ancient Slavery and the Ideal of Man* (Oxford 1974), p.42, says of the Delphic manumission inscriptions that they point to the impoverishment rather than to the prosperity of the population. F. Bömer, *Untersuchungen über die Religion der Sklaven in Griechenland und Rom*, vol. II (Wiesbaden 1960), also offers an economic interpretation of the Delphic information. For example, the increase in conditional release is said to be caused by the law of supply and demand (ibid., pp.39-40,46). Scarcity of slaves had set a premium on their value so that their masters sought not only their value but their labour as well. This scarcity and its consequent effect on the number of manumissions recorded at Delphi in the first century BC is also usually attributed to Greece's declining economic circumstances. However, Hopkins, op.cit., p.134, doubts that this was the reason given the incidence of manumission in Thessaly. One may also ask whether the patterns of practice at either site can properly be used as a barometer of local fortunes or, for that matter, of the economic fortunes of Greece as a whole.

Table 11.2: Percentage of female slaves manumitted

Place	Period II BC	I BC
Delphi	59.3%	62.3%
Thessaly	50.0%	44.8%

Another interesting difference between Thessaly and Delphi can be observed. The frequency of female manumission at Delphi (see Table 11.2) is much higher than that in Thessaly. If the results for each site are summed over the two periods, the difference is highly significant.[92] The question is how best to account for the higher frequency of female manumissions at Delphi. Were there proportionately more female slaves in 'Delphic society' and do the statistics just reflect this? Perhaps, but it must be remembered that a large number of those manumitted at Delphi were not from there.[93] Or should the significant difference between Delphi and Thessaly be accounted for by the fact that at Delphi sacral manumission was practised (i.e. the manumission was sanctioned and guaranteed by the deity and its sanctuary – see *New Docs* 6 [1992] §10) whereas in Thessaly the manumission was civic? The question also needs to be asked whether the use of Delphic manumission was a matter of choice, and if so, whose choice (i.e. the master or the slave). A. Kränzlein, 'Bemerkungen zu Form und Inhalt der delphischen Freilassungen', *RIDA* 27 (1980), pp.81-91, has argued the importance of the *paramone* clause in the Delphic text. C.W. Tucker, 'Women in the Manumission Inscriptions at Delphi', *TAPA* 112 (1982), pp.225-36, points to specific provisions when the newly-freed person was female (i.e. concerning the status of children born under *paramone* and

92 Pooling the results for the two periods gives a p-value of 0.0018, i.e. a 1 in 556 (approx.) chance that the difference could arise randomly. This must be considered a significant difference.

93 Hopkins, op.cit., p.138 n.10, gives the sampled percentage of known non-Delphic manumittors as: 201-174 BC = 55%; 152-125 BC = 22%; and 100-53 BC = 16%.

the provision of a child to the manumittor at her release from *paramone*). Did such provisions increase the likelihood of female manumission? The evidence suggests not. It has already been shown in the previous entry (*New Docs* 6 [1992] **§10** Table 10.2 and point 9) that there was no significant association between the variables of sex and type of release. In other words, the fact that a slave was female did not significantly affect the likelihood of conditional release. However, the *paramone* clause, penalty provisions (e.g. beating, sale, loss of freedom etc.) and stipulations regulating the provision of a child to the manumittor suggest to Bömer (pp.34,38-44) that the god Apollo did not primarily function to protect slaves by sanctioning and guaranteeing their freedom, for clearly such provisions exploited them. Indeed, the priests by sacral manumission seem instead to have given sanction to exploitation.[94] Perceiving the tension between the cult's humanising and moralising influence on the one hand and its participation in the exploitation of slaves on the other, Bömer attempts to explain it (p.37) as a lack of agreement between theory and practice. **S.R.L.**

94 Note also that the inscriptions use the *terminus technicus* σῶμα to describe the slave. One wonders whether there was a connection between the decline in the use of sacral manumission at Delphi (see above) and the degree of exploitation associated with it.

BUSINESS TRANSACTIONS

§12 'Even the winds and the waves obey him' Matt.8.27: Acts of God in Shipping Contracts

Provenance unknown — Augustan Period

Ed.pr. — B. Kramer, M. Erler, D. Hagedorn and R. Hübner, *P. Köln* III 147 (Opladen 1980), pp.101-107.

The upper and lower lines as well as part of the left bottom edge are lost. The papyrus measures 20.3 x 10.2 cm and is dated paleographically.

[± 10]. [.]. [± 40]	...
[.]. . . . . νων πρ[.]ς̣. . . [.]. . .[± 28]	...
τὴν συνάλλαξιν ἐντὸς τοῦ χρόνου .[.] .. [..]. [± 23]	the contract within the time ...
σὺν τοῖς σκεύε̣σι ἐπ̣ὶ τῶ̣ν κατ[ὰ] Ἀ̣λε[ξ]ανδρε[ίαν ὅρμων] ἐ̣μ̣ μ̣η̣δ̣ε̣νὶ κατα-	with its equipment at anchor in Alexandria in no way damaged,
βεβλαμμένα πλὴν τριβῆς καὶ σ(κ)ήψεως, πλὴν ἐὰν μή τι βίαιον ἐκ θεοῦ	except for wear and tear, except unless some act of God
γ[έ]νη[τ]αι κατὰ χιμῶνα ἢ πυρὸς ἀπὸ γῆς πάθῃ τὸ̣ π̣λ̣ο̣ῖ̣ο̣ν ἢ ὑπὸ πολεμίων	occur by storm or the boat suffer fire from land or be stripped bare by enemies
ἢ λῃστῶν περισπασθῇ ὃ κα[ὶ] συμφανὲ̣ς καταστ̣ή̣σ̣ω̣. ἐὰν δέ τι τούτων	or pirates, which also I will prove. If I transgress any of these (conditions),
παραβαίνω, ἐκτείσω σοι τά τε βλάβη καὶ ὃ ἐὰν ὀφιλήσω πρὸς τὰ τῶν	I will pay you the damages and whatever I owe for the
ναύλων μέρη σὺν ἡμιολίαι καὶ ἄλλας \`ὡς´ ἴδιον χρέος ἀργυρίου δραχμὰς πεντακοσία[ς]	portions of the rent with the 50% penalty as well as the other, as a private debt, five hundred silver drachmae
καὶ ἱερὰς Καίσαρι δραχμὰς διακοσίας χωρὶς τοῦ μένειν κύρια τὰ προγεγραμ(μένα),	and two hundred drachmae sacred to Caesar, apart from what is written above remaining valid,
τῆς πράξεως σοι οὔσης ἔκ τε ἐμοῦ καὶ ἐκ τῶν ὑπαρχόντων μοι πάντων	the action for recovery being to you from me and from all the property belonging to me
καθάπερ ἐγ δίκης ἀκύρων οὐσῶν ὧν ἐὰν ἐπενέγκωι πίστεων πασῶν	as one does when bringing a lawsuit,[95] all guarantees which I bring
καὶ πάσης σκέπης. ἐὰν δέ τι παρασυγγράφω, ἐξέστω σοι ἐγβάλλοντά με	and every protection being invalid. If I break the contract in any (detail), let it be lawful for you, ejecting me

---

95 For the meaning of this expression see H.J. Wolff, 'Some Observations on πράξις', *XIIth Int. Congr. of Pap.* (Toronto 1970), pp.527-35.

ἐκ τῆς μισθώσεως ἐνχρόνου οὔσης	from the lease though current,
ἑτέρῳ μεταμισθῶσαι καὶ εἰσ-	to lease it to another and
πράσσειν τὸ ἐσόμενον ἀφεύρεμα	to exact the future loss
παρὰ τὴν ἐξαναμίσθωσιν	on account of the new lease
ὑ̣π̣ὲ̣ρ̣ ὧν καὶ ἐν ἡμέραις	for which also within five business (?)
χ̣ρ̣ημ̣α̣τ̣ι̣ζούσαις πέντε ἀφ' ἧς ἐάν μοι προ-	days from whenever you de[clare] to me
[είπ̣ης ± 18]τ̣ὴ̣ν̣ ἀσφ[άλ]ειαν	[...] the surety
ἀνυπερθέτως.	immediately.

....

6 χειμῶνα 8 ἐκτίσω, ὀφειλήσω 12 ἐπενέγκω 13 ἐκβάλλοντί

According to the editors, the document is the earliest example (by more than 500 years) of the lease of a boat for a short period of time. A comparison is made with *BGU* IV 1157 (10 BC), *P. Lond.* III 1164 (AD 212) and *P. Oxy.* XVII 2136 (AD 291). However, in all these deeds the lease periods are much longer, i.e. 50-60 years, and the rent is calculated and paid in advance. For these reasons the editors argue that the longer-period lease, called a μισθοπρασία, resembled a sale transaction more than a lease.[96]

In the above document the lessee guarantees the return of the boat undamaged but for the exceptions of wear and tear and τι βίαιον ἐκ θεοῦ. What is meant by the latter phrase is specified as storms, fires and attacks by enemies or pirates. The editors note parallels to the *Digest* (see *Dig.*4.9.3.1 – shipwreck and piracy, 19.2.15.1 – attack by enemy, and 19.5.17.4 – fire). See also *Dig.*19.2.25.6: *vis maior, quam Graeci* θεοῦ βίαν *appellant*. The expression τι βίαιον ἐκ θεοῦ or θεοῦ βία designates events which lie beyond the control and foresight of the lessee. On the questions of liability in shipping contracts and of the relationship between the Roman *receptum nautae* and shipping contracts from Egypt see further C.H. Brecht, *Zur Haftung der Schiffer im antiken Recht* (Munich 1962) and reviewed by B.R. Rees, *JHS* 84 (1964), pp.186-7 and L. Casson, *AJP* 86 (1965), pp.330-2. On the risk to the *fiscus* posed by a fraudulent claim relating to the loss of a ship carrying the *annona* and the measures taken to guard against it, including the torture of the ship's sailors or their children, see A.D. Manfredini, 'Les naviculaires et le naufrage', *RIDA* 33 (1986), pp.135-148 and example b) below.

Clauses limiting liability in the case of loss or damages caused by θεοῦ βία are found in other contracts involving ships. A.J.M. Meyer-Termeer, *Die Haftung der Schiffer im griechischen und römischen Recht* (Zutphen 1978), pp.117-20, discusses such clauses of limitation in relation to three freight contracts:[97]

---

96 The editors also differentiate *P. Köln* III 147 from *SB* XIV 11552 (AD 221) and *MChr* 341 (AD 236). In these later papyri the lessor is at the same time the ship's skipper. He undertakes to transport the lessee's goods by return voyage in his ship.

97 There is some uncertainty regarding the status of the expression in freight contracts. R. Hübner, *P. Köln* III, p.103 n.4, questions the reading of *P. Laur.* I 6 describing it as palaeographically unsure. Two further objections are also raised against the restoration, namely that no surety could have been given against the danger but only against its consequences and that θεοῦ βία and attacks of an enemy are not events of the same order. A question also stands over the reading of the expression Διὸς βία in *P. Oxy. inv.* 21 3B25G (cited by Meyer-Termeer, op.cit., p.118). Its viability seems to depend on the reading of *P. Laur.* I 6. On the basis of *P. Köln* III 147 the following reading of *P. Oxy. inv.* 21 3B25G has been suggested: πλὴν ἐάν, ὃ μὴ γεί[νοιτο, ἐκ Δι]ὸς βίαιόν τι συμβῇ κτλ.

a) *P. Laur.* I 6 *ll.* 7-11 (AD 97/8 – 116/7):

ἄχρι οὗ παραγενόμενος ẹ[ἰς 'Αλεξάνδρειαν παραδώσῃ τὰ]
ἐμ{βε}βληθησόμενα σῶα ạ̓[κακούργητα ἀπὸ ναυτι-]
κῆς κακουργίας, ἐὰν μή τịṣ ḳ[ίνδυνος ἢ βλάβος]
γένηται ἤτοι ἀπὸ Διὸς βίας αλ[... ἢ λῃσ-]
τῶν ἐφόδου.

until he is present [in Alexandria and hands over the]
freight safe [uninjured by any]
injury [at sea], unless some [risk or damage]
happen either by an act of Zeus [... or]
attack of [pir]ates.

b) *P. Oxy. inv.* 21 3B25G (AD 176) – cited by Meyer-Termeer (p.118):

καὶ πλεύσῃ τὸν πλοῦν ... πλὴν ἐάν, ὃ μὴ γεί[νοιτο, Διὸς βί]ạς αἰτιόν τι συμβῇ ἢ πυρὸς ἀπὸ γῆς ἢ χιμώνος ἢ κακούργων ẹ̓πịβα[λ]λọ́ṇṭωṇ, ὃ συμφανὲς ποιήσας ἀνεύθυνος ἔσῃ σὺν καὶ τῇ ναυτίạ.

and he will sail the boat ... except if, may it not happen, some cause of Zeus' act occur or of fire from the land or of storm or of enemy attacking, which once proving you and your crew will be guiltless.

c) *P. Oxy.* I 144 *ll.*10-12 (AD 580):

καὶ ταῦτα
ἑτοίμως ἔχω καταγαγεῖν ἐν 'Αλεξανδρείạ δίχα θεοῦ βίας
καὶ τῶν κατὰ ποταμὸν κινδύνων καὶ ἐπηρειῶν κτλ

and these
I am prepared to bring to port in Alexandria apart from an act of God
and the risks of the river and assaults etc.

The reason for the ability of the skipper to limit his liability is not stated explicitly in any of the freight contracts; however, on the basis of *P. Oxy.* I 144 Meyer-Termeer suggests that one reason may have been the value of the cargo itself. In most freight contracts the skipper contracted with the state and as a result was placed in a weaker bargaining position (see pp.90-103, where 77% of freight contracts, by my reckoning, are between the skipper and the state). In other words, it was usual for the skipper to accept liability for any loss. However, in *P. Oxy.* I 144 the high value of the cargo (2205 gold solidi) placed the skipper in a stronger bargaining position over against the state. Meyer-Termeer suggests that he simply could not afford to accept the liability in this instance.

P. Oxy. XXII 2347 *ll.*10-11 (AD 362) is another type of document again. It is a deed of surety whereby Aurelius Zeuxios guarantees that Aurelius Horoptoleeis, the skipper of a Hellenic vessel, will transport and deliver his cargo and letters of consignment to the required authorities and when requested his vessel also. The guarantee concerning the vessel's delivery is qualified by an exemption in the case of an act of God.

καὶ ὁπόταν αἱρῇ παραδοῦναι αὐτὸν
τὸ αὐτοῦ πλοῖον μετὰ καὶ τῆς τούτου ἐξαρτίσẹọς ἐὰν ὑποδέξηται χωρὶς θεοῦ βίας.

and (on condition) that whenever you choose, he will hand over his vessel with also its equipment, if he takes charge (of any), apart from an act of God.

Another relevant deed is *P. Lond.* V 1714 (AD 570). In form the deed appears to involve the lease of a vessel; however, the editor notes: 'but as no rent is mentioned and the lessee undertakes to discharge any commission entrusted to him by the owner and to carry his goods ... it is possible the agreement is less a lease than a contract of service'. At *ll.*45-6 the lessee agrees to restore the vessel[98] apart from an act of God.

ἀ]π̣ο̣κ[α]τ̣αστῆσαι [ὑ]μῖν δίχα θεοῦ
[βίας ἄνευ οἱασδήποτ]ε ῥᾳδιουργίας καὶ ἀπενεγκεῖν ὑμῖν κτλ

to restore (it) to you apart from
[an act] of God [without any] fraud [whatsoever] and to return to you etc.

The only known document using the expression without reference to shipping is *P. Oxy.* XXXIV 2721 *ll.*22-26 (AD 234), a work contract between Aurelius Ptollion and Aurelius Heras, village presidents, and Antinous son of Hermias, the supervisor of a musical troop. The Aurelii contracted the services of Antinous' troop to help celebrate a festival. Part of the agreement concerns their transport from the Oxyrhynchite nome by three donkeys.

καὶ	and
τοῦτον ἅμα τοῖς ἄλλοις παραλήμ-	they will take him with the others,
ψονται χωρὶς θεοῦ βίας ἀπὸ τοῦ Ὀξυ-	apart from an act of God, from the
ρυνχείτου διὰ ὄνων τριῶν καὶ ἀπο-	Oxyrhynchite nome by three donkeys and
καταστήσουσι εἰς τὴν κώμην κτλ	return (them) to the village etc.

Meyer-Termeer, op.cit., pp.131-2 nn.63 and 66), considers that the expression Διὸς βία was replaced by the Christian expression θεοῦ βία beginning in the fourth century AD. Accordingly, the use of θεοῦ at *Dig.*19.2.25.6 (cited above) is considered to be a Christian interpolation into the text. In view of the readings τι βίαιον ἐκ θεοῦ in *P. Köln* III 147 and χωρὶς θεοῦ βίας in *P. Oxy.* XXXIV 2721 Meyer-Termeer's hypothesis must be reconsidered. The expression 'act of God' appears to have predated the rise of Christianity to the status of the empire's official religion. It was used contemporaneously with the expression 'act of Zeus'.

Thank-offerings to the gods for a safe return have already been discussed in *New Docs* 3 (1983), pp.58-9, and 4 (1987), pp.113-7. Such offerings were retrospective and arose as a response to an act of deliverance – σωθεὶς ἐκ μεγάλου κινδύνου. The clause limiting liability was different. It provided protection against a future contingency, the loss of a ship or its cargo. However, behind both thank-offerings and clauses limiting liability lies a similar perception of travel and its attendant risks. In case of deliverance the gods were to be thanked; in case of destruction the contracting party was to be protected from any liability for the loss arising from the act of God. Deliverance or destruction at sea are in the hands of God.

Such a view of travel may prove of interest for more than Paul's journeys by sea, cf. in particular Acts 27.1-44 and 2Cor.11.26 and the discussion in the above *New Docs* 3 (1983) passages. It may also inform the interpretation of the miracles in which Jesus stilled storms at sea. In particular, it may throw light on the disciples' response to such miracles. If a storm at sea was perceived to be an 'act of God', then the words 'What kind of man is this? Even the winds and the waves obey him!' (Matt.8.27, Mark 4.41, Luke 8.25) take on a new significance. Indeed, such a miracle to the Graeco-Roman audience, at least, offered a proof of

98 Meyer-Termeer, ibid., p.132, states that it is unclear whether the vessel or its freight is referred to. Two arguments suggest to me that the reference is rather to the vessel. First, the document itself formally represents the lease of a vessel, i.e. the document concerns the vessel. The transporting of freight is a condition of the lease but not its subject matter. Second, the similar expression τι βίαιον ἐκ θεοῦ occurs in another lease of a vessel, i.e. *P. Köln* III 147.

Jesus' divinity. Indeed, in Matthew's second account of a miracle at sea (Matt.14.22-33) the disciples utter the confession: 'Truly you are the son of God'. **S.R.L.**

§13 Self-Help and Legal Redress: The Parable of the Wicked Tenants

Theadelphia 16 Sept. AD 44

Ed.pr. — O. Montevecchi, 'Affitto di terreno', *Aegyptus* 54 (1974), pp.64-71.

The papyrus measures 10 x 28.3 cm. The suggested readings of D. Hagedorn have been accepted into the text.

Bib. – *SB* XIV 11279; N. Lewis, *BASP* 13 (1976), p.169; D. Hagedorn, *ZPE* 28 (1978), p.283.

Μ`η΄(νὸς) Σ`ε΄(βαστοῦ) ιθ̄ ὀφ(είλει) (ὀβολοὺς) ε̄.	In the mo(nth) of Se(bastos) 19, he ow(es) 5 (obols).
Ἔτους πέμπτου Τιβερ̣ί̣[ου Κλαυ]δ̣ί̣ο̣υ̣ Κ̣α̣ί̣σ̣α̣ρ̣ο̣[ς Σεβαστοῦ]	In the fifth year of Tiberi[us Clau]dius Caesar [Augustus]
Γερμανικοῦ Αὐτοκράτορος μηνὸς Σεβαστοῦ ἐνν[εακαιδε-]	Germanicus Imperator, in the month of Sebastos, on the nine[teenth day]
κάτῃ ἐν Θε(α)δελφείᾳ τῆς Θεμίστου μερίδος τ̣ο̣ῦ Ἀ̣[ρσινο-]	in Theadelphia in the district of Themistos of the A[rsinoite]
είτου νομοῦ. Ἐμίσθωσεν Ἡράκλεια Χάρητος ὡς [(ἐτῶν)]	nome. Herakleia, daughter of Chares, about
εἴκοσι δύο οὐλῆι μήλωι ἀριστερῶι μ̣ε̣τ̣ὰ̣ κ̣[υρίου τοῦ]	twenty-two [years of age], scar to the left cheek, with her
ἑαυτῆς ἀνδρὸς Ἀπολλωνίου Ἰσιδώρου [ὡς ἐτῶν τ]ρ̣ι̣ά̣-	husband Apollonios, son of Isidoros, [about th]irty-three [years of age],
κοντα τριῶν οὐλῆι ὀφρύι ἀριστερᾷ Αὐνῇ Ἁρθώτ̣ο̣υ	scar to left eyebrow, [acting as guardian], has leased to Aunes, son of Harthotos,
Πέρσῃ τῆς ἐπιγονῆς ὡς ἐτῶν εἴκοσι πέντε οὐλὴ ὑπὸ	Persian of the descent, about twenty-five years of age, scar under
ὀ̣φ̣ρ̣ύ̣ι̣ ἀριστερᾷ τὸν ὑπάρχοντα αὐτῇ περὶ Θεαδέλ-	left eyebrow, her catoecic estate about
φειαν κλῆρον κατοικικὸν ἀρουρῶν ἓξ ἢ ὅσαι ἐὰν	Theadelphia of six arouras or as much as
ὦσι ἐν μιᾷ σφραγεῖδι. Ἡ μίσθωσις ἥδε· εἰς ἔτη τέσερα	they are in one parcel. This is the lease: for four years
ἀπὸ τοῦ ἐνεστῶτος πέμπτου ἔτους Τιβερίου Κλαυδίου	from the present fifth year of Tiberius Claudius
Καίσαρος Σεβαστοῦ Γερμανικοῦ Αὐτοκράτορος, ἐκφορίου	Caesar Augustus Germanicus Imperator, at a rent paid in kind
τὸ μ̣ὲ̣ν̣ πρῶ[τον] ἔτος ἑκάστης ἀρούρης, σὺν ᾗ λήμψεται	for the first year for each aroura, with which
ὁ μεμισθωμένος πυροῦ ἀρτάβης μιᾶς, πυροῦ ἀρταβῶν	the lessee will take one artaba of wheat (for seed), of five artabas of wheat,

πέντε, ἐπὶ δὲ τὰ λοιπὰ ἔτη τρία κατ᾽ ἔτος ἑκάστης	and for the remaining three years yearly for each
ἀρούρης, σὺν αἷς λήμψεται ὁ μεμισθωμένος σπερ-	aroura, with which the lessee will take for
μάτων πυροῦ ἀρτάβης μιᾶς, πυροῦ ἀρταβῶν ἕξ, καὶ	seed one artaba of wheat, of six artabas of wheat, and
θαλλῶν κατ᾽ ἔτος ἄρτων ἀρτάβης μιᾶς, πάντων δὲ	at an annual gratuity of one artaba of bread, and all
τῶν ἐκφορίων κατ᾽ ἔτος μέτρωι δρόμωι τετρα-	the rents in kind annually (being) at the four-*choinikes* measure
χοινίκωι θησαυροῦ Καισίου ἀνυπολόγως παντὸς	of Kaisios' granary, free from every
ὑπολόγου καὶ ἀκινδύνως παντὸς κινδύνου. Τὰ δ᾽ ἔργα	liability and safe from every risk. All the workings
πάντα τοῦ κλήρου τούς τε χωματισμοὺς καὶ ποτισμοὺς	of the estate – the maintenance of dykes, watering,
καὶ βοτανισμοὺς καὶ τῶν ἄλλων γεωργικῶν ὑπουργιῶν	weeding and the other agricultural duties –
πάντα ἐπιτελείτω ὁ μεμισθωμένος κατ᾽ ἔτος ἐκ τοῦ ἰδίου	let the lessee annually perform all these at his own expense
καὶ ἀναπαύσεται κατ᾽ ἔτος τὸ ἥμισυ μέρος τοῦ κλήρου	and he will cause a half part of the estate to lie fallow annually
χόρτωι ἢ ἀράκωι εἰς κατάβρωμα καὶ κοιτασμὸν προ-	with grass or chickling for the feeding and folding
βάτων. Μὴ ἐξέστωι οὖν τῶι μεμισθωμένωι ἐντὸς τοῦ	of sheep. Therefore, let it not be lawful for the lessee within the
χρόνου προλειπεῖν τὴν μίσθωσιν ἄλλωι, τ̣ὰ̣ δ̣ὲ̣ κ̣α̣τ̣᾽ ἔ̣τ̣ο̣ς̣	period to abandon the lease to another and
ἐ̣κ̣φ̣ό̣ρ̣ι̣α̣ ἀποδότωι ὁ μεμισθωμένος τῆι Ἡρακλείᾳ	let the lessee pay the annual rent in kind to Herakleia
ἐ̣ν̣ [μηνὶ Παῦνι ἐν τῆι κώμηι], καὶ μετὰ τὸν προκίμενον χρόνον	in [the month of Pauni in the village,] and after the aforesaid period
παραδότωι ὁ μεμισθωμένος τῇ Ἡρακλείᾳ τὸν κλῆρον	let the lessee return to Herakleia the estate
[κ]αθαρὸν ἀπὸ θρύου κ̣α̣λ̣ά̣μ̣ο̣υ̣ ἀγ̣ρ̣ώ̣σ̣τ̣ε̣ω̣ς̣ δείσης πάσης.	clear of rush, reed, grass and all slime.
Ἐὰν δέ τι τούτων παρ[αβ]ῆι [ὁ μεμ]ι̣σ̣θ̣ω̣μ̣έ̣ν̣ο̣ς̣ ἀποτεισάτω τά τε	If the lessee transgresses any of these (conditions), let him pay both
βλάβη καὶ τὰ δαπανήματα δειπλᾶ καὶ ἐπίτειμ`ο´(ν) χαλ`κ´(ου) [(ταλ.)] ε̄, τῆς	the damages and the expenses twofold and a penalty of 5 bronze talents, the
πράξεως οὔσης̣ τῇ Ἡρακλείᾳ ἔκ τε τοῦ μεμισθωμένου καὶ βε-	action for recovery being to Herakleia and from the lessee, and

βαιούτωι τὴν μίσθωσιν καὶ ἀπὸ δημοσίων. Ἡ συγγραφὴ κ(υρία).	let Herakleia guarantee the lease also with the public officials. The agreement is valid.
(m. 2) Ἡ̣ρ̣ά̣κ̣λ̣ε̣ι̣α̣ Χάρητος μετὰ κυρίου τοῦ ἀνδρός μου	(m. 2) I, Herakleia, daughter of Chares, with my husband
Ἀπολλωνίου τοῦ Ἰσιδώρου μεμίσθωκα κα-	Apollonios, son of Isidoros, acting as guardian, have leased
[θὼς πρόκειτ]α̣ι̣. Ἀπολλώνιος ἔγραψα ὑπὲρ	[as aforesaid]. I, Apollonios, have written for
τῆς γυναικός μου [μὴ εἰδυίης] γράμ[ματα].	my wife [who is il]literate.
(m. 3) Αὐνῆς Ἁρ[θώτ]ου Πέρσης τῆς ἐπιγονῆς μεμίσθωμαι	(m. 3) I, Aunes, son of Har[thot]os, Persian of the descent, have leased
παρὰ τῆς Ἡρακλείας τὸ̣ν̣ προγεγρ(αμμένον) κλ(ῆρον) ἀρουρῶν ἓξ ἢ ὅσαι	from Herakleia the aforementioned estate of six arouras, or as many
[ἐὰν ὦσι περὶ Θεαδέλ]φειαν εἰς ἔτη δ̅ ἀπὸ τοῦ ἐνεστῶτος ἔτους	as [they are, about Theadel]phia for 4 years from the present year
ἐκφορίου τὸ μὲν πρῶτον ἔ̣τ̣ο̣ς̣ ἑ̣κ̣ά̣σ̣τ̣η̣ς̣ ἀρούρης σὺν ᾗ λ-	at a rent in kind for the first year for each aroura, with which
ή(μψομαι) πυροῦ ἀρτάβης μιᾶς πυροῦ ἀρταβῶν πέντε, ἐπὶ δὲ τὰ λοιπ[ὰ]	I will take one artaba of wheat, of five artabas of wheat, and for the remaining
ἔτη τρία κατ' ἔτος ἑ̣κ̣ά̣σ̣τ̣η̣ς̣ ἀρ̣ο̣ύρης σ̣ὺ̣ν̣ α̣ἷ̣ς̣ λ̣ή̣μ̣ψ̣ο̣μ̣α̣ι̣	three years annually for each aroura, with which I will take
πυροῦ ἀρτάβης μιᾶς πυροῦ ἀρταβῶν ἓξ πάντων μέτρ`ω´(ι)	one artaba of wheat, of six artabas of wheat by the
δ[ρόμωι τετρ]αχ[οινίκωι θησαυροῦ Κ]α̣ι̣σ̣ί̣ο̣υ̣ [καὶ θαλλῶν]	[four-*choinikes*] measure [of Kaisios' granary and for a gratuity]
ἄρτων ἀρτάβης μ̣ι̣ᾶ̣ς̣ [...]	of one artaba of bread [...]
(Back) Α[ὐ]ν̣ῆ̣ς̣ Π̣ε̣ρ-	A[u]nes, Per[sian]
[σης τ]ῆ̣ς̣ ἐ̣π̣(ιγονῆς) (ταλ.) ε̣.	of the descent, 5 (talents).

4-5 Ἀρσινοίτου 6 & 8 οὐλή 12 σφραγῖδι, τέσσαρα 29 ἐξέστω 30 προλιπεῖν τὴν μίσθωσιν <μηδὲ μεταμισθοῦν μηδενὶ> ἄλλωι (N.Lewis) 31 ἀποδότω 33 παραδότω 36 διπλᾶ, ἐπίτιμον 37 βεβαιούτω

In the above lease Aunes leased from Herakleia an estate of six arouras for a period of four years. The rent was to be paid in kind and varies from five artabas per aroura in the first year to six artabas per aroura in the subsequent years. In each year the lessee retained (probably for sowing the next crop) one artaba of wheat. In addition to the rent in kind the lessor received a gratuity of one artaba of bread. The other terms of the lease concern the maintenance of the estate, abandonment of the lease before its expiry and the due date for the payment of the rent. Herakleia also possessed the right of action for damages and losses against the lessee who assumed the fictitious designation of Πέρσης τῆς ἐπιγονῆς (for the significance of this expression see *New Docs* 6 [1992] §1) and in return guaranteed that the lessee would not be disturbed in his cultivation of the estate either by herself or by a third party (*ll.*37-8 – see also

Taubenschlag, *Law*, p.361 and H.J. Wolff, 'Consensual Contracts in the Papyri?', *JJP* 1 [1946], pp.63-5). From the above deed it is clear that the interests of the lessor were adequately protected. In order to appreciate more generally the protection afforded the owner within the lease agreement, one might profitably consider the terms imposed on the lessee, e.g. the maintenance of dykes, watering, weeding etc.

D. Hennig, 'Die Arbeitsverpflichtungen der Pächter in Landpachtverträgen aus dem Faijum', *ZPE* 9 (1972), pp.111-131, discusses the types of terms to which a tenant was subject when leasing agricultural land. Land care was a vital concern in leases of agricultural land for it affected the tenant's ability to pay his rent and the landlord's ability to re-let the property on termination of the lease agreement. In this matter the short duration of lease agreements (one to three years) was an important consideration, for a tenant had a shorter period in which to make good any arrears or damages. Nor was personal execution always a viable option, for a tenant might own little or no property. The landlord also had to consider returns on future lease agreements. A maximal rate of return would, of course, depend on the land's continued productivity.

The terms vary according to the type of land and its use. Vineyards, date and olive groves, orchards and gardens naturally required more careful cultivation as the plants themselves constituted an ongoing investment. Land used for the cultivation of grains and fodder (i.e. crops planted annually) involved primarily an obligation of care for the land itself. The lease agreement stipulated the obligations of the tenant. They included:

i. The obligation to do all necessary works in their season (pp.113-5): τὰ δὲ γεωργικὰ ἔργα πάντα ἄξω καὶ ἐπιτελέσω κατ' ἔτος.
Special obligations could be specified:
- **a.** repair of canals, dams and locks in the irrigation system (pp.120-1);
- **b.** artificial watering (pp.121-2);
- **c.** weeding (pp.122-3).

ii. The obligation to avoid causing damage (pp.115-7): βλάβος μηδὲν ποιῶν.

iii. The obligation to bear all relevant costs of maintenance (p.117).

iv. At the termination of the lease (after the final harvest) the tenant was obligated to hand over the land in a good condition[99] (pp.123-30): καὶ μετὰ τὸν χρόνον παραδώσω τὰς ἀρούρας καθαρὰς ἀπὸ θρύου καλάμου ἀγρώστεως δείσης πάσης. In longer leases this often required that some of the land be left fallow.

Most of these obligations find expression in the above example of a lease agreement. For further information on leases see J. Herrmann, *Studien zur Bodenpacht im Rechte der gräco-ägyptischen Papyri* (Munich 1958).

Agricultural duties also appear to have been specified in the lease agreements of Palestine (see *m. B. Meṣ.* 9.1-10 and *t. B. Meṣ.* 9.1-33). General regulations appear to have governed the methods of cutting, uprooting, ploughing and the sharing in the land's produce by the tenant and landlord (*m. B. Meṣ.* 9.1, 7), the obligation of the tenant to weed (*m. B. Meṣ.* 9.4) and to work the property (*m. B. Meṣ.* 9.5), the reduction in rentals in the case of a natural calamity (*m. B. Meṣ.* 9.6), the duration of leases which extend into the Sabbatical year (*m. B. Meṣ.* 9.10), the payment of rent (*t. B. Meṣ.* 9.8) and subletting (*t. B. Meṣ.* 9.33). The wording of lease agreements covered such matters also as the reductions in rentals where the property was adversely affected by the loss of water supply or the cutting down of trees (*m. B. Meṣ.* 9.2), the rental return of the property when left fallow (*m. B. Meṣ.* 9.3), the type of crops that

---

99 One might compare leases of land with leases of other property with regard to the condition of the object at the end of the lease period.

could be planted or the produce that could be gathered (*m. B. Meṣ.* 9.8-9) and the duties of the lessee (*t. B. Meṣ.* 9.13). The latter is expressed thus in the contract:

> אנור ואזרע ואחצד ואדוש ואוקים כריא
> קדמך ואנת תיתי ותיסב פלגא בעיבורא
> ובתיבנא ואנא בעמלי ובנפקת ידי פלגא
> **I shall plough and sow and harvest and thresh and place a pile**
> **before you and you will come and take half in grain**
> **and in straw and I for my labour and my outgoings a half.**

If the above discussion has demonstrated a degree of similarity between the conditions of lease agreements in Egypt and Palestine, the result can be further confirmed by a reading of *DJD* II 24, an agricultural lease from Palestine in Hebrew and dated AD 133. Of this deed it is remarked (p.123): 'It is interesting to note that the autonomous administration of the revolutionaries had faithfully continued the Graeco-Roman administrative routine, only changing the language of the deeds'.

The *praxis*-clause (see *ll.*37-8 of the above lease) deals with the agreement's execution in case of default by the promisor (e.g. the debtor or lessee). H.J. Wolff, 'The *Praxis*-Provision in Papyrus Contracts', *TAPA* 72 (1941), pp.418-38, maintains a separation between the concepts of duty and liability in Greek and Hellenistic law so that the promisor's liability did not follow immediately from the duty created by the transaction or *res* but was constituted by a particular clause in the agreement, i.e. the *praxis*-clause. See further H.J. Wolff, 'Consensual Contracts in the Papyri?', pp.56-71. In other types of deed lacking a *praxis*-clause, it is argued, liability was established outside the agreement by laws (νόμοι), edicts (προστάγματα) or regulations (διαγράμματα) and losses were claimed under a more general action for damages, i.e. the βλάβης δίκη. But in those instruments not covered by such legislation the liability of the promisor was constituted as one of the terms of the agreement. As such the person who had the right to initiate action had to be named, though he (or she) did not have to be a party to the agreement. The execution was usually against the person and his (or her) property.

How might an execution in case of default proceed? As a first step the person possessing the right of execution might seek personal satisfaction from the promisor. If the parties agreed, a private arbitrator could be appointed to settle the dispute (see J. Modrzejewski, 'Private Arbitration in the Law of Greco-Roman Egypt', *JJP* 6 [1952], pp.239-56). If the attempt to seek personal satisfaction failed, the creditor could petition the relevant authority seeking assistance to enforce his rights under the contract. The bailiff (πράκτωρ ξενικῶν) would then serve a writ (διαστολικόν) on the defaulter. Three options were open to the defaulter at this point. Under the coercion of the authorities he might pay the liability (i.e. the amount owed and a penalty) and the matter would be settled. Alternatively, he might take no action whatever. If so, after a specified time (ten days) the stages of execution were undertaken – the designation of the defaulter's property (= παράδειξις); the seizing of the defaulter's property by the state (= ἐνεχυρασία); the auction of the defaulter's property to the highest bidder (= προσβολή); the conveyance to the creditor (= καταγραφή); and the entering into possession by the creditor (= ἐμβαδεία). The third option was for the defaulter to object (= ἀντίρρησις) to the action and to petition the authorities protesting his innocence. If this happened, then the case required a judicial decision (δική) which found either for or against the defendant. If the latter, the decision did not order performance by the promisor (i.e. the defaulter) but determined the promisee's right to execution (see H.J. Wolff, 'Some Observations on *Praxis*', *Proceedings of XIIth International Congress of Papyrology* [Toronto 1970], pp.527-35). It did this by writing to the bailiff to take the necessary steps to effect enforcement. See further Taubenschlag, *Law*, pp.531-7, *BGU* XIV 2376 and the discussion of procedures at *BGU* XV 2472-3. For the preparation of a suit against defaulting lessees see W.L. Westermann and E.S. Hasenoehrl, *Zenon Papyri: Business Papers of the Third Century BC Dealing with Palestine and Egypt* (NY 1934), pp.132-144.Despite the coercive powers of the civil authorities and the judicial powers of the courts and officials, an element of self-help pervaded much of the legal procedure. This extended beyond the mere attempt to seek satisfaction before making an appeal to the authorities. Even in such cases as theft or assault it was up to the wronged party to petition the authorities to investigate the matter. Moreover, when a favourable *subscriptio* had been given by the authorities, it could be left to the petitioner to communicate the decision to the *strategos* for further action or even to one's opponents. See further J.D. Thomas, *The Epistrategos in Ptolemaic and Roman Egypt* vol.II (Opladen 1982), pp.121, 134, who also cites M. Humbert, 'Juridiction du préfet d'Égypte' in *Aspects de l'Empire romain*, ed. N. Burdeau et al. (1964), p.129 (non vidi).

Like the lease conditions discussed above, the right of execution arose from the nature of the commercial transaction and thus was not confined to the Greek law of Egypt only. For example, one might cite the expression שלימן למלקח לך – 'you have the right to take for yourself' – in fifth century BC Aramaic loan agreements (see A. Cowley, *Aramaic Papyri of the Fifth Century BC* [Oxford 1923 – reprinted Osnabrück 1967], no.10, *ll.*8-9//16-17). A question arises as to whether the remedy relied solely on an act of self-help or whether an appeal to the administrative and judicial authorities was possible if self-help failed. From the OT it appears that the creditor was able to seize the property which was offered as the loan's pledge (i.e. if he did not already have it in his possession) or in the case of the debtor's insolvency to reduce him to servitude for six years. However, as Palestine came increasingly under Hellenistic influence, administrative and judicial procedures changed. E. Schürer, *The History of the Jewish People in the Age of Jesus Christ*, vol.II, revised and edited by G. Vermes, F. Millar, M. Black (Edinburgh 1979), pp.52-80, discusses the various types of Hellenistic influence on the Jewish regions. Particular emphasis is placed on the effects of trade and commerce - see also M. Hengel, *Judaism and Hellenism* (London 1974), pp.32-57. In *New Docs* 6 (1992) **§1** and **§4** Hellenistic influence in such matters as marriage (e.g. E. Bickerman, 'Two Legal Interpretations of the Septuagint', *RIDA* III [1956] = *Studies in Jewish and Christian History* [Leiden 1976], pp.201-215 and his discussion of the *kethubah*) and testamentary gifts (cf. R. Yaron, *Gifts in Contemplation of Death* [Oxford 1960], p.18) has been touched on. Such penetration into the family is worth noting, though one hastens to add that it was not without adaptation. Be that as it may, the Hellenistic influence here is also considered to be the result of economic changes. Another influence, this time in the realm of administration, is discussed in *New Docs* 6 (1992) **§16**. The adoption of an Hellenistic administrative system, again, was most probably motivated by an economic concern, i.e. taxation to finance the government. The rise of Hellenistic power and influence had thus created a situation to which the Jewish territories had to adapt in many different ways. However, it is important to observe that this was not necessarily achieved by a wholesale adoption of Greek practices. Rather, it appears that there was either an adaptation of a Jewish practice to the prevailing situation or an adoption of a modified form of a Greek practice. Another area of Hellenistic influence appears to have been in the area of the judicial system, especially where it concerned commerce. Judicial functions were carried out by village and city courts and the Sanhedrin. According to Schürer, op.cit., pp.185, the local councils had a judicial and policing function – cf. Josephus, *BJ* 2.273, *m. Sheb.* 10.4, *m. Soṭa* 1.3, *m. Sanh.* 11.4, Mark 13.9. A. of the Schalit, *König Herodes* (Berlin 1969), pp.223-56, discusses various pieces of evidence for the influence of Greek and Roman law in Herod's kingdom. In view of Josephus, *AJ* 16.9-10 (§271) and *m. Ket.* 13.1, he observes traces of Greek law in the areas of legal obligation and the right of execution (καθάπερ ἐκ δίκης): 'in money matters no one in the first century of the Christian era in Jerusalem was entitled to take the law into his own hands, and there is no reason to think that in the first century BC the legal situation may have been any different' (p.256; my translation). The right of execution by judicial decision secured the creditor-class against the debtor-class of Palestinian society. As further examples of the increasing role of the court in commercial and other civil cases one can note the *logion* concerning the debtor and his creditor (Matt.5.25-26 and Luke 12.57-59; note the steps in the legal procedure, i.e. a preliminary hearing before a magistrate, ἄρχων, followed by a decision of the judge, κρίτης) and the introduction of the *prozbol* (פרוזבול = προσβολή) by Hillel which secured a loan against annulment in the sabbatical year (*m. Shev.* 10.3-4). As well, one may note other legal procedures which appear to protect the debtor and required a decision of the court (בית דין), e.g. to exact a payment (*m. B. Meṣ.* 1.6) or to acquire a pledge subsequent to the making of a loan (*m. B. Meṣ.* 9.13). R.S. de Franch, *Études sur le droit palestinien à l'époque évangélique* (Fribourg 1946), notes other accompanying changes, e.g. the practice of placing pledges on persons (e.g. children) and imposing servitude on the insolvent debtor gave way to pledges on immovables and other property (e.g. land and slaves), work contracts and the introduction of the debtor's prison. There was also a corresponding change in legal concepts. For example, whereas the servitude of the insolvent debtor was a remedy to compensate the creditor, the debtor's prison acted as an incentive to encourage compliance with the agreement.

A chronologically relevant deed is *DJD* II 18 (especially *ll.*6-8), a loan agreement in Aramaic dated AD 55 – 6.

ואפשר בתמ[ימותא]
ושנת שמטה דה והן כן לא אעבד תשלומ[תא]
לך מנכסי ודי אקנה לקובליך

... and it (i.e. the loan) will be redeemed in full,
though it is a sabbatical year. And if then I do not perform, payment
(is) yours from my goods and whatever I acquire (is) for your repayment.

The deed both makes reference to the *prozbol* (*l.*7) and the right of execution (*ll.*7-8). The clause itself does not make clear whether the creditor could petition the judical authorities to enforce payment, when self-help failed. However, in view of the evidence cited above and the presence of the *praxis* or execution clause in deeds of a later date from Palestine (see *DJD* II 114 *ll.*17-21 dated AD 171, 115 *ll.*16-17 dated AD 124, *P. Yadin* 11 *ll.*22-27 dated AD 124, 18 *ll.*24-27 dated AD 128, 21 *ll.*24-27 dated AD 130) it seems reasonable to assume that he could. In other words, it seems probable that in first-century Palestine a person could petition officials to assist and to give judgement when self-help failed.[100] The question therefore is not whether the right existed or not but how effective it was. J.D.M. Derrett, 'Law and Society in Jesus's World', *ANRW* II 25, 1 (1982), pp.477-564, argues that the administration of law was ineffective with the result that individuals resorted to self-help rather than to the petitioning of authorities for assistance (so also Hengel – see below).

Some of the parables of Jesus assume the use of a lease agreement as part of their social and economic background. In this respect particular attention needs to be paid to Matt.21.33-46 (et par.), the parable of the landlord who lets his vineyard to tenants and goes off to a far land. This parable in particular has played a central role in the discussion over the nature of the genre. Is it a parable or an allegory? Indeed, how are these figures of speech to be distinguished? A

---

100 In both Egypt and Palestine another method commonly used by the creditor to secure a debt was the mortgage or ὑποθήκη over the debtor's property, e.g. *P. Yadin* 11 dated AD 124. M. Gil, 'Land Ownership in Palestine under Roman Rule', *RIDA* 17 (1970), p.37, argues that for a loan to profit from *prozbol* it had to be secured by a mortgage. Be that as it may in the later period, it is clear from *DJD* II 18, a deed (dated AD 55 – 6) referring to the *prozbol* (though not by name) but not secured by a mortgage, that this was not necessarily the case in the earlier period.

working distinction will be assumed in the discussion which follows. Both the parable and the allegory have two (if not more) levels of meaning, i.e. their literal and metaphorical meanings. However, whereas the parable has a single point of contact between the two levels of meaning, the allegory has multiple points of contact between them. To illustrate the difference M. Lattke (per litt.) offers the following helpful diagram. I equate "Sache" with the story's metaphorical meaning and "Bild" with its literal meaning.

Diagram 13.1: Parable and Allegory

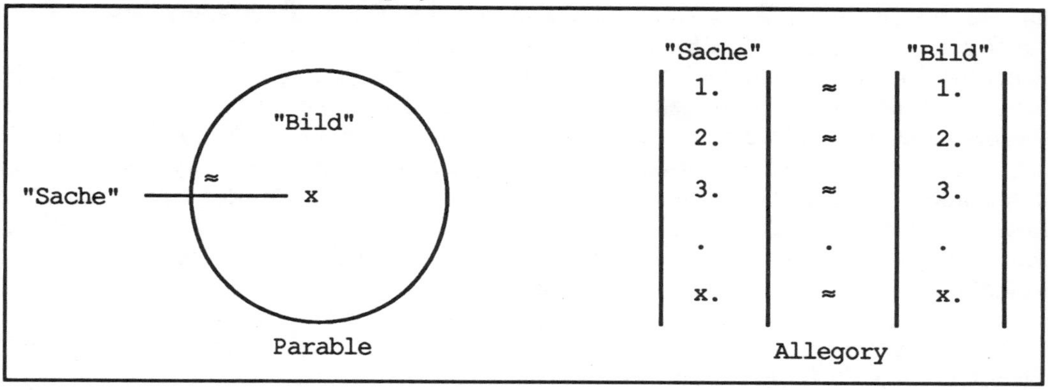

There is a danger in the analysis of parables and allegories which needs to be stated and thereby, one hopes, avoided. In parables there tends to be a single metaphorical meaning which determines the choice of the illustration as a whole. As a result the illustration can be drawn more readily from real events. In allegories the metaphorical meaning is more complex (i.e. it has multiple points of contact with the literal meaning) and thus cannot readily find a real event to provide an appropriate vehicle for itself. As a result the metaphorical meaning tends to tell the story, so to speak, and the illustration, though perhaps at its core an historically probable event, gathers around itself unrealistic details. However, it does not follow that all allegories have such unrealistic details nor that all parables are realistic. At most the presence of unrealistic details may permit one to assume the working hypothesis that the illustration is an allegory. However, the hypothesis must be tested against the evidence.

Through the ages the illustrations of Jesus had been interpreted predominantly as if they were allegories. However, A. Jülicher, *Die Gleichnisreden Jesu I – II* (Tübingen 1910 – reprinted Darmstadt 1969), C.H. Dodd, *The Parables of the Kingdom* (London 1935) and J. Jeremias, *The Parables of Jesus* (Trowbridge 1972) argued that such interpretations misconceive the true nature of Jesus' illustrations which, as they believed, concerned real-life situations both in their telling and in their content. Jeremias, ibid., pp.12-13, has observed:

> The hearers find themselves in a familiar scene where everything is so simple and clear that a child can understand, so plain that those who hear can say, 'Yes, that's how it is'.

In consequence, for Dodd, op.cit., p.10, the parables offered an opportunity to study everyday life under the Roman Empire in a way which was only second to the opportunity offered by the papyri of Egypt. Where allegory occurs in the gospel tradition it is understood by the above scholars as a later accretion to the tradition. As such the distinction between parable and allegory became a means to distinguish the genuine from what was not.

How does this distinction affect the parable of the wicked tenants? The problem is that the story appears to be an allegory, i.e. God = landlord; vineyard = Israel; tenants = the nation's leaders; the landlord's servants = the prophets; and the son = Jesus. Is the parable then genuine? For Dodd, op.cit., pp.96-102, some expansion of the parable has occurred, e.g. the series of servants sent to collect the rent and the testimonium at the end concerning the stone[101] that the builders rejected. Nevertheless, the basic outline of the story remains realistic. The story concerned an absent landlord[102] who sent his servants in season to collect the rent on the estate. After the servants' failure the owner sent his son, thinking that he would thereby gain their respect. However, the tenants rose up against the son and killed him. So the story goes. Is the extremity of the tenants' action against the son real to life? Dodd answers the question first in terms of the political climate of Palestine and a supposed association between agrarian discontent and nationalistic feelings, and second by virtue of an inner logic[103] in the story itself. In this Jeremias, op.cit., pp.70-77, also concurs. Dodd, accordingly, argues for a genuine core within the parable. But problems persist. Dodd fails to distinguish in a convincing manner the form of the parable from that of allegory. For example, he holds that the initial allusion to Isa.5.1-2 assists the audience to understand that the vineyard and its tenants represent Israel and its leaders respectively. Also Dodd's placing of the parable in the life context of Jesus' last days in Jerusalem and its supposed association with sayings foretelling his impending death further suggest that Jesus understood the son to be a representation of himself. In other words, the vineyard and persons of the parable have allegorical applications. Jeremias remedies the two problematic areas in Dodd's argument. First, the parable's opening allusion to Isa.5.1-2 is also considered to be part of a secondary allegorising activity. Second, the parable's application is located in Jesus' vindication of his message to the poor. In other words, the vineyard and persons of the parable represent themselves. The point of the parable is the exclusion of the former tenants and their replacement by new tenants.

Here a point of contact between this parable and the protection of the landlord's interests in a lease must be made. A major difficulty arises in Jeremias' interpretation of the parable within its *Sitz im Leben* in the ministry of Jesus and concerns the incongruity of the parable and its supposed function. If Jesus had intended the parable to deal with the exclusion of one social group and the inclusion of a new group, then a simple story of the failure of the tenants to meet their contracted duties to the landlord might have sufficed. We have noted above the provisions in the lease which secured the landlord against his tenant. The loading of the parable with added and complicating details gives the semblance of allegory. Indeed, the story is quite different from the simplistic description of the parable offered by Jeremias and quoted above. It implies an understanding of the complexity of politics and nationalistic feelings. Moreover, such forces may well interfere with the message itself, for it is not clear whether the audience would perceive the point of the parable if deprived of its allegorical elements, i.e. deprived of those elements which are supposed to have been added later. Indeed, if agrarian discontent and nationalism were widespread, would not the audience have sided with the tenants against their landlord? Also the import of the parable as a story to vindicate Jesus' mission to the poor would be confused by the audience, for the rich/poor distinction would be drawn between the landlord and his tenants rather than between the old and new tenants. It is not surpising then that in a later edition of his work Jeremias changed the parable's application so that it became a 'threat of judgement to the leaders of the people'.

More recently, K. Snodgrass, *The Parable of the Wicked Tenants* (Tübingen 1983), has questioned the dichotomy between parable and allegory and argued that Jesus could indeed have used allegory in his teaching. This permits him to reintegrate into the parable many of the

---

101 The testimonium only fits its present context in the parable if one assumes a play (in Hebrew) on the words stone (אבן) and son (בן).

102 Dodd assumed that the landlord was a foreigner, though ἀπεδήμησεν does not necessarily imply this.

103 C.H. Dodd and M. Hengel (see below) appeal to the parable's inner logic to explain some problematic facets of the narrative. What is thought to be unrealistic, they argue, does not arise from the story's metaphorical meaning but from its literal meaning and thus should not be used to show the presence of allegory. That judgement, however, must await a decision on the story's metaphorical meaning and how suited to this the narrative's alleged unrealistic facets are.

features which were considered by Dodd and Jeremias to be secondary, e.g. the allusion to Isa.5, the number of sendings in Matthew,[104] the saying about the stone rejected by the builders. For Snodgrass the parable occupies an early position in the gospel tradition and may well have been uttered by Jesus in his conflict with the Jewish leaders in Jerusalem. The allegorical connections are clear: the landlord of the vineyard is God; the vineyard represents the relationship between God and his people; the tenants are the Jewish leaders; the servants are the prophets; the son is Jesus himself. Like Jeremias' later interpretation the parable concerned the threat of judgement against the Jewish leadership. Despite accepting the parable as essentially allegorical Snodgrass maintains that its details are historically probable (see pp.31-40 in particular). He states: 'the events of the story were quite common and understandable in the early Palestinian culture'.

There are essentially three problematic areas in the parable which must be clarified or explained before it can be seen as historically probable. They are:

1. Given that a vineyard did not become productive before five years, it is unlikely that tenants would lease a newly planted vineyard.[105]
2. What can account for the tenants' behaviour towards the landlord's servants and their belief that they could get hold of the son's inheritance by killing him?
3. Why did the landlord continue to send his servants and later his son (Matt.21.37 et par.), when he knew the reception shown to the others? Were there no other remedies or courses of action available to him? Were there no other avenues of redress available to him?

To dismiss problems which centre on **1** above Snodgrass, ibid., pp.32-3, cites *P. Oxy.* XIV 1631 (third century AD), i.e. a deed which shows, according to his argument, that a landlord might lease his vineyard to tenants. *P. Oxy.* XLVII 3354 (AD 257) is a parallel example in the material culled for 1980/81. Unfortunately, the deeds are not leases but labour agreements which specify in detail the contractors' agricultural duties in regard to the vineyard. That this is so can be seen from the simple fact that wages are paid to the workers, i.e. rents are not collected from them. *P. Oxy.* XIV 1631, therefore, cannot properly be used to support any argument against **1** above. This is not to say that the leasing of a vineyard never occurred. For examples see J.D.M. Derrett, 'The Parable of the Wicked Vinedressers', *Law in the New Testament* (London 1970), pp.293-4 n.4. What is of interest and future relevance is the fact that leasing was not the only avenue whereby the owner might cultivate the vineyard.

In addressing the problem areas **2** and **3** Snodgrass rests substantially on Derrett, op.cit., pp.286-312 and M. Hengel, 'Das Gleichnis von den Weingärtnern Mc 12 1-12 im Lichte der Zenonpapyri und der rabbinischen Gleichnisse', *ZNW* 59 (1968), pp.1-39. Derrett seeks to show that 'the behaviour of all parties is reasonable and human' (p.288). Taking note of the fact that for the first few years there was little return on a vineyard, he interprets each sending as an annual event which coincides with the harvest. However, as the cost of cultivation, which fell in part to the landlord to pay (see the lease agreement above), was greater than the estate's income, for the first three years the tenants turned the servants away taking what possessions they had as both payment for and security against what they were owed by the landlord (p.297). This not only set a rebellious precedent but in view of the law of *ḥazaqah* (חזקה) led the tenants to believe that a claim to ownership of the estate might lie by virtue of their unhindered possession of it.[106] The arrival of the landlord's son signalled to the tenants that he

[104] Snodgrass considers Matthew's version of the parable to be the earliest.

[105] The sequence of aorists joined by paratactic καί in Mark 12.1 suggest that the vineyard was leased soon after its planting. Moreover, the various arguments in support of the historical reality of the parable (see especially Derrett's argument below) rest on the assumption that the vineyard was new.

[106] E. Bammel, 'Das Gleichnis von den bösen Winzern (Mk 12, 1-9) und das jüdische Erbrecht', *RIDA* 6 (1959), pp.11-17, had previously drawn attention to the relevance of the law of *ḥazaqah* for understanding the parable. See the discussion of his argument in *New Docs* 6 (1992) §4. According to *m. Qid.* 1.5, immovable property (i.e.

had become the vineyard's owner[107] and was about to instigate a claim against them (the servants/slaves being legally incapable). They resolved to kill him so that their possession might proceed unhindered.

There is an initial difficulty with such an argument, for insofar as it seeks to account for the behaviour of the landlord (3) and his tenants (2), it also makes the leasing of the vineyard (1) more problematic. For example, in support of the argument that a landlord faced problems if he let his vineyard before it was redeemed, Derrett (p.301) cites *m. Soṭa* 8.2 and 4 which concern the exemption of such owners from military service. Equally, it shows the improbability that the owner of a new vineyard would lease it before it was redeemed. Moreover, there are inherent commercial problems with the proposed leasing arrangement. Why would a landlord lease a vineyard and the tenants accept the lease when the property was not commercially viable for some years? Such a lease would amount to economic nonsense.[108] Would it not be more feasible to enter into a labour contract (cf. *m. B. Meṣ.* 9.11) thereby not relinquishing possession for a set period and incurring the possible and no doubt also foreseen risk? When the vineyard became economically viable, then, and not before, would a lease be entered into. The papyrological evidence seems to support this suggestion (see the discussion on *P. Köln* III 144 at *New Docs* 6 [1992] §24).

Derrett's account of the tenants' behaviour remains difficult to comprehend and highlights a problem faced by any argument which seeks to explain a parable's difficulties by an appeal to the characters' motives. Intentions are hard to prove and disprove. This is made more complicated when the beliefs which underlie the action, as in the case of the tenants, are fanciful. How can one argue against an intentional reconstruction, for any problem with it can be ascribed to a misdirected belief? Even so, an attempt to highlight the problems must be made. According to Derrett, the tenants must assume that the landlord would take no other step to rectify the situation than the annual sending of the servant. Is this likely? Would the owner not petition the authorities both to investigate his claim (both regarding the non-payment of rent and the treatment of his servants) and to take the necessary action (see *y. B. Bat.* 3.3 on such complaints and their effect on usucaption). Regardless of what action the local officials took, the complaint itself proved that the landlord had neither disappeared (see לא נשתקעו הבעלים – 'the owners had not disappeared', *y. Kil.*7.4) nor forsaken his property. In other words, *ḥazaqah* would not apply (see *m. B. Bat.* 3.2 and *b. B. Bat.* 35b). Similarly, the landlord's holding of a duly signed lease agreement[109] would equally preclude the tenants' claim, for the tenant was expressly excluded from acquisition by *ḥazaqah* under such circumstances (*m. B. Bat.* 3.3 and *y. B. Bat.* 3.5). The tenants' claim to ownership could only be valid if the lease agreement never came to light and they alleged that a sale or gift had occurred or that the property had been pledged for a debt.[110] However, the landlord's continued interest in the

houses, land and slaves) could be acquired by money (i.e. sale), by written deed (i.e. a gift or a division of an inheritance) or by *ḥazaqah* (i.e. the seizure of abandoned property or the property of a proselyte who died without heirs – see further *t. Ket.* 4.16, *m. B. Bat.* 3.3, 4.9).

107 In rabbinic law only a person with an interest in the estate could initiate a legal action concerning it. It is thus assumed that the owner had given his son the vineyard as a gift 'from today and after death' – see *New Docs* 6 (1992) §4 and §5 for a discussion of gifts in contemplation of death.

108 The commercial sense of the lease agreement will depend on other factors such as the overall length of the tenancy (i.e. a longer lease would permit the tenant to recoup his losses) and the stringency of the requirement that the landlord take an annual rent. However, it is in both these areas that difficulties arise.

109 See *m. B. Bat.* 10.4, *P. Muraba'at* 24, Z.W. Falk, *Introduction to Jewish Law of the Second Commonwealth* vol.II (Leiden 1978), pp.220-4, and the above discussion on clauses in Palestinian lease agreements; Derrett, p.294, also assumes that a written deed would have been in existence. It is of interest to note that in Judaea loan agreements were registered, no doubt as written deeds, in the Jerusalem records office (Josephus, *BJ* 2.427 [AD 66]; cf. also *BJ* 6.354, 7.61).

110 The concept of sale includes the acquisition (in case of default) of an item pledged by a loan or mortgage agreement. It might be suggested that the tenants alleged that they were the absent owner's creditors and that they

property as witnessed by his sending of the servants to collect the rent weighed against such a course of action by the tenants, for the deed or witnesses might be produced at any time to refute the claim. It might be replied that the tenants acted from a mistaken belief of what was legally and practically feasible. Indeed this is possible but then the reconstruction becomes impossible to refute historically.

This last point brings us to another difficulty in Derrett's argument. From reading his account one would think that rabbinic law actually served the person who acted with fraudulent intent.[111] This is not the case. The law of *ḥazaqah*, as Gil, op.cit., p.14, describes it, 'expresses the aspiration to reach a legal recognition of a real circumstance. It is apparently the striving to insure the victory of common sense and of public interest over sanctified rights'. There is also another difficulty. The Mishnah was itself a compilation of earlier rulings and opinions at various stages of development. However, it is not always possible to know the details or form of a particular ruling at any one point in time. The law of *ḥazaqah* is a case in point. The legal concept went through stages of development.[112] At first it indicated the act of possessing either by drawing/taking in the case of movable property or by the enjoyment of the produce in the case of immovable property. According to *m. B. Bat.* 3.3, the usurper (unless an heir) needed to enter a plea that the property was either sold or given to him (see also *y. B. Bat.* 3.3). There is no mention of a three-year period. Indeed, *m. Ket.* 2.2 assumes that the usurper's claim was overturned if disproved by witnesses. This teaching is ascribed to R. Joshua, a second-generation teacher (AD 80 – 120). Here, then, ownership was established by a plea until refuted. According to *m. B. Bat.* 3.1, a period of three years of uninterrupted possession established ownership; there is no mention of entering a plea. The definition as to what constitutes the three-year period is ascribed to R. Ishmael and R. Akiba, third-generation teachers (AD 120 – 140). The two concepts of *ḥazaqah* appear somewhat inconsistent, i.e. the need to enter a plea which was subject to falsification by witnesses is not consistent with the view that mere uninterrupted possession for a defined period was sufficient. According to *m. B. Bat.* 3.2, R. Judah, a fourth-generation teacher (AD 140 – 165), argued that the three-year period applied only if the owner lived at some distance from his property. His view was not accepted. Instead, in the case where the owner did not live in the same province as the property the law of *ḥazaqah* did not apply. Some rabbis, however, tried to confine this rule to times of upheaval only (*y. B. Bat.* 3.3). The above discussion is sufficient to illustrate that the law of *ḥazaqah* went through various stages of development in the first and second centuries AD. However, it is not possible to know with any certainty the particular form it took in the earlier

---

had been given the vineyard as security. As such, they were entitled to enjoy its fruit in lieu of interest. Also if the debt was not repaid, they could acquire possession of it (see *m. B. Meṣ.* 5.3). The difficulty with this suggestion is that there was no deed of loan upon which to base the claim. Indeed, the opposite was the case. The landlord had in his possession a deed which proved that they were tenants.

111 For example, the citing of *m. Ket.* 13.7 might mislead the reader – 'If a man goes overseas even the path leading to his field *may* be annexed by an adjoining owner and, not knowing which or how to recover it, he may have his choice between buying another right of way or "flying through the air" to get to his field'. The use of 'may' seems to imply permission within the context of Derrett's discussion. But this is surely not its meaning at *m. Ket.* 13.7. The reason for the ruling is that the path was lost (note there is no question here of a three-year period) and the former owner no longer knew who had actually committed the illegal act. The dispute between Admon and the Sages at *m. Ket.* 13.7 cannot be used as an example of the law of *ḥazaqah* in the pre-tannaitic period (i.e. before AD 10).

112 The consensus of opinion dates the law of *ḥazaqah* as relatively late. Gil, op.cit., p.16, argues that it was a product of Graeco-Roman influence and consequently a 'late concept in the Jewish legal tradition'. Also S. Freyne, *Galilee from Alexander the Great to Hadrian 323 BCE to 135 CE* (Delaware 1980), pp.168-9, alleges that the law of *ḥazaqah*, like the law of confiscation (סיקריקון), first occurred in the period of Roman *dominium* when the Jewish law yielded to the imperial pressure to recognise use rather than absolute ownership. Z.W. Falk, op.cit., pp.246-7, states that the law 'perhaps dates from a later stage of the halakah', though it 'certainly antedates the destruction'. See further *m. Git.* 5.6, *t. Git.* 5.1 and *m. Kil.* 7.6.

half of the first century in Galilee. Indeed, to use the law's developed form in an attempt to understand Jesus' parable runs the risk of being anachronistic. A similar risk also arises with the use of rabbinic parables, which derive from the later period, to illustrate the function of the law of *ḥazaqah* in Galilee at the time of Jesus.

The use of the law's developed form has affected Derrett's interpretation of the parable, especially where the issue of ownership after three (or four) years of uninterrrupted possession is concerned. The evidence for this legal condition depends on the understanding that each sending was an annual event; however, this interpretation of the parable hangs on the slenderest of threads. It is argued that 'πάλιν ("again" at Mark 12.4) suggests a repetition in circumstances closely resembling the first, i.e. on the next appropriate occasion (καιρῷ), in other words, the next year' (p.298). It should be noted that πάλιν is only used by Mark for the second sending of a servant. The third sending, which Derrett also assumes to have been on the next appropriate occasion (καιρῷ), is narrated without it: καὶ ἄλλον ἀπέστειλεν (Mark 12.5). The argument, I suggest, is suspect in other ways as well. The adverb πάλιν marks a repetition of the action but not necessarily its attendant circumstances. Consider for example John 10.17: τίθημι τὴν ψυχήν μου, ἵνα πάλιν λάβω – I am laying down my life, that I may take (it up) again. Clearly, the use of πάλιν here does not imply a repetition in circumstances! Why then should the second sending in the parable imply a repetition in circumstances? Moreover, there is no indication that the original hearers would so understand the parable, though here one would need to have recourse to the parable's Aramaic *Vorlage*. The natural assumption is that the landlord would make a second attempt to collect his rent immediately upon hearing of the tenants' refusal.

The above difficulties relating to the dating of the law of *ḥazaqah* do not necessarily rule out the possibility that a tenant might seek to take illegal possession of his landlord's estate. It only means that the developed form of the law cannot properly (i.e. without appropriate qualification) be used to understand the attempt. The parable of the wicked tenants may thus still have an historical core. Indeed, the papyri show that attempts to acquire illegal possession were not confined to Palestine. For example, *P. Oxy*. XLIX 3464 (dated AD 54-60) is an application for summons against certain persons who had formerly taken illegal possession of a vineyard and who were now again attempting to do the same. Clearly, the issues of disputed ownership and illegal possession are not confined to any one time or place. Here also a *logion* of Jesus, which seems to allude to illegal possession (though in a religious rather than commercial sense), proves of interest:

> ἀπὸ δὲ τῶν ἡμερῶν Ἰωάννου τοῦ βαπτιστοῦ ἕως ἄρτι ἡ βασιλεία τῶν οὐρανῶν βιάζεται, καὶ βιασταὶ ἁρπάζουσιν αὐτήν. (Matt.11.12)

The use of βιαζόμενος (middle participle) in *SB* V 8033 *l*.15 (*circa* 165-158 BC) and *P. Tebt*. I 6 *ll*.31-32 (140 – 39 BC) to denote illegal possession or usucaption of immovable property suggests a plausible meaning for the same verb (passive) at Matt.11.12.[113] The paratactic extension of the verse (i.e. καὶ βιασταὶ ἁρπάζουσιν αὐτήν) further confirms this meaning.

Hengel, op.cit., seeks to show that the parable would not sound improbable when judged by the standards and expectations of its ancient hearers. He places the parable in a Galilean context where foreign ownership of land was extensive and where the estates of absentee landlords were let to tenant farmers. The absence of a landlord was bound to cause problems, and as evidence Hengel cites rabbinic parables (p.23). Of particular interest is the proposition that the landlord invariably had to resort to self-help in order to remedy a contractual failure. Starting from the parable of the widow and unjust judge (Luke 18.1-8), Hengel observes the reluctance of the authorities to intervene. How much more so, he argues, when the plaintiff was

113 See also Taubenschlag, *Law*, p.446 n.82, for βία 'directed against immovables'.

but one individual who lived afar off and the defendants were numerous and a politically volatile group. Authority would naturally choose the way of least resistance (p.26) and refrain from intervention as far as possible. Hengel cites the Zenon papyri, *P. Cair. Zen. I* 59018 and *P. Cair. Zen.* I 59015 (mistakenly cited as *P. Cair. Zen.* I 50915 by both Hengel and Snodgrass), which concern two separate instances to illustrate his point. To explain the sending of the son, however, Hengel appeals to Dodd's argument based on the parable's inner logic (pp.30, 32). It may appear unusual to the hearer but not without sense given the legal context of disputed ownership. Here Hengel appeals to Derrett's arguments as outlined above. The feasibility of the argument rests on the choice of starting point (for Hengel the parable of the widow and unjust judge) and the interpretation of the papyri. But another construction can be placed on the evidence. The following *logion* could instead be chosen as the point of departure:

> ἴσθι εὐνοῶν τῷ ἀντιδίκῳ σου ταχὺ, ἕως ὅτου εἶ μετ' αὐτοῦ ἐν τῇ ὁδῷ, μήποτέ σε παραδῷ ὁ ἀντίδικος τῷ κριτῇ καὶ ὁ κριτὴς τῷ ὑπηρέτῃ καὶ εἰς φυλακὴν βληθήσῃ· ἀμὴν λέγω σοι, οὐ μὴ ἐξέλθῃς ἐκεῖθεν, ἕως ἂν ἀποδῷς τὸν ἔσχατον κοδράντην.
>
> (Matt.5.25-26; cf. Luke 12.58-59)

The parable assumes an effective administration which intervenes to assist the aggrieved party of a private contract. The defaulter is placed in the debtor's prison as a means to enforce payment – so also Matt.18.30. For a further discussion of the liability to personal execution in first-century Palestine based on a study of the available evidence see R.S. de Franch, *Études sur le droit palestinien à l'époque évangélique* (Fribourg 1946). The parable of the widow and judge may be explained as an instance of an unjust and corrupt official who disregarded the petitions of the poor. That such officials existed cannot be denied.[114] However, as the practice of petitioning in Ptolemaic and early Roman Egypt shows (see the discussion in *New Docs* 6 [1992] **§18**), the administration was perceived to be interested in the rights of the petitioner.[115] This would not have been so if it regularly disregarded its petitioners. Indeed, orderly government required officials to take an interest in all matters which had the potential to disturb civil order – cf. Schalit, op.cit., pp.223 ff., and his discussion of Herod's use of slavery to deal with the problem of brigandage (Josephus, *AJ* 16.1.1). Herod Antipas was no different; he ruled Galilee by the grace of Rome and would naturally seek to guard against any practice which was likely to lead to social unrest. Here also Josephus' administrative policy on his assumption of the control of Galilee is informative; he appointed seven magistrates for each town and a central body of seventy ἄρχοντες to decide more important and capital cases (*BJ* 2.571). The orderly government of Galilee required a system of justice which was able to decide disputed matters and then to enforce its decisions. Moreover, in terms of the parable of the wicked tenants it must be borne in mind that the landlord of the vineyard, unlike the widow, possessed a higher social status which meant that even a corrupt official would be more likely

---

114 D.J. Crawford, 'The good official in Ptolemaic Egypt', *Das ptolemäische Ägypten* (Mainz am Rhein 1978) pp.195-202, suggests two reasons for official corruption in Ptolemaic Egypt. They were: a) the expectations within personal relationships, e.g. favours and benefits granted to friends and relatives; and b) the fact that positions were not salaried. However, any study into the extent of official corruption faces a difficulty, namely a bias within the evidence. Petitioners were much more likely to write about official corruption than about an experience of official fairness! Such was the nature of petitions.

115 The evidence for the use of self-help in Graeco-Roman Egypt is ambiguous, cf. R. Taubenschlag, 'Selfhelp in Greco-Roman Egypt', *Opera Minora* (Warsaw 1959), pp.135-41. It was permitted in some areas (e.g. the apprehension of a slave, the expulsion of a wife, a parent's taking of his/her child, a parent's dissolution of his/her daughter's marriage etc.) but illegal in others (e.g. the creditor's right to imprison his/her debtor). Apart from the question of the legality of self-help, the establishment of judicial mechanisms to settle contractual disputes and the evidence for the resort to administrative authorities and courts of law by parties to such contracts indicate its declining significance.

to attend to his petition. From this starting point the evidence of the Zenon papyri may be construed quite differently.

Palestine — c.5th April 258 BC

Ed. – C.C.Edgar, *P. Cair. Zen.* I 59018 (Cairo 1925 – reprinted Hildesheim 1971), p.38.

	[Ἀλέξαν]δρος Ὀρύαι χαίρειν. ἐκομισάμην τὸ παρὰ σ[οῦ] ἐ]π̣ιστόλι[ον],	[Alexan]dros to Oryas greeting. I received the letter from you
	[ἐν ὧι ὑ]π̣έγρ[α]ψάς μοι τήν τε παρὰ Ζ̣ήνωνος πρὸς Ἰεδδοῦν γεγρ[αμμένην],	[in which] you copied for me also the letter from Zenon to Jeddous,
	[ὅπως ἂν], ἐὰμ μὴ ἀποδιδῶι τἀργ[ύ]ρ̣ιον Στράτω̣νι τῶι παρὰ Ζήνωνος [πα]-	[that] if he did not repay the money to Straton, Zenon's [representative],
4	[ραγενο]μένωι, ἐνέχυρα αὐτοῦ π̣[αραδ]ε̣ίξωμεν αὐτῶι. ἐγὼ μὲν [ο]ὖ̣ν	we might assign his pledges to him. Now I
	[ἄρρωστ]ος ἐτύγχανον ἐ[[χ]]$^{\kappa}$ φαρμακείας ὤν, συναπέστειλα̣ [δὲ Στ]ράτωνι	happened to be [ill] from medicine, [but] sent along with Straton
	[παρ' ἡ]μῶν νεανίσκον καὶ ἐπιστολὴν ἔγρ[α]ψ̣α πρὸς Ἰεδδοῦν. παραγενόμενοι	one of our servants and wrote a letter to Jeddous. Returning,
	[οὖν εἶπ]όν μοι μηθένα λόγον πεποιῆσθαι τῶι ἐπιστο[λίωι μου], αὐτοῖς δὲ	[then], they told me that he took no account of [my] letter, but
8	[χεῖρας] προσενεγκεῖν καὶ ἐγβα̣λ̣[εῖ]ν ἐκ τῆς κώμης. γέγραφα ο̣ὖ̣ν σοι.	laid [hands] on them and threw (them) from the village. Wherefore I have written to you.
	ἔρρωσο. L κ̄ζ̄, Περιτίου ἐμβολίμου κ̄.	Farewell. Year 27, Peritios intercalary 20.
	(Back) Ὀρύαι.	To Oryas.

The reconstruction of the letter indicates that Zenon had sent an underling, Straton, with a letter to Oryas, an official in Palestine, asking him to assist in procuring money or pledges from Jeddous, a local Jewish 'sheikh'.[116] Oryas properly referred the request to the local official Alexandros. The latter, claiming to be unwell, did not expedite the request himself but sent a νεανίσκος (slave?) with a letter to accompany Straton. Jeddous took no account of the letter. Instead he assaulted the νεανίσκος and Straton and drove them out of the village. It may be suspected that Jeddous' act was prompted by an attempt made by the others to seize pledges against him.[117] *P. Cair. Zen.* I 59018 is Alexandros' letter to Oryas relating his actions and

---

116 So *CPJ* 6 and C. Orrieux, *Les papyrus de Zenon* (Paris 1983), p.48. S. Freyne, op.cit., pp.29, 156-7, compares Jeddous with the Tobias met in other Zenon papyri and suggests that the Ptolemaic government probably relied on the compliance of such people to administer the territory.

117 Orrieux, op.cit., p.48, suggests another interpretation. He surmises that Jeddous was offended by the rank of the persons sent to deal with him.

Jeddous' response to his letter. Much has been made of the fact that Alexandros did not expedite the matter himself but pleaded ill-health and sent the νεανίσκος in his stead. In view of Jeddous' response it is assumed that the local official did not want to get personally involved. It has also been suggested that by the expression γέγραφα οὖν σοι – 'therefore I have written to you' – Alexandros declined further responsibility. Both are matters of interpretation. The fact that this letter found its way into Zenon's archive suggests that Straton actually brought it back to Egypt when he returned. There is, however, no reason to suspect that Straton questioned Alexandros' excuse. Indeed, he was on hand to refute it or at least cast doubt upon it. Even so Alexandros did act. The emphasis of *P. Cair. Zen.* I 59018 falls on Alexandros' letter to Jeddous rather than on his sending of the νεανίσκος. It is the letter bearing Alexandros' name and authority which Jeddous disregards. No doubt it was in Alexandros' interest to emphasise in this letter to his superior the measures which he had undertaken. Even so, it is difficult to see how one can argue that Alexandros avoided involvement. Also the lack of information concerning the contents of Oryas' letter to Alexandros, the resources immediately available to the local official and the eventual outcome of the dispute make it difficult to offer a decisive interpretation of the letter. Perhaps Alexandros had no personnel on hand to enforce execution and Oryas, aware of this, asked to be informed of any difficulties. If so, on being informed of Jeddous' response Oryas may have arranged for a bailiff (no doubt accompanied) to be sent to enforce execution. The risk inherent in any attempt to establish a more general administrative practice on the basis of one official's actions may also be highlighted. Even allowing that Alexandros feigned sickness and wished to avoid Jeddous' wrath, we cannot conclude that the majority of officials acted in this way. On the contrary *P. Cair. Zen.* I 59018 shows that Zenon believed and trusted that the administration of Palestine was both willing and able to expedite his request. Nor should it be assumed that intimidation by a powerful local figure was confined to Palestine. For example, *P. Fouad* 26 (AD 157 – 159) shows a similar problem with intimidation in Egypt. However, the petitioner here did not perceive the problem to be insurmountable for he sought the assistance of a higher authority for a trial elsewhere. No doubt in the case of *P. Cair. Zen.* I 59018, if Alexandros failed, there were other official avenues available to Zenon to realise his request.

Alexandria
259 – 258 BC
Ed. – C.C.Edgar, *P. Cair. Zen.* I 59015 verso (Cairo 1925 – reprinted Hildesheim 1971), pp.34-36.

The writer's corrections to the letter, which appear above *ll.* 4, 10, 12, 18, 19, 23 and 33, have been incorporated into the following text. The still visible text which they replace has been omitted.

Column I

Πασικλεῖ. εἰ ἔρρωσαι, καλῶς ἂν ἔχοι· ὑγιαίνομεν δὲ	To Pasikles. If you are well, it is good. We are in good health
καὶ αὐτοί. ἀνήγγελλέν μοι Κρότος γεγραφέναι σε αὐτῶι	also. Krotos has told me that you wrote to him
ὅτι οἱ παῖδες οἱ ἀποδράντες μηνυτρίζοιντο	that the runaway slaves are reported
εἶναι παρὰ τῶι Κολλοχούτωι καὶ τῶι Ζαιδήλωι τῶι ἀδελφῶι	to be with Kollochoutos and his brother Zaidelos
καὶ αἰτοίησαν [[μνᾶν]], ἐφ' ὧι ἀνάξουσιν, ἀργυρίου (δραχμὰς) ρ̄.	and that they have demanded 100 silver drachmae for returning (them).
καλῶς ἂν οὖν ποιήσαις τὴμ πᾶσαν σπουδὴν	Therefore, kindly make all haste

ποιησάμενος τοῦ συλληφθῆναι αὐτοὺς	to apprehend them
⟦ἵνα καὶ ο̣ι̣α̣. . ο̣ι̣⟧ καὶ παραδ̣ο̣ὺς Στράτωνι	and hand (them) over to Straton
τῶι κομίζοντί σοι τὸ ἐπιστόλιον. τοῦτο γὰρ	who is bringing you this letter. For
ποιήσας εὐχαριστήσ[εις ἡμῖν.] ὃ δ' ἂν ἀνηλώσηις	by doing this you will gratify [us]. Whatever you spend,
[δώσ]ομεν. πεπραμέ[νη δ' ἐστὶν ἀλ]α̣βαστροθήκη	we [will pay] (you). The alabaster chest has been bought
[. . . . .]σ̣αι· εἰ δὲ μὴ [βούλει,] ἐπίστειλον.	[...] If you do not [want] (it), write.
[ὁ δὲ πρ]ι̣[ά]μ̣ενος ἀποδώσει. [καὶ σὺ δὲ ἐάν τινος]	[The purchaser] will give (you it). [And if you]
[χ]ρείαν ἔχη[ις] τῶν ἐν τ[ῆι χώραι, γράφε ἡ]μῖν·	have need [of anything] in [the *chora*, write] to us,
π̣οιήσομεν γὰρ φιλικῶ[ς]. ἔρρ[ω]σο.	for we will oblige (you) as a friend. Farewell.
Ἐπικράτει. ἐπιδημήσαντες ἐμ Μαρίσηι ἐπρ̣[ιάμεθα]	To Epikrates. Whilst staying at Marise we bought
ἐκ τῶν Ζαιδήλου σώματα, ⟦[ὧν ἀποδεδρά̣[κασιν] ⟧	slaves from the (stock) of Zaidelos.
⟦[ἀδελ⟧ ἡμῶν δ' εἰς Αἴγυπτον εἰσπορευομέ̣[νων]	Whilst we were returning to Egypt
ἀπέδρασαν [α]ὐ̣τ̣ῶ̣ν̣ παῖδες γ̄, τούτων ἀ̣δελφο̣ὶ δύο, ⟦[οἳ ὀνομα⟧ ὧν [τὰ ὀνόματα]	3 of the slaves, of whom two are brothers, ran away, whose names
καὶ τὰς εἰκόνας ὑ̣π̣ο̣γέγραφά σοι. προσήγγ[ελται δὲ]	and characteristics I have written below for you. It is reported
ἡμῖ̣ν̣ ε̣ἶ̣να̣ι̣ τ̣[ούτους παρ]ὰ Κολλοχούτωι τ̣. . [	to us that [they] are [with] Kollochoutos [...]
καλ̣[ῶς ἂν οὖν ποιήσαις τὴμ π]ᾶσαν σπουδὴν π[οιησάμενος]	Kindly [make] all haste
[τοῦ συλληφθῆναι αὐτο]ὺ̣ς καὶ παραδοὺς [Στράτωνι.]	[to apprehend them] and hand (them) over [to Straton.]
[ὃ δ' ἂν ἀνηλώσηις τοῖς ἀ]ναγαγοῦσιν α .. [ ]	[Whatever you spend on those] returning [...]
[ ]υ̣. . ι̣αι τουτ̣[ ]	[...]
Column II	
Πεσιστράτωι. εἰ ἔρρωσαι, καλῶς ἂν ἔχοι· ὑγιαίνομεν δὲ	To Peisistratos. If you are well, it is good. We are in good health
καὶ αὐτοί. ἀνήγγελλεν ἡμῖν Κρότος γεγραφέναι	also. Krotos has told us that Pasikles wrote
Πασικλῆν μηνυτρίζεσθαι τοὺς ἀποδράντας	to report the runaway

παῖδας [[τ̣]] ὧν ἐπριάμεθα [[π̣α̣ρὰ]] ἐμ Μαρίζηι	slaves which we bought in Marise
τῶν Ζαιδήλου. γεγράφαμεν οὖ‹ν› ἀξιοῦντες	of the (stock) of Zaidelos. Therefore we have written asking (him)
τὴμ πᾶσαν ἐπιμέλειαν ποιήσασθαι	to take all care
ὅπως ἂν συλληφθῶσιν καὶ παραδῶι αὐτοὺς	that they be apprehended and he (i.e. Pasikles) hand them over
Στράτωνι τῶι τὰς ἐπιστολ[[η]]ὰς ὑμῖν	to Straton who is bringing the letters
κομίζοντι. διὸ καὶ σὺ καλῶς ἂν ποιοῖς	to you. Wherefore, do you also kindly
ὑπομιμνήσκων τε αὐτὸν καὶ συνσπουδάσ‹ας›	remind him and lend assistance
ὅπως μὴ διαφύγωσιν [[οἱ παῖδες]]. καὶ σὺ δὲ εὐχαρισ-	that they may not escape. Also you will gratify
τήσεις ἡμῖν γράφων, [[τίνων]] ἐάν τι βούληι τῶν	us by writing, if you want anything
ἀπὸ τῆς χώρας· φιλικῶς γάρ σοι ποιήσομεν.	from the *chora*, for we will oblige you as a friend.
ἔρρωσο.	Farewell.
Ἐπαινέτωι. παῖδές [[ἡμῖν]] τινες τ[υγχά]ν̣ουσιν	To Epainetos. Some slaves happen
ἀποκεχωρ̣ηκότες ἡμῶν, οἳ προσηγγελ̣μ̣έ̣ν̣ο̣ι̣ εἰσὶν	to have run away from us, who are reported
ἐν τῆι Ἰδ[ο]υ̣μαίαι. ἀπεστάλκαμεν δὲ ἐπ' αὐτὸ	to be in Idoumaia. We have sent Straton to attend to this.
Στράτωνα. καλῶς ἂν οὖν ποιήσαις σ[υ]ντάξας τῶι υἱ‹ῶι›	Therefore, kindly order your son
μὴ ἐνοχλεῖν αὐτὸν τὰ κατὰ τὰς λειτουργίας, ὅπως συν̣λάβηι τοὺς παῖδας.	not to trouble him with any liturgy, that he may apprehend the slaves.
Ἄμμωνι. τὴν αὐτήν.	To Ammon. The same.
[[ὅπως Δωροθέωι καὶ Δημαινέτωι]]	
καλῶς ἂν οὖν ποιήσαις γράψας Δωρ[ο]θέωι καὶ Δημαινέτωι	Kindly write to Dorotheos and Demainetos
ὅπως μὴ ἐνοχλῆται τὰ κατὰ τὰς λειτουργίας.	that he not be troubled with any liturgy.

The papyrus is a draft of five letters to be written to officials in Palestine over the matter of some runaway slaves. Whilst in Palestine Zenon had purchased some slaves but on the journey to Egypt three of them had escaped and returned to Kollochoutos and his brother Zaidelos, from whom they had been purchased. Pasikles, one of the local officials to whom Zenon wrote, had informed Krotos, Zenon's agent, of their whereabouts and he in turn had informed Zenon. Kollochoutos and Zaidelos demanded 100 drachmae possibly as the cost of recovery (contra Hengel, op.cit., p.27, who holds this sum to be a renewed purchase price). In one sitting Zenon now wrote to five officials in order that they might assist in the regaining of the runaways. The letters thus present a special case of self-help, for Zenon wrote to officials who were personally known to him and of whom he could ask a favour. As a rule self-help was also the first step taken by the creditor or injured party in Graeco-Roman Egypt to recover any loss or damage (see above).

Zenon wrote one letter to Pasikles, who in the first place was the source of information concerning the slaves' whereabouts, and another to Epikrates asking them to seize the slaves and turn them over to Straton, any expenses being met by Zenon. A third letter was written to Peisistratos asking him to remind and assist Pasikles so that the slaves may not escape. Two other letters were written to the officials, Epainetos and Ammon, requesting that Dorotheos, Demainetos and the son of Epainetos (if another person), no doubt local officials, not hinder the task by imposing liturgies on Straton. The latter letters are of interest because they seem to imply that the administrative system, or at least that aspect of the administrative system which was concerned with forced labour or service, operated effectively, a fact which Zenon had to anticipate if he wished to regain the slaves. Moreover, Zenon trusted that he could use his official acquaintances to expedite the request. This trust may not have been misplaced for the slaves were regained. Hengel suggests that Zenon paid the one hundred drachmae; however, lack of information about the method by which the slaves were regained makes any certainty on this point difficult. Nor should it be thought that Zenon pleaded with the officials in the same manner as the widow of Lk 18. It must be borne in mind that all five letters were sent at the same time and not consecutively in response to refusals. This can be attributed to a desire to expedite the matter and may not in itself reflect any assumed inadequacy in the officials. Indeed, the action is easily explicable if one accepts Orrieux's suggestion (op.cit., pp.48-9) that Kollochoutos and Zaidelos were nomads living on the borders of the Ptolemaic territories. Zenon, no doubt, appreciated the difficulty of recovering the lost slaves and accordingly sought the help of several contacts and friends. Nor should it be thought that Zenon, like the widow in the parable, pleaded with his correspondents. Rather, the requests are made by way of the polite, though forceful, command καλῶς ἂν ποιήσαις – 'kindly see that'.

The only possible confirmation for Hengel's interpretation is found in the letter to Peisistratos where Zenon asks him to remind and assist Pasikles. But again this may be interpreted differently. Zenon knew his correspondents. We have already noted that Pasikles had informed Zenon's agent of the slaves' whereabouts. Moreover, in the concluding lines of the letter to Pasikles Zenon informed him that the alabaster chest (?) had been bought and that if he did not want it, he should write. Zenon also asked whether there was anything else he would like, indicating that he would oblige him as a friend – ποιήσομεν γὰρ φιλικῶ[ς]. In all probability Zenon's letter to Peisistratos was not prompted by any doubt regarding the operation of the administrative system generally but by his knowledge of Pasikles' character. After all, the correspondence was not an official petition but a personal letter addressed to an official whom Zenon knew and of whom he could ask a favour. It is also to be noted that in the same letter to Peisistratos no request is made that he remind Epikrates as well. This further suggests that Zenon's request was motivated by a personal knowledge of Pasikles' character. As such, this letter (as do all the other letters) offers more information on the nature and use of friendship than on the administration of the province.

A final query of a more general character needs also to be raised. It has been observed above that the use of rabbinic parables and *halakoth* to interpret Jesus' parables poses the risk of anachronism. Later traditions cannot be used to explain the parable of the wicked tenants without justification and supporting argument. A similar unease should also be felt when earlier documents are used to illustrate the parable's historical context. The Zenon papyri predate the parable of the wicked tenants by almost three hundred years. In the intervening period governments and empires had come and gone; political institutions, legal systems and religious beliefs had evolved. As a result it is difficult to establish a degree of continuity sufficient to justify the use of the Zenon papyri. The effectiveness of the legal system of first-century Galilee must be determined by whatever surviving evidence there is for the period, i.e. the NT, Josephus and the few pieces of documentary evidence.

The discussion has shown that the attempt to explain the behaviour of either the landlord or his tenants by rabbinic or papyrological evidence faces difficulties. The particular conditions which applied to the law of *ḥazaqah* and their operation in early first-century Galilee are uncertain. The Zenon papyri offer neither a contemporaneous nor unambiguous picture of the administrative situation in Palestine. The papyrological evidence itself suggests that new vineyards were worked by contract labour rather than leased to tenants. It follows that there are features in the story which appear improbable and unrealistic. This is not to say that it lacks an historical core (i.e. the illegal possession of a landlord's estate by his tenants) nor that it could not have been told by Jesus. The illustrations of Jesus, like the משלים of the OT, consisted of both parables and allegories.

S.R.L.

§14 'Having cancelled the bond which stood against us': Col.2.14 and the *Cheirographon*

Oxyrhynchus 11 Oct. AD 122 and 10 Dec. AD 123

Ed.pr. — B. Frid, *P. Ups.Frid* 3 (Bonn 1981), pp.31-39.

The papyrus sheet (30.5 x 15 cm) is well preserved. It has been folded several times. The presence of a *kollesis* indicates that it has been cut from a roll.

Θῶνις Ἁρθώνιος τοῦ Πετοσείριος	Thonis, son of Harthonis, grandson of
μητρὸς Ταυσοράπιος ἀπ'	Petosiris, my mother being Tausorapis,
Ὀξυρύγχων	from the city of Oxyrhynchus,
πόλεως Πέρσης τῆς ἐπιγονῆς	Persian of the descent, to Dionysios, son
Διονυσίῳ Πασίωνος τοῦ Πασίωνος	of Pasion, grandson of Pasion
ἀπὸ τῆς αὐτῆς πόλεως χαίρειν.	from the same city, greeting.
Ὁμολογῶ ἔχειν παρὰ σοῦ	I acknowledge that I have received from
διὰ χειρὸς ἀρ-	you in cash
γυρίου δραχμὰς δισχειλίας, γείνονται	two thousand silver drachmae, total
ἀργυρίου δραχμαὶ δισχείλιαι	two thousand silver drachmae of
κεφαλαίου αἷς οὐδὲν προσῆκται, τόκου	principal to which nothing has been added,
δραχμιαίου ἑκάστης μνᾶς τοῦ	at an interest of a drachma for each mina
μηνὸς ἑκάστου ἀπὸ τοῦ ἑξῆς μηνὸς	for each month from the next month of
Ἁθὺρ καὶ ἀποδώσειν σοι τὸ κεφά-	Hathyr and that I will repay to you the
λαιον καὶ τοὺς τόκους τῇ τριακάδι	principal and the interest on the thirtieth
τοῦ Μεσορὴ τοῦ ἐνεστῶτος	day of Mesore of the present
ἑβδόμου	seventh
ἔτους Ἁδριανοῦ Καίσαρος τοῦ	year of Hadrian Caesar, the
κυρίου χωρὶς ὑπερθέσεως·	lord, without delay.
εἰ δὲ μή, ἐκτείσω	If not, I will repay

σοι ταύτας μεθ' ἡμιολίας σὺν τοῖς καὶ τοῦ ὑπερπεσόντος χρόνου ἴσοις	to you these (moneys) at the one and one half (penalty) ratio together also with the equivalent
δραχμιαίοις τόκοις ἑκάστης μνᾶς κατὰ μῆνα, τῆς πράξεώς σοι οὔ-	drachma interest for the excess time for each mina monthly; the action for recovery being to you
σης ἔκ τε ἐμοῦ καὶ ἐκ τῶν ὑπαρχόντων μοι πάντων μὴ ἐλαττου-	both from me and from all property belonging to me; no loss being suffered
μένου σου τοῦ Διονυσίου ἐν τῇ πράξει, ὧν ἄλλων ὀφείλω σοι σὺν τῷ	by you, Dionysios, in the action for recovery for what other (money) I owe you together with
υἱῷ μου Παήσει καθ' ἕτερον χειρόγραφον ἀργυρίου δραχμῶν δισ-	my son Paesis in accord with the *cheirographon*, two thousand silver drachmae
χειλίων κεφαλαίου ὡς περιέχει. Κυρία ἡ χεὶρ πανταχῇ ἐπιφερομένη	of principal, as it stands. The instrument is valid everywhere it is produced
καὶ παντὶ τῷ ὑπὲρ σοῦ ἐπιφέροντι. (Ἔτους) ζ Αὐτοκράτορος Καίσαρος Τραιανοῦ	and for everyone producing (it) on your behalf. In year 7 of Imperator Caesar Trajan
Ἁδριανοῦ Σεβαστοῦ Φαῶφι τεσσαρασκαιδεκάτῃ. (m. 2) Θῶνις Ἁρθώνιος	Hadrian Augustus, Phaophi fourteenth. (m. 2) I, Thonis son of Harthonis,
τοῦ Πετοσίριος ἔχω παρὰ τοῦ Διονυσίου τὰς τοῦ ἀργυρί-	grandson of Petosiris, have received from Dionysios the
ου δραχμὰς δισχιλίας κεφαλαίου καὶ ἀποδώσω σὺν τοῖς	two thousand silver drachmae of principal and I will repay together with the
ἀπὸ τοῦ ἑξῆς μεινὸς Ἁθὺρ δραχμιαίοις τόκοις τῇ τρια-	drachma interest from the sixth month Hathyr on the thirtieth
κάδι τοῦ Μεσορὴ τοῦ ἐνεστῶτος ἔτους μὴ ἐλατ-	of Mesore of the present year; no loss being suffered
τουμένου αὐτοῦ ἐν αἷς ἄλλαις ὀφίλω αὐτῷ σὺν τῷ	by him in what other (money) I owe him together with
υἱῷ μου Παύσι καθ' ἕτερον χιρόγραφον δραχμαῖς	my son Pausis in accord with the other *cheirographon*,
δισχιλίαις ὡς πρόκιται. Ἔτους ἑβδόμου Αὐτοκράτορος	two thousand drachmae, as aforementioned. In the seventh year of Imperator
Καίσαρος Τραιανοῦ Ἁδριανοῦ Σεβαστοῦ Φαῶφι τεσ-	Caesar Trajan Hadrian Augustus, Phaophi
σαρεσκαιδεκάτῃ. (m. 3) Διονύσιος ὁ προγεγραμμένος	fourteenth. (m. 3) I, Dionysios, the aforewritten,
ἀπέχω παρὰ τοῦ Θοώνιọς τὰς προκειμένας	have received back from Thonis the aforementioned

ἀργυ(ρίου) (δραχμὰς) δισχειλίας καὶ	two thousand sil(ver drachmae) and the
τοὺς τόκους καὶ οὐδὲν	interest and no claim
ἐνκαλῶ [π]ερὶ οὐδενὸς ἁπλῶς.	do I make concerning anything absolutely.
Ἔτους ὀγδόου	In the eighth year
Αὐτοκράτορος Καίσαρος Τραιανοῦ	of Imperator Caesar Trajan
Ἁδριανοῦ Σεβαστοῦ	Hadrian Augustus,
Χοίακ ιγ̄.	Choiak 13.

....

1 Πετοσίριος 4 δισχιλίας, γίνονται, δισχίλιαι 8 ἐκτίσω 13-14 δισχιλίων 16 τεσσαρεσκαιδεκάτῃ 19 μηνός 21 ὀφείλω 22 χειρόγραφον 23 πρόκειται 26 Θώνιος 27 δισχιλίας 28 ἐγκαλῶ

The text consists of three parts. The first is a *cheirographon* (*ll*.1-16) drawn up and ruled off by a scribe. The *cheirographon* was a private document written in the form of a personal letter to the addressee, i.e. 'X to Y greeting' (*ll*.1-3), though without the customary farewell ἔρρωσο. As such it was written in the subjective style, e.g. *l*.3 Ὁμολογῶ ἔχειν παρὰ σοῦ and *ll*.8-9 εἰ δέ μή, ἐκτείσω σοι. The *kyria* clause (*ll*.14-15), though only first attested in such deeds in 133 BC (*P. Lond*. II 220 col. II), was regularly added thereafter. The document is dated at the end (*l*.16). In the *cheirographon* the issuing party acknowledged (though not necessarily as a *homologia*) that he/she had entered into the attested arrangement with its attendant obligations. The *cheirographon* was perhaps the easiest form of document to draw up as no witnesses were required (cf. the six-witness *syngraphe*) and it could be written *in situ* either by the person himself/herself or by a local scribe (cf. for example, the notarial *syngraphe* which was drawn up in the notary's office with the certificate of the *agoranomos*). When completed, the *cheirographon* was handed to the addressee/creditor (or perhaps to an independent party) much as an IOU. In the Ptolemaic period the deed might be registered in exceptional cases (see *P. L. Bat*. XXII 32, 34 and the editor's note on p.25 and J. Mélèze-Modrzejewski, 'Le document grec dans l'Égypte Ptolémaïque', *Atti del XVII Congr. Intern. di Papirologia* [Naples 1984], p.1179). In the Roman period the *cheirographon* was never registered (ἀναγράφειν) as such but could achieve the status of a public document (δημόσιος χρηματισμός) by insertion into the Alexandrian archives (the procedure of *demosiosis* dates from the late first-century AD) or by insertion into the nome archives through the *agoranomos* (the procedure of *ekmartyresis* dates from the third-century AD) – see H.J. Wolff, *Das Recht der griechischen Papyri Ägyptens* (Munich 1978), p.39 and 129-35. The primary problem with the *cheirographon* was that it lacked an independent witness or witnesses to the transaction and as a result its probative value was diminished. For this reason certain types of transaction were not documented by it, though this changed somewhat in the later period (see Wolff, pp.111-2). The *cheirographon* tended instead to document 'simple transactions of everyday life – receipts, credit in cash and kind, purchase of livestock' (p.111). Regarding its origin Wolff (p.110) surmises that the *cheirographon* derives from a common archetype which the Greek scribes of the Near East and Egypt independently developed.

The second part of *P. Ups.Frid* 3 is Thonis' *hypographe* or subscription (*ll*.16-25), i.e. Thonis' summary of the *cheirographon*. Together these first two parts form one document, the loan deed. The document concerns a loan of 2000 drachmae made to Thonis by Dionysios. The interest charged (*ll*. 5-6) on the loan is 12%, the maximum rate according to the *Gnomon of the Idios Logos* §105 (*BGU* V 1210). The second document and third part of the present papyrus is the receipt (*ll*.25-30) issued by Dionysios. It states that the loan had been repaid.

Deeds were cancelled in various ways. A deed could be cancelled by the issuing of a receipt, as above. In those cases where the creditor had more than one loan outstanding to the same debtor, he was usually careful to note that the repayment of one loan did not cancel the other (e.g. see *P. Turner* 17 *ll.*19-21 below). Clearly, this is not the case in the receipt of *P. Ups.Frid* 3, though another loan is known to have existed (*ll.*12-14 and 21-22). From this we may surmise that the other loan had already been repaid. A bearer bond, i.e. a deed stating as above that 'the instrument is valid everywhere it is produced and for everyone producing it on your behalf' (*ll.*14-15; cf. Tobit 5.2-3), might be cancelled by the handing back of the deed itself (cf. also *y. Qid.* 3.4). In this case the deed was frequently scored through or crossed (χιάζειν) for annulment, e.g. *P. Flor.* 61 and 65, *P. Oxy.* II 362, 363, X 1282. *P. Ups.Frid* 3 was cancelled by both the issuing of a receipt and the crossing through of the deed (see *P. Ups.Frid* Plate 3; no doubt the deed was also handed back to the debtor). A similar multiple cancellation is illustrated by *P. Turner* 17. For a discussion of receipts see H.-A. Rupprecht, ***Studien zur Quittung im Recht der gräco-ägyptischen Papyri*** (München 1971), especially pp.57ff.

Oxyrhynchus — AD 69

Ed.pr. – W.E.H. Cockle, *P. Turner* 17 (London 1981), pp.83-88 (= *P. Lond. inv.*1565).

The papyrus document measures 11.8 x 18.8 cm. It is described as written 'in a small cursive hand very rubbed in places'. The number 7 at the top of the document is a docket number.

(m. 3) ζ̄	(m. 3) 7
(m. 1) Ἰμούθης Ἁρθώθο̣υ τοῦ Θοώνιος ἱερακοβοσκὸς καὶ	(m. 1) Imouthes, son of Harthothes, grandson of Thoönis, hawk-feeder and
ἱερακοτάφος κ̣α̣ὶ̣ β̣υ̣σ̣σ̣ουργὸς τῶν ἀπὸ Ὀξυρύγχω̣ν̣	hawk-burier and linen-worker of the city of Oxyrhynchus,
πόλεως Ἁρθοώνι[ει] Ἁρθοώνιος τοῦ Ἁρθοώ̣ν̣ιος	to Harthoönis, son of Harthoönis, grandson of Harthoönis,
θεαγῷ κ̣α̣ὶ̣ ἱερακοβ[οσ]κῷ χαίρ̣ειν. [ὁ]μολογῶ ἀπέχ(ειν)	image-bearer and hawk-feeder, greeting. I acknowledge that I have received
παρὰ σοῦ ἐπὶ τοῦ π̣[ρ]ὸ̣ς Ὀξ̣υ̣ρύγχων πόλει Σαραπ̣ιεί(ου)	from you at the Sarapeum near the city of Oxyrhynchus
διὰ τῆς Σαραπ̣ί̣ω̣νος καὶ Ἀμμω̣νίου τῶν	through the bank of Sarapion and Ammonios who
συνεσταμέν[ω]ν̣ ὑπὸ Διονυσ̣[ί]ο̣υ̣ ωσδεπ̣ι̣τ̣ις̣ .[ ]	are contracted by Dionysios as ? [...]
Φαύστου καὶ τ̣ῶν μ[ε]τ̣όχων τρα̣[πέζ]ης ἀργυ[ρί]ο̣υ̣	of Faustus and his partners
Σεβαστοῦ ν̣ο̣μ̣[ίσμ]ατος δ̣ρ̣α̣χ̣[μὰς ἑκατὸν ± 5]	[one hundred ...] drachmae of silver imperial coin
κεφαλαίου καὶ τ[ό]κους καθήκοντ̣α̣ς̣ [κατὰ μῆνα]	of principal and interest due [monthly]
ἃς εὐχρήστησά σοι καὶ Ὀννώ̣φ̣[ρει ± 7]	which I lent to you and Onnophris [...]
κατὰ χειρόγρ[α]φον καὶ διαγραφὴ̣[ν τῆς τοῦ προ-]	according to the *cheirographon* and *diagraphe* [of the]
γεγραμμένου Διονυσίου καὶ τῶ[ν μετόχων]	bank [of the afore]mentioned Dionysios and his [partners]

τραπέζης τῶι Σεβαστῷ μη[νὶ τοῦ διελθόντος τρισ-]	in the month of Sebastos [of the past]
καιδεκάτου ἔτ[ο]υς Νέρωνος [ὅπερ αὐτόθι ἀνα-]	[thir]teenth year of Nero [which here]
δέδωκά σοι [[.]] κεχιασμένον ε[ἰς ἀκύρωσιν καὶ ἀθέτ(ησιν).]	I have given to you crossed-through [for cancelling and annulling].
[κα]ὶ οὐδέν σοι ἐγ[κ]αλῶ οὐδέ σοι [ἐγκαλέσω περὶ οὐ-]	[And] I neither make nor [will make] any claim against you [concerning]
δενὸς ἁπλῶς μέχρι τῆς ἐ[νεστώσης ἡμέρας κατὰ μηδ(ὲν)]	anything absolutely until the [appointed day,] with me [in no way]
μὴ ἐλαττουμένου μου ἐν [τῆι πράξει ὑπὲρ ὧν ἄλλων]	disadvantaged in [the action for recovery on behalf of what other (moneys)]
ὀφείλει ὁ προ[γεγ]ραμμένος ʽΑ[ρθοῶνις κα-]	the aforementioned H[arthoönis] owes according
θ' ἑτέρας ἀσφαλείας. κυρία ἡ [συγγραφή. ἔτους $\bar{\alpha}$]	to the other securities. The [agreement] is valid. [In year 1]
Μάρκου Ὄθων[ο]ς Καίσαρος Σε[βαστοῦ 7-8]	of Marcus Otho Caesar [Augustus, ...]
τρίτηι καὶ εἰκοστῆι. (m. 2) [Ἰμούθης ʽΑρθώθου]	twenty-third (day). (m. 2) I, [Imouthes, son of Harthothes,]
[[.]] ἀπέχω [πα]ρὰ σοῦ ἀρ[γυρίου]	have received back from you
δραχμὰ[ς] ἑκατὸν [± 5 κεφαλ-]	one hundred [silver] drachmae
αίου καὶ [τοὺ]ς τόκ[ους. καὶ οὐ-]	of [principal] and [its] int[erest. And no]
δὲν ἐ[γκαλ]ῶ [καθὼς πρόκειτα-]	[claim do I make as it is stated above.]
ι. (ἔτους) [$\bar{\alpha}$] Αὐ[τοκράτορος Μάρκου]	In (year) [1 of Imperator Marcus]
Ὄθ[ωνος Καίσαρος Σεβαστοῦ]	Oth[o Caesar Augustus]
[7-8 $\overline{\kappa\gamma}$.]	[... 23]

....

22 χείρ for συγγραφή (?) as in *P. Yale* I 63

The above receipt acknowledges the repayment of a loan between Imouthes, the lender, and Harthoönis and Onnophris, the borrowers. All parties are priests of the Horos/Apollo cult. The loan document had been crossed for annulment (see *l.*17) and a receipt in the form of a *cheirographon* issued.

The above papyri provide good examples of the type of document and legal procedure assumed in Col.2.14. The writer of Colossians uses the metaphor of a commercial loan to interpret the redemptive work of Christ. According to the metaphor Christ has cancelled the debt which stood against us (Col.2.14): ἐξαλείψας τὸ καθ' ἡμῶν χειρόγραφον τοῖς δόγμασιν ὃ ἦν ὑπεναντίον ἡμῖν. For a recent discussion of the interpretation of the verse see R. Yates, 'Colossians 2,14: Metaphor of Forgiveness', *Biblica* 71 (1990), pp.248-59.

Deissmann, *LAE*, pp.336-7, suggests a further contact between the metaphor and the work of Christ. He sees in the expression 'nailing it to the cross' a reference to the procedure whereby a document was cancelled, as in the above cases, by crossing it (see Taubenschlag, *Law*, p.420). Unfortunately, the play on words, though possible in German (Kreuz – kreuzen) and English (cross – cross), is impossible in Greek (σταυρός – χιάζειν). A visual connection between the letter chi and the crucifix is suggested by the use of tilted chi in the spelling of certain words (see *New Docs* 3 [1983], pp.133-4 and *New Docs* 4 [1987], pp.236-8). However, the perception of a connection appears to be considerably later than the dating of the epistle itself. In other words, the author of Colossians may not have been conscious of any visual connection at all. Indeed, σταυρός was one of the *nomina sacra* (see C.H. Roberts, *Manuscript, Society and Belief in Early Christian Egypt* [London 1979], p.27 and p.35 n.3; also the entry for σταυρός in LSJ p.1635) which was represented by the symbol tau (i.e. T and not X). Clearly, this letter afforded a closer visual approximation.

The syntactic relationship between the words τοῖς δόγμασιν and Col.2.14 has posed something of a problem to NT scholars. How are the words connected with the rest of the sentence and what do they mean?. C.F.D. Moule, *The Epistles of Paul the Apostle to the Colossians and to Philemon* (Cambridge 1968), p.98, has suggested four possible syntactic relationships: a) to an implied γεγραμμένον = 'consisting of, or written in terms of, decrees'; b) to ἐξαλείψας = 'having cancelled the bond by keeping God's decrees'; c) to ὃ ἦν ὑπεναντίον ἡμῖν = 'opposed to us by means of or because of its adverse decrees'; and d) as an instrumental dative = 'by means of decrees'. Though the choice between competing relationships cannot be made by a consideration of syntax alone, it may be possible both stylistically and semantically. A probabilistic argument is based on the author's use of expansion, i.e. the use of clauses and word groups which expand an initial expression (e.g. Col.1.5, 12-13, 13-15, 23, 27-29, 4.7-8, 9, 10). In the case of Col.2.14 τὸ χειρόγραφον is the initial expression which is expanded by τοῖς δόγμασιν and then ὃ ἦν ὑπεναντίον ἡμῖν. Compare Col.1.5 where the initial expression is τὴν ἐλπίδα which is expanded first by τὴν ἀποκειμένην ὑμῖν ἐν τοῖς οὐρανοῖς and then by ἣν προηκούσατε ἐν τῷ λόγῳ κτλ. The stylistic argument by making τοῖς δόγμασιν an expansion of τὸ χειρόγραφον suggests the translation 'the *cheirographon* with its regulations'.

The semantic argument starts from the observation that there is a difficulty with the *cheirographon* metaphor of Col.2.14. Though a copy of the *cheirographon* might be registered in the *grapheion* or registry office, it was essentially a private deed and as such was not displayed or posted publicly. Clearly, the expression προσηλώσας αὐτὸ τῷ σταυρῷ, though referring to the crucifixion, also implies the notion that the *cheirographon* is publicly displayed as cancelled (see v.15 which expands the idea, the antecedent of αὐτῷ being τῷ σταυρῷ). The usual verbs to express public display, i.e. ἐκτίθημι or προτίθημι, are not used here. However, J. Reynolds, *Aphrodisias and Rome* (London 1982), pp.90-91, argues that in Rome the *senatus consulta* (= τὰ δόγματα; see H.J. Mason, *Greek Terms for Roman Institutions* [Toronto 1974], pp.126-31) which concerned treaties were inscribed on bronze tablets and 'displayed in (or near) the temple of Capitoline Jupiter'.

> ... ἀνακειμένο[υ] δὲ ἐ[ν Ῥώμη]ι ἐν τῶι ἱερῶ[ι τοῦ] | Διὸς τοῦ Καπετωλ[ίου πί]νακος [χ]αλκο[ῦ καὶ] | ἐν αὐτῶι κατατετα[γμένων] τοῦ [τε γε]γονότος [δ]όγματος [ὑ]πὸ τῆς [συγκλή]του περὶ τῆς συμμα[χ]ίας ὁμοίως δὲ καὶ τῆ[ς συνθήκ]ης *Syll.*[2] 694 *ll.*24-6. (129 BC)
>
> **... a bronze plate being set up in the temple of Capitoline Jupiter in Rome [and] on it being drawn up [both] the decree issued by the [senate] concerning the alliance and in a like manner also the [treaty].**

> ... ὅπως τε τοῦτο δόγμα τῆς συνκλήτου [καὶ τὸ ὅρκιον τὸ πρὸ]ς τὸν δῆμον τὸν Πλαρασέω[ν καὶ Ἀφροδεισιέων ἐπ]ιγενησόμενον δέλτοις χαλκείαις ἐνχαρα[χθέντα ἐν ἱερῷ Δίο]ς ἐν Ῥώμῃ ἐν τῷ Καπετωλίῳ ἀ[νατιθῶσι κτλ]
> J. Reynolds, *Aphrodisias and Rome* 8, *ll.*90-2 (39 BC)
>
> **... that they may set up both this decree of the senate [and the treaty which] will be made [with] the Plarasian [and Aphrodisian] people engraved on bronze plates [in the temple of Jupiter] in Rome on the Capitolium etc.**

The allied city also erected a copy of the same decree for public display. For example, Reynolds, *Aphrodisias and Rome* 8, goes on to speak of displaying the treaty in the sanctuary of Aphrodite and (depending on the text's restoration) in the market place as well (see *ll*.92-3). In the light of the practice of posting such δόγματα, *Syll.*[2] 764 *ll*.8-10 (45 BC) are of interest. The text speaks of the nailing (προσηλῶσαι) of a bronze plate on which the matters agreed to by the senate were written.

> ... ἅ τε αὐτοῖς πρό|τερον ὑπὸ τῆς συγκλήτου φιλάνθρωπα συγκεχωρημένα ἦν, ταῦτα ἐν δέλ|τωι χαλκῆι γεγραμμένα προσηλῶσαι ἐξεῖναι, ὅταν θέλωσιν·
> **... and that, whenever they wish, they be allowed to write on a bronze plate the benefactions, which were agreed formerly by the senate, and nail it up.**

Similarly, Diod.Sic., *Hist.* 12.26.1 speaks of the nailing of the Twelve Tables of Roman law engraved in bronze on the rostra before the senate. The spoils of war (in particular the armaments of the enemy) were also nailed to be displayed in temples and public buildings, e.g. Diod.Sic., *Hist.* 11.25.1, 12.70.5, 13.19.3. For the nailing of a person's name and lock of hair in the temple see Lucian, *Syr.D.*60.12. The nailing of a criminal in crucifixion was also a form of public exhibition.[118]

The problem with the metaphor of the *cheirographon* or bond was simple: as a private document it was neither displayed nor a matter for public knowledge. The expression τοῖς δόγμασιν, i.e. decrees, regulations or even *senatus consulta*, forms the bridge, as it were, between the metaphor of the *cheirographon* and the following clauses. Δόγματα were a matter of public knowledge (see Luke 2.1, Acts 16.4, 17.7, also Josephus, *AJ* 14.197-8, *SB* III 7246 *l*.16, IV 7457 *ll*.24,47, V 8267 *l*.52, VI 9528 *l*.3, *P. Oxy*. XXXIV 2710 *l*.6, *P. Fay*. 20 *l*.22). For this reason also it is preferable to understand τοῖς δόγμασιν as referring to the *cheirographon* and translate the expression rather freely by 'the *cheirographon* with its regulations'. The metaphor of the *cheirographon* is thereby expanded by the use of τοῖς δόγμασιν which in turn facilitates the notion of public display.

S.R.L.

118 The term προσηλῶσαι has a metaphorical usage in philosophical works, i.e. the nailing of the soul to the body and its pleasures. Here, however, the notion of exhibition is absent.

ROMAN ADMINISTRATION

§15 'And everyone went to his own town to register' Luke 2.3

Arsinoite nome 21 Feb. AD 168

Ed.pr. — A. Swiderek, 'ΟΙ ΤΩΙ ΟΝΤΙ ΑΝΑΚΕΧΩΡΗΚΟΤΕΣ', *Festschr. 150jähr. Bestehen Berl. Aeg. Museums* (Berlin 1975), pp.425-29.

Bib. – N.Lewis, 'The Tax Concession of AD 168', *ZPE* 38 (1980), pp.249-254; *SB* XIV 11374 (*P. Berol. inv.* 16036).

['Αντίγρ]αφον ἐπιστολῆς.	[Co]py of a letter.
[Βαιη]νὸς Βλοστιανὸς Φωκίωνι στρα(τηγῷ) 'Αρσιονοΐτου Θε(μίστου) καὶ Πολ(έμωνος) μερίδω(ν) χα(ίρειν)	[Baie]nus Blastianus to Phokion, *strategos* of the Arsinoite nome in the districts of The(mistes) and Pol(emon), gr(eeting).
[τὰ] ἐπικεφάλεια τῶν ἀνακεχωρηκότων ἀπόρων συνήθως	[The] capitation-taxes of those without means who have fled, customarily
[ἐκ μ]ερισμοῦ εἰσφερόμενα συνχωρῶι πρὸς τὸ παρὸν	collected [from] an assessment, I grant for the present
[ἐπ]ισκεθῆναι, ἵνα οἱ ἐν ἀναχωρήσι ὄντες ἐπανέλθωσι	to have been suspended that those in flight may return
εἰς τὴν οἰκίαν καὶ οἱ ὄντες συμμένειν δύνονται	home and those being (at home) may be able to remain there;
καὶ ὅπως τοῦτο πάντες εἰδῶσι τῆς ἐπιστολῆς μου	and that all may know this, (I order) that a copy of my letter
τὸ ἀντίγραφον προτεθῆναι ἔν τε τῇ μητροπόλι καὶ	be posted both in the Metropolis and
καθ' ἑκάστην κώμην. Προσήκει δὲ καὶ σὲ μὴ μόνον	in each village. It is your duty not only
ταῖς τῶν πρακτόρων καὶ τῶν ἄλλων πραγματικῶν	to pay attention to the reports of the *praktores* and of
προφωνήσεσει προσέχειν, ἀλλὰ ἐπιμελῶς ἐξετάζε[ιν]	the other officials but to examine carefully
τίνες εἰσὶ οἱ τῷ ὄντι ἀνακεχωρηκότες [...]	who are those who have really fled [...]
προθέντα καὶ τὴν γραφὴν δημοσίᾳ ἐν ταῖς κώμαις	having posted also the list publicly in the villages
ὅθεν ἕκαστοι ἀνεχώρησαν. Εἰ γὰρ πρὸς τὸ παρὸν	whence each fled. For if for the present
ἀναγκαία ἐγένετο ὑπέρθεσις τῆς εἰσπράξεως, ἄλλου	a postponement of the collection has become necessary,
προνοηταίον ἐστίν, μηδὲ ὕστερον τοὺς ἐπι-	care must be taken for another matter, that later the
χωρίους κατ[αβα]ρεῖσθαι εἰσφοραῖς τῶν οὐκ ἀνακε-	inhabitants not be burdened by the taxes of those who have not
χωρηκότων.	fled.

Ἐρρῶσθ(αί) ‹σε› βούλομαι.	I wish you farewell.
(Ἔτους) η̄ ὅλων Μεχεὶρ κ̄ϛ̄.	In year 8 of so and so, Mecheir 26.

....

2 Βλαστιανός 3 ἐπικεφάλια 5 ἐπισχεθῆναι, ἀναχωρήσει 6 δύνωνται 8 μητροπόλει 11 προσφωνήσεσι 16 προνοητέον

The above document is a copy of an edict of the prefect, Baienus Blastianus, concerning the suspension/postponement of capitation-taxes. The copy of the edict was probably made in the office of the *strategos* (see Swiderek, op.cit., p.426). *P. Strassb.* I 239 is a more fragmentary copy of the same edict. Since the two copies of the letter differ (especially at the ending), Swiderek postulates that a similar letter had been sent to each *strategos* by the prefect but that the text was extended by comments of the regional authorities.

The Roman taxation system was a heavy burden to Egyptian peasants. It reached into every facet of their life. There were taxes on land, grain, animal, capitation, trade, customs, transport, manumission etc.. N. Lewis, *Life in Egypt under Roman Rule* (Oxford 1983), p.160, estimates that their number was 'considerably in excess of a hundred'. The burden of taxation (and the various liturgies placed on individuals) was such that many persons turned to flight. See *New Docs* 2 (1982), p.42, for the question 'Shall I be a fugitive?' which was asked of the oracle.

H. Braunert, 'ΙΔΙΑ: Studien zur Bevölkerungsgeschichte des ptolemäischen und römischen Ägyptens', *JJP* 9/10 (1955/6), pp.211-328 especially pp.240ff., deals with ἀναχώρησις and the concept of *idia*. The use of flight to avoid the burdens of taxation, the performance of liturgies and the cultivation of state land was endemic in Egypt and the Romans were forced to combat it administratively.[119] Those who had fled were pursued, their property confiscated and any shortfall exacted from their relatives or associates, whether by the state itself in the case of directly raised taxes or by the tax-farmers who themselves had to make good any shortfall. Such measures, however, did not succeed in discouraging flight, and whole villages were depopulated. Amnesties and the remittance of taxes were offered to induce a return of runaways. According to Braunert, the Romans attempted another remedy in the reign of Nero. This involved the creation of a stronger bond between the individual and the community in a particular place by the introduction of the concept of *idia*, i.e. a person's fiscal/legal domicile or the community in which he was registered. So defined, the *idia* became the place where the individual fulfilled his obligations to the state. At the same time, the word ἀναχώρησις is first met as a *terminus technicus* to describe flight from one's fiscal/legal domicile. From the period AD 104-216 several edicts ordering the return of οἱ ἀνακεχωρηκότες to their *idia* survive. Even so this measure also failed to restrain flight. To insure the *fiscus* against further loss other measures were introduced in the reigns of Trajan and Hadrian. In particular, a tax assessment (μερισμός) was made for each *idia* and any shortfall arising from individuals who failed to pay – i.e. those who were without means (ἄποροι) or those who had fled (ἀνακεχωρηκότες) – was met by the other tax-payers of the *idia*. The μερισμὸς ἀνακεχωρηκότων shifted the burden of any shortfall to a wider tax base, i.e. from the relatives of the runaway to his *idia* as a whole. The burden of cultivating state land (see *P. Berl.Leihg.* 7) and performing liturgies was similarly allocated to the *idia*. It was, no doubt, hoped that these measures would both guarantee the likelihood of recouping losses and induce the community itself to restrain any abuse. However, as the evidence of remittances and

---

119 The flight of agricultural workers was not a new occurrence in the Roman period. It was also present in Ptolemaic and Pharaonic Egypt. See, for example, G. Posener, 'L' ΑΝΑΧΩΡΗΣΙΣ dans l' Égypte pharaonique', *Le monde grec* (Brussels 1975), pp.663-9. He concludes that the root cause of ἀναχώρησις in both Ptolemaic and Pharaonic Egypt was the excess and rigidity of taxation.

amnesties shows, this measure also failed to remedy the situation. Persons continued to run away and the authorities continued to call them back to their *idia* by offering the inducements of amnesties and the remittance of taxes. See Swiderek, ibid., pp.428-9, who cites as examples of the situation *BGU* II 372, *P. Oxy*. XXIV 2413 and *BGU* III 903 (to which we can now add the above papyrus, *SB* XIV 11374). In her view 'the authorities were no longer in control of the situation'.

The above edict is of particular interest for the light it throws on the μερισμὸς ἀνακεχωρηκότων and the μερισμὸς ἀπόρων. Whilst Swiderek argued that the present edict could be used to argue the identity of the two assessments, Lewis, op.cit., and *BASP* 17 (1980), pp.63-64, takes issue with such an interpretation. He holds that there were two lists of ἄποροι and two assessments; one assessment was for the ἄποροι who had fled and the other was an assessment for the ἄποροι who did not flee. Thus Lewis understands by τῶν ἀνακεχωρηκότων ἀπόρων *l*.3 the former class of ἄποροι. He further sees confirmation for the conjecture in *ll*.5-6 where, as he argues, a distinction is made between the ἄποροι who fled and those who did not.

Lewis further argues that the edict concerns a cancellation (rather than postponement) of the capitation taxes. The reason for such an interpretation is basically logical. He maintains that a postponement of taxes would not have the desired effect of attracting fugitives back to the villages. To defend the interpretation, however, he must adduce evidence to show that both ἐπέχω (*l*.5) and ὑπέρθεσις (*l*.15) do not take their usual meaning of 'delay' or 'postponement'. The linguistic evidence deduced is not without its difficulties. For example, to derive the meaning of 'cancellation' for ὑπέρθεσις he appeals to a meaning sometimes attested for its cognate verb. However, an attestation for the verb, which incidentally can also mean 'to delay', is not an attestation for its cognate noun. The argument's error is what J. Barr, *The Semantics of Biblical Language* (Oxford 1961), calls the 'root fallacy'. Although cognates historically share a common root, past (or diachronic) derivation cannot be determinant of present (or synchronic) meaning, for in time a cognate may take on a new meaning (i.e. polyseme) not shared by its derivative (and vice versa) or at the point of its formation the derivative may take on only one meaning of its cognate.

One may also note that a cancellation of the taxes is not without its 'logical' difficulties. Lewis, op.cit., p.251, states:

> But an outright forgiveness, or cancellation, of the taxes due would benefit both the fugitive, who could return with a clean slate, and the remaining population, which would be spared the additional impost of the merismos.

The statement is correct so far as it goes. However, it fails to give due recognition to the fact that a cancellation of the taxes may be seen to benefit the fugitives most (after all those who had not fled had paid their taxes) and thus act as an inducement to future flight. See A.C. Johnson, *Roman Egypt* (Baltimore 1936), p.546, for evidence concerning variation in the annual rate of the μερισμὸς ἀνακεχωρηκότων within the fourteen-year cycle.

The above edict tells the *strategos* not only to pay attention to the reports of the officials but to examine carefully who are really fugitives. Lists of fugitives were made and these, no doubt, were used to calculate the μερισμὸς ἀνακεχωρηκότων. *P. Oxy*. II 251-3 and *P. Mich*.X 580 are notifications of disappearance and ask that the person be registered ἐν τῇ τῶν ἀνακεχωρηκότων τάξει. The procedure of registration was possibly similar to that of the notification of death (see *New Docs* 6 [1992] §16; the two notifications also share the same form). A village official was asked to verify the truth of the notification and upon his certification the person's name was entered on the list of fugitives. The names of persons, who were absent on business or who owned property in two or more districts but paid capitation taxes in one district only, might incorrectly be notified and placed on the list of fugitives. Other persons may contrive with village officials to have their names placed on the list of fugitives and thereby to avoid paying their taxes.[120] Seeing that the burden of unpaid tax fell to the other villagers, the government hoped to enlist their assistance in maintaining a correct list of fugitives. Accordingly, the edict (*ll*.13-14) commanded that the list be posted publicly in the villages whence they had fled.

One needs to distinguish two types of publishing or posting of official documents (see F. Millar, *The Emperor in the Roman World, 31 BC – AD 337* [London 1977], pp.252-9). The first mode sought permanency and was inscribed in stone or on a bronze plaque. The second mode[121] was temporary in nature and was written on a white-painted wooden board (λεύκωμα = *album*). The division was both physical and functional. Permanent notices were erected to proclaim from generation to generation the feats and/or status of a person, people or city. The communities of the empire had inscribed those decrees and letters which concerned their interests. The temporary notices, like the list of absentees mentioned by the above papyrus, concerned the day-to-day operation of government.

The latter form of posting is either used or possibly alluded to several times in the New Testament. First, there is the notice of the charge placed on the cross, 'The king of the Jews' (Mark 15.26 et par.). It was probably written on wood. Second, the posting of a notice is alluded to at Col.2.13-14. The verses speak of the *cheirographon* (a papyrus document) being nailed to the cross/stake. See *New Docs* 6 (1992) §14 for further discussion. Third, an allusion to the practice is also probably made at Rom.3.25. In particular note the use of the terms προέθετο (v.25) and ἔνδειξιν (vv.25, 26). It is of interest to observe that all three cases of allusion to or practice of posting relate to the crucifixion.

A matter of some importance for the Lukan birth narrative concerns the connection between the edicts calling for the return of absentees to their *idia* and the edicts which announced the census year. Luke, when speaking of the census of Quirinius and the journey of Joseph and Mary from Nazareth to Bethlehem, states: καὶ ἐπορεύοντο πάντες ἀπογράφεσθαι, ἕκαστος εἰς τὴν ἑαυτοῦ πόλιν – 'And everyone went to his own town to register' (Luke 2.3). Associating edicts of census and reintegration[122] Deissmann, *LAE*, pp.279-81, comments: 'That this was no figment (nicht rein fingiert) of St. Luke or his authority, but that similar things took place in that age, is proved by an edict of G. Vibius Maximus, governor of Egypt, 104 AD'. V. Martin, 'Recensement périodique et réintégration du domicile légal', *Atti del IV Congresso Internazionale di Papirologia* (Milano 1936 – reprinted 1976), pp.225-50, addresses the question of the connection between the census and reintegration edicts with particular reference to G. Vibius Maximus' edict, *P. Lond.* III 904.

120 One might compare the issue of official corruption with regard to tax lists with the statement at *SifNum* 134 – 'a man who is registered in the imperial records, even if he pays out much money (in bribes), it is impossible [for him] to have himself removed [from the records]' (trans. D. Sperber, *A Dictionary of Greek and Latin Legal Terms in Rabbinic Literature* [Jerusalem 1984], p.173).

121 For example, petitions to officials with their subscriptions were posted for a set period. Thereafter, the papyrus was taken down and filed within its roll in the archive where it could continue to be consulted and transcripts of it made by the petitioner. See A.A. Schiller in W.L. Westermann, *Apokrimata* (New York 1954), pp.41-2. See further W. Turpin, 'Apokrimata, Decreta, and the Roman Legal Procedure', *BASP* 18 (1981), pp.145ff., who argues that such practice extended to the posting of the oral *decreta* of court cases.

122 Edicts of reintegration are defined as those edicts which commanded persons to return to their ἴδιαι. To this group belong also edicts expelling Egyptians from Alexandria and calling them to return to their nomes. M. Hombert - Cl. Préaux, *Recherches sur le recensement dans l'Égypte romain* (Leiden 1952), pp.63-70, equate the ἰδία, ἐφέστιον and place of fiscal domicile (i.e. place of registration) and argue that such edicts are calls to individuals to return to their fiscal domicile. The reason for such edicts is clearly the threat posed to agriculture and the *fiscus* by the movement of persons.

Alexandria (?) AD 104

Ed.pr. – F.G. Kenyon and H.I. Bell, *P. Lond.* III 904 (London 1907) (= *Select Papyri* §220).

The papyrus appears to be the surviving part of an official letter book. It contains three letters. The first is a receipt issued to a *strategos*. The second is a letter to the same *strategos*. The present document, a rescript from the prefect, is the third letter. It is badly mutilated at the bottom. The restorations and text of *Select Papyri* §220 have been used together with the restorations of *ll.*38-41 suggested by W. Schubart, *Aegyptus* 31 (1951), p.153.

Column II

Γ[άιος Οὐί]βιο[ς Μάξιμος ἔπα]ρχ[ος] Αἰγύπτ[ου λέγει·]	G[aius Vi]biu[s Maximus, pre]fect of Egypt, [says:]
τῆς κατ' οἰ[κίαν ἀπογραφῆς ἐ]νεστώ[σης]	The house-by-house [registration being] at hand,
ἀναγκαῖόν [ἐστιν πᾶσιν τοῖ]ς καθ' ἥ[ντινα]	[it is] necessary [for all those who] for whatsoever
δήποτε αἰτ[ίαν ἀποδημοῦσιν ἀπὸ τῶν]	reason [are outside their]
νομῶν προσα[γγέλλε]σθαι ἐπα[νελ-]	nomes to be ord[ered] to return
θεῖν εἰς τὰ ἑαυ[τῶν ἐ]φέστια, ἵν[α]	to their own hearths, that
καὶ τὴν συνήθη [οἰ]κονομίαν τῆ[ς ἀπο-]	they may complete also the customary arrangement
γραφῆς πληρώσωσιν καὶ τῇ προσ[ηκού-]	of registration and apply themselves
σῃ αὐτοῖς γεωργίαι προσκαρτερήσω[σιν.]	to the husbandry which be[fits] them.
εἰδὼς μέντο[ι ὅ]τι ἐνίων τῶν [ἀπὸ]	Knowing, however, that
τῆς χώρας ἡ πόλις ἡμῶν ἔχει χρε[ίαν],	our city has need of some people from the country,
βούλομ[αι] πάντα[ς τ]οὺς εὔ[λ]ογον δο[κοῦν-]	I wish all who th[ink] they have a sensible
τα[ς] ἔχειν τοῦ ἐνθάδε ἐπιμένιν [αἰ-]	[re]ason to remain here
τίαν ἀπογράφεσ[θ]αι παρὰ Βουλ. . . [. . .]	to register themselves before Boul ... [...]
Φήστῳ ἐπάρχω[ι] εἴλης, ὃν ἐπὶ το[ύτῳ]	Festus, *praefectus alae*, whom I have appointed for th[is],
ἔταξα, οὗ καὶ τὰς [ὑ]πογραφὰς οἱ ἀποδ[εί-]	whose subscriptions also those
ξαντες ἀναγκ[αίαν α]ὐτῶν τὴν παρου[σίαν]	demonstrating the necessity of their presence
λήμψοντα[ι κατὰ τ]οῦ[τ]ο τὸ παράγγελμ[α]	will receive [in accord with] this edict
ἐντὸς [τῆς τριακάδος τοῦ ἐν]εσ[τ]ῶτος μη-	before [the thirtieth day of the pr]esent
νὸς Ἐ[πείφ, τοὺς δὲ ἄλλους ἐ]πανελθεῖν	month of E[peiph; but the others] (I order) to return

μεθ' ἡ[μέρας .. · ἐὰν δέ τις χωρὶ]ς ὑπογραφῆ[ς]	after [X days. If anyone] is found [without] a subscription
τοῦ ἐπ' ἴλ[ης τεταγμένου ε]ὑρεθῆι οὐ	of the [appointed official] of the *ala*,
μετρίω[ς ζημιωθήσεται. εὖ γὰ]ρ οἶδα κτλ	[he will be punished] severely. [For well] do I know etc.

....

31 ἐπιμένειν   33 ἴλης

Martin, op. cit., argues that there is no necessary connection between the census and reintegration edicts.[123] On the one hand, the census was directed at all residents of Egypt; it only required the declarant's temporary presence at the place of registration; it had a limited time-span in view, for registration had to take place before the end of following year. On the other hand, the reintegration edicts were directed at a limited section of the Egyptian population, i.e. farmers and agricultural workers who had absconded; their object was the regularisation of a problem by encouraging the absentees to remain in their *idia*; the edict envisaged no time limitation to its effectiveness. The question, then, is whether the government availed itself of the opportunity afforded by the census to renew the reintegration edict, as H. Braunert, *Die Binnenwanderung* (Bonn 1964), p.167, states: 'their general connection with the provincial census held every 14 years must be above all quite clear'. Martin discusses several problems with such an interpretation. First, census edicts, though none survive, do not appear to have included clauses regulating reintegration. Instead, this was the subject-matter of separate edicts. However, the issuing of such edicts was not contemporary with the issuing of the census edicts, as one would naturally expect, but either sufficiently before or after them to make one suspect that the two are only connected by chronological coincidence. For example, the edict of Septimius Severus and Caracalla (*P. Cattaoui* II = *SB* I 4284) was issued six months before the census year. An edict of Subatianus Aquila (*P. Flor.* I 6) was probably issued about eighteen months after the calling of the census and that of Valerius Datus (*BGU* I 159) a little before the tenth month of the census year. The occurrence of a time delay is critical to any hypothesis which seeks to find a direct association between the taking of a census and the reintegration edict, for the simple reason that it has failed to account for those who may have already made their census declaration.

Second, reintegration edicts were not issued only in or near census years, e.g. the edict of Sempronius Liberalis (*BGU* II 372 of AD 154 – referred to also in *P. Fay.* 24). Third, not all census edicts appear to have been accompanied by a reintegration edict. Martin argues the latter point from the silence of *P. Lond.* III 924 (= *WChr.*355). Fourth, in documents which either contain or refer to reintegration edicts the action seems motivated by agricultural and related fiscal concerns, i.e. there is no evident connection with the census. For example, in AD 215 Caracalla ordered the expulsion of Egyptians from Alexandria that they may return to the cultivation of the soil (*P. Giss.* II 40 col. ii). The edict fell within the census period but no mention was made of the latter. Rather, the order only witnesses to the general troubles of the times. Fifth, the edicts of Sempronius Liberalis, Subatianus Aquila and Valerius Datus (i.e. *BGU* II 372, *P. Gen.* 16 and *BGU* I 159 respectively) are associated with the commencement of the prefect's term of office. The same also applies to the edict of Vibius Maximus (*P. Lond.* III 904) and possibly to another edict by Subatianus Aquila (*P. Flor.* I 6). In other words, the

123 It should be observed that the term ἰδία is absent from *P. Lond.* III 904. However, Hombert - Préaux, op.cit., pp.67-70, argue from *P. Oslo* III 111 and *P. Oxy.*XVII 2106 that by the third or fourth century AD the term ἐφέστιον had acquired a technical meaning and indicated one's fiscal/legal domicile, i.e. where one was registered. They further argue that the meaning well suits the use of the same term in *P. Lond.* III 904. In other words, ἐφέστιον in *l.*24 is equivalent to ἰδία.

chronological coincidence between the census and reintegration edicts may reside in the simple fact that a change of prefect occurred in the course of the period of census-taking. In this regard it is important to note that the reintegration edicts of Subatianus Aquila (*P. Gen.* 16) and Valerius Datus (*BGU* I 159) were issued in the census years AD 201/2 and AD 215/6 respectively but that the census edicts, as indicated by two early census declarations, were issued by their predecessors, Q. Maecius Laetus and Aurelius Antinous. It is Martin's contention that the supposed connection between the census and reintegration edicts results from the interpretative function played by *P. Lond.* III 904. However, when the reintegration edicts are considered by themselves, the question of their connection with census edicts appears problematic. What then of *P. Lond.* III 904?

G. Vibius Maximus made a connection between the census and reintegration edicts (*l.*20) but this does not appear to be the result of any habitual connection between the two (see arguments above). Martin notes in particular that *P. Lond.* III 904 is not directed to all persons living in Egypt but only to those living in Alexandria.[124] In other words, it is a particular rather than a general edict regarding the return of absentees. His argument rests on a careful reading of the text, i.e. a) the opposition between πόλις and the nomes of the χώρα seems to indicate that Alexandria is being referred to; and b) the use of ἀποδημεῖν ἀπὸ τῶν νομῶν (*ll.*22-3) instead of εἶναι or διατρίβειν ἐπὶ τῆς ξένης appears to indicate that the persons are not in other nomes but in Alexandria itself. As such, Martin compares *P. Lond.* III 904 with the edicts of Caracalla and Subatianus Aquila which deal with the expulsion of Egyptians from Alexandria (e.g. *P. Flor.* I 6 and *P. Giss.* II 40 col. ii). However, in contrast with those edicts a considerable focus (*ll.*28ff.) in Vibius Maximus' edict concerns exemptions for persons whose services were necessary to the city. In view of *P. Giss.* 40 Braunert, *Die Binnenwanderung*, p.172-4, suggests that those permitted to remain in Alexandria were pig-traders, river-skippers and the reed-collectors for the bath-houses. Be that as it may, on the basis of his reconstruction of *ll.*37-40 Martin offers the following tentative reconstruction of the procedure.[125]

a. The person whose services were necessary was to register (ἀπογράφεσθαι in *l.*32) with the *praefectus alae* in Alexandria to receive his subscription.

b. Not exempted from the obligation to return to his nome to complete the census declaration, he made the journey, lodged the declaration and received a second subscription made this time by the local official. This acknowledged the completion of the census declaration.

c. The person could then return to Alexandria.

Braunert (p.170, n.245) follows instead Schubart's reconstruction of the text (reproduced above). He concludes that those whose services were required in Alexandria were not required to return to their *idia* but could make their census declaration instead in Alexandria.

The above discussion draws attention to the difficulties inherent in any appeal to reintegration edicts to explains details of Luke's birth narrative. First, the reintegration edicts issued between AD 104 and 216 addressed a particular economic concern in Egypt and were not always connected nor of necessity connected to the taking of a census. The concern itself was the loss to the *fiscus* resulting from the absenteeism of farmers and agricultural labourers. The edicts are thus directed at these persons. If so, before the documentary evidence of Egypt can be

124 So also H. Braunert, *Die Binnenwanderung*, p.169. Braunert places the edict within the context of a more general tendency of migration from the χώρα to the cities.

125 The reading of *ll.*37-40 offered by Martin is:

ἐντὸς [τῆς τριακάδος τοῦ ἐν]εσ[τ]ῶτος μηνὸς Ἐ[πείφ εἰς Ἀλεξάνδρειαν ἐ]πανελθεῖν
μεθ' ἧ[ς λήψονται ἐπὶ τόποι]ς ὑπογραφῆ[ς]
τοῦ ἐπὶ τ[ῇ λαογραφίᾳ κτλ

before [the thirtieth day of the pr]esent
month of E[pheiph] to return [to Alexandria]
with the subscription, which [they will receive in (their) districts,]
of the (official) for [the poll-tax] etc.

used to argue for a similar procedure in Palestine, it must be shown that some analogous economic situation existed there. Census edicts alone do not permit one to suppose the use of reintegration edicts as well. The incidence of brigandage and a movement of persons to the cities may well argue for an analogous situation in Judaea (see Josephus, *AJ* 18.274, 20.124; also M.Goodman, *The Ruling Class of Judaea* [Cambridge 1988], pp.60-4). However, one must also reckon with a chronological difference (AD 6 in Judaea as opposed to AD 104 in Egypt) and the fact that the political concept of *idia* in Egypt is rather particular. It has already been argued above that the concept of *idia* gradually developed from its Ptolemaic origins to become a political remedy of Roman Egypt in the course of the first century of occupation. It appears rather peculiar that the Romans would use such a remedy immediately with their annexation of Judaea.[126] Second, reintegration edicts envisaged the permanent return of persons to their fiscal domiciles. Only in exceptional cases does it appear that the return was to be temporary. Indeed, if the return were only temporary, then the edict would in no way achieve its objective, namely to rectify the problem of absenteeism. In Luke's narrative, however, we observe that Joseph and Mary returned to Nazareth after the completion of their census obligations (Luke 2.39). For this reason alone, Augustus' census edict (Luke 2.1-3) cannot be construed as including a reintegration edict. If Joseph and Mary were required to return to Bethlehem to complete the census, then it must be for another reason. It is to a discussion of this that the next entry turns.

S.R.L.

§16 The Provincial Census and Jesus' Birth in Bethlehem

Oxyrhynchus — 11 Jan. AD 133
Ed.pr. — T. Carp, *P. Oxy.* XLVII 3336 (London 1980), pp.66-68.

[(vac.?)]	
α̣[± 20]	[...]
π̣ᾳρ̣ᾲ [Στεφάνου Στεφάνου καὶ ὣς]	from [Stephanos, son of Stephanos, and however]
χρημ(ατίζω) [± 15 'Ο-]	I am called [... from]
ξ(υρύγχων) πόλε[ως. κατὰ τὰ] κ̣ε̣λ̣(ευσθέντα)	the city of Oxyrhynchus. [According to the matters] commanded
ὑπὸ Φλαυίου Τιτιανοῦ τοῦ	by Flavius Titianus,
κρατίστου ἡγεμόνος ἀπογρ(άφομαι)	*vir egregius, praefectus*, I register
πρὸς τὴν τοῦ διελ(θόντος) ῑϛ̄ (ἔτους) 'Αδριανοῦ	for the house-by-house census of the past year 16 of Hadrianus
Καίσαρος τοῦ κυρίου κατ' οἰκί(αν)	Caesar, the lord,
ἀπογρ(αφὴν) {απογρ( )} ἐμαυτὸν	myself
ἀπογρ[α]φόμενο(ν) εἰς οἰκί(αν) (πρότερον)	being registered in a house (formerly)

126 One must be careful to distinguish between different uses of the term *idia*. Not every use represents a reference to a politically defined region or group of people. For example, John 1.11 can be cited – εἰς τὰ ἴδια ἦλθεν, καὶ οἱ ἴδιοι αὐτὸν οὐ παρέλαβον.

Τνεφẹρσọ́ιτος Σαρα( )
καὶ
Ạ. . . . . . ( ) Θώνιος καὶ ἄλ(λων)
ẹ̓π̣' ἀ̣μ̣φọ́δ(ου) Δρόμ(ου) Θοήριδος
(vac.) [.]. . . . . . .vac.)
αὐτὸς ἐγὼ Στέφανος ὁ
(προ)γεγρ(αμμένος)
ἄτεχ(νος) ο(ὐλή) (vac.)
καταγι(νόμενος) ἐν
ἡμίσει μέρει οἰκί(ας)
(πρότερον)
Εὐδαιμονίδος Ἀμμωνίο(υ)
ἐπ' ἀμ(φόδου) Βο(ρρᾶ) Δρόμ(ου)
(ἐτῶν) ῑζ̄.
(γίνεται) ἀνὴ(ρ) ᾱ.
καὶ ὀμνύω Αὐτοκράτορα
Καίσαρα Τραιανὸν Ἁδριανὸν
Σεβαστὸν ἐξ (ὑγιοῦς) καὶ ἐπ'
ἀλ(ηθείας)
ἐπιδεδωκ(έναι) τὴν προκ(ειμένην)
ἀπογρ(αφὴν) καὶ μηθ(ὲν) διεψε(ῦσθαι)
ἢ ἔνοχ(ος) εἴην τῷ ὅρκῳ. (ἔτους) ῑζ̄
Αὐτοκράτορος Καίσαρος
Τραιανοῦ Ἁδριανοῦ
Σεβαστοῦ, Τῦβι ῑς̄. (m. 2) Στέφανος
Στε[φ]άνου ἐπιδέδωκα καὶ ὀ-
μόμεκα τὸν ὅρκον. χρόνος
ὁ αὐτός.

belonging to Tnephersois, daughter of
Sara( ), and
A [ ], (son ?) of Thonis, and others,
in the quarter of the Thoeris Road,
[...]
I myself, Stephanos, the
aforementioned,
without trade, scar (vac.),
dwelling in
a half share of a house
(formerly) belonging to
Eudaemonis, daughter of Ammonios,
in the quarter of the North Road,
17 years of age.
(Total) 1 man.
And I swear by Imperator
Caesar Traianus Hadrianus
Augustus that from (a sound mind) and in
truth
I have delivered the above
registration and falsified nothing
or may I be liable to the oath. In year 17
of Imperator Caesar
Traianus Hadrianus
Augustus, Tybi 16. (m. 2) I, Stephanos,
son of Stephanos, have delivered and
sworn the oath. The same
date.

....

31 ὀμώμοκα

The forms of census declaration varied greatly from district to district. However, M. Hombert - Cl. Préaux, *Recherches sur le recensement dans l'Égypte romain* (Leiden 1952), p.100, give the following general outline (see also S.L. Wallace, *Taxation in Egypt* [New York 1969], pp.100-104, who gives a slightly different form):

1. The address:
- **a.** addressee(s)[127]
- **b.** declarant[128]

---

127 Hombert - Préaux, ibid., pp.84-97, distinguish three types of declarations: 1) originals or signed declarations; 2) duplicates or unsigned declarations; and 3) copies made later than the declaration for whatever reasons. Originals are addressed to a single addressee. Duplicates either have multiple addressees (i.e. in the Fayum and at Oxyrhynchus) or a single addressee (in other regions). Copies and extracts of declarations appear to be predominantly concerned with proof of civil status, e.g. their use in ἐπικρίσεις at Arsinoe and Hermoupolis or in the determination of priestly descent (see ibid., pp.144-7).

128 The name of the declarant is introduced by παρά. Profession and status/origin may also be given. See further Hombert - Préaux, ibid., pp.102-8.

2. The body of the declaration:
- **a.** the announcement of the type of declaration (i.e. proprietor or tenant)[129]
- **b.** the introduction formula to the list of inhabitants[130]
- **c.** the list of inhabitants with their details[131]
- **d.** the mention of other immovables, i.e. land, houses etc.
- **e.** final formula[132] – διὸ ἐπιδίδωμι

3. Oath[133]
4. The signature of declarant or another signing for him[134]
5. The date[135]
6. Subscriptions[136]

The declaration could be lodged either in the year of the prefect's announcing the census or in the following year.[137] Most lodgements, however, occur in the second year (see Hombert - Préaux, op.cit., pp.76-84). Hombert - Préaux, op.cit., pp.131ff., also describe the administrative processing of the declarations. The declaration (original or duplicate) became a numbered κόλλημα which was pasted to the roll or τόμος (generally in date order). The rolls were composed of declarations from the same village or, in the case of larger towns, the same quarter. An exemplar of the roll was deposited in the δημοσία βιβλιοθήκη of each nome. Duplicates were circulated to other relevant officials who would make a check[138] or ἐξέτασις on the declaration's details, especially age. The rolls with their collated declarations were then used to make lists, the predominant, though not the sole, function of which appears to have been fiscal. Lists were updated on a yearly basis; the names of those whose age had exceeded the taxable age-range (14 to 62 years) or who had been notified as having died (see below) were removed from the tax lists,[139] whilst the names of those who had become liable were added to them. From AD 33/4 to AD 257/8 the Romans took a census in Egypt every fourteen years. Before AD 33/4 the census was also taken but the evidence does not permit the

129 Hombert - Préaux, ibid., p.109 classify declarations according to whether they deal with the idea of proprietorship (ὑπάρχει) or the idea of declaration (ἀπογράφομαι). An indication of the edict's year and a reference to a former declaration may also be included. See ibid., pp.108ff.

130 The formulae vary greatly. See Hombert - Préaux, ibid., pp.113-4.

131 The names of the inhabitants were given together with other details, e.g. age, profession, distinguishing features, fiscal status, status libertatis, mention of a former declaration and mention of a declaration of birth. See Hombert - Préaux, ibid., pp.114-23.

132 Hombert - Préaux, ibid., pp123-4.

133 Hombert - Préaux, ibid., pp.124-27.

134 Another would sign for the declarant when he was illiterate. Signed declarations are classified as originals by Hombert - Préaux, ibid., pp.84-5. They are always made to a single addressee and probably formed part of a τόμος. See also ibid., pp.128-9.

135 Hombert - Préaux, ibid., p.127.

136 A subscription was made by an official and is found on duplicates, i.e. unsigned declarations, with single or multiple addressees. The duplicate with subscription may either function as a receipt of registration returned to the declarant or as the official's mark that he had seen the declaration in its administrative travels (see Hombert - Préaux, ibid., pp.130-1). In view of the penalties specified by the *Gnomon of the Idiologos* (§58-63), one might expect that the declarants would want some proof of registration.

137 The dates for the issuing of the census edicts can only be approximated. This is done by taking the dates of the earliest census declarations and allowing a sufficient period for the issuing of the edict and its publication. According to this method it is estimated that the census edicts were issued early in the second semester of the census year.

138 E.g. see the discussion of *P.Ross.Georg.*II.12 by Hombert - Préaux, ibid., pp.143-4.

139 The names of those who had been declared as without means (ἄποροι) or as runaways (ἀνακεχωρηκότες) were also removed from the tax lists and placed on lists of similar persons. The latter lists were then used to calculate the μερισμός. See further the discussion in *New Docs* 6 (1992) **§15**.

conclusion that the fouteen-year cycle was then in existence.[140] The fundamental connection between the taking of the census and the system of taxation in Egypt can be seen in the use of a fourteen-year cycle. As each male became liable to the poll-tax at the age of fourteen, the cycle permitted the administration to include all liable males in its tax lists. Lists of minors in age order were kept to update the tax lists. The lists of minors were also updated by the removal of the names of those who had reached the taxable age and by the addition of the names of those registered in birth declarations.

As stated above, the death of a taxpayer had to be notified.[141] See the discussion on *P. Mich.* VI 579 concerning the notification's form and its compulsory nature (also *New Docs* 2 [1982], p.16). On the procedures of notification see P.J. Sijpesteijn, 'A Document concerning Registration of Deaths', *ZPE* 52 (1983), pp.282-4. Below is printed a scribe's draft copy of a notification of death.

Provenance unknown — Second or third century AD

Ed.pr. – R.P. Salomons, P.J. Sijpesteijn, K.A. Worp, *P. Amst.* 32b (Zutphen 1980), pp.63-64.

The death notice is the second part of two drafts prepared by the same scribe. The former part, not reproduced here, is a clause from a lease of land. The whole papyrus measures 8.1 x 7.7 cm. The right edge of the papyrus is broken. The missing portions of the text can be restored using other notifications of death. I have amended and completed the last two lines using *SB* XIV 11586 and 11587.

4	[[Κωμογρ(αμματεῖ) κώμης Μούχ̣[εως]]]	[[To the komogr(ammateus) of the village of Mouch[is]]]
	Κωμογρ(αμματεῖ) κώμης Βουκ[όλων]	To the komogr(ammateus) of the village of Bouk[oloi]
	παρὰ Ἥρωνος Μ̣άρω̣νος [ἀπὸ κώμης].	from Heron, son of Maron, [from the village].
	Ὁ συγγενής μου Δ̣[ ]	My kinsman, [N.N.],
8	τελῶν τὰ ἐπιτελ[ούμενα ἐπὶ τῆς προκει-]	paying the pre[scribed (taxes) in the aforementioned]
	μένης κώμ̣ης ἐτ[ελεύτησεν τῷ ἐνεστῶ-]	village has die[d in the present]
	τ̣ι μηνὶ Μ[εσορ]ῆ̣. Διὸ ἀ̣[ξιῶ ταγῆναι αὐτοῦ]	month of M[esor]e. Wherefore [I ask that his]
	[τὸ ὄνομα ἐν τοῖς τετελευτηκόσι.]	[name be registered among the dead.]

A birth could also be registered; however, such registrations usually involve the children of parents belonging to the privileged classes, e.g. priests at Socnopaiou Nesos and Tebtunis, members of the gymnasium class at Oxyrhynchus, metropolites at Arsinoe etc. (see Hombert - Préaux, op.cit., p.117). Wallace, op.cit., p.105, suggests that a birth notice or ὑπόμνημα ἐπιγεννήσεως played a function in procuring for the child the same privileged fiscal position; it also functioned to procure an education in the gymnasium. The following document is an abstract of a birth notice. Whilst the birth was registered on 13 Aug. AD 186, a copy of the original registration was made in red ink some time later (after AD 195 as indicated by the use of the titulature *divus* for Commodus). The notice concerns a family which possessed both

140 For a discussion of the commencement and termination dates of the fourteen-year cycle see Hombert - Préaux, ibid., p.47-53.

141 As the master was liable for the poll-tax on his slaves, the death of a slave was also notified, e.g. *P. Oxy.* XLIX 3510 (= *ZPE* 30 [1978], pp.198-200).

Antinoite and Roman citizenship. The editor suggests that the great-grandfather of the child, M. Lucretius Clemens, was granted his Roman citizenship as a veteran soon after AD 130. On the obligations of Roman citizens towards a provincial census see Hombert - Préaux, op. cit., pp.56-7; H.Braunert, 'Der römische Provinzialzensus und der Schätzungsbericht des Lukas-Evangeliums', *Historia* 6 (1957), p.192-200; and id., 'Cives romani und ΚΑΤ' ΟΙΚΙΑΝ ΑΠΟΓΡΑΦΑΙ', *Antidoron Martino David Oblatum* (= *P. Lugd.-Bat.* XVII, Leiden 1968), pp.11-21.

Philadelphia? After AD 195?
Ed.pr. — A.K. Bowman, *P. Turner* 29 (London 1981), pp.132-139.
The papyrus (21.5 x 26 cm) is written in red ink with borders at its top and left side. It is an extract from the Antinoite birth register.

Μᾶρκος Λουκρήτιος Μίνωρ Μάρ-	Marcus Lucretius Minor, son of Marcus
κου Λουκρητίου Διογένους	Lucretius Diogenes, of the
Ἁδριάνιος	Hadrianian tribe
ὁ καὶ Ζήνιος ὡς (ἐτῶν) μ̅δ̅	and Zenian deme, about 44 years of age,
ὑπὲρ υἱοῦ	for his son,
Μάρκου Λουκρητίου Διογένους	Marcus Lucretius Diogenes,
μηνῶν ε̅ (ἡμίσους) εἰς Μεσορὴ κ̅	5 and a half months, on Mesore 20,
κ̅ϛ̅ (ἔτους)	in year 26
Θεοῦ Κομμόδου. γνωστῆ-	of *divus* Commodus. Guarantors:
ρες Μᾶρκος Ἰούλιος Διογένης	Marcus Julius Diogenes
Ματίδιος ὁ καὶ Μαρκιάνιος	of the Matidian tribe and Marcianian deme;
Μᾶρκος	Marcus
Ἀντώνιος Οὐάλης Ὀσειραντι-	Antonius Valens of the Osirantinoan tribe
νόιος ὁ καὶ Βειθυνιεὺς Γάϊος	and Bithynian deme; Gaius
Λογγεῖνος Μᾶρκος Ματίδιος	Longinus Marcus of the Matidian tribe
ὁ καὶ Δημητριεύς.	and Demetrian deme.

The Provincial Census and the Birth of Jesus

Luke is the only gospel to record that the birth of Jesus coincided with the taking of a census. Matthew records no such census. Four primary difficulties are perceived to exist for Luke's account. They are:

1. Luke's dating appears inconsistent. On the one hand, allowing for gestation periods and age differences between Jesus and John, Jesus' birth must be dated in or soon after the death of Herod the Great (i.e. 4 BC). See Matt.2.1, 3, Luke 1.5, 26, 39-41. On the other hand the census when Quirinius was legate of Syria (Luke 2.2) must be dated AD 6/7.
2. The provincial census was ordered by the local governors (proconsuls, prefects or legates) and not Caesar. Also there is no evidence for a world census. The provincial census was taken on a province-by-province basis.
3. Though Judaea became a Roman province in AD 6, Galilee only became one in AD 39. There is then no plausible reason for Joseph and Mary to travel to Bethlehem in Judaea to register in the provincial census.
4. A person registered for the census in the place where he/she lived – however, according to Luke, Joseph and Mary lived in Nazareth (Luke 2.39).

Various arguments have been adduced in an attempt to circumvent the four difficulties. On the debate see H. Braunert, 'Der römische Provinzialzensus ...', *Historia* 6 (1957), p.192-

214; A.N. Sherwin-White, *Roman Society and Roman Law in the New Testament* (Oxford 1963), pp.162-71; G. Ogg, 'The Quirinius Question Today', *ET* 79 (1967-8), pp.231-6; R.E. Brown, *The Birth of the Messiah* (London 1977), pp.547-56; J.A. Fitzmyer, *The Gospel According to Luke I – IX* (New York 1981), pp.399-405 (pp.415-7 give a relevant bibliography); and R. Syme, *The Augustan Aristocracy* (Oxford 1986), pp.337-41. The major problem with arguments in support of Luke's accuracy is that they rely heavily on a reconstruction of historical events for which no direct evidence is offered. The principal example of this is the attempt to establish a former governorship of Syria by Quirinius. Opposed to such arguments is the attempt to understand Luke's use of the census as a mere literary device, e.g. a vehicle to reconcile divergent traditions which spoke of a birth in Bethlehem (emphasising a Davidic origin) but childhood in Nazareth.

Two questions concerning censorial methods may be of relevance to an assessment of Luke's account. They are:

1. Who was obliged to make a declaration?

2. Where was the declaration lodged?

Both questions are relevant to a discussion of Luke 2.1-5. If Joseph could lodge his wife's declaration, then there was no need for Mary, who was pregnant, to make the dangerous journey. If Joseph could have lodged the declaration where he lived in Nazareth (I leave aside the difficulty that Galilee was not as yet a Roman province), again there was no need to make the journey. Answers to these questions might be gained by an analysis of the census returns in Roman Egypt, though one must always bear in mind that Judaea was not Egypt so that census procedures may have been different there.

A preliminary difficulty in the provincial census needs to be noted. It concerns the ambiguity caused by the fact that the census sought to enumerate persons (mainly for tax purposes) but it did this by property on a house-by-house (κατ' οἰκίαν ἀπογραφή) basis. Proprietors of immovable property and heads of households whether as proprietors or tenants of the property of residence[142] were the ones who lodged census declarations, not individuals. Generally speaking, the head of a household declared all persons living under his roof. Vacant houses and lands also required the declaration of their owners. It was this incongruity between purpose and procedural base which led to confusions regarding who should declare and where. One also needs to distinguish between subjective declarations (i.e. as in *P. Oxy*. XLVII 3336 where there is a personal declaration by the person submitting the census return – also with associated declaration of personal details) and objective declarations (i.e. where there is no such personal declaration by the person submitting the return – the property and its inhabitants, if any, are declared).

According to Hombert - Préaux, op.cit., pp.56-63, the general rule[143] was that the head of a household declared all those living under his roof. Clearly, the house-by-house basis of the census meant that one person could declare for another. For example, a father might declare his adult son if the latter continued to live under his roof. Of further interest are those cases of objective declarations made by one person on behalf of another, e.g. a husband for his wife, a soldier's wife for her husband, a widow for her children, children for parents, a guardian for his charges, tenants for their proprietors, proprietors for their tenants and agent-slaves for their

142 The lodgement of census declarations by tenants is evidenced in particular at Memphis. Hombert - Préaux, op.cit.,p.57, describe the responsibility of the proprietor as being the countersigning and guaranteeing of the declaration.

143 This is not to say that in particular cases it was clear who should declare. For example, if a woman owned property, it might be declared by her husband or parent or again she might declare it herself assisted or unassisted by her κύριος. Hombert - Préaux, op.cit., pp.59-60, observe that there was a lack of precision concerning who should declare.

masters. For the use of agents by absentee proprietors and *libertini* see further examples in J.G. Keenan, 'Census Return of Herakleides Son of Didymos the Younger', *CE* 46 (1971), pp.120-8 and C.A. Nelson, 'Census Returns from Arsinoe', *ZPE* 9 (1972), pp.245-58.

Lacking any census edict, one is left to ascertain from the returns themselves the factors which determined the place of lodgement. The question is whether this coincides with the declarant's place of residence, the place where he holds civil status[144] or the property's situation. We return to the ambiguity between person and property noted above. Did the property determine the place of lodgement or did the person?

Hombert - Préaux, op.cit., pp.63-76, deal with the question of lodgement. In the countryside they note that all three (i.e. residence, place of civil status and property's situation) tend to coincide. In other words, there was a degree of stability there. Apart from objective declarations which were lodged in the district of the property's situation, there is only one exception. *P. Berl.Leihg.*16 consists of five subjective declarations lodged at Theadelphia by persons, three of whom at least (i.e. individuals lodging declarations B, C and D – declarations A and E are too fragmentary) neither lived nor owned property there but who had originally come from there. It is argued that civil status determined the place of lodgement in these cases.[145] In contrast with the countryside, it is unusual in the cities for all three to coincide. In conformity with *P. Berl.Leihg.*16 some declarations were lodged in quarters (the ἄμφοδον was a fiscal domicile) where the declarant held civil status when the property's situation was in another quarter (see Hombert - Préaux, op.cit., p.72 n.1, for relevant papyri). However, other declarations were lodged in the quarter of the property's situation when that was not the same as the owner's fiscal domicile (see Hombert - Préaux, op.cit., p.72 n.2, for relevant papyri). Other declarations were lodged in quarters which neither coincide with the property's situation nor with the owner's fiscal domicile. All these cases, however, concern tenanted property and the declaration was lodged at the place of the tenants' fiscal domicile (i.e. where they were registered formerly). Hombert - Préaux, op.cit., pp.72-3, conclude that there was no clear rule as to where the census declarations were to be lodged and suggest that perhaps it was a matter of choice. A study of μετάβασις, or the change in one's fiscal domicile, also shows a similar want of coincidence between situation of property, place of residence and fiscal domicile.

H. Braunert, 'ΙΔΙΑ: Studien zur Bevölkerungsgeschichte des ptolemäischen und römischen Ägypten', *JJP* 9/10 (1955/6), pp.211-328 especially pp.306ff., argues from a reassessment of *P. Harr.* 70 and *P. Cornell* 16 that in Arsinoe tenants, though they were living in one district, might be declared in another. In these cases the determining factor was the fiscal domicile or *idia* where the tenants had been registered and declared in the previous census. Thus Braunert sees in the two papyri further confirmation that 'it is the place of their previous declaration which determines the place where they are declared' (Braunert, op.cit., p.311 and Hombert - Préaux, op.cit., pp.74 – my translation). Other nomes, however, pose something of a problem and on the basis of the wording of *PSI* X 1112 (from Oxyrhynchus and dated AD 229/30) Braunert suggests that here at least the situation of the house played a more decisive role. He surmises that outside Arsinoe the lodgement procedure was simplified. Persons lodged their declarations where they lived and the authorities later grouped them by their *idia*. Braunert further argues that the reign of Nero was decisive for the development of the census. It is from this period that the census declaration was called the κατ' οἰκίαν ἀπογραφή[146] and the

---

144 Hombert - Préaux, op.cit., pp.67-70, argue that the terms ἰδία and ἐφέστιον indicated the place where the person was registered and held his fiscal domicile (see the discussion in *New Docs* 6 [1992] §15).

145 T. Kalén, the ed. pr. of *P. Berl.Leihg.*16, suggests that the lodgement of the declarations at Theadelphia supports the view that individuals had to return to their *idia* (cf. discussion in *New Docs* 6 [1992] §15) to make their declarations.

146 H. Braunert, 'Zur Terminologie der Volkszählung im frühen römischen Ägypten', *Symbolae R.Taubenschlag dedicatae* III (Bratislava 1957), pp.53-6, 61, 64, argues that in the earlier principate the census was designated as either an ἐπίκρισις or an εἰκονισμός.

expression ἀναγραφόμενος ἐπὶ τοῦ ... ἀμφόδου was first used. He argues that in the reign of Nero the census declaration was first associated with the concept of *idia* and the population's fiscal/legal domicile or place of registration defined accordingly. It was the place where a person lived at the time of the *epikriseis* of AD 54/5 and AD 61/2 which determined his *idia* and consequently place of registration. But this is not to say that a person could not change his *idia*. By the term μετάβασις is meant the change in one's *idia* resulting from a change in status or permanent residence.

No census declaration appears to have been sent by the declarant to the place of lodgement. Instead, they appear to have been delivered in person. This fact seems to be consonant with the hypothesis of U. Wilcken, *Grundzüge und Chrestomathie der Papyruskunde* (reprinted Hildesheim 1963) pp.193-4, that all declarants had to present themselves in person to register their personal details, i.e. profession, status and age. Wilcken bases his hypothesis on the edict of G.Vibius Maximus requiring persons to return to their hearths (i.e. *P. Lond.* III 904 – see previous entry) and the restoration of καὶ ἀπὸ ἀ[παρ]αστάτ(ων) ὕστερον εἰκο(νισθέντων) – 'and from those (minors) not appearing in person later having their personal details registered' – in the tax-list *P. Lond.* II 261 *l*.39. Hombert - Préaux, op.cit., pp.75-6, criticise the hypothesis on several accounts. First, *P. Lond.* II 261 comprises a list of minors who had not had any former administrative contact and who were to have their personal details registered. The question is whether one can use this papyrus to draw more general conclusions. Might not such an appearance be required only for the initial registration? Second, the edict of Vibius Maximus with its call for persons to return to their hearths is adequately explained as an edict which sought to remedy ἀναχώρησις. There is no reason to interpret it as an order requiring appearance for the registration of personal details. Other considerations also raise questions concerning such a practice. For example, there does not appear to be any system of registration. Also, Hombert - Préaux cite *P. Oxy.* VIII 1157 in which a husband writes to his wife and asks her to make the declaration for him. Clearly, it cannot be assumed that there was a registration of personal details in this case. Lastly, Hombert - Préaux raise questions over the mechanics of such an exercise requiring the absence of persons from their homes and work.

H. Braunert, 'Zur Terminologie der Volkszählung im frühen römischen Ägypten', *Symbolae R.Taubenschlag dedicatae* III (Bratislava 1957), pp.53-66 especially pp.56-62, opposes the interpretation of Hombert - Préaux. He argues that the census required the personal presence of all declarants for the registration of their personal details, i.e. name, filiation, age, fiscal status and profession. For example, see *P. Oxy.* XLVII 3336 (reproduced above) where the declarant states his name, father's name, age, distinguishing features (left blank) and lack of profession. Braunert also makes several responses to the arguments of Hombert - Préaux. First, he notes that in *l*.10 of *P. Lond.* II 261 a registration of distinguishing features can be implied for adult males also. The relevant phrase is οἱ καὶ εἰς [τὸ ῆ ?] (ἔτος) ἰκο(νισθέντες) ἄνδ(ρες) ϙ. Second, all census declarations submitted by representatives or agents are of the objective type. Unlike the subjective declaration, these did not require the personal presence of the declarant to register his personal details. Third, against the observation about the want of any system in the registration of distinguishing features Braunert does not develop an argument but cites with approval the observation of J. Hasebroek, *Das Signalement in den Papyrusurkunden* (Heidelberg 1921), p.6. However, in his article, 'Der römische Provinzialzensus ...', *Historia* 6 (1957), p.205, Braunert makes two further points. Against the mechanical problems alleged by Hombert - Préaux he notes that only a few persons would be affected by the procedure of personal notification and registration; most people registered where they lived. Also it is observed that in antiquity the difficulty of identification provided an impetus for the registration of such details. Fourth, on *P. Oxy.* VIII 1157 Braunert makes two points. The first and rather strained point is that in this private letter the writer's belief that his wife could declare for him does not show that she could in practice. In other words, the writer may have been mistaken about official policy in this area. The second and stronger point relies on the rather late date of the letter (third century AD) and the likelihood that the whole tax system was in a state of transition. If so, one can conclude little from the letter about earlier tax policy.

Braunert also adduces an argument in direct support of his thesis. The term εἰκονίζειν occurs both in second century documents where officials write and sign for illiterate declarants (further examples cited in *BGU* XV 2475) and in Ephebic registrations. He concludes that the declaration of personal details by presenting oneself before an official in the nome's *grapheion* for identification was called εἰκονισμός. The use of the same term in connection with the census (see *P. Lond.* II 261, *Stud.Pap.* II, p.27, *BGU* II 562 and *P. Lond.inv.* 2196 = op.cit., p.66) implies for Braunert a similar procedure during the census-taking. Further, in support of the argument that declarants made their census declarations in person Braunert cites *P. Ross.Georg.* II 12, a list of names based on census declarations and stating also filiation, age and distinguishing features (written in a second hand). One can add to these examples evidence from several newly published extracts from census registers. See O.M. Pearl, 'An Unpublished Text: *P. Mich.inv.* 5806, Copy of a Sale', *Atti del XVII Congresso Internazionale di Papirologia* 3 (Naples 1984), p.1063 where extracts from the εἰκονισμός, i.e. census register with personal descriptions, are offered as proof of title. Also see P.J. Sijpesteijn, 'Auszug aus einem Zensusregister', *ZPE* 55 (1984), pp.299-300, for another example of an extract from an εἰκονισμός (Arsinoe AD 175-188) and P.J. Sijpesteijn, 'Extracts from a Census Register', *ZPE* 57 (1984), pp.119-20.

The procedure involved in the notification and registration of personal details is central to the treatment of Luke's account of the census under Quirinius given by H. Braunert, 'Der römische Provinzialzensus ...', *Historia* 6 (1957), pp.192-214. In this he follows Wilcken, op.cit., p.134. Braunert's own analysis of the development of the provincial census in Egypt clearly shows the effect which regional considerations had on its form and procedure. The Roman administration not only adopted the bureaucracy and its procedures which were at hand but also adapted these to its own purposes and to the various crises that developed. For example, the issuing of reintegration edicts and the application of the *idia* concept are adaptations to particular exigencies in the administration of Egypt. It is then not surprising that Braunert does not attempt to connect the Lukan birth narrative to the reintegration edicts. However, Braunert does argue that the provincial censuses of Egypt and of Judaea do share the same procedure with regard to the registration of personal details, i.e. personal details were registered and the declaration had to be made in person. The alleged reason for the similarity is to be found, as Braunert argues (pp.197-8), in the common desire behind every provincial census to facilitate the gathering of taxes and the particular adaptation of the provincial census to the census of *cives Romani*. It is, therefore, argued that the provincial census of Judaea, like that in Egypt, required the personal presence of the declarant to register with the authorities his or her personal details. At the same time the provincial census in Judaea also accommodated itself to regional factors. First, as well as men aged fourteen years and older, women aged twelve years and older were taxed (so for Syria generally – *Dig.* 50.15.3). Consequently, Braunert argues for a twelve-year census-cycle and the requirement that females also register their name, filiation, age and fiscal status in person (see p.206 n.3 for references). This, no doubt, will explain why Mary accompanied Joseph. Second, Braunert alleges that Quirinius adopted a regional procedure when, according to Luke, he decided to register persons by their ancestry. So both Joseph and Mary were required to return to Bethlehem.

Braunert's argument is problematic at several points. There is no attempt to show that registration by ancestry was at all feasible. Do the biblical references which Braunert (p.207) gives really translate into a defined administrative procedure?[147] When the Romans removed Archelaus in AD 6, they had to 'invent', as M. Goodman (*The Ruling Class of Judaea* [Cambridge 1988], pp.109-110) argues, a new aristocracy. They did this around the office of the high priest (Josephus, *AJ* 20.251). The services of the high priest Joazar were used in the taking of the census – see Josephus, *AJ* 18.3. Josephus (*BJ* 2.405) also seems to imply that the Sanhedrin was responsible for the collection of taxes in Judaea. Might it not be reasonable to assume that a traditionally Jewish method of census-taking (Ex.30.11-16) was adapted for the provincial census? In other words, was there a requirement to register by tribe and ancestry? There are, however, problems with the suggestion. First, it is unclear to what extent the religious rulers were involved in the actual process of census-taking. Probably only the occupants of the highest administrative echelons were changed; the administrative structure of Archelaus' Judaea would then be left intact and used by the Romans to collect the census. Second, it is difficult to see that a registration by ancestry was at all feasible. Those of a priestly family might know their ancestry (e.g. *CD* 4.5-6). For example, Josephus recounts his ancestry from a Hasmonaean great-grandfather, Simon, as recorded in the public registers (Josephus, *Vita* 1-6). However, as priests occupied the highest order of the caste system (*m. Qid.*4.1 and *m. Hor.*3.8) and ancestry was an essential condition of their status and function (*m. Qid.* 4.4), their knowledge of ancestry cannot be considered to be typical.[148] On the other hand, Paul, the zealous Pharisee, knew that he was of the tribe of Benjamin (Phil.3.5). Goodman, ibid., pp.68-9, describes Paul's knowledge of his ancestry as 'an exception'. Braunert (p.207 n.3) refers to the lists of Israelites returning from Babylon (Ezra 2.1-63). However, here it may be noted that some descendants could not find their family records and were excluded from the priesthood. Braunert also cites in support of his argument the genealogies of Matt.1.2ff. and Luke 3.23ff. However, these lists are not without difficulties. Discrepancies between the lists and their evident theological function are relevant considerations here. The examples, it seems, only point to a genealogical interest in particular sections of Palestinian society (i.e. the social elite and members of new religious movements) and even here uncertainties arise. But what of the vast mass of the population, the עם הארץ or people of the land? Did they know their ancestry? The historical upheavals of exile, captivity and migration and the conversions of and intermarriage among subject populations would render the process unworkable. The debate between Rabban Gamaliel and R. Joshua (second generation teachers, i.e. AD 80-120) over the acceptance of an Ammonite proselyte (*m. Yad.* 4.4) may be cited to illustrate the point. R. Joshua argues that 'long ago Sennacherib, king of Assyria, came up and confused all the nations [beyond recognition]'. His view was accepted and the proselyte admitted.[149] Mention may also be made of the presence of Greek cities and the gentile inhabitants of Judaea more generally. The slaves of Jewish households, the children of such slaves, foundlings, freedmen and proselytes will also have posed a problem for registration by ancestry – see again the list of castes at *m. Qid.* 4.1. Though ancestry in the Mishnah continued

147 As further support for Braunert's contention one can note that the Qumran community appears to have been administratively organised by tribes, thousands, hundreds, fifties and tens (*CD* 13.1, *1QM* 2.3-4 and 5.12-13 – see also *CD* 14.3-6, *1QS* 2.19-24 and Y. Yadin, *The Scroll of the War of the Sons of Light against the Sons of Darkness* [Oxford 1962], pp.59-61). In adopting this system the Qumran sect were trying to revive an older patriarchal system, e.g. Ex.18.13-27. However, one can ask whether this system was any longer feasible in contemporary Judaean society as a whole (see below). Even at Qumran it may be asked how members were assigned to tribes and subdivisions. Was it by ancestry and birth or by merit?

148 The *epikrisis* of youths of the *gymnasium* class (see the discussion in *New Docs* 6 [1992] §17) may be cited as a somewhat similar instance in Graeco-Roman Egypt. To be a member of that socially elite group, one needed to demonstrate his ancestors' membership of the class. At Oxyrhynchus the boy's ancestry was usually traced back through the archives of the *gymnasium*.

149 It should also be noted that although the Jews of Alexandria were divided into tribes or phylae, the division was administrative and bore 'no relation to the Jewish tribes of old' – E.R. Goodenough, *The Jurisprudence of the Jewish Courts in Egypt* (New Haven 1929 – reprinted Amsterdam 1968), pp.216-7.

to determine a child's status in the caste system, the determination depended on the caste of its parents and the validity of their marriage. In this regard it is significant that the list of castes names only one tribe, i.e. the Levites. Other tribal divisions play no part in the social arrangement. The caste and ancestry of the majority of the population was simply Israelite. This is yet another indication of the breakdown in the traditional structure of society.

The most probable policy would be for the Romans to adopt the administrative procedures used by the previous rulers. M. Hengel, *Judaism and Hellenism* (London 1974), pp.18-23, maintains that the Ptolemies introduced their system of administration and taxation into Palestine and that it continued to operate down to the Roman times. A. Schalit, *König Herodes* (Berlin 1969), pp.195-6, argues that the Greek administrative system by toparchies was itself an adaptation of the earlier Persian system. The Ptolemies further extended the system and this in turn was retained by the Seleucids. For tax reasons the Hasmonaeans had retained the Hellenistic administrative system by superimposing the toparchies on the religious division of their territories – so Schalit, 'Domestic Politics and Political Institutions' in *The World History of the Jews: The Hellenistic Age*, ed. Schalit (Jerusalem 1972), pp.265-8, 280. According to Schalit, *König Herodes*, pp.201-14, the Hasmonaeans distinguished between Jewish and non-Jewish regions under their control. In the Jewish regions the system of toparchies was maintained, though their number increased to twenty-four to coincide with the division of priests (1Chron.24.7-18). Gabinius also retained the toparchies but attached them to the various Sanhedrins. Herod substantially took over the Hasmonaean division of the kingdom between Jewish and non-Jewish regions. The system of toparchies, now nineteen in number, was retained in the Jewish regions and their structure of authority (στρατηγός, τοπάρχης, τοπογραμματεύς, κωμάρχης, κωμογραμματεύς) further hellenised (Schalit, pp.215-23).[150] Schalit also surmises that Herod held a census or ἀπογραφὴ ἀνθρώπων every six years in which was also registered an inventory of movable and immovable property (pp.272-81). No doubt the census was carried out by the officials of each toparchy on a village by village basis.[151] E.M. Smallwood, *The Jews under Roman Rule* (Leiden 1976), p.152, argues that the structure used to collect the land and capitation taxes in AD 6 was the already existing toparchic administration system.[152] Similarly, M. Stern, 'The Herodian Dynasty and the Province of Judea at the End of the Period of the Second Temple' in *The World History of the Jewish People: The Herodian Period*, ed. M. Avi-Yonah (Israel 1975), pp.166-7, argues that the Romans 'largely adopted the methods of tax collection used in Judea under the previous régime' and in this 'they were assisted by the local administrative institutions'. Since the census formed the basis for the calculation of the capitation tax of each toparch, it seems to follow, I suggest, that the same institutions would have been used to collect the census. The administrative division into toparchies also continued well after the period of Roman annexation – see E. Schürer, *The History of the Jewish People in the Age of Jesus Christ*, vol.2, revised and edited by G. Vermes, F. Millar, M. Black (Edinburgh 1979), pp.190-6. From all this it seems to follow that registration by ancestry was an improbable course of action in the taking of the census.

---

150 Similarly, M. Stern, 'The Reign of Herod' in *The World History of the Jewish People: The Herodian Period*, ed. M. Avi-Yonah (Israel 1975), pp.92-95, argues for the retention of the toparchies under Herod with a strengthening of the Hellenes in the administration and army of the kingdom.

151 A.H.M. Jones, *The Herods of Judaea* (Oxford 1967), pp.85-92 and 168-9, also maintains that these regional divisions formed the basis of the system of taxation under Herod the Great.

152 Concerning the Lukan dating of the nativity Smallwood, ibid., pp.568-71, argues that the Romans took a census of the client kingdom of Herod when Sentius Saturninus was legate of Syria (9-6 BC). Luke, however, confused this census with that taken by Quirinius in AD 6 and mistakenly dated Jesus' birth by this later event. Unfortunately, the evidence for an earlier census (i.e. Tertullian, *Adv.Marc*.iv.19.10 and an argumentation dependent on the gospel narrative itself) is rather insecure.

Braunert's argument faces still other difficulties. First, he finds (p.207) support for his position in the citation of Eusebius, *Hist.Eccl.* 3.20, that Jesus' family in Domitian's time possessed property in Bethlehem. If so, the place of declaration/registration may have been determined by the situation of the property. The difficulty here is that Eusebius' statement is accepted uncritically. The birth narrative gives no indication that Jesus' family owned property in Bethlehem; indeed, Mary gave birth in a stable (Luke 2.7) as she had no other lodging. Second, Hombert - Préaux's criticism (op.cit., p.76) regarding the mechanical difficulties caused by the necessity of registration in person also presents problems, it seems to me, for Braunert's argument. In view of the preceding paragraphs it can no longer be asserted that only a few persons would be involved in the general disruption to agriculture and business (so Braunert, pp.205-6). One must remember the historical upheavals and the effects these had on the dispersion of the population through the centuries. Braunert (p.206) tries to avert the difficulty by citing the instance of the annual journey to Jerusalem to celebrate the passover. No doubt the continuance of such a practice was permitted as a Roman concession to Jewish religious sensibilities. However, it is another matter to suggest that the Romans instituted a policy requiring similar migrations. Third, it is difficult to see how registration by ancestry would indeed satisfy the fiscal purposes of the Roman census. The registration of Joseph and Mary in Bethlehem would not facilitate the collection of their taxes in Nazareth. Indeed, one might postulate that copies of declarations or lists of taxpayers were made at the point of declaration (or some other place) and then sent to the bureau in the declarant's place of residence. But then why not have Joseph and Mary make their declarations there in the first place? Moreover, such a procedure assumes a bureaucratic structure equivalent to or even greater than that which prevailed in Egypt. Fourth, Braunert (p.208) argues in favour of Luke's account that later writers, whether Christian, pagan or Jewish, do not criticise it. The problem with this argument is that it disregards the process whereby any pertinent literature was preserved. The churches had, no doubt, an interest in preserving traditions like that reported by Eusebius but less interest in preserving more critical traditions. The argument also seems to assume the existence of a standard procedure for the taking of a provincial census against which any aberrant procedure might be judged. In fact the procedures, as Braunert himself argues, varied both from province to province and within the same province in the course of time. Any potential critic, writing some generations after the event and aware of these variations, would need precise information on the provincial census held in Judaea before offering a criticism. Lastly, Braunert (p.212) places the birth of Jesus in the last years of Herod's reign and suggests (pp.212-4) that Luke's dating by the census of Quirinius arises from his use of source material possibly of 'zealot' provenance. His solution, however, raises still further difficulties, for it seems to undermine much of his preceding argument. For example, the only substantive evidence for a registration by ancestry in the Roman census of AD 6 is Luke 2.4. Other evidence is very much a matter of conjecture. However, Braunert's solution appears to break the historical nexus between the census of AD 6 and the circumstances surrounding Jesus' birth.[153]

As well as the historical reconstructions, there are also linguistic arguments which seek to vindicate the accuracy of Luke. The chief of these is the claim that interpreters have misunderstood πρώτη (Luke 2.2). For example, F.M. Heichelheim, *Roman Syria* (New Jersey

---

[153] The question arises as to why Luke should either create or use the census-motif in his narrative. A prevalent explanation involves seeking the motive in Luke's redactional stance, be it theological, political or social. For example, H.R. Moehring, 'The Census in Luke as an Apologetic Device', *Studies in New Testament and Early Christian Literature*, ed. by D.E. Aune (Leiden 1972), pp.144-60, sees the census-motif as providing an example of Mary's and Joseph's obedience to the rule of Rome in contradistinction to the response of the 'zealots'. He ties this interpretation to other facets in Luke and Acts which also show an apologetic function. Christianity thus does not appear to be anti-Rome and as such should be considered the *religio licita* instead of Judaism.

1959), p.161, (= vol.4 in *An Economic Survey of Ancient Rome*), interprets the verse: 'This census was the first before (= πρώτη) that under the prefectureship of Quirinius in Syria'. Also A.J.B. Higgins, 'Sidelights on Christian Beginnings in the Graeco-Roman World', *Evangelical Quarterly* 41 (1969), pp.197-206 (esp. pp.198-201), argues that πρώτη should be translated as 'earlier than' or 'before'. Accordingly, he translates the verse: 'This census was before Quirinius' governorship of Syria'. The translation depends on the declining use of πρότερος – note, however, Homer, *Il.*13.502, 18.92 – and its replacement by πρῶτος (see *LSJ*, p.1535 and *BDF* §62). We can leave aside those instances (e.g. Homer, *Il.* 13.502, 18.92, Diod. Sic., *Hist.* 1.42.1, Matt.21.28, Acts 1.1, 7.12, 12.10, Rev.20.5, 21.1) where πρῶτος is equivalent to πρότερος with the meaning 'first of two' but has no dependent genitive.

a. Athenaeus, *Deipn.* 4.630c
πρώτη δ' εὕρηται ἡ περὶ τοὺς πόδας κίνησις τῆς διὰ τῶν χειρῶν.
Movement of feet was found before that of hands.

b. Aelian, *De nat.anim.* 8.12
... οἱ πρῶτοί μου ταῦτα ἀνιχνεύσαντες.
... those having investigated these things before me.

c. Plutarch, *Cato Minor* §18
... οὔτε γὰρ πρῶτός τις ἀνέβη τῶν συναρχόντων εἰς τὸ ταμιεῖον Κάτωνος
οὔτε ὕστερος ἀπῆλθεν.
... for neither did any of his colleagues attain the treasury earlier than Cato nor did any quit it later.

d. *IG* 12 (5).590.5
... ὃς ἔφθασας ἀλόχου πρῶτος [εἰ]ς μακάρων χῶρον ἐλθεῖν μοῖραν ἀναπλήσας·
... (you) who prior to your wife attained the place of the blessed having fulfilled your fate.

e. John 1.15; also John 1.30, 15.18 and *PGM* II, p.113, *l*.50
... ὅτι πρῶτός μου ἦν.
... because he was before me.

f. Manetho, *Apotel.* 1.329-30 (= 4.404-5)
τηνίκα φυομένων βρεφέων γεννήτορα πρῶτον
μητέρος εἰς 'Αΐδην πέμψει νεκυηπόλος Αἶσα.
Then will deathly fate send to Hades
the father of growing babes before (their) mother.

H. Braunert, 'Der römische Provinzialzensus ... ', p.212, makes two criticisms of the interpretation of Luke 2.2 which construes ἡγεμονεύοντος τῆς Συρίας Κυρηνίου as dependent on πρώτη. The first concerns Acts 5.37 where 'the census' clearly refers to the census under Quirinius. The second concerns the interpretation of the Lukan sentence by other authors of antiquity. In particular he notes that the Suidas[154] and John Chrysostom understood πρώτη at Luke 2.2 to mean 'first'. Sherwin-White, op.cit., p.171, offers a passing criticism stating that the 'suggestion ... that πρώτη in Luke 2.2 means πρότερον could only be accepted if supported by a parallel in Luke himself'. This criticism has little force. Since a speaker's performances are only part of his/her linguistic competence, one cannot deduce from absence in performances a corresponding absence in linguistic competence. Moreover, though many other linguistic items are used only once by an author, we do not doubt his/her competence for each of these. Ogg, op.cit., pp.232-3, makes a more important criticism. The problem, as he sees it, is that in the Greek language as a whole there are no similar examples of a dependent participial

[154] Braunert states that the Suidas (= αὕτη ἡ ἀπογραφὴ πρώτη ἐγένετο) took over the precise wording of Luke 2.2 (= αὕτη ἀπογραφὴ πρώτη ἐγένετο). The difference between the two versions, however, is significant. The insertion of the article clearly changes πρώτη from an attributive (Luke) to a predicative (Suidas) adjective and the deep structure of the sentence is transformed.

phrase. Another problem with the participial phrase should also be noted. The temporal expression 'before' generally describes the event or process as complete and takes the aorist form of the verb. In other words, Luke might have been expected to say: πρὶν Κυρήνιον τὸν τῆς Συρίας ἡγέμονα γενέσθαι – 'before Quirinius became governor of Syria' or something similar. The participle's tense (or, better, aspectual) form, however, is present.

One reply to the above criticisms is that an ellipsis of the word 'census' has occurred after πρώτη. In other words, Luke intended to say: 'This was the census before the census which occurred when Quirinius was governor of Syria'. There is one severe linguistic problem with this particular suggestion. If ellipsis were to have occurred, it would need to have been marked or felt in some way or other. Ellipsis can only be proposed if a sentence or clause is linguistically incomplete. In other words, it is determined by linguistic, not historical concerns. Where ellipsis does occur in the above examples (i.e. Athenaeus, *Deipn.* 14.630c) we note that it is marked by the definite article τῆς. The effect of this is to make the clause incomplete. However, Luke 2.2 shows no linguistic incompleteness which would lead one to suggest an instance of ellipsis. By way of concluding, it must be observed that the problem with all arguments which seek to understand πρώτη as meaning 'before' is that they disregard the most natural and intuitive way of interpreting the sentence. First, the participial phrase reads intuitively as a genitive absolute indicating the time when the census occurred. Second, the position of πρώτη after ἀπογραφή but separated from the participial phrase by ἐγένετο naturally makes it read as the postpositioned ordinal adjective 'first'. And it should be noted that Luke shows no distinct preference one way or other in the placing of the ordinal adjective. He places it 16 times before its noun (Luke 9.22, 12.38 (2x), 13.32, 24.7, 21, 46, Acts 10.30, 40, 12.10 (2x), 20.18, 23.23, 27.19?, 27, 33) and 12 times after (Luke 1.26, 36, 59, 18.33, 23.44 (2x), Acts 2.15, 3.1, 7.8, 10.3, 9, 30?). Accordingly, Luke 2.2 finds its closest structural parallel in the temporal clause:

ὡς δὲ τεσσαρεσκαιδεκάτη νὺξ ἐγένετο διαφερομένων ἡμῶν ἐν τῷ Ἀδρίᾳ (Acts 27.27)

S.R.L.

§17 The Preservation of Status and its Testing

Oxyrhynchus 4 Aug. AD 272

Ed.pr.— V.P.McCarren, *P. Mich.* XIV 676 (Chico 1980), pp.9-19.

The papyrus (19.3 x 29.9 cm) is broken at the top and partially on the left edge (*ll*.1-9 and *ll*.31-33). There are several holes and serious lacunae as well. Familiar formulae have been used to restore lost portions of text.

[± 19] ..ιτω [± 8] τους ε. [± 15	
] ου.κος [± 8]	
[± 17]. φίλου. [± 4 μετ]ηλλαχ[ό]τος	[...] friend [...] dead
καὶ [± 9] Μάρκος Αὐρ[ήλιος	and [...] Marcus Aurelius
Θ]ῶνις	Thonis,
[μητρὸς Θερμου]θίου ὢ[ν πρὸ]ς τὸ	[his mother being Thermou]thion, for the
ἐ[νεστὸς γ̄ (ἔτος) (ἐτῶν)] ιδ̄,	[present year 3] being 14 [years of age,]
οὐλ(ὴν) μὴ ἔχ[ων . . . .]μεὺς	without scar, an apprentice [...].
μανθάνων. ὅθεν	Wherefore,

4 [παραγενό]μενος πρὸς τὴν τού[του ἐπίκ(ρισιν)] δηλῶ κατὰ τὴν γενομένην τῷ ε̅ (ἔτει) θε[οῦ] Ο]ὐεσ(πασιανοῦ) τῶν	[having been present] at his examination I declare that in accord with the examination which occurred in year 5 of *divus*[155] Vespasian of those
[ἐκ τοῦ γυμ]νασίου ἐπίκ(ρισιν) ἐπικ(εκρίσθαι) τ[ὸ]ν ṭ[οῦ πάππ(ου) αὐ]τ[ο]ῦ προσβ(αίνοντος) πρόπ(αππον) Ἀπολλώνιον ἐπ' ἀμφ(όδου) Πλατίας	[from the gym]nasium the great-grandfather of the grandfather of the candidate, Apollonios, was examined in the quarter of Platia
[ἀκολούθ]ω̣ς αἷς ‹ἐ›πήνεγκεν ἀπο̣δε̣ί̣[ξεσι], καὶ τὸν τοῦ πατρὸς αὐτοῦ πρόπ(αππον) Δι[ο]ν̣ύ̣[σι]ο̣ν̣ τὸν	[in accord with] the proofs which he offered, and that the great-grandfather of his father, Dionysios, also called
[καὶ ± 6 π]ροσβ(αίνοντα) τῷ δ̅ (ἔτει) θεοῦ Τρα̣[ι]ανοῦ ἐπικ(εκρίσθαι) ἐπ' ἀ]μφ(όδου) τοῦ αὐτ[ο]ῦ, καὶ τὸν πρόπ(αππον) αὐτοῦ Διογένην	[...], candidate in year 4 of *divus* Trajan, was examined in the same quarter, and that his great-grandfather, Diogenes,
8 [προσβ(αίνοντα) τ]ῷ ι̣α̅ (ἔτει) θεοῦ Αἰλίου Ἀντων[ίνο]υ ἐ[πι]κ(εκρίσθαι) [ἐπ'] ἀμφ(όδου) τοῦ αὐτοῦ, καὶ τὸν πάππ(ον) αὐτο̣[ῦ] Ἀμοῦν	[candidate] in year 11 of *divus* Aelius Antoninus, was examined [in] the same quarter, and that his grandfather, Amous,
[± 8 πρ]οσβ(αίνοντα) τῷ κα̅ (ἔτει) θεοῦ Κομόδ[ο]υ ἐπ[ι]κ(εκρίσθαι) ἐπ' ἀμφ(όδου) τοῦ αὐτοῦ, καὶ τὸν πατέρα αὐ[τ]οῦ Κοπρέα	[...], candidate in year 21 of *divus* Commodus, was examined in the same quarter, and that his father Kopreus,
π[ροσβ(αίνοντα) τ]ῷ ε̅ (ἔτει) ṭῆς μετὰ θεὸν Σεο[υῆ]ρον Ἀντωνίνον βασιλίας ἐπικ(εκρίσθαι) ἐπὶ τα[ῖ]ς προκειμέ-ναις [ἀποδ(είξεσιν)] ἐπ' ἀμφ(όδου) Λουκίων Π[αρε]μ(βολῆς), καὶ τὸν τοῦ προπάππ(ου) τῆς μητρὸς \`τοῦ´ αὐτοῦ προσβ(αίνοντος) πρόπ(αππον)	[candidate] in year 5 of the reign after *divus* Severus Antoninus, was examined on the above [proofs] in the quarter of the Lucians' barracks, and that the great-grandfather of the great-grandfather of the mother of the same candidate,
12 Σεραπί[ων]α Θεωνίνου ἐν εἴδ̣ι̣ [τῶν] ṭῷ γ̅ (ἔτει) καὶ ϛ̣̅ (ἔτει) Νέρωνος ὑπὸ Κουρτίου Παυλίνου	Sarapion, son of Theonis, in the category of those examined in year 3 and year 5 of Nero by Curtius Paulinus,
χη̣λιάρχ[ο]υ ἐπικ(εκριμένων) ἐπ' ἀ̣μφόδ(ου) Μυροβαλάνου, καὶ τὸν τοῦ πάππ(ου) αὐτῆς πρόπαππ(ον) Θέω̣να προσβ(αίνοντα)	*chiliarchos*, in the Myrobalanus quarter, and that the great-grandfather of her grandfather, Theon, candidate

155 The names of all but two emperors are prefixed by the epithet θεός = *divus* (for the discussion of the terms see H.J.Mason, *Greek Terms for Roman Institutions* [Toronto 1974], pp.124-5). The two exceptions are the names of Nero and Domitian. From the time of Augustus the title was given to the dead emperor by a decree of the Roman senate. To withhold the decree or *relatio inter deos* effectively annulled the former emperor's acts.

τῷ δ̄ (ἔτει) Δ[ο]μ[ι]τιανοῦ ἐπικ(εκρίσθαι) ἐπ' ἀμφ(όδου) τοῦ αὐ[τ]οῦ, καὶ τὸν τοῦ πατρὸς αὐτῆς πρόπαππ(ον) {αὐτῆς}	in year 4 of Domitian, was examined in the same quarter, and that the great-grandfather of her father,
Σαραπίω[ν]α προσβ(αίνοντα) τῷ ιε̄ (ἔτει) θεοῦ [Τρ]αιανοῦ ἐπικ(εκρίσθαι) ἐπ' ἀμφ(όδου) τοῦ αὐτοῦ, καὶ τὸ πρόπαππ(ον) αὐτῆς	Sarapion, candidate in year 15 of *divus* Trajan, was examined in the same quarter, and that her great-grandfather,
Ε̣ὔφελλι̣ν̣ [π]ρ̣οσβ(αίνοντα) τῷ κᾱ (ἔτει) θ̣εοῦ Αἰλί[ο]υ Ἀντωνίνου ἐπικ(εκρίσθαι) ἐπ' ἀμφ(όδου) τοῦ αὐτοῦ, καὶ τὸν πάππ(ον) αὐτῆς	Euphellis, candidate in year 21 of *divus* Aelius Antoninus, was examined in the same quarter, and that her grandfather,
Ἄντι. . . . προσβ(αίνοντα) τῷ λβ̄ (ἔτει) θε[οῦ] Κομό[δ]ου ἐπικ(εκρίσθαι) ἐπ' ἀ[μ]φ(όδου) Μυροβαλάνου, καὶ τὸν πατέρα	Anti[...], candidate in year 32 of *divus* Commodus, was examined in the Myrobalanus quarter, and that her father,
αὐτῆς Σα[ρ]απίωνα πρ[ο]σβ(αίνοντα) τῷ δ̄ (ἔτει) θεοῦ Ἀλεξάνδρου ἐπικ(εκρίσθαι) ἐπὶ ταῖς αὐταῖς ἀποδ(είξεσιν) ἐπ' ἀμφ(όδου)	Sarapion, candidate in year 4 of *divus* Alexander, was examined on the same proofs in the quarter
Βορρᾶ Δ[ρό(μου)]. παρέσχ[ο]ν δὲ τῆς ἐπ̣ι̣κρίσεως γνωστῆρας καὶ ὀμνοίω τὴν Αὐρηλιανοῦ	of the North Road. I have provided witnesses of the examination and I swear by the fortune of Aurelianus
Καίσαρος τ[οῦ] κυρ[ί]ου Σεβαστοῦ τύχην ἀληθῆ εἶναι τὰ προγεγραμμένα καὶ εἶναι τὸν	Caesar, the lord Augustus, that the aforewritten (matters) are true and that Thonis is
Θῶνιν φ[ύσ]ι τοῦ Κοπρέως καὶ τῆς Θερμούθιον υἱὸν καὶ μήτε θέσι μήτε ὑπόβλητο(ν)	the natural son of Kopreus and Thermouthion and neither by adoption nor by substitution,
μηδὲ ἀλλο[τ]ρίαις ἀσφαλίαις ἢ ὁμονυμίαις καιχρῆσθαι ἢ ἔνοχος εἴην τῷ ὅρκῳ.	nor has he used another's credentials or identity of names or may I be liable to the oath.
(ἔτους) γ̄ Αὐτ[οκ]ράτορος Καίσαρος Λουκ[ί]ου Δομιττίου Αὐρηλιανοῦ Γουθθικοῦ Μεγίστου	In year 3 of Imperator Caesar Lucius Domitius Aurelianus Gothicus Maximus
Εὐσεβοῦς Εὐτυχοῦς Σεβαστοῦ Μεσορὴ ιᾱ.	Pius Felix Augustus, Mesore 11.
(m. 2) Αὐρήλιο[ς] Σεύθης ἐπιδέδωκα καὶ ὤμ‹ο›σα τὸν ὅρκον ὡς	(m. 2) I, Aurelius Seuthes, have submitted and sworn the oath as
πρόκειται. Αὐρήλιος Δίδυμος ὁ καὶ Σαραπίων ἔγραψα ὑπὲρ αὐτοῦ	aforementioned. I, Aurelius Didymos, also called Sarapion, have written (it) for him
μὴ εἰδ[ό]τος γράμματα.	since he is illiterate.

28 (m. 3) Αὐρήλιος Σαραπίων Διογένους μητρὸς Ἑλένης ἀπὸ τῆς
πόλεως γνωστεύω τὸν Θῶνειν ὄντα φύσι υἑὸν τοῦ
Κοπρέως καὶ τῆς Θερμουτẹίου ὡς πρόκειται.
(m. 4) [Α]ὐρήλιος 'Αμόις 'Αφυνχίου μητρὸς 'Ạῴλεẉς
32 [± 3]ẉς συṿγνωστεύω τὸν Θῶνιν ὡς πρόκει-
[τα]ι. (m. 5) Αὐρή[λ]ιος 'Ιοῦστος 'Ηρακλάμμωνος μητρὸς ῎Ισειτος
συνγνω[σ]τεύω τὸν [Θ]ῶνειν ὡς πρόκειται.

(m. 3) I, Aurelius Sarapion, son of Diogenes, my mother being Helene, from the
city, witness that Thonis is the natural son of
Kopreus and Thermouthion as aforementioned.
(m. 4) I, Aurelius Amois, son of Aphunchios, my mother being Aolis,
[...] act as joint witness for Thonis as aforementioned.
(m. 5) I, Aurelius Justus, son of Heraklammon, my mother being Iseis,
act as joint witness for Thonis as aforementioned.

....

5 Πλατείας 6 ἀπήνεγκεν 9&17 Κομμόδου 10 βασιλείας 11 Λυκίων 12 εἴδει 13 χιλιάρχου 19 ὀμνύω 21 φύσει, Θερμουθίου, θέσει 22 ἀσφαλείαις, ὁμωνυμίαις, κεχρῆσθαι 23 Δομιτίου, Γουθικοῦ 25 ὤμοσα 29 Θῶνιν, φύσει, υἱόν 30 Θερμουθίου 32 συγγνωστεύω

The form of the Oxyrhynchus *epikrisis* is discussed by C.A.Nelson, *Status Declarations in Roman Egypt* (Amsterdam 1979), pp.26-30. Its elements are:

1. The introductory formula:
- **a.** dative of addressees, either officials of the nome in the early period or municipal office holder in the later period;
- **b.** the name of the declarant, i.e. the parent, brother or guardian – παρὰ N, son of N and N, ἀπ' 'Οξυρύγχων πόλεως.

2. The declaration:
- **a.** a declaration that the *epikrisis* is made in accord with the decrees – κατὰ τὰ κελευσθέντα περὶ ἐπικρίσεως τῶν προσβαινόντων εἰς τοὺς ἐκ τοῦ γυμνασίου;
- **b.** the conditional statement εἰ εἰσιν τοῦ γένους τούτου;
- **c.** a statement that the boy is eligible for the *epikrisis* – ἐτάγη ἐπ' ἀμφόδου N ὁ υἱός μου N + identifying features or δηλῶ τὸν υἱόν μου N (mother identified) γεγονέναι (age) εἰς τὸ ἐνεστὸς x^th^ (ἔτος) + identifying features;
- **d.** the declaration ὅθεν παραγενόμενος πρὸς τὴν τούτου ἐπίκρισιν δηλῶ κατὰ τὴν γενομένην (date) τῶν ἐκ τοῦ γυμνασίου ἐπίκρισιν ἐπικεκρίσθαι τὸν πατέρα (or other relative).

3. The credentials showing that the boy's ancestors were members of the *gymnasium* class.

4. An oath of the declarant that the child is his natural legitimate son and that the ancestry is not that of another.

5. Conclusion:
- **a.** date;
- **b.** signature – N ἐπιδέδωκα καὶ ὀμώμοκα (here ὤμοσα) τὸν ὅρκον;
- **c.** names and statement of witnesses (usually three in number).

On the basis of the formal analysis, it can be seen that elements **1** to **2.b** of the present *epikrisis* are missing.

N. Lewis, *Life in Egypt under Roman Rule* (Oxford 1983), p.211, defines ἐπίκρισις as 'the process for determining admissibility to a special status, civilian or military'. Nelson, op.cit. pp.3-9 and 40-46, argues against any military purpose. An *epikrisis* was conducted to ascertain an individual's status and thus the privileges to which he was entitled. *Epikriseis* involving veterans are part of this general process. When a veteran decided to settle in a particular area, he underwent an *epikrisis* to establish his status and privileges (see also the discussion in *New Docs* 6 [1992] **§19**). Another type of *epikrisis* concerned the examination of youths (males aged fourteen years or slightly younger) of privileged families. It is argued that the significance of the child's age resided in the fact that at the age of fourteen the boy became liable for poll-tax. Different types of *epikrisis* occur within nomes and between nomes. However, Nelson sees two purposes in the establishment of status. One is purely fiscal and establishes the person's entitlement to a lower rate of poll-tax (e.g. the *epikrisis* of metropolites);[156] the other deals primarily with status and entitles the person to educational and vocational opportunities (e.g. the *epikrisis* to the *gymnasium* class).[157] For this reason there can be an overlap between the two types of *epikrisis*, i.e. a person may undergo two *epikriseis*. However, the *epikrisis* of the κάτοικοι in the Arsinoite nome, Nelson, op.cit., pp.36-39, argues, was used for both fiscal and status purposes.

Between the years AD 33/4 and AD 257/8 a census was taken every fourteen years in Egypt. For a discussion of the *termini* see M.Hombert – Cl.Préaux, *Recherches sur le recensement dans l'Égypte romain* (Leiden 1952), pp.47-53. By collating the returns for each household lists of minors in age order (starting with boys of thirteen years of age) were compiled. This information was probably used to update on a yearly basis the regional tax lists. The fiscal aspect of the *epikrisis* of a fourteen-year-old male addressed his impending liability to pay the poll-tax by establishing his exemption or partial exemption from its payment. However, a question remains concerning Nelson's differentiation between the fiscal function and educational/vocational function of the *epikrisis*. How does one explain the concurrent decline of both types of *epikrisis* towards the end of the third century? The decline of the fiscal *epikrisis* can be readily explained by the changing system of taxation before the introduction of the system of indiction in AD 312 (on the decline of the census see the discussion by Hombert – Préaux, ibid., pp.52-3). By contrast no explanation is offered for the similar decline of the *epikrisis* whose function was solely educational/vocational. Perhaps the social upheavals at the end of third century led both to the change to the fourteen-year census cycle (as suggested by Hombert – Préaux, ibid., p.53) and to an end in the use of all *epikriseis*.

The above papyrus is an *epikrisis* for membership of the *gymnasium* class at Oxyrhynchus (for other *epikriseis* to the *gymnasium* class see Nelson, op. cit., p.26). Element **3** of the *epikrisis* involved the demonstration that the youth's paternal and maternal ancestors were members of the *gymnasium* class, with membership being traced back to the list drawn up in AD 4/5 and its revision in AD 72/3. After the latter date admission to the *gymnasium* seems to have been closed. The present *epikrisis* is declared by the boy's guardian. His father was no doubt dead. Theonis' genealogy is traced back on his father's side six generations to an *epikrisis* in AD 72/3 and on his mother's side by eight generations to two *epikriseis* in years AD 56/7 & 58/9. It is usual for the father's genealogy to be traced further back than that of the mother.

---

156 The amount of the poll-tax or λαογραφία was not uniform in Roman Egypt. Some persons were exempt (e.g. Roman citizens, some priests, officials, games victors, scholars etc. and, initially, the citizens of Alexandria). The citizens of a metropolis (οἱ ἀπὸ μητροπόλεως), the *gymnasium* classes of Oxyrhynchus and Hermopolis (οἱ ἀπὸ γυμνασίου) and the κάτοικοι paid a reduced poll-tax (some may have paid none). The unprivileged population of the Egyptian villages and countryside, however, paid a higher rate of poll-tax, usually double that of the citizens of the metropolis.

157 For example, candidates for the municipal magistracy were probably drawn from the *gymnasium* class. Nelson, op.cit., p.35, argues that the *gymnasium* class at Oxyrhynchus was a more elite group than the metropolites. Nelson argues a similar status distinction between the ephebic and *gymnasium* classes. However, J.E.G. Whitehorne, 'The Ephebate and the Gymnasial Class in Roman Egypt', *BASP* 19 (1982), pp.171-84, disagrees with Nelson's assignment of lower status to the ephebic class. It is argued that ἐφηβεία and its cognates either are used to describe youths in training before admission to full membership of the *gymnasium* or relate to the attempts of Alexandrian citizens living outside Alexandria to have their sons educated in the local *gymnasium*.

The condition that the youth's paternal and maternal ancestors belong to the *gymnasium* class was a strong incentive for marriage to be endogamous. Frequencies of consanguine marriages in the χώρα and the cities confirm this tendency (see Table 17.1: Consanguine and Other Marriage):[158]

Table 17.1: Marriage by Region and Source

Region	Source	Marriage: Consanguine	Marriage: Other
Chora	Census	13	69
	Epikrisis	-	-
City	Census	18	36
	Epikrisis	7	18

An analysis of the table shows a strong association between one's region of registration (i.e. *chora* or city) and the type of marriage (i.e. consanguine or other) entered into. See Appendix ii). Those living and registering in the cities were more probably of the privileged classes. This group also shows a significantly higher proportion of consanguine marriages.

One might note here the types of regional difference regarding proof of civil status. At Oxyrhynchus the boy's ancestry was usually traced back through the archives of the *gymnasium* (see above). At Arsinoe and Hermoupolis extracts from previous census declarations sufficed, e.g. *SB* XIV 11270 (Arsinoe, AD 96 or 98). S.L.Wallace, *Taxation in Egypt* (New York 1969), p.105, suggests that another element in the procurement of entry to the privileged *gymnasium* class was the birth notice or ὑπόμνημα ἐπιγεννήσεως. *P. Ups.Frid* 6 is such a birth notice.

Oxyrhynchus July/Aug. AD 273

Ed.pr.– B.Frid, *P. Ups.Frid* 6 (Bonn 1981), pp.63-72.

The document (measuring 14.8 x 8.8 cm) is incomplete; it lacks a top, bottom and part of the upper left hand margin. Only a few letters are missing from the right margin. The editor has restored the opening lines on the basis of similar documents.

[τῷ Ν.Ν. φυλάρχῳ τῆς λαμπρᾶς Ὀξυρυγχιτῶν πόλεως τοῦ ἐνεστῶτος ἔτους δ̅ παρὰ Αὐρηλίου Πλουτάμμωνος Σαραπίωνος]	[To N.N. *phylarchos* of the illustrious city of Oxrhynchus, in the present year 4, from Aurelius Ploutammon, son of Sarapion,]
κ̣αὶ τῆς τούτου γενομένης καὶ ἀπηλ̣[λ]αγμένη̣ς	and his former and divorced
γυναικὸς Αὐρηλίας Ἰσιδώρας Παυσα-	wife Aurelia Isidora, daughter of Pausanias,
νίου ἀμφοτέρων ἀπὸ τῆς αὐτῆς πόλεως.	both from the same city.
Βουλόμεθα πρώτως ἀναγραφῆ̣ναι ἐφ' ἧς	We wish to have registered for the first time in the house which

158 Hombert – Préaux, op.cit., p.152, gathered their data from census and *epikrisis* declarations. In Table 17.1 the count data for the χώρα have been grouped and the count data for the cities have been grouped. Though the data could be updated, their sample is sufficiently large to permit statistical observations to be made.

ἔχει Αὐρήλιος Ἀπολλώνιος ὁ καὶ Διονύσιος	is owned by Aurelius Apollonios, also called Dionysios,
γυμνασίαρχος βουλευτὴς τῆς αὐτῆς	*gymnasiarchos*, councillor of the same
πόλεως ἐπ' ἀμφόδου Παμμένους Παραδί-	city, in the quarter of Pammenes' garden,
σου οἰκίας τὸν γεγονότα ἡμεῖν ἐξ ἀλλή-	the son born to both of us,
λων υἱὸν Αὐρήλιον Παυσεῖριν (δωδεκάδραχμον)	Aurelius Pauseiris, (*dodecadrachmos*),
ἀπὸ γυμ(νασίου) ὄντα πρὸς τὸ ἐνεστὸς δ̅ (ἔτος) (ἐτῶν) ι̅γ̅.	of the *gymnasium* class for the present year 4 aged 13 years.
Ἐπιδιδόντες τὸ ὑπόμνημα ἀξιοῦμεν τα-	Submitting the memorandum we ask that
γ̣ῆ̣ναι αὐτὸν διὰ τῆς καταχωριζομένης	he be registered by means of the list of minors
ὑπὸ σοῦ γραφῆς ἀφηλίκων ἐν τῇ τῶν	compiled by you in the
ὁμηλίκων τάξει ὡς καθήκει καὶ ὀμνύω	division of the same age as is appropriate and I swear
τὸν ἔθιμον Ῥωμαίοις ὅρκον μὴ [ἐψεῦ-]	the oath customary to the Romans not to have lied.
σθαι. (Ἔτους) δ Αὐτοκράτορος Καίσαρος Λ[ουκίου]	In year 4 of Imperator Caesar Lucius
Δομιττίου Αὐρηλιανοῦ Γουνθικοῦ Μεγ[ίστου]	Domitius Aurelianus Gothicus Maximus
Εὐσεβοῦς Εὐτυχοῦς Ἀνεικήτου Σεβαστ[οῦ Μ]ε-	Pius Felix Invictus Augustus, Mesore.
σορή. (m. 2) Αὐρήλιος Πλουτάμμων	(m. 2) I, Aurelius Ploutammon,
Σαραπίωνος ἐπιδέδωκα.	son of Sarapion, have submitted.
(m. 3) [Α]ὐρηλία Ἰσιδώρα Παυσανίου	(m. 3) I, Aurelia Isidora, daughter of Pausanias,
[ἐ]πιδέδωκα. Αὐρήλιος Διόσκο-	have submitted. I, Aurelius Dioscoros,
[ρος] ἔγρ[α]ψα̣ [ὑπὲρ αὐτῆς] μ̣ὴ	have written (it) [for her since she
[εἰδυίης γράμματα]	is illiterate.]

....

8 παραδείσου 9 ἡμῖν 10 Παυσῖριν 15 ὀμνύομεν 18 Δομιτίου, Γουθικοῦ 19 Ἀνικήτου

On registration (*l*.5) and the preparation of lists for taxation purposes see *New Docs* 6 (1992) **§16**. The editor of *P. Ups.Frid* 6 calls for a reconsideration of Wallace's interpretation regarding the use of birth notices from Oxyrhynchus. Can they have functioned to procure entry to the privileged *gymnasium* class? He lists the extant birth notices from Oxyrhynchus and notes several problematic areas. They are:

1. the registration of girls;
2. the registration of boys aged thirteen years;
3. some declarations lack the designation of the boy as δωδεκάδραχμος ἀπὸ γυμνασίου (i.e. liable to the lower twelve-drachma poll-tax).

The first two factors are easily explained. The registration of girls would arise from the need to prove membership of the *gymnasium* class in the boy's maternal family as well as his paternal family. The registration of boys aged thirteen years seems to prove nothing against the hypothesis if one supposes that the registration of birth had occurred and been accepted before their *epikrisis*. The third factor, however, is difficult. If the registration was to serve as a proof of the youth's parentage for the purpose of *epikrisis*, then the omission of the child's privileged status on registration is problematic.

Status in the NT

The *epikrisis* illustrates an ancient society's awareness of and care in guarding status and privilege. The context may be important for an understanding of Paul's treatment of status. For example, Paul's apparent inversion of status conventions should be understood against the background of the importance attached to them in antiquity. Two examples can be cited. The first forms part of Paul's 'boasting' to the Corinthians (2Cor.11.22): Ἑβραῖοί εἰσιν; κἀγώ. Ἰσραηλῖταί εἰσιν; κἀγώ. σπέρμα Ἀβραάμ εἰσιν; κἀγώ. On the status significance of the terms 'Hebrew', 'Israelite' and 'seed of Abraham' see D. Georgi, *The Opponents of Paul in Second Corinthians* (Edinburgh 1987), pp.41-60. Like Paul, Josephus recounts his high priestly ancestry (Josephus, *Vita* 1-6). M. Goodman, *The Ruling Class of Judaea* (Cambridge 1988), p.67, observes of the Jews: 'Important social categories for them were based on religious status: a man felt himself to be an Israelite, a Levite or a priest, a proselyte or a natural-born Jew'. It needs to be stressed that the status indicators for Paul are Jewish rather than Roman (see discussion of Paul's possession of Roman citizenship in *New Docs* 6 [1992] **§20**). What follows the Jewish status indicators in 2Cor.11.22 is a list of the shame and humiliations suffered by Paul as a servant of Christ, i.e. imprisonments, floggings, stonings etc. (see also 1Cor.4.6-13). J.T. Fitzgerald, *Cracks in an Earthen Vessel: An Examination of the Catalogues of Hardships in the Corinthian Correspondence* (Atlanta 1988), argues that in listing his hardships Paul was using a linguistic convention to demonstrate his integrity as a true apostle and to show the power of God in human frailty.

> *Peristasis* catalogues serve to legitimate the claims made about a person and show him to be virtuous because *peristaseis* have a revelatory and probative function in regard to character. Since it is axiomatic in the ancient world that adversity is the litmus test of character, a person's virtuous attitude and action while under duress furnish the proof that he is a man of genuine worth and/or a true philosopher. They distinguish him from the person who owes his high standing to Fortune as well as from the person who feigns virtue and knowledge. (p.203)

Also important for an understanding of the catalogues of hardships is Paul's attitude to his sufferings. P. Marshall, *Enmity in Corinth: Social Conventions in Paul's Relations with the Corinthians* (Tübingen 1987), pp.351-64, points to the anguish experienced by Paul over his humiliation and shame and argues that the model of 'Cynic inversion' gives an insufficient account of it. However, these have instead become for Paul 'the marks of (his) apostleship and God's approval' over against those who criticise him (p.364). The source of the criticism, it is argued, was Paul's rejection of the Corinthian gift but acceptance of the gift of support from the Philippians. But we might note that Paul could write in a similar vein to this church also:

> περιτομῇ ὀκταήμερος, ἐκ γένους Ἰσραήλ, φυλῆς Βενιαμίν, Ἑβραῖος ἐξ Ἑβραίων, κατὰ νόμον Φαρισαῖος, κατὰ ζῆλος διώκων τὴν ἐκκλησίαν, κατὰ δικαιοσύνην τὴν ἐν νόμῳ γενόμενος ἄμεμπτος. [ἀλλὰ] ἅτινα ἦν μοι κέρδη, ταῦτα ἥγημαι διὰ τὸν Χριστὸν ζημίαν. ἀλλὰ μενοῦνγε καὶ ἡγοῦμαι πάντα ζημίαν εἶναι διὰ τὸ ὑπερέχον τῆς γνώσεως Χριστοῦ Ἰησοῦ τοῦ κυρίου μου, δι' ὃν τὰ πάντα ἐζημιώθην, καὶ ἡγοῦμαι σκύβαλα, ἵνα Χριστὸν κερδήσω κτλ (Phil.3.5-8)

Such statements by Paul which contrast the conventions of status and his experience in Christ show the tension within his own consciousness. In the *epikrisis* the boy's privileged status was traced back through several generations. His status afforded him social, political and educational advantages. Paul also was aware of the advantages afforded him by his birth and this was not negated by his experience in Christ. For Paul social distinctions remained valid, as has been argued with regard to slavery (see *New Docs* 6 [1992] §6). However, the example of Christ (e.g. Phil.2.6-8) and the prospect of a superior advantage had relativised in Paul's consciousness the advantages afforded by privileged status.

S.R.L.

§18 Petitions, Social History and the Language of Requests

Provenance unknown AD 130 (?)

Ed.pr. — A. Lukaszewicz, 'A Petition from Priests to Hadrian with his Subscription', *Am. Stud. Pap*. XXIII (Chico 1981), pp.357-361 (= *P. Berol. inv*.16546).

The papyrus sheet (14 x 11.5 cm) contains the final section of a petition to Hadrian. It is only broken along the left edge. A space at its top indicates that the petition was written in several columns. The present fragment is the only surviving column.

	[... διὸ δεόμεθά σε,]	[Therefore, we ask you,]
	[Σω]τ̣ῆρα καὶ Εὐεργέτην, ἐλεῆσαι ἡμᾶ̣ς	[sa]viour and benefactor, to pity
	καὶ τὸν ἡμέ-	us and our
	[τερ]ον θεὸν Σόξειν καὶ ἐπιτρέψαι	god, Soxis, and to permit
	κ̣[α]ὶ̣ ἡμεῖν ἃ̣ς ποιού-	us also to collect
	[με]θα ὑπὲρ τοῦ ἱεροῦ δαπάνας παρὰ	the expenditure which we make on the
	[τ]ῶν αὐτῶν κω-	temple from the same
4	[μη]τῶν λαμβ̣ά̣ν̣ειν ἵνα δυνηθῶ[μ]εν τὰς	villagers that we may be able to perform
	ὑπηρεσίας	our services
	[ποι]εῖσθαι καὶ τὰ ὀφειλόμενα τῶι	and pay without fault what is owed to the
	φίσκωι ἀμέμπτω[ς]	*fiscus*
	[ἀπο]διδόναι ἐκ τῆς σῆς εὐεργεσίας.	by your beneficence.
	(vac.) διευτύχει.	Farewell.
	[ἀ]ντίγρ(αφον) ὑπογρ(αφῆς).	Copy of a subscription.
	ὑπέγραψ(α). προτεθήτωι̣.	I have subscribed. Let it be posted.
	(vac.)	
8	[Αὐτ]ο̣κράτωρ Καῖσαρ [Τρ]αιανὸς	Imperator Caesar Traianus
	Ἁδριανὸς Σεβαστὸς	Hadrianus Augustus
	[ἱ]ερεῦσι (vac.) [ ]τ̣ο̣ς [ ]	to the priests ...

The petition was a letter addressed to an official which might be used by him in the decision-making process. As a result it gave the petitioner access to the judicial/administrative powers of government. Letters of petition also tend to be highly formulaic. J.L.White, *The Form and Structure of the Official Petition* (Missoula 1972), has distinguished the following formal elements:

1. Opening:

a. salutation – To A from B;
b. lineage of petitioner;
c. vocation of petitioner;
d. residence of petitioner.

2. Background: a description of the state of affairs giving rise to the petition.
3. Petition, e.g. 'I request, therefore, that you write to the *strategos* to investigate the matter, if it pleases you, that I may obtain justice':

A. **a.** the verb of petition, e.g. 'I request' – δέομαι or ἀξιῶ;
b. the conjunction between the formal elements of the background and petition, e.g. 'therefore' – οὖν, διό or ὅθεν;
c. pronominal object (i.e. the address to the official), e.g. 'you';
B. **d.** the request to the official, usually an infinitive clause, e.g. 'to write to ...';
e. the anticipated action of the official, e.g. 'to investigate the matter';
f. a qualification to e, e.g. 'if it pleases you';
C. **g.** statement regarding anticipated justice, e.g. 'that I may obtain justice'.

4. Closing: εὐτύχει.

According to White's paradigm, the above fragmentary petition contains only the formal elements **3.B**, **3.C** and **4**; however, element **3.A** can safely be restored to read 'Therefore, we ask you'. However, R.R.I. Harper (per litt.) raises questions over the usefulness of White's paradigm. In particular he notes the relatively small sample size (seventy-one petitions) on which the paradigm is based; the absence of any 'particular reference to the habit of using introductory sentence before the actual exposition of the case in petitions to high officials', e.g. in *BGU* I 168 and *P. Oxy.* XVII 2131; and the neglect of such variables as time of creation, subject matter and the official's rank and their effect on the petition's form (see below). Harper thus indicates the need for a more detailed study of petitions in the Roman period along the lines of A. Di Bitonto's study of Ptolemaic petitions (*Aegytus* 47 [1967], pp.5-57 and *Aegyptus* 48 [1968], pp.53-107).

R.L.B. Morris, 'Reflections of Citizen Attitudes in Petitions from Roman Oxyrhynchus' in *Am. Stud. Pap.* XXIII (Chico 1981), pp.363-70, uses petitions submitted to government officials to study 'individual perceptions of rights and the role of government'. The study leads him to qualify the view that Roman rule was always overly oppressive. He concludes that during the first century the government was perceived to be interested in the rights of the petitioner. Where complaints concerned government administration, they were made against officials and not the government itself. During the second century, however, Morris notes a change in attitude. Rather than seeing the government as the guardian of their rights, as they had done previously, petitioners now perceived themselves as being oppressed by government. Appeals were made on the basis of pity or veiled threats (especially to abandon home and land, i.e. to cause financial loss to the *fiscus*). Morris assigns the change in attitude to 'a growing problem of economic and administrative instability'. Government liturgies and taxes were a heavy burden reducing many individuals to poverty and flight. See *New Docs* 6 (1992) **§15** on these problems and the use of reintegration edicts to address the problem.

Using as a sample those petitions of the first and second centuries (total number 44) presented by White, one can observe significant changes over the period. These either confirm or extend Morris' conclusions. For example, one notes a significant change in the subject matter of petitions. Table 18.1 illustrates the change away from petitions which predominantly concern private matters (e.g. theft, damages, assault and fraud) towards petitions which concern public matters. It is important to note that two of the three petitions classified as 'other' and occurring in the second century AD concern guardianship, also a form of liturgy (the third petition concerns patrimony).

Table 18.1: The subject matter of petitions

	Period	
Subject Matter	I AD	II AD
Theft,[159] damages, assault & fraud	28	2
Private commercial	3	2
Tax, liturgies & against officials	1	6
Other	0	3

Morris' hypothesis substantially depends on the appeal to pity or the use of veiled threats in petitions of the latter period. However, Harper (per litt.) sees the need for a degree of perspective when assessing such matters. For example, he points to the use of threats against government revenue in both Ptolemaic (e.g. *BGU* VIII 1836, *P. Lille* I 8, *P. Petrie* II 2 1, *P. Rein.* I 18, *P. Tebt.* I 41, 50, 53, III 782, 786, 787) and Byzantine petitions (e.g. *P. Oxy.* XXVII 2479) and suggests that they may well have been 'a reflection of perennial and inherent problems in the nature of the ancient economy, as much as a barometer of government oppression or social unrest at a particular point in time'. On the other hand, Harper feels that the value of appeals to pity is equivocal as 'petitions were in their nature a documentary supplication'. Petitioners routinely portrayed themselves as pitiable in an attempt to gain a sympathetic hearing. On the basis of Tables 18.1 and 18.2 three further points, I believe, should be made.

First, the relationship between the type of arguments used and the petition's official addressee is important and must be borne in mind when assessing petitions. For example, most of the petitions of the first century are addressed to the chief of police or *strategos*. In these instances the petitioner asks either that he might obtain justice – ἵνα τύχω τῶν δικαίων – or that the offending party might be punished – πρὸς τὴν ἐσομένην ἐπέξοδον. However, when a centurion is addressed (see White's petition no.33 = *P. Ryl.* 141 of AD 37) appeal is made to the preservation of public order – ἵνα μηδὲν τῶν δημοσίων διαπέσῃ. When the official is a person of high rank, appeal is made to his beneficence – ἵνα ὦμεν εὐεργετημένοι (see White's nos.45 and 47 = *P. Ryl.* 119 and *P. Graux* 2 of AD 54-67 and AD 55-59 respectively). In other words, the argument used by a petitioner seems to depend on the official's status and/or function.

Table 18.2: The addressees of petitions

	Period	
Addressee	I AD	II AD
Strategos, Chief of Police	27	6
Epistrategos, Prefect[160]	1	5
Other (centurion, council, *exegetes* etc.)	3	2

159 Note that one petition in the earlier period concerns a double complaint of theft and breach of contract. It is counted twice.

160 The *epistrategoi* and prefect of Egypt were Romans of equestrian rank. On the grouping of these officials see J.D. Thomas, ibid., pp.141-2 and 180-1.

Second, petitions of the latter period were addressed more frequently to higher officials (see Table 18.2). J.D. Thomas, *The Epistrategos in Ptolemaic and Roman Egypt*, part 2 (Opladen 1982), p.140, observes that 'there was no rigid distinction between the types of case which could come in the first instance to strategos, epistrategos or prefect'. Nevertheless, the nature of the complaint and the position held by the petitioner's opponent seem to have played an important role in determining the official to be petitioned. The evidence adduced by N. Lewis, *The Compulsory Public Services of Roman Egypt* (= *P. Flor.* XI, Florence 1982), pp.122-7, is of further relevance. His Table 5 is a list of petitions which protest liturgies. It also shows a highly significant difference between the number of such petitions from the first century AD and their number from subsequent centuries, e.g. two petitions from 1 to 100 AD, forty one petitions from 101 to 200 AD and sixteen from 201 to 300 AD. The evidence further supports the count data of Table 18.1. Moreover, Table 5 also shows, as N. Lewis, ibid., pp.100-1, has himself observed, the tendency of petitioners to address their protests against liturgies to higher officials, 'generally to the prefect or the epistrategos, occasionally also to the dioiketes or other high official'. The observation is relevant to the point at hand. Since the status and function of the addressee may well have affected the type of argument used by the petitioner, an increase in the appeal to an official's beneficence or function (e.g. the prefect's role of protecting the *fiscus*) will be expected in the later periods because of the change in the topics and addressees of petitions. It will also be noted that petitions were increasingly directed against a hardship caused by the administration itself. Under these circumstances the official was no longer addressed as a third and independent party to the dispute itself. This change would also affect the type of argument used by the petitioner to gain a favourable hearing.

Third, whilst in the earlier period petitions were predominantly made by the persons from the lower social strata (e.g. farmers, villagers, clerks, estate agents, an oil-maker, a wine-press lessee, a slave), the later period saw a marked increase in petitions from persons of a higher social status (e.g. metropolites[161] or children of metropolites, estate owners, a veteran, a physician). In other words, a further dimension can be added to Morris' interpretation, namely that the sample of second-century petitions witnesses an extension in the use of petitioning to the more privileged strata of society. Attempts to curtail or to ignore both privileges and exemptions as well as the imposition of liturgies in the harder economic times of the second century were no doubt contributing factors to this observable change.

In the above discussion White's examples of petitions have been used as a sample on which observations were made. Before any more general observation can be inferred, one will need to know how randomly his selection was made. Even conceding randomness in White's selection, a further question stands over the randomness in papyrological finds themselves. For example, a skew in the data can easily be caused by the finding of a large number of petitions stemming from one particular office. Leaving aside the question of randomness, the above observations may still be used to ask questions of and seek parallels and contrasts in other petitions of the period. For example, the above petition from the priests to Hadrian shows several of the features common to other petitions of the second century. The petitioners appeal to the emperor's beneficence and mercy and express a veiled threat against the *fiscus* if their request is not granted. Also it is to be noted that the petitioners, as priests, are of a privileged social status and that their appeal is to the highest authority of the empire. Another papyrus also shows interesting parallels.

---

161 Metropolites belonged to a more privileged stratum of society. They underwent an *epikrisis* which entitiled them, as privileged city-dwellers, to a reduced rate of poll-tax.

Karanis? After 27 July AD 179

Ed.pr.– L.C.Youtie, 'Petition to an Epistrategos', *ZPE* 42 (1981), pp.81-88.

The papyrus (12.5 x 31 cm) consists of four fragments which were found separately. A petition had formerly been made to the prefect and a copy of this (*ll*.17-33 reproduced below) with the prefect's subscription was then transmitted by the petitioner to the *epistrategos*.

[Τίτωι Πακτουμηΐ]ωι Μάγνωι ἐπάρχῳ Αἰγύπ(του)	[To Titus Pactumei]us Magnus, prefect of Egypt,
[παρὰ Ἰουλίας Ἡ]ραΐδος Ἀντινοΐτιδος	[from Julia] Herais, an Antinoite,
[καὶ ὡς χρηματίζω]ι. προσφέρ̣[ω] σοι, ἡγεμὼν	[and however I am called.] I bring to you, prefect
[κύριε, πρᾶγμα τῆς] σ̣ῆς ἐκδικίας̣ δεόμενον.	[lord, a matter] requiring your decision.
[ἐπειδὴ] Ἡ̣ρακλείδης Ἀμμωνίου	[Since] Herakleides, son of Ammonios,
μισθωτ[ὴς] καταλοχισμῶν Ἀρσιν[ο]-	tax-farmer of the land register of Arsinoite
ε̣ί̣του καὶ ἄλλων νομῶν αὐθάδη τρ[ό]πο̣ν	and other nomes, possessing a self-willed manner
κεκτημέ[ν]ος ἐβιάσατό με βουλη-	has intimidated me wishing
θεὶς ἀπ̣α̣ι̣τ[ῆ]σαί με οὐ δεόντως τέλος	to demand payment from me unnecessarily of a tax
μὴ ὀφειλ[ό]μενον βασιλικοῦ ὑπολ[όγου]	not owed on unproductive state (land),
ὑπὲρ τοῦ τοι̣[ού]τ̣ου μηδεπώποτε τ̣έλους	(seeing that) tax on such (land) never
καταβληθ[έν]τος ἀναγκαίως ἐπὶ σέ, τὸν	is paid, perforce (then) to you, the
σωτῆρα, κατέφυγον καὶ ἀξιῶ κελεῦσα̣ι	saviour, have I fled and ask that (you) order
γ̣ρ̣[α]φῆ̣ν̣α̣ι τ[ῷ] τ̣ῶν Ἑ̣πτὰ Νομῶν ἐ̣π̣ι̣[στρ]α̣(τήγῳ)	that the *epistrategos* of the Seven Nomes be written to
ἀ[κ]οῦσαί μου πρὸς αὐτὸν ὅπως μηδὲν	to hear me against him that no
βί[αι]όν μοι ὑ̣πὸ τοῦ Ἡρακλείδου γείνηθαι	act of force might occur against me at the hands of Herakleides
κ̣α̣ὶ [ὦ] ε̣ὐεργετημένη.	and I may receive your benefaction.
διευτύχει. Ἰουλία Ἡραῒς	Farewell. I, Julia Herais,
δι(ὰ) [τ]οῦ υἱοῦ Γα[ί]ου Ἰουλίου Πρείσκου ἐπιδέδωκα.	have submitted (the petition) through my son, Gaius Julius Priscus.

Julia Herais had first petitioned the prefect of Egypt, Titus Pactumeius Magnus. She received his subscription to write to the *epistrategos* (*ll*.35-6 not reproduced here) and this she now does. Included in this new petition to the *epistrategos* is a copy of the original petition to the prefect and his subscription, i.e. *ll*.17-34 reproduced above. Again the document shows several features in common with the type of petitions to be found in the second century. First, the addressee of the petition is the highest Roman authority in Egypt. Second, the petitioner is a metropolite and member of a privileged stratum of society. Julia's son, Gaius Julius Priscus, is a witness at an *epikrisis* of an ephebe in AD 168/9 (*SB* IV 7427) and in AD 172-4 is shown as a landholder in the tax rolls of Karanis. He bears a Roman name. Third, the petition calls on the prefect as saviour to show his beneficence. Finally, the petition concerns the matter of tax on unproductive state land and thus deals with a topic central to the plight of second-century Egypt. With many farmers absconding from their lands and the burden of tax falling on those who remained behind, it was no doubt a temptation for tax-farmers, in order to assure an adequate collection of revenues, to levy taxes against all lands. See further the discussion in *New Docs* 6 (1992) **§15**.

Petitions and the NT

The above discussion has highlighted some of the information concerning social conditions and attitudes which can be gathered from the papyrological evidence of petitions. The study by Morris has drawn attention to the changed attitude to Roman government between the first and second centuries. His evidence relates to Egypt and Oxyrhynchus in particular. An even sharper differentiation in the attitude to Rome can be perceived in the texts of the NT. For example, in Rom.13.1-7 Paul advised his readers to submit to the governing authorities as agents established by God, to pay their taxes and dues, and to show reverence and honour to the authorities (so also Tit.3.1 and 1Pet.2.13-17). However, in Rev.17-18 a diametrically opposed picture of Rome emerges. She was no longer perceived as the agent of God to punish evil but as the great prostitute and perpetrator of evil and violence on earth. In the NT, however, the change cannot be ascribed simply to the chronological distance between Paul and Revelation and an increasing awareness of the burden of Roman government. For one thing there may not be so great a time span between 1Peter and Revelation; yet 1Peter still shows an approving attitude to the governing authorities. The difference in the NT is due rather to the experience of persecution and the emergence of the apocalyptic genre with its traditional motifs and view of the world order.

Diagram 18.1

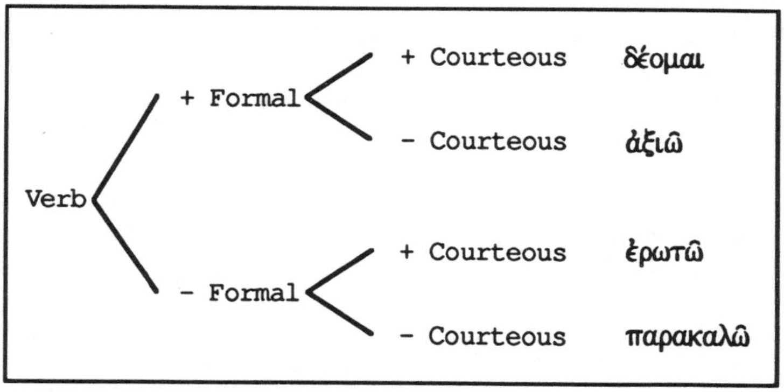

The language of petitions is of further relevance to the study of the NT. D. Hartman, *Social Relationships and Letter Writing in the Early Roman Empire: The Use of Petitions/Requests in Paul and the Papyri* (unpublished Macquarie thesis), discusses four verbs of petitioning (i.e. ἀξιῶ, δέομαι, ἐρωτῶ and παρακαλῶ) and their use in the documentary sources. Using Hartman's analysis of the papyrological evidence, it seems possible to distinguish the four verbs along two dimensions: a) the *formal aspect* distinguishes between verbs used predominantly in petitions to officials (i.e. ἀξιῶ and δέομαι) and those used predominantly in private letters (i.e. ἐρωτῶ and παρακαλῶ); b) the *courteous aspect* distinguishes between the verbs which are more courteous and humble (δέομαι and ἐρωτῶ) and those that are less so (ἀξιῶ and παρακαλῶ). Diagram 18.1 (above) is a schematic construct placed on Hartman's discussion. Caution, however, needs to be exercised in using it. This is so for two reasons. First, the sample used in the analysis is limited to non-literary, documentary texts. One will need to broaden the sample by the inclusion of literary texts of both the same and different genres before the schema can be considered definitive. An expanded analysis may indeed require some modification. Second, other variables besides the two specified may bear on the writer's choice of verb. For example, regional scribal practice may significantly affect the choice of verb in petitions to officials. This appears to be so in the case of ἀξιῶ at Oxyrhynchus. Bearing in mind these cautions let us accept for the time being the schema as a working hypothesis.

The schema is based on predominant usage so that it does not follow that each verb cannot be used in a different context (i.e. in a context expecting a different set of aspects). For example, δέομαι can be and is used in personal letters – its usage is not confined to the petitioning of administrative officials or persons of higher social status. However, when the verb is uttered outside its usual context, the schema suggests that the use must be marked. Knowing which parts of speech are marked and unmarked provides the non-native speaker with an insight into the author's intentionality. It is here that the native speaker with his/her intuitive sense of the language usually has a distinct advantage over the non-native speaker. Hartman gives the following occurrences of the verbs of petitioning in the NT:

δέομαι:	2Cor.5.20, 10.2, Gal.4.12
ἀξιῶ:	None
ἐρωτῶ:	Phil.4.3, 1Thess.4.1, 5.12, 2Thess.2.1, 2John 5
παρακαλῶ:	Rom.12.1, 15.30, 16.17, 1Cor.1.10, 4.16, 16.15, 2Cor.2.8, 6.1, 10.1, Eph.4.1, Phil.4.2, 1Thess.4.1,10, 5.14, 2Thess.3.12, 1Tim.2.1, Phlm.9,10, Heb.13.19,22, 1Pet.2.11, 5.1, Jude 3

Why did Paul use δέομαι at 2Cor.5.20, 10.2, Gal.4.12? Its use appears marked in terms of both the formal and courteous aspects of the verb. Hartman suggests that the strained relations between Paul and the two communities in Corinth and Galatia may account for its use. However, this cannot have been a determining reason since elsewhere in Paul's letters to the Corinthians he used παρακαλῶ (1Cor.1.10, 4.16, 16.15, 2Cor.2.8, 6.1, 10.1). To account then for the use of δέομαι one must look at its particular context in Paul's plea to the communities. The use is marked and thus may draw attention to the earnestness of Paul's plea, e.g. δεόμεθα ὑπὲρ Χριστοῦ καταλλάγητε τῷ θεῷ – 'We implore you on Christ's behalf: be reconciled to God' (2Cor.5.20); Γίνεσθε ὡς ἐγώ, ὅτι κἀγὼ ὡς ὑμᾶς, ἀδελφοί, δέομαι ὑμῶν – 'I implore you, brothers, become as I am because I have become as you' (Gal.4.12). Again, it may follow the umarked παρακαλῶ and thereby indicate the ascending tone in Paul's plea, e.g. Αὐτὸς δὲ ἐγὼ Παῦλος παρακαλῶ ὑμᾶς διὰ τῆς πραΰτητος καὶ ἐπιεικείας τοῦ Χριστοῦ ... δέομαι δὲ ... – 'I, Paul, appeal to you by the meekness and gentleness of Christ ... I implore you ...' (2Cor.10.1-2). Of course, no great interpretational crux depends on understanding Paul's use of δέομαι. However, an understanding of marked and unmarked word usage does offer an invaluable insight into the author's intentionality where intuition fails.

S.R.L.

§19 Name and Status: A Veteran seeks Tax Exemption

Provenance unknown 10 Jan. AD 149

Ed.pr. — M.H. Eliassen, *Am. Stud. Pap.* XXIII (Chico 1981), pp.329-333.

The papyrus sheet (14 x 17.3 cm) is well preserved except for its right edge. Its photograph indicates folding. The letter claiming exemption was written by Aurelius Petronius. As taxation was the concern of the prefect and his office, Aurelius Petronius was probably an official or imperial freedman attached to the prefect's office.

[᾿Αν]τ̣ίγραφον. Αὐρήλιος Πετρώνιο̣ς [. . . .]	Copy. Aurelius Petronius [...]
Δ̣ι̣ο̣φάντωι βασιλικῶι γραμματεῖ [᾿Αρσ(ινοίτου) ῾Ηρ(ακλείδου)]	to Diophantos, royal scribe of the district [of Herakleides
μ̣ερίδος χαίρ(ειν). ᾿Αχιλλᾶς ῾Αρποκράτο̣[υς]	of Arsinoe], greeting. Achillas, son of Harpokrates,
[ἱ]ππεὺς εἴλης Οὐοκουντίων πρὸ τῆ[ς στρα-]	cavalryman of *ala Vocontiorum* , before his [military service]
[τ]είας κληθεὶς ᾿Οροννοῦς ῾Ραπαλ̣ι̣ω̣[. .]ς	called Oronnous, son of Rhapalion,
μ̣ητρὸς Ταμεστρεμφι ἀπὸ κώμης Συνγνα̣	his mother being Tamestremphis, from the village of Syngnas,
[ἐ]δηλώθη ἐστρατεῦσθαι ἔτεσι πλείο̣σ̣[ι εἴκο-]	has been shown to have served for more than [twenty-]
[σ]ι̣ πέντε· ἀκόλουθον οὖν ἐστί γρ(άψαι) κ̣ατὰ	five years. Therefore, it is consistent to write that in accord with
τὴν χάριν τοῦ μεγίστου Αὐτοκράτορος	the favour of the most excellent Imperator
περιαιρεθῆναι αὐτὸν ἐκ τῆς δόσε-ως ἐπικεφαλίων.	he has been removed from the payment of capitation tax.
(m. 2) ᾿Ερρῶσ(θαί) σε εὔχομαι	(m. 2) I pray that you are well.
(m. 3) (῎Ετους) ιγ̄ Αὐτοκράτορος Καίσαρος Τίτου Αἰλίου ῾Αδριανοῦ ᾿Αντωνείνου Σεβαστοῦ Εὐσεβοῦς Φαῶφι δ̄	(m. 3) In year 13 of Imperator Caesar Titus Aelius Hadrianus Antoninus Augustus Pius, Phaophi 4.

Achillas was a veteran of the auxiliary cavalry unit or *ala Vocontiorum*. As a veteran and therefore presumably a Roman citizen he ought to have been exempt from capitation taxes. How then is the above request for exemption (*ll*.8-11) to be explained? The editor suggests that the anomaly arose from a delay in the processing of Achillas' military discharge and his resumption of civilian life. The process usually consisted of three stages:

missio	discharge usually in December – January
diploma	document providing evidence of military service and citizenship perhaps received some months after the *missio*

epikrisis examination and registration of the veteran by the prefect or one of his officers usually in spring[162]

As the process could take up to one year, the editor suggests that the veteran was granted the privilege of exemption for the year of discharge. For the history of citizenship rights for veterans of auxiliary units see P.A. Holder, *The Auxilia from Augustus to Trajan* (Oxford 1980), pp.46-63 and D.B. Saddington, *The Development of the Roman Auxiliary Forces from Caesar to Vespasian* (Harare 1982), pp.187-92.

Roman soldiers were prohibited from marrying during service and the restriction was not eased till the reign of Septimius Severus, i.e. AD 197 (Herodian 3.8.5). However, in the earlier period in view of the length of military service emperors tended to turn a blind eye to the family relationships formed by their soldiers. For example, Claudius' reform of the army included the issuing of a diploma granting not only citizenship to a soldier of 25 or more years service[163] but recognition of his marriage or *conubium* and civic rights to the soldier's wife, children and descendants. The reform should probably to be dated to the census of AD 47-48. Under Trajan the maximum period of service was probably brought into line with the granting of the diploma. In other words, after 25 years of service the auxiliary obtained both his discharge and citizenship. Antoninus Pius, during whose reign the above document was written, removed from the diploma the grant of citizenship to the soldier's children born before his release from military service.

The editor relates the grant of exemption and the above change in the military diploma to two factors, the emperor's sense of justice and his relative freedom from reliance on the military. G.L. Cheesman, *The Auxilia of the Roman Imperial Army* (1914 – reprinted Rome 1968), pp.32-34, interpreted the change in the military diploma as an attempt to remove an anomalous situation; the auxiliary's children born before his release from military service were recognised as citizens whereas the children of the Household Troops were not so recognised. For Cheesman the situation of a legionary's children was uncertain. In interpreting Antoninus Pius' motive, the present editor understands the anomalous situation to include the children of legionaries also. However, *BGU* I 140, a rescript of Hadrian dated AD 119 and dealing with the problems of illegitimacy and the rights of inheritance among the children of soldiers who die in service, implies that a legionary could legitimate his marriage (and thus the status of his children) after his release from service. See further the discussion of *SB* 5217 by C.A. Nelson, *Status Declarations in Roman Egypt* (Amsterdam 1979), pp.45-6. The papyrus concerns the *epikrisis* of a child before the prefect of Egypt. Nelson suggests that the mother declared the child because the father, possibly a soldier, had died and was thus unable to legitimate the marriage or his son's status.

No matter how Antoninus Pius' motives are interpreted two factors made the question of a soldier's family an issue. The first was a soldier's length of service (i.e. at least 25 years). The

---

162 C.A. Nelson, *Status Declarations in Roman Egypt* (Amsterdam 1979) pp.40-46, argues against a military *epikrisis*. Instead, it is argued, the *epikrisis* of veterans has to do with their desire to settle in a particular province and to gain the status and privileges to which they were entitled as veterans. Of the papyri published in 1980/81 *P. Wash.*3 (early third century AD) is possibly a list of veterans who had undergone such an *epikrisis* under the auspices of the prefect of Egypt. There is, however, a dispute as to the interpretation of the document. The editor of *P. Wash.*3, V.B. Schuman, interprets it as a list concerned with 'citizenship or residence rights or entrance to the privileged *gerousia* class'. For this class of citizens see E.G. Turner, 'The gerousia of Oxyrhynchus', *Archiv für Papyrusforschung* 12 (1937), pp.179-86. Nelson, op.cit., pp.64-5, at first shared Schuman's interpretation in view of the advanced age of the persons involved. However, since the *epikrisis* was made before the prefect and the persons involved bore Roman names, Nelson, op.cit., pp.viii-ix, later changed his interpretation and argued that the document concerned the settlement of veterans.

163 S. Dusanic, 'The issue of military diplomata under Claudius and Nero', *ZPE* 47 (1982), pp.149-71, argues against the generally held view that Claudius introduced grants of citizenship to all auxiliary veterans who had served 25 years. He contends that grants of citizenship remained conditional upon a particular military achievement.

period was such that one could not reasonably expect a soldier to abstain from forming a family. The second factor was the stationing of legions and *auxilia* in permanent bases. The policy was begun by Augustus but reached its culmination in Hadrian's change from the expansionist policies of his predecessors; the army was now used to guard and police the empire's borders (see E. Birley, 'Hadrianic frontier policy', *Carnuntina, Römische Forschungen in Niederösterreich III* [Graz-Köln 1965], pp.25-33 = *The Roman Army* [Amsterdam 1988], pp.12-20). The change in policy meant that soldiers and their units were located in one place for long periods of time. In the course of the second century recruitment to legions and *auxilia* also became more local. Accordingly, the soldier's more settled existence afforded him the opportunity to form a family. It also presented the authorities with the difficult task of maintaining military discipline in the face of the growing involvement of soldiers in the pursuits and practices of civilian life (for Hadrian's efforts to maintain military discipline see Dio, *Hist.*69.9 and Script.Hist.Aug., *Had.*10).[164] The hardship caused by the demands of military service and discipline is alluded to at 2Tim.2.3-4: 'Endure hardship with us like a good soldier of Christ Jesus. No one serving as a soldier gets involved in civilian affairs – he wants to please his commanding officer'.

The Social Composition of the Early Church

The above papyrus also illustrates Holder's observation (op.cit., p.55) that 'it is impossible to determine the legal status of an auxiliary from his name alone'. For example, Holder cites cases where peregrines assumed the Roman *tria nomina* on recruitment or where citizens indicated filiation by the use of the father's cognomen. In the present document the veteran, though presumably a Roman citizen, is designated by the Greek name 'Achillas son of Harpokrates'. The names in the above document also illustrate another important aspect of military service. Before military service Archillas was called Oronnous son of Rhapalion. As an Egyptian by birth he possessed low rank and social status in Egypt. However, military service and the award of Roman citizenship had given Achillas a rank in society which was not consonant with his status as indicated by his racial origins.

E.A. Judge, *Rank and Status in the World of the Caesars and St.Paul* (Canterbury 1982), p.9, defines the categories of rank and status thus:

> 'Rank' is meant to denote any formally defined position in society, while 'status' refers to positions of influence that may not correspond to the official pattern of social order. Status tends to convert itself into rank, and rank is the fossilised status of the past, defending itself against the aspirations of those who have only status, often newly acquired.

It is Judge's contention that status dissonance was inverted in the community of the early church. From a consideration of the proportion of Latin cognomina among the names of Paul's acquaintances it is argued (ibid., p.12-13) that many of them probably held Roman citizenship. Moreover, it is deduced (ibid., p.13) from the types of Latin *cognomina* that citizenship was probably gained through military service (citizenship arising from manumission is given a lower profile in the analysis). Accordingly, individuals of a high rank, i.e. Roman citizens, but of low status were members of the Pauline churches. The situation of dissonance is further reflected and affirmed in the message of Paul. Judge, 'Cultural Conformity and Innovation in Paul: Some Clues from Contemporary Documents', *Tyndale Bulletin* 35 (1984), p.12, argues that Paul 'while accepting rank ... repudiated the status conventions which permitted people to exploit the system to private advantage'.

---

164 See also R. MacMullen, *Soldier and Civilian in the Later Roman Empire* (Cambridge, MA 1967). MacMullen demonstrates how from the second century the Roman soldier became increasingly involved in civilian work (e.g. farming, building, manufacturing, the administrative tasks of policing and revenue collection etc.) rather than his military duties.

The method adopted by Judge involved the comparison between the proportion of Latin names in a list of Paul's acquaintances and the proportion of Latin names in lists of non-Romans drawn from the provinces, i.e. a list of names with the names of identifiable Roman citizens excluded. Given the sample size, a significant difference was found to exist between the two proportions (i.e. 1/3 for the Pauline list and 1/30 for the provincial lists). The significant difference is accounted for in terms of an assumed presence of Roman citizens in the Pauline list. However, before the conclusion may be drawn two points need to be considered. First, if the names of Roman citizens are added back to the provincial lists, is the difference between the two proportions no longer significant? If the difference is still significant, then Roman citizenship may not be the only nor even the dominant variable needed to explain the difference between the proportions. The method's underlying assumption appears to be that by eliminating Roman names a bias is created in the list and that as a consequence any difference between the two lists (i.e. the provincial or the Pauline) must be due to this structural bias. The important question is whether there was a bias in either list in the first place. These observations lead to the second consideration. Are both lists really obtained by random sampling and thus comparable? For example, perhaps many of the names in the Pauline list belong to persons living in Rome or in a Roman colony whereas this is not the case with the provincial list. Another possible bias is to be found in the epistolary and social conventions regarding the naming of individuals in letters. Convention dictated that Paul mention by name community members of higher social status.[165] This naturally would create a bias in his list. In other words, sociopolitical or even chronological factors may bear on the question of name use and mention. Such is the case within Latin *cognomina* themselves (see I. Kajanto, *The Latin Cognomina* [Helsinki 1965] for the geographical aspect pp.18-19, 37, 49-50, 54-55 and for the political/social aspect pp.48, 62-70).

G.H.R. Horsley, *New Docs* 5 (1989), pp.108-111, adduces further evidence chronologically relevant to the debate. In his discussion of a list of names of donors to the erection of a toll house in Ephesus (i.e. *I. Eph.*Ia.20), he notes that although half the identifiable names belong to Roman citizens, the ratio of Latin to Greek names is approximately equal to that found among Paul's acquaintances. Moreover, since only two Latin names are held by non-Romans who were probably slaves, it is reasonable to conclude, it is argued, that the similarity of ratios should be accounted for by the presence of Roman citizens among Paul's acquaintances. However, there are three areas of the methodology which need comment. First, the exclusion of Semitic and indigenous names from both lists appears unnecessary. Since the proportion of persons who possess Roman citizenship is the central concern, it might be preferable to compare the number of Latin names with the number of all non-Latin names. Second, since it is reasonable to assume a positive correlation between status and wealth, the use of the legible part of the Ephesus list to establish the ratio of Latin to non-Latin names is potentially biased.[166] The reason for this is that the names on the list of donors are not ordered randomly but according to the amount given with the names of the smaller donors now mostly illegible. Third, the fact that the difference between the ratios is insignificant does not necessarily imply that the two ratios are determined by the same factors. Again it will be

---

165 If Paul did follow the convention of addressing prominent community members, it may prove relevant to the question of status inversion. Regard will also need to be taken of another factor. The naming of individuals in the letters may also have depended in part on Paul's knowing them personally. However, again this could be biased. When Paul writes to a church which he has neither founded nor visited, it is the leaders and prominent persons of those churches with whom Paul would be acquainted. Again, when writing to a familiar church, Paul does not address all persons known to him. One may suppose that it is the leaders and prominent persons whom he would tend to address.

166 This is not to say that Roman names cannot appear on side B of the stone. It is also relevant that the bias caused by the listing of names by the donation's value works against the hypothesis. Thus once recognised it does not prejudice the results.

important to ascertain whether socio-political factors apart from Roman citizenship affect the name use and mention.

The above discussion highlights the difficulties inherent in any analysis of social structure based on the use and mention of names. The difficulty in obtaining unbiased samples has been adequately discussed already. The above papyrus illustrates another important difficulty, namely that of determining a person's legal status by name alone. For example, if the name 'Achillas, son of Harpokrates' had occurred in a provincial list rather than in the present papyrus, it would not have been identified as belonging to a person possessing Roman citizenship. Indeed, it is the enlarged context afforded by the papyrus itself which permits the identification of legal status. A similar context, however, is frequently absent from name lists like the one designating contributors to a toll house at Ephesus.[167] Another difficulty is posed by P.R.C. Weaver's recent article, 'Where have all the Junian Latins gone? Nomenclature and Status in the Early Empire', *Chiron* 20 (1990), pp.276-304, to which Judge has himself referred me. Weaver argues that the number of slaves freed informally[168] or children born to parents or a mother possessing only Junian status is significantly higher than had been formerly thought.[169] For Rome he gives a rough estimate of the status distribution among children born of at least one freed parent:[170] Roman citizen 40%; Junian Latin 43%; and slave 17%. Furthermore, since the opportunities to manumit formally or to convert status from Junian Latinity to Roman citizenship were more restrictive in the provinces, Weaver argues that the percentage of Junian Latins would be higher there than in Rome itself. Now the significance of Junian Latinity for the present discussion is that though they were not Roman citizens, they bore the *tria nomina*. We have already noted above Holder's doubt that the legal status of an auxiliary can be determined from his name alone. Citizenship was not routinely given to veterans of auxiliary units until Claudius' reform; however, even before this reform the army had acted as a Romanising influence with many soldiers adopting Latin names. In other words, the use of a Latin name by either a soldier or a freedman did not necessarily imply the possession of Roman citizenship. Socio-political factors apart from Roman citizenship did affect name usage. Thus any decision concerning a person's legal status based on the use of the *tria nomina* alone is hazardous. As Weaver observes (p.279): 'the use of the *tria nomina* without tribal indication does not necessarily imply Roman citizenship'.

Though this result may seem somewhat negative, in reality it is not so. The high proportion of Roman names among Paul's addressees still needs some explanation. Could many of them have been soldiers, veterans (i.e. without Roman citizenship)[171] or persons holding Junian Latinity? Indeed, might it not be the case that, besides the so-called God-fearers, Paul's converts were Jewish members of diaspora synagogues who had been Romanised either by employment in the army or by servitude in Roman families? To such a group the Christian

---

167 G.H.R. Horsley (per litt.) points out to me that not all the individuals in *I. Eph.*Ia.20 are without a context but that a few are evidenced in other inscriptions from Ephesus. This may permit a further confirmation of the assignment of civil status.

168 Informal manumission before the *lex Junia* was either *manumissio inter amicos* (i.e. when a master declared his slave free before friends) or *manumissio per epistulam* (i.e. when the master gave his slave a certificate of freedom). Formal manumission was either *vindicta* (i.e. by the Quiritary owner assisted by a Roman magistrate), *censu* (i.e. by declaration for a census) or *testamento* (i.e. by a will).

169 See also A.J.B. Sirks, 'Informal Manumission and the Lex Junia', *RIDA* 28 (1981), pp.247-76, who suggests an economic reason for the prevalence of informal manumission.

170 The percentage figures are fuzzy as a certain amount of calculated guess-work is involved in their derivation.

171 It cannot at the time of Paul's writing be assumed that many auxiliary veterans would have possessed Roman citizenship. It was only in the reign of Claudius that major changes in the army were effected, i.e. length of service was restricted to 30 years (reduced to 25 years under the Flavians); the soldiers' marriages were recognised and their children given citizenship at the same time as them (restricted under Antoninus Pius); command and career structures, i.e. the *tres militiae*, were put in place for the equestrian officers; and, what is significant in the present instance, Roman citizenship was granted universally after 25 years of service.

message may well have appeared attractive. On the one hand, their past employment or service will have marginalised them within the synagogue. Both the army and slavery potentially involved the individual in cultic and moral practices which the synagogue disdained.[172] On the other hand, the veteran or freedman did not receive full acceptance into the citizenship of those whom he had served and whose values he had either adopted or come to recognise. The message that 'you are all one in Christ Jesus' (Gal.3.28) might be thought by such a person to address the political, social and religious distinctions experienced in his own life.

S.R.L.

§20 Claudius Lysias (Acts 22) and the Question of Paul's Roman Citizenship

Sebaste in Phrygia — Third century AD

Ed.pr. — M. Speidel, 'Legionaries from Asia Minor', *ANRW* II 7 2 (1980), pp.730-746 (= *Roman Army Studies* 1 [Amsterdam 1984], pp.45-63).

[Κατ]ὰ τὰ πολλάκις [δόξ-]	[In accord with] the matters often [decreed]
αντα τῇ βουλῇ καὶ τ̣[ῷ]	by the council and the
δήμῳ Αὐρ(ήλιον) 'Αττικὸν οὐ-	people, Aurelius Atticus,
ετρανὸν ληγιῶνος δε-	veteran of *legio*
κάτης Γεμίνης ἐκ	*X Gemina*, like
προγόνων ἀρχι-	his forefathers, a magistrate
κὸν καὶ βουλευ-	and councillor,
τὴν ἡ πατρὶς τὸν	(is honoured by) his country
(vac.) ἑαυτῆς	(as) her
[εὐε]ργέτην.	benefactor.

The published evidence, in Speidel's view, leaves the incorrect impression that Asia Minor's contribution to military recruitment was inconspicuous. He contends that the evidence itself is skewed. Using local tombstones and dedications, he argues instead that Asia Minor's contribution to recruitment for legions stationed on the Euphrates frontier was not insignificant – 'the *Oriens* ... formed an army district by itself, supplying its legions and *auxilia* with its own recruits' (p.730). Asia Minor also supplied recruits to other Eastern, African and Danubian legions. As *legio X Gemina* was stationed at Vindobona (= Vienna) in Upper Pannonia, the above inscription (cut in the base of a statue) is in part offered as evidence for Speidel's thesis.

It has generally been held that the majority of legionaries after their service of twenty to twenty-five years settled in the province where they had served. The extended period of absence from their place of origin, the creation of familial bonds and the opportunities to acquire grants of land in the frontier provinces are thought to have facilitated this. The present inscription, however, illustrates that settlement in the province of military service was not always the case. Aurelius Atticus returned to his home town and was later honoured by its citizens. As legionary service offered the citizen an opportunity to attain higher social status, an

---

172 The sages assumed that both male and female captives and slaves were subject to sexual abuse – see *m. Hor.*3.7 and *m. Ket.*1.4. As an indication of the disdain in the case of priestly marriage see Josephus, *AJ* 13.10.5.292, *m. 'Ed.* 8.2, *m. Ket.* 2.9, *t. Ket.* 3.2, *b. Qid.* 66a. Cf. also Philo, *Leg. ad Cai.* 155.

important factor in a legionary's decision to return home, according to Speidel, was his 'prospects of social status'.[173]

The above inscription, it is argued, also gives an indication of the regard in which military service was held by the upper classes (and thus presumably all classes); Aurelius Atticus, a member of a local aristocratic family, entered upon the military career of legionary. However, the fact that he never reached the centurionate should not be construed as evidence for the status of the ordinary legionary *per se* in the eyes of a member of the local aristocracy (contra Speidel). The inscription reveals the view of the council and people, not that of Aurelius Atticus himself. Aurelius Atticus may well have entered upon his military career in the hope of advancement through the ranks but was prevented in this by either aptitude or opportunity. One must also bear in mind the growing 'militarisation' of the civil service during the third century. A military career did not confine the recruit to a purely military service in the provinces but opened up to him various other avenues of advancement (see R. MacMullen, *Soldier and Civilian in the Later Roman Empire* [Cambridge, MA 1967], pp.65ff. and 99-118). The inscription also indicates the dissonance caused by the imposition of Roman rule in the status systems of antiquity. The inscription witnesses to the attempt made by a person of local status to obtain a position within the status system of the Roman Empire. Military service was the vehicle to achieve such an objective. Thus both the above inscription and the preceding papyrus (see *New Docs* 6 [1992] §19) illustrate two aspects of the social dissonance experienced in societies under Roman rule. In the case of the inscription we find an individual of higher local but lower Roman rank. In case of the papyrus the situation is reversed. Achillas, son of Harpokrates, was of lower local but higher Roman rank.

The former dissonance (i.e. higher local but lower Roman status) may manifest itself at times in the NT. For example, it may explain Luke's account of both Claudius Lysias' purchase of Roman citizenship at such a great cost and the soldier's subsequent surprise at Paul's citizenship (Acts 22.25-8). Indeed, one may even speak of a Lukan sensitivity to such dissonance. Saddington, op.cit., p.190, suggests that Claudius Lysias had purchased citizenship 'before entry into a military career as a means of reaching a better position than that of an ordinary auxiliary'. The cost of the purchase may indicate that he was a person of considerable status before his entry into the army. The name he adopted indicates that he probably was a Greek who acquired his citizenship during the reign of Claudius (AD 41-54). A purchase of citizenship during the reign of Claudius is further supported by Dio Cassius' account.

συχνοὺς δὲ δὴ καὶ ἄλλους καὶ ἀναξίους τῆς πολιτείας ἀπήλασε, καὶ ἑτέροις αὐτὴν καὶ πάνυ ἀνέδην, τοῖς μὲν κατ' ἄνδρα τοῖς δὲ καὶ ἀθρόοις, ἐδίδου. ἐπειδὴ γὰρ ἐν πᾶσιν ὡς εἰπεῖν οἱ Ῥωμαῖοι τῶν ξένων προετετίμηντο, πολλοὶ αὐτὴν παρά τε αὐτοῦ ἐκείνου ᾐτοῦντο καὶ παρὰ τῆς Μεσσαλίνης τῶν τε Καισαρείων ὠνοῦντο· καὶ διὰ τοῦτο μεγάλων τὸ πρῶτον χρημάτων πραθεῖσα, ἔπειθ' οὕτως ὑπὸ τῆς εὐχερείας ἐπευωνίσθη ὥστε καὶ λογοποιηθῆναι ὅτι κἂν ὑάλινά τις σκεύη συντετριμμένα δῷ τινι πολίτης ἔσται.

A great many other persons unworthy of citizenship were also deprived of it, whereas he granted citizenship to others quite indiscriminately, sometimes to individuals and sometimes to whole groups. For inasmuch as Romans had the advantage over foreigners in practically all respects, many sought the franchise by personal application to the emperor, and many bought it from Messalina and the imperial freedmen. For this reason, though the privilege was at first sold only for large sums, it later became so cheapened by the facility with which it could be obtained that it

173 The same can be said of service in the *auxilia*. Not only did the *auxilia* attract the enlistment of Roman citizens but also in terms of function and pay there was little difference between service in the *auxilia* and legions. For pay see M. Speidel, 'The Pay of the Auxilia', *JRS* 63 (1973), pp.141-147 (= *Roman Army Studies* [Amsterdam 1984], pp.83-89); for deployment and professionalism see D.B. Saddington, *The Development of the Roman Auxiliary Forces from Caesar to Vespasian* (Harare 1982), pp.179-86.

came to be a common saying, that a man could become a citizen by giving the right person some bits of broken glass. Dio Cassius, *Hist*.60.17 (Loeb Translation)

If Luke's account is to be believed, then Claudius Lysias by AD 57 (R. Jewett, *Dating Paul's Life* [London 1979], p.102) had advanced to the rank of tribune. This rank was usually held by an equestrian officer and formed the second stage in his military career (i.e. *militia secunda*). Unlike the tribunate of the legion, however, the command of a milliary unit afforded the officer a greater degree of independence and appointment was usually by the emperor himself (see E. Birley, 'Alae and Cohortes Milliariae', reprinted in *The Roman Army* [Amsterdam 1988], p.360). It would seem that Claudius Lysias had realised his ambitions. Paul's situation was another matter again. Though a Roman citizen by birth, he did not appear to show any of the marks of status and rank that the tribune had come to expect in a citizen. Instead, the apostle was implicated in a disturbance of order, had been arrested by the authorities and was about to be flogged.

Recently W. Stegemann, 'War der Apostel Paulus ein römischer Bürger?', *ZNW* 78 (1987), pp.200-29, has raised again the question of Paul's citizenship.[174] After considering several problematic areas in the assumption, he concludes that 'it is extremely improbable that the apostle Paul had possessed Roman citizenship' (p.228). The book of Acts is the only NT document to refer to Paul's citizenship status (see discussion pp.201-13). Stegemann holds that these references are either redactionally introduced or unnecessarily assumed. For example, the unnatural delay in Paul's notification of his status to the authorities (Acts 22.25; see also Acts 16.37), the subsequent delay in his release (Acts 22.30), the improbability of Claudius Lysias' disclosure of the bribe before his subordinates and Paul (Acts 22.28) and the improbability of his promotion through the ranks are noted in the case of Acts 22.22-29. Stegemann acknowledges the references (i.e. Dio Cassius, *Hist*.60.17 and other references regarding the granting of citizenship) which give to the Lysias incident the appearance of verisimilitude but concludes that Luke had actually stylised his account to fit these reports (p.206). How then did the author of Acts come to attribute Roman citizenship to Paul? According to Stegemann, it arose from a misunderstanding concerning the reason behind Paul's being sent as a prisoner to Rome to stand trial. Luke congenially assumed that Paul was sent to Rome because he exercised the Roman citizen's right of appeal to Caesar. Stegemann instead suggests that Paul was sent to Rome because his case was both problematic and politically sensitive.

More generally, Stegemann argues that when the epistles speak of the trials and punishments endured by Paul (see especially 2Cor.11.24-5), they provide information which seems inconsistent with the assumption of his possession of Roman citizenship (pp.221-4). Also, the restricted practice of granting citizenship to the local Hellenised/Romanised aristocracy does not fit well with the picture of Paul's (and his family's) strict adherence to Judaism and his lowly craft as disclosed in the epistles (pp.213-221, 224-8). That Paul nowhere uses the *tria nomina* is also adduced as evidence against his posession of citizenship. These last few arguments are perhaps Stegemann's weakest and have received recent criticism. The absence of any mention of his *tria nomina* indicates very little (see M. Hengel, *The Pre-Christian Paul* (London 1991), pp.8-10; cf. also *New Docs* 6 [1992] §19). H.W. Tajra, *The Trial of St.Paul* (Tübingen 1989), pp.81-9, argues that there need be no tension between Paul's possession of Roman citizenship and his being a Pharisee (so also Hengel, op.cit., pp.11-13).[175] Also Paul's craft is interpreted by his adherence to the rabbinic tradition in which the disciple was encouraged to follow a humble trade (cf. Hengel, op.cit., pp.15-7). Paul's trials

---

174 For a bibliography of the debate see M. Hengel, *The Pre-Christian Paul* (London 1991), pp.101-2 n.58.

175 Tajra does recognize a tension between citizenship of a Greek city and Paul's Pharisaic upbringing especially as the former involved participation in the local cults and educational system (pp.16,80). Consequently, he argues that Paul was not a citizen of Tarsus (pp.78-80).

and punishments can also be explained. E.R. Goodenough, *The Jurisprudence of the Jewish Courts in Egypt* (New Haven 1929 – reprinted Amsterdam 1968), pp.34-35, had already argued that 'Jews acted precisely in the spirit of Philo' (i.e. 'Philo's call to lynching apostates') 'and, without reference to any Roman tribunal, freely followed their own instincts in dealing with heretics'. On the other hand, Hengel, op.cit., pp.6-7, suggests that in some instances Paul may not have wished to disclose his citizenship 'in order to follow Christ in his suffering' or because its mention 'would have been more of a hindrance'. Hengel also questions whether circumstances would have always allowed magistrates to attend to the issue of Paul's citizenship. Another line of attack is taken by S.M. Baugh, *Paul and Ephesus: The Apostle among his Contemporaries* (University of California, Irvine, Ph.D. thesis 1990). He uses the epigraphical evidence from Ephesus to argue against the hypothesis that either Paul's craft or religious upbringing would preclude his possession of Roman citizenship. In particular, he objects to the strict stratification of status in ancient society and the assumption that the possession of Roman citizenship implied membership of the social elite. Even so, Paul's role as teacher and his possession of Roman citizenship allowed him to associate with those members of the elite who valued such characteristics (i.e. the Asiarchs of Acts 19.31).

The debate over Paul's citizenship presents a clear case of the under-determination of evidence. Paul may have chosen not to disclose his citizenship and/or magistrates may not have always paid regarded to it. Clearly, we just do not know. Yet the author of Acts indicates that Paul was not averse to disclosing his citizenship and that Roman officials were acutely aware of Paul's rights as a Roman citizen. Hengel, op.cit., p.7, also suggests that 'a trial lasting around five years is almost inconceivable in the case of a Jewish provincial without means'. However, one cannot infer from this that Paul was a Roman citizen. Other factors need also to be considered. For example, Acts 24.26-7 indicates that two years of Paul's imprisonment were due to Felix's corruption. Moreover, it needs to be borne in mind that in all likelihood Paul travelled and was maintained at his own or his church's expense. Rome did not have to pay for this. Lastly, delays need also to be reckoned between Paul's arrival in Rome and his hearing. In support of Paul's citizenship Hengel, op.cit., p.10, also argues that 'geographically this bearer of a rare Roman name thinks entirely in Roman categories, and in his world-wide plans for mission has only the empire and its provinces in view'. Again, it is difficult to know what to conclude from this. Surely provincials who travelled as Paul did thought in the same geographical categories. Roads, sea routes and other lines of communication, no doubt, were important factors in determining one's geographical perspective.

The strongest element in Stegemann's argument remains his literary analysis of the Lukan scenes in which Paul lays claim to Roman citizenship. Due to the under-determination of other evidence the debate needs to focus more carefully on this area. Other entries in the present volume also bear on the debate over Paul's citizenship. For example, *New Docs* 6 (1992) §4 takes issue with F. Lyall's argument (see *Slaves, Citizens, Sons* [Grand Rapids 1984]) that many Pauline metaphors are better understood if interpreted by Roman law. Lyall's underlying assumption is that Paul was a Roman citizenship who knew the legal system under which he lived. The discussion of the annulment of wills and Paul's use of metaphor at Gal.3.15 is also relevant (see *New Docs* 6 [1992] §5). The metaphor does not rely on Roman legal practice. Again, *New Docs* 6 (1992) §1 observes that when Paul gave practical advice on matters of legal import (i.e. marriage and divorce) his thinking did not show a particularly Roman legal perspective. *New Docs* 6 (1992) §17 also deals with a relevant matter. Here it is observed that when Paul boasted to the Corinthians and Philippians (i.e. members of Roman colonies) his boasting was based on a Jewish rather that Roman valuation of status. Again, these results are not sufficient to settle the question of Paul's citizenship. However, the last points indicate that if Paul was indeed a Roman citizen, it was of little importance to him. Paul's *Weltanschauung* was that of a Jewish Christian and not a Roman citizen. **S.R.L.**

§21 A Soldier's Letter Home

Provenance unknown AD 84-96

Ed.pr. — H.M. Cockle, *P. Turner* 18 (London 1981), pp.89-92.

Πετρώνιος Οὐάλης Πτολεμα̣[ίωι]	Petronius Valens to Ptolemaios,
τῶι τ̣ιμιωτάτωι π̣ατρὶ̣ χαίρ̣[ειν.]	my most honoured father, greeting.
πρὸ̣ μ̣ὲ̣ν πάντ̣ω̣ν εὔχομαί σ̣ε̣ ὑ̣γ[ιαί-]	Most of all, I pray you are well,
νειν ὡ̣ς καὶ ἐ̣π' Ἀ̣λεξανδρείας η[ὐξάμην]	as at Alexandria I also [prayed]
παρ̣ὰ̣ τ̣ῷ Σ̣αρ̣άπιδι διαμῖναί σε εἰ̣ς π̣ο̣λ̣-	to Sarapis that you live for many
λὰ ἔτη ἕως αὐξήσας ἀποδώσῳ τ̣ὰ̣ς	years until having grown up I return your
χάριτας· ἄξιο̣ς ἶ γὰρ τ̣ο̣ύτων ἀγαθῶ̣ν. γι-	kindnesses; for you are worthy of these good things.
νώσκειν δέ σε θέλω ὅτι τῆι ἰκάδι ἐ̣γε-	I wish you to know that on the twentieth I returned
νό̣μ̣ην εἰ̣ς π̣α̣ρ̣ενβολὴν πρὸ δέκα ἡμε-	to barracks ten days before
ρ̣ῶν τοῦ κομιάτου μου. ἐρωτῶ οὖν σ̣ε,	my furlough. Therefore I ask you,
π̣ά̣τ̣ε̣ρ, ἵ̣να ἀ̣νακκάσῃς 'Αλ̣ι̣μαν διόξε	father, to compel Alima to pursue
τὰ ἱ̣μάτια καὶ̣ δ̣ώσις αὐτῇ̣ ἀξίαν σου	(the matter of) the clothes and give her
πορφύρα̣ν κ̣α̣τ̣ὰ̣ κ̣ιθῶνα μ̣ό̣νον ἐπι-	purple worthy of you for one tunic only
δὴ πρὸ̣ς ὀψόν̣ι̣ο̣ν̣ .[± 7]υ. τὸ οὖν	since for pay [...] therefore
π̣αρεχόμενο̣ν̣ ἀξ̣ι̣ῶ̣.[± 8 · ἐλπί-]	being provided I ask [...]
ζ̣ω γ̣ὰ̣ρ τοῦ κυρίου Σ[αράπιδος θ̣έλοντος]	for I [hope], the lord [Sarapis willing,]
προκόψαι καὶ̣ ἀποδόσ̣ῳ [± 10]	to gain a promotion and will repay [...]
τ̣ας. πέμ̣ψω δέ σ̣ο̣ι̣ δ̣ι̣ὰ̣ Ν.[± 10]	[...] I will send you by N [...]
[.]. υτ̣ο̣ς καὶ ἐ̣ρινᾶ̣ [± 14]	[...] and wool [...]
[. . . . .]αι π̣α̣ν[± 15]	[...]
[. . . . .].ν̣α̣. .[± 15]	[...]
In right margin (upwards)	
22 [ ]ν Σαβῖνον. γίνωσκε δὲ ὅτι ἔλ[α]βά σοι .ξ.[.]	[...] Sabinus. Know that I took for you [...]
[ ]. .λε. . .ικον. μὴ οὖν ἄ̣[λ]λως ποιήσις ἵν[α]	[...]. Therefore do not act otherwise that ...
[(ἔτους). . . Δομιτιανο]ῦ̣ Κ̣αίσαρ̣ο̣ς τ̣ο̣ῦ κ̣υρ̣ί̣ο̣υ μ[ηνὸ]ς Γερμανικοῦ κε̅.	[in year ... of Domitian] Caesar, the lord, in the month of Germanicus, 25.
(Back and upwards)	
[ἀπ]όδο̣ς [Πτ]ο̣[λε]μαίῳ πατρί.	Give to Ptolemaios, my father.

5 διαμεῖναί 7 εἶ 8 εἰκάδι 9 παρεμβολήν 10 κομμεάτου 11 ἀναγκάσῃς, διῶξαι 12 δώσῃς 13-4 χιτῶνα, ἐπειδή 14 ὀψώνιον 17 ἀποδώσω 22 ἔλαβον 23 ποιήσῃς

A sense of filial respect and duty figures prominently in the letter's greeting and wish for the addressee's health (*ll*.1-7). Petronius addresses his father with the superlative epithet τιμιώτατος and recounts how he offered prayers for his health to Sarapis. Petronius also expresses a sense of obligation when he states a desire to repay his father's kindnesses, for the father is thought 'worthy of these good things' – note the lexical cohesion (ethical) between the words τιμιώτατος, χάρις, ἄξιος, ἀγαθός and ἀποδίδωμι.[176] Nevertheless, the greeting and health wish, as usual, draw heavily on epistolary convention. For example, see the greeting and health wish in *CPR* 19 *ll*.2-5 (also = *New Docs* 1 [1981], p.56): χαίρειν καὶ διὰ παντὸς ἐρρωμένον διαμένειν ὅλῳ τῷ σώματι ἰς μακροὺς χρόνους. This can also be seen in regard to the *proskynema* formula and the use of the disclosure formula γινώσκειν δέ σε θέλω ὅτι to mark the transfer to the body of the letter (see J.L. White, *The Body of the Greek Letter* [Missoula 1972], pp.2-4).

The editor suggests that the above soldier and C. Petronius Valens of the *cohors II Thracum* (*CIL* III 12074) may possibly be one and the same individual. The latter's auxiliary unit is known to have been stationed in Judaea in AD 86 (*CIL* XVI 33) and in Egypt in AD 105 (H.-G. Pflaum, *Syria* 44 [1967], pp.339-62 = M.M. Roxan, *Roman Military Diplomas 1954-1977*, pp.40-1). Even if the soldiers are identical, the dating of the unit's transfer will depend on whether one assumes that the papyrus was written in Egypt (i.e. a transfer date prior to AD 96 – contra Pflaum) or outside Egypt (i.e. the transfer date could be as late as AD 105).

On the meaning of the temporal expression πρὸ δέκα ἡμερῶν τοῦ κομιάτου μου *ll*.9-10, which has NT parallels (e.g. John 12.1), see L. Rydbeck, *Fachprosa, vermeintliche Volkssprache und neues Testament* (Uppsala 1967), pp.62-77. H.M. Cockle understands the clause ἐπιδὴ πρὸς ὀψόνιον κτλ (*ll*.13-14) to refer to μόνον and translates it 'since for my pay'. The clause explains, then, why Petronius only requests one garment. The problem with the translation, however, is that the usual prepositional phrase meaning 'for pay' is εἰς ὀψώνιον (see Athen., *Deipn*.4.19, Dio Hal., *Antiq.Rom*.9.17.1, 9.36.2, 9.59.4, Plutarch, *Lyc*.12.2, 82.222, Polyb., *Hist*.1.72.6, 5.89.4 and the documentary papyri *SB* V 7642 *l*.2, *P. Iand*. VIII 146 *ll*.6-7, *P. Mil*. 33 *l*.6, *P. Ross.Georg*. V 154/6 *ll*.1, 10, *UPZ* II 158a *ll*.6, 42). Roman soldiers up till the reign of Domitian, when this papyrus was written, received three stipendia a year in early January, May and September (see G.R. Watson, *The Roman Soldier* [London 1969], p.91 and R.O. Fink, *Roman Military Records on Papyrus* [1971], p.246). Domitian increased military pay with the institution of a fourth stipendium (Suetonius, *Life of Domitian* 7.3: *addidit et quartum stipendium militi, aureos ternos*). On the basis of Dio 67.3.5 it has been argued that Domitian increased the pay by a third rather than adding a fourth stipendium. See G.R. Watson, 'The Pay of the Roman Army, Suetonius, Dio and the Quartum Stipendium', *Historia* 5 (1956), pp.332-340, for the arguments in favour of a fourth stipendium. Fink, op.cit., p.253 n.27, believes that the payment of a fourth stipendium was, however, short-lived. Soon after the reign of Domitian the army reverted to three stipendia a year. Can πρὸς ὀψώνιον be construed as a temporal expression (see LSJ p.1498) in which Petronius states that he will soon receive his pay and that when this is received he will ask (see ἀξιῶ at *l*.15) for something else? If so, the above papyrus (dated 22 September) in conjunction with *P. Gen.lat*. 4 might afford documentary evidence for the payment of four stipendia effective 1 January, 1 April, 1 July and 1 October. The suggestion, though historically attractive, lacks linguistic support. I know of no similar temporal expression in Greek. On the

---

176 At first sight, the inclusion of the term ἀποδίδωι in the list may raise a doubt. However, it should be borne in mind that it describes the reciprocal obligation required by a giver of the receiver. This is so not only in commercial transactions such as the making of loans or the giving of dowries but also in personal relationships such as in the family, as here, or among friends. On the obligation to repay the benefits conferred by friends see P. Marshall, *Enmity in Corinth: Social Conventions in Paul's Relations with the Corinthians* (Tübingen 1987), pp.9-13.

other hand, πρός does appear to be used occasionally to indicate a payment for something, e.g. *l*.23 of *P. Amst*. 40 in *New Docs* 6 (1992) §1 and *l*.8 of *P. Köln* III 147.

P. Oxy. XLVII 3333 is another document in the culling for years 1980/81 dated in the reign of Domitian (i.e. 1 Feb. AD 92). It is a request for payment of salary by 32 desert guards (not soldiers) for the past month of Tybi; it permits a comparison of salaries between legionaries, auxiliaries and guards (see Table 21.1). The annual salaries are given in Egyptian drachmae with the information of legionary and auxiliary salary taken from M. Speidel, 'The Pay of the Auxiliary', *JRS* 63 (1973), pp.141-7. Note that a guard's salary was paid on a monthly basis.

Table 21.1: Comparison of Annual Salaries

	Basic Legionary	Basic Auxiliary	Guard
Salary	1200 dr.	800-1000 dr.	240 dr.

P. Grenf. II 43 (also dated AD 92) gives the salary of a guard in the metropolis of Arsinoe as 40 dr. each month (here 20 dr. each month). An expectation by the authorities that a guard would supplement his salary in one way or another may be one reason for the comparative salary difference. The question of stoppages and deductions from salaries will also need to be considered.

Petronius Valens writes to his father to expedite the matter of a piece of clothing. Deductions for such items as his food, armour, clothing and shoes etc. and if a cavalryman, the cost of keeping his mount, were made from a soldier's pay (see *P. Gen.lat*. 1 and *P. Fay*. 105). Before his stipend was credited to the military treasury, the cost of such items was deducted. As the rate of deductions for food and clothing seems somewhat high, A.C. Johnson, *Roman Egypt* (New Jersey 1959), p.671, has suggested that 'neither food nor clothing were provided at cost'. Watson, op.cit., p.337, argues against this. He maintains that Johnson's method of comparative costings was inappropriate (Johnson used the cost of items for estate labourers) and that in all probability food and clothing were a matter of individual choice. In other words, soldiers had a higher standard of living than estate labourers and therefore spent more on food and clothing. Granting Watson's argument, pay and stoppages were, nevertheless, a source of discontent to soldiers.[177] Clothing provided from home would reduce the amount of deductions from a soldier's stipend. It is not surprising, then, to find letters sent home asking for such items. See also *P. Mich*.VIII 467 *ll*.16-23 and 468 *ll*.23-29 where Claudius Terentius requests that his father[178] send clothes and armaments. The practice of deducting the cost of clothing

177 See Tacitus, *Annals* 1.17.6. Tacitus also speaks of the soldiers' discontent arising from corruption and bribery, especially with regard to the avoidance of fatigues. Another example of corruption is found in *P. Mich*.VIII 468 *ll*.35-41 where Claudius Terentianus states his transfer from the *classis Augusta Alexandrina* to a legionary cohort will require the payment of money – hic a[ut]em sene aer[e] | [ni]hil fiet. Soldiers also took bribes from civilians – see C. Wessely, *Stud. Pap*. XX 75 (third to fourth century AD) where a list of requisitions and bribes made to soldiers is drawn up by an agent for his master; cf. also Luke 3.14.

178 Claudius Terentius addresses Claudius Tiberianus as father. However, Terentius also calls Ptolemaios 'father' (see *P. Mich*.VIII 467.32 and 468.46-7). The editor suggests that Tiberianus may have been his adoptive father. However, he also acknowledges the loose use of familial titles. For example, in each of *UPZ* I 65.3, *P. Mich*.III 209 and *SB* III 6263 the letter writer addresses his brother as father. See also *P. Oxy*. X 1296 which addresses 3 persons as father, 2 as mother and several brothers and sisters; *P. Oxy*. XLVIII 3396 which addresses 3 persons as father and 2 as mother; and *P. Oxy*. LVI 3859 which addresses greetings to 14 brothers, 5 sisters and 2 mothers, but in this case only 1 father. The phenomenon can be observed in the NT also. The use of 'brother' needs no mention. Paul calls himself father at 1Cor.4.15, though there the title's metaphorical meaning is evident. Of more direct relevance is Rom.16.13 where Paul greets Rufus καὶ τὴν μητέρα αὐτοῦ καὶ ἐμοῦ. There is clearly a loose use of familial titles to indicate 'respect and affection'.

from the military stipend, I suggest, may also help to explain the behaviour of the Roman soldiers when they cast lots for Jesus' garment at the crucifixion (Matt.27.35, Mark 15.24, Luke 23.34, John 19.23-24).

S.R.L.

§22 The Size of the Roman Garrison in Jerusalem

P.A. Holder, *The Auxilia from Augustus to Trajan* (Oxford 1980), seeks to provide a comprehensive survey of our knowledge of the *auxilia* and thereby to redress an imbalance which has been caused since the appearance of G.L. Cheesman's *The Auxilia of the Roman Imperial Army* (1914 – reprinted at Rome, 1968) by the proliferation of individual studies. Holder's conclusion, op.cit., pp.140-3, provides a useful summary of his work.

The study is of particular interest to NT studies in that until AD 70, when *legio X Fretensis* was stationed in Jerusalem, Judaea as an imperial province was solely garrisoned by auxiliary troops. The use of *auxilia* for such purposes was a visible indicator that the peregrine units had been integrated into the Roman military and administrative system. The NT provides the names of two of these units.[179] The centurion Cornelius is said (Acts 10.1) to belong to the *coh. Italica* and the centurion Julius to *coh. Augusta* (Acts 27.1). However, as evidence for the movement of auxiliary units is largely wanting, locations and dates cannot be determined with any precision (but see the table of provincial dispositions in D.B. Saddington, *The Development of the Roman Auxiliary Forces from Caesar to Vespasian* [Harare 1982], pp.251-2). Auxiliary units were generally composed of peregrine soldiers (i.e. they lacked Roman citizenship) and for much of the first century the basis of a unit's grouping was ethnic. In Judaea the auxiliary units were primarily drawn from the non-Jewish cities of Sebaste and Caesarea. The military and administrative headquarters were located with the prefect/proconsul in Caesarea.

Holder, op.cit., pp.5-13, divides the *auxilia* into the following functional types (a century consisting of eighty men and a *turma* of between thirty and thirty-two cavalrymen):

Unit	No. of Centuries	No. of turmae	Total
cohors peditata	6	-	480
cohors equitata	6	4	600
cohors peditata milliaria	10	-	800
cohors equitata milliaria	10	8	1040
ala	-	16	512
ala milliaria	-	24	768

Holder, op.cit., pp.5-6, follows E. Birley, 'Alae and Cohortes Milliariae', reprinted in *The Roman Army* (Amsterdam 1988), pp.349-364, in arguing that there is no evidence for a pre-AD 70 dating of milliary units. Two points are brought to bear. First, it is noted that the earliest pieces of documentary evidence for a cavalry unit (*ala Flavia milliaria* – *ILS* 1418) and for a cohort (*coh. I Britannica milliaria* and *coh. I Brittonum milliaria* – *CIL* XVI 31) are dated AD

179 See further the discussion of the units' identification in D.B. Saddington, *The Development of the Roman Auxiliary Forces from Caesar to Vespasian* (Harare 1982), pp.137-8. Some difficulty arises with the disposition of Cornelius' unit in Judaea. If his conversion is dated AD 41-4 when Herod Agrippa was king, then there was no Roman procurator in Judaea and presumably no Roman troops either. Saddington, ibid., p.99, surmises that Claudius had left the Roman troops to the new king in order to support his reign. F. Jackson and K. Lake, *The Beginnings of Christianity* 5 (London 1933), p.443, tentatively suggest that Cornelius had already retired from military service.

81 and AD 85 respectively. Second, it is argued that the full spelling of the term *milliaria* in the early evidence indicates its novelty. It was later abbreviated to the sign ∞. Accordingly, Holder concludes that the supposed literary evidence for the existence of *milliariae* before AD 70 results from Josephus' exaggeration of unit sizes.[180] However, Josephus is not the only author to be considered. Luke tells of Paul's arrest by Claudius Lysias, a tribune and supposedly a commander of a milliary unit. The event can be dated approximately to AD 57.

E.M. Smallwood, *The Jews under Roman Rule* (Leiden 1976), p.147 n.14, holds that the Jerusalem garrison after AD 44 was a *cohors equitata*. However, E.Haenchen, *The Acts of the Apostles* (Oxford 1971), p.616, states that Claudius Lysias, the χιλίαρχος or *tribunus militum* (see H.J. Mason, *Greek Terms for Roman Institutions* [Toronto 1974], pp.163-4) of the garrison in Jerusalem at the time of Paul's arrest (Acts 21.31-3, 37, 22.24, 26-9, 23.10, 15, 17-19, 22, 24.22), commanded a unit of approximately 1,000 men. In other words, he commanded a *cohors equitata milliaria* of 800 infantry and 240 cavalry. Two arguments can be made for the presence of the larger milliary unit.

a. Claudius Lysias' title implies the command of a milliary unit. A χιλίαρχος or *tribunus militum* commanded a milliary unit whereas an ἔπαρχος or *praefectus* (see Mason, ibid., p.138-40) commanded a *quingenaria* unit.
b. The size of Paul's bodyguard consisting of 200 foot soldiers, 70 cavalrymen and 200 δεξιολάβοι[181] seems improbable if the auxiliary unit was a *cohors equitata* (i.e. 600 men). One must assume that the Jerusalem garrison was left rather depleted.

Further evidence might be adduced to support an earlier dating of milliary units.

c. In a military diploma (*CIL* XVI 31) dated AD 85 a *coh. I Brittonum milliaria* is mentioned. Saddington argues that the milliary unit may go back to AD 60, i.e. by counting back a minimum of twenty-five years (for years of military service) from the date of the diplomata. See Saddington, op.cit., pp.158, 174 (with slight qualification) and 195.

However, none of these arguments is conclusive. Against the first argument one notes that there are exceptions. For example, C. Julius Victor (probably Tiberian or late Augustan period) is described in *CIL* XIII 1042-5 as a *tribunus militum* of an auxiliary cohort. Saddington, op.cit., p.62, comments: 'the title was on occasion given as an honour, and may not imply that the cohort was in fact milliary'. The commander of *coh. I Ligurum* was also a tribune (see Saddington, op.cit., p.146). Further, one might also consider whether or not Luke's use of the title χιλίαρχος, if indeed he intended to indicate the commander of a milliary unit, is anachronistic. Against the second argument one must contend with the possibility that Luke exaggerated the escort's size to emphasise the danger to Paul. Finally, against the third argument it can be noted that it assumes the continuity of the unit's existence as *milliaria* and of the soldier's service in that unit. However, both Holder, op.cit., pp.6 and 12-13 nn.6, 7 and 9,

---

180 E.g. Josephus, *BJ* 3.67 where ten of the twenty-three cohorts are said to be milliary (ἀνὰ χιλίους πεζούς). The size of auxiliary units is also indicated by the use of the term χιλίαρχος to describe their commanders, e.g. *AJ* 20.6.2.132 and *BJ* 2.12.6.244.

181 There is uncertainty as to what the term δεξιολάβοι denotes. LSJ gives the meaning 'spearmen'. The meaning 'led horses' has been suggested to me, i.e. that three horses were led by each cavalryman and were intended for the speedy return of the infantry. In support of this suggestion the numerical agreement (i.e. 200) can be noted. But some questions remain unanswered. Where were the horses from? Since each cavalryman was responsible for his own horse (i.e. feed and equipment), the number of horses in each unit would not much exceed the number of cavalrymen. Also if the infantry could ride and haste was of the essence, why did they not ride in both directions? Cf. the separate mention of infantry and δεξιολάβοι (Acts 23.23) which seems to imply that they did not ride from Jerusalem.

and Birley, op.cit., pp.350 and 356, argue that milliary units could be formed from the smaller *quingenaria* units. The continuity of a unit's existence over a twenty-five-year period cannot be assumed from the diplomata themselves. More particularly, Holder, op.cit., pp.6 and 13 n.8, argues that *coh. I Brittonum milliaria* was first raised in the Flavian period (i.e. later than AD 69). In other words, the continuity of a soldier's service in the same unit cannot be assumed.

A criticism can also be levelled against Holder's and Birley's argument that the full spelling of the term *milliaria* in the early evidence indicates its novelty at that date (i.e. early AD 80s); for one finds even in AD 103 a full spelling (*coh. I Vangionum* – *CIL* XVI 48). If a full spelling in AD 103 after some twenty-two years (assuming the creation of milliary units in approx. AD 81) does not indicate novelty, why should a full spelling in AD 81 after twenty-four years (assuming a creation date for milliary units by AD 57) indicate novelty? The argument is clearly subjective as novelty relies on the user's consciousness. Essentially, then, Holder's argument is reduced to one which concerns the want of documentary evidence before AD 81.

The under-determination of the evidence does not permit a definite conclusion regarding the dating of milliary units. The answer depends on several variables and one's disposition to accept or deny their import. The first documentary evidence for milliary units does not appear till the AD 80s. Against this one needs to ask several questions. Has chance deprived us of earlier documentary evidence? Were milliary units at first not indicated as such in inscriptions?[182] Again, what credence can be placed in the literary evidence of Josephus and Acts, especially since documentary evidence may be wanting? Indeed, can the suggested earlier dating of milliary units derived by counting back years of service in military diplomata and the literary evidence of Josephus and Acts be used to corroborate each other? As stated above, the answers to these questions depend on one's disposition towards them.

S.R.L.

---

182 For example, *coh. I Britannica* in a diploma of AD 84 (*CIL* XVI 30) is not designated as milliary; however, in the diploma of AD 85 (*CIL* XVI 31) it is so designated. Birley, op.cit., p.356, comments: 'one cannot exclude the possibility that it was merely the title *milliaria* and not the unit of that size which, from AD 85 onwards, became officially recognised in this and other cases'.

JUDAICA

§23 The Goliath Family at Jericho

Jericho — Late I AD

Ed.pr. — R. Hachlili, 'The Goliath Family in Jericho: Funerary Inscriptions from a First Century AD Jewish Monumental Tomb', *Bulletin of the American Schools of Oriental Research* 235 [1979], pp.31-73, nos.3, 9, 14; *SEG* 31 (1981), 1405-7).

1. Θεοδότου ἀπελευθέρου βασιλίσσης 'Αγριππείνης σορός
The ossuary of Theodotos, freedman of Queen Agrippina

2 'Ιωεζρος 'Ιωεζρου Γολιαθου
Yehoezer son of Yehoezer Goliath

3. ΑΒΓΔ
ΕΖ
ΗΘ
- - - -
Φ

These are only three of a total of thirty-two inscriptions dating to the first century AD which have been discovered in an unusually large double-chambered tomb excavated in the Jewish necropolis at Jericho. (See the full discussion of the cemetery in R. Hachlili and A. Killebrew, 'Jewish funerary customs during the Second Temple period in the light of excavations at the Jericho necropolis', *PEQ* 115 [1983], pp.109-32.) The inscriptions occur on fourteen of the twenty-two limestone ossuaries found within the tomb, some of which bear the same inscription twice, or even three times. Most of the texts were incised but two were written, one with ink and the other with charcoal. Seventeen of the inscriptions are Greek and the remaining fifteen are in the Hebrew script.

To judge from its size, the elaborate nature of its design with courtyard and two chambers each containing several loculi and, in addition, the plastered walls bearing painted decoration in the first chamber, the tomb must have belonged to a wealthy family. Its inclusion within the Jewish necropolis and the fact that all the names on the ossuaries except one (Theodotus, which is a Greek translation of the Hebrew name Nathanel) are Jewish, indicate that the family was Jewish.

It has been possible to discover something of the structure of the family interred within the tomb, primarily from the familial relationships revealed in the texts, but to a lesser extent also from an analysis of skeletal remains and the original position of the ossuaries. Three generations of the family are represented. Yehoezer, son of Eleazar and his wife Shlomsion were the founders of the tomb; with them were buried their six sons together with their wives and fourteen offspring. If there were any daughters born to Yehoezer and Shlomsion, they were buried elsewhere; probably, by analogy with other family tombs investigated in Israel, in their husband's tomb if they had married. Yet the female side of the family is given some prominence by the appearance of Shlomsion's name on the ossuary of her granddaughter where a patronymic might have been expected. The anthropological examination of the bones has revealed that Shlomsion lived until her sixties while Yehoezer her husband died at the early age of about thirty-five. Therefore, in the opinion of Hachlili, this text may attest her important status in childrearing after his early death. Among the offspring of the third generation there is one female buried in the tomb. Even though she died at the age of forty she was, presumably, unmarried.

Inscription 1, which appears twice in Greek on ossuary VIII, is the only one in which an historical figure is mentioned. Identification of Theodotos' patron Queen Agrippina as Agrippina the Younger, wife of the Roman emperor Claudius between AD 50-54, provides a chronological indication for the lifetime of Theodotos. Considering the palaeographic and anthropological evidence and allowing for the lapse of the time between the generations, Hachlili places the tomb's use in the years between AD 10-70 (p.62).

Despite the Jewish context of his burial, Theodotos' funerary inscription retains the traditional format of epitaphs of freedmen, recording solely his status and his patron's name. It differs from others in the tomb also by its formal and well-executed letters. Theodotos alone of all the family is described by a Greek name, all other Jewish names in the Greek inscriptions are not translated but transliterated. All these features mark out the exceptional course his life took when compared with other family members. Hachlili suggests (p.33) that, since Theodotos belonged to a wealthy family of Jericho, he was probably taken to Rome as a political prisoner. Many who were enslaved during the imperial period, regardless of race, adopted Greek names and this probably explains therefore, the apparent anomaly of his Greek name. There is no indication that any of his five brothers suffered the same fate however, and the occasion on which Theodotos might have been enslaved is unknown. He must already have been an adult for, according to the other remains found, he already had two children. The evidence does not reveal either how long he was enslaved or at what date he was free to leave Agrippina's service and return, as he did, to his family. However, if Agrippina was indeed well disposed towards the Jewish community as Josephus (*AJ* 20.135) records, this might explain Theodotos' manumission. In his book *The Pre-Christian Paul* (London/Philadelphia, 1991, p.13), Martin Hengel argues that the ascription to Theodotos of his freedman status in the tomb illustrates the respectability of his standing on his return to Judaea, not only in the eyes of his family but also of the community at large. He suggests also (p.14) that the burial of this man with his Jewish relatives provides an example of how other Jewish families which had obtained Roman citizenship, such as Paul's, could nevertheless combine sucessfully their new rank with their ancestral religion.

The most striking aspect of Inscription 2 is the appearance of the word 'Goliath'. It appears in fact on a total of five ossuaries in both Greek and Hebrew. Hachlili believes this is the only attested usage of the name outside the references to 'Goliath the Philistine' in the LXX; where it occurs in the Hebrew script Goliath is spelt exactly as it is written in the Hebrew Bible and LXX. Since the name is included in the identification of male burials in the tomb over two generations it appears to have been adopted as a family name and, even if it commenced as a nickname of one individual only, must have later been embraced by the family as a whole. That it was connected to a physical characteristic of this family is nevertheless likely, for study of the skeletal remains of four male members of the family has revealed that they were unusually tall (p.52).

Additional names referring to a physical characteristic, or to profession such as scribe, priest, are not uncommon among Jews. Nevertheless it is unusual for additional names of either type to be passed from generation to generation and Hachlili believes (p.53) this is the strongest argument for thinking Goliath became a family name rather than a nickname.

Inscription 3 was drawn with charcoal inside the lid of Ossuary VI containing a female of approximately forty years of age. The lid of the ossuary was found standing so that it faced the entrance of the tomb. Hachlili (p.47) supposes that the removal of the lid from its ossuary and its placement opposite the tomb's entrance was a deliberate act which occurred at some point during the use of the tomb but not necessarily at the time of the ossuary's deposition.

Although the form of some of the letters is unusual, the most likely interpretation of this inscription is as a Greek abecedary; it is the first so far to have been found in Israel according to Hachlili (p.48), although several Hebrew ones survive. The usual interpretation of abecedaries is that they were writing exercises, however it appears to Hachlili (p.48) that the position of the Goliath abecedary indicates the letters may have been viewed as having some magical significance since Pythagorean belief in the creative power of letters and numbers was known to the Jews. This view is endorsed by L.Y. Rahmani ('Some remarks on R. Hachlili's and A. Killebrew's "Jewish funerary customs"', *PEQ* 118 [1986], p.97). Alternatively, although in Hachlili's opinion less probably, the letters may have related in some way to the ordering of burials in the tomb.

Whether or not this is the case, the presence of such a high proportion of Greek inscriptions in the tomb draws attention once again to the extent of Hellenization in Israel in the first century AD (Hachlili p.62). Recent discussions of this topic include *New Docs* 4 (1987), p.233; *New Docs* 5 (1989), pp.19ff and, in this volume, **§13** on the penetration of Greek legal concepts into Judaism. In his recent monograph, *The 'Hellenization' of Judaea in the First Century after Christ* (London/Philadelphia 1989) Martin Hengel supports the view that Judaea was a bilingual society at that time (p.9), and proceeds in the subsequent discussion to explore the consequences of this for the New Testament.

The reason for the exhumation of the dead and the placing of their bones in ossuaries appears to be due to the desire to leave the body free of pollution and in the state of greatest purity (M. Goodman, *The Ruling Class of Judaea* [Cambridge 1987], p.104; Hachlili and Killebrew, ibid., p.129). Concerning the question of the origin and extent of such notable changes to traditional burial customs as represented by the ossuaries of the Goliath tomb in the period late I BC – AD 70 there has been less consensus. Rahmani (op.cit., pp.96-100) argues against it being a feature of external influence or even common over a wide area of Judaea. Goodman (ibid., pp.88-89), however, believes the burial habits of most inhabitants changed and that this change was related to messianic beliefs owing much to Hellenistic, Mesopotamian and Iranian influences.

R.A. Kearsley

§24 A Work Contract of Jewish Soldiers

Arsinoites 3 Feb.152 BC

Ed.pr. — B. Kramer, M. Erler, D. Hagedorn and R. Hübner, *P. Köln* III 144 (Opladen 1980), pp.86-94.

The document, written in duplicate, survives in three fragments (6 x 14.5 cm, 6 x 5 cm and 6 x 7 cm). Only the second section (*ll*.14-34) is translated below – *ll*.29-34 concern the particular details of cultivation but are very fragmentary. Gaps in *ll*.14-28 can partly be filled by comparison with the duplicate, though not exactly the same, text of *ll*.1-8. Even so the text is problematic. At the beginning of *l*.25 the reading suggested by the editors (p.91) has been inserted in the text.

[Βασιλευόντων Πτολεμαίου καὶ Κλεοπάτρας τ]ῶ̣ν̣ Πτολεμ̣α̣ί̣ου καὶ Κλεοπάτρας θεῶν Ἐπιφ̣ανῶν ἔτο[υς ἐν]ά̣τ̣[ου καὶ εἰκοστοῦ ἐφ' ἱερέως Δημητρίου]

[τοῦ Στρατονίκου Ἀλεξάνδρου καὶ θεῶν Σωτ]ήρων κ̣α̣ὶ θ̣ε̣ῶ̣ν̣ Ἀ̣δ̣ε̣λ̣φ̣ῶ̣ν̣ καὶ θεῶν Εὐεργετῶν καὶ [θεῶ]ν̣ Φιλοπ[ατόρ]ων καὶ θεῶ̣ν̣ Ἐ̣π̣[ιφανῶν καὶ θεῶν]

[Φιλομητόρων ἀθλοφόρου Βερενίκης Εὐεργέτιδος] Ε̣ἰ̣[ρ]ή̣ν̣η̣ς̣ τ̣ῆ̣ς̣ Διοσκουρίδου κανηφόρου Ἀ̣ρ̣σ̣[ιν]ό̣ης [Φι]λ̣α̣δ̣[έλφ]ου Κ̣λεοπάτρας [τῆς Πτολεμ]α̣ί̣ο̣[υ]

4 [ἱερείας Ἀρσινόης Φιλοπάτορος Δημαρίου τῆς] Μ̣ητρ[ο]φ̣ά̣ν̣ους μ̣η̣ν̣[ὸ]ς Πανήμου ἑβδόμ̣η̣ι̣ Τ̣[ῦβι] ἑ̣β̣δ̣ό̣μ̣η̣ι̣ ἐ̣[ν τῆι] Ἀλεξ̣ά̣ν̣δ̣ρ̣ο̣υ̣ ν̣(ή)σ̣ω̣ι̣ τ̣ῆς Θ̣ε̣[μ]ί̣στο̣[υ]

[μερίδος τοῦ Ἀρσινοίτου νομοῦ. ὁμολογοῦσι Σίμων] Θ̣ε̣ο̣δ̣ώρου καὶ ο̣ἱ̣ σ̣υ̣μ̣μ̣έ̣τ̣ο̣χ̣ο̣ι̣ α̣ὐ̣[τοῦ Ἰου]δ̣α̣ῖ̣ο̣ι̣ τ̣ῶ̣ν̣ . . . . τακτ̣ό̣μ̣ι̣σ̣θ̣ο̣ι̣ . . . .

[± 14 Εὐάρχωι Ἡλιοδώρου Αἰακιδεῖ] τ̣ῶ̣ν̣ περὶ αὐλὴν διαδόχων ἐ̣ξειληφέ̣[ναι πα]ρ̣' α̣ὐ̣τοῦ τὰ ἀ̣μ̣πελικὰ ἔ̣ρ̣γ̣α̣ π̣ά̣ν̣τ̣α̣ . . . . του . [.]

[± 20 Μελαγκόμαι τῶι ἀρχισ]ω̣μ̣α̣τ̣ο̣φ̣ύ̣λ̣α̣κι καὶ στρατηγῶι ἀ̣μ̣πελῶν̣ι̣ π̣[ρότ]ε̣ρον Λ̣ά̣μ̣π̣ρου λεγομέν̣ω̣ι μ̣[ισ]θ̣ο̣ῦ̣

8 [τὴν ἄρουραν ἑκάστην χαλκοῦ νομίσματος δραχμῶν χιλί]ω̣ν̣ ἑπτακοσίων ...

[± 38] ...

[± 38] ... [. . .]α̣τ̣α̣β̣λ̣η̣ . . . τ̣η̣ν̣χορηγ [. .] . . . .

[± 38] ... [. . .]χ̣ε̣ι̣π̣ε̣ . . . . σ̣ι̣π̣ο̣ . τ̣ . κα . . . . .

12 [± 38] . . . . καὶ ἐν τῶ̣ι̣ Π̣α̣χ̣ὼ̣ν̣ [μηνὶ] τὸν μισθὸ̣ν̣ ὃ̣ν̣ προσοφείλε̣ι̣ ἐγ λόγου, ἐν δὲ μη̣ . . .

[± 38]μ̣α̣τ̣α̣ Εὔαρχος Σ̣ί̣μ̣ω̣ν̣ι̣ καὶ τοῖς συμμετόχο̣[ις.]

[βασιλευόντων Πτολεμαίου] καὶ Κλεοπάτρας τῶν Π[το]λεμαίου καὶ Κλεοπάτρας θεῶν	[In the reign of Ptolemy] and Cleopatra, children of Ptolemy and Cleopatra, gods
[Ἐπιφανῶν ἔτους ἐνάτου] καὶ εἰκοστοῦ ἐφ' ἱερέως Δημ[ητρίου] τ̣οῦ Στρατονίκου Ἀλεξάνδρου	[Epiphaneis, in the] twenty-[ninth year], when Demetrios, son of Stratonikos, was priest of Alexander
16 [καὶ θεῶν Σωτήρων καὶ θ]εῶν Ἀδελφῶν καὶ θεῶν Εὐεργ[ετῶ]ν̣ καὶ θεῶν Φιλοπατόρων	[and of gods Soteres and] of gods Adelphoi and of gods Euergetai and of gods Philopatores
[καὶ θεῶν Ἐπιφανῶν κ]αὶ θεῶν Φιλομητόρω̣ν̣ ἀ̣θ̣λ̣ο̣[φόρου] Βερενίκης Εὐεργέτιδος	[and of gods Epiphaneis] and of gods Philometores, *athlophoros* of Berenice Euergetis being
[Εἰρήνης τῆς Διοσκουρ]ί̣δου κανηφόρου Ἀρσινόης [Φιλ]αδέλφου Κλεοπάτρας τῆς	[Irene, daughter of Dioskour]ides, *kanephoros* of Arsinoe Philadelphos being Cleopatra, daughter
[Πτολεμαίου ἱερεία]ς Ἀρσινόης Φιλ[ο]π̣ά̣τ̣ο̣ρος Δημ̣α̣ρίου τῆς Μητροφάνου[ς]	of [Ptolemy, priestess] of Arsinoe Philopator, being Demarios, daughter of Metrophanes,
20 [μηνὸς Πανήμου ἑ]βδόμη̣ι̣ Τ̣ῦβι ἑβδόμηι ἐν τ̣ῆ̣[ι] Ἀλεξάνδρου ν̣ή̣σ̣ωι τῆς	[in the month of Panemos,] the seventh, (in the month of) Tybi, the seventh, in the island of Alexander of the
[Θεμίστου μερίδος το]ῦ Ἀρσινοίτου νομοῦ. ὁμο[λογ]ο̣ῦσι Σ̣ί̣μων Θεοδώ̣ρου καὶ	[district of Themistos] of the Arsinoite nome. Simon, son of Theodoros, and
[οἱ συμμέτοχοι αὐτο]ῦ̣ Ἰουδαῖοι τῶ̣ν̣ . . . . [τ]α̣κ̣[τ]ό̣μισθ̣ο̣ι̣ . . . . . ω̣ . . . . ε̣ο̣υ̣	[his partners], Jews of the ... (being) *taktomisthoi* ...
[± 16] Εὐάρχωι Ἡλι̣ο̣δώρου Αἰακιδεῖ τῶν περὶ αὐλὴν διαδόχων	[...] acknowledge to Euarchos, son of Heliodoros, of the *demos* Aiakideus, of the court *diadochoi*

24	[ἐξειληφέναι παρ' αὐτ]ο̣ῦ̣ τ̣ὰ ἀμπελικὰ ἔργα π̣ά̣ντα̣ τοῦ εὑρεθησομ̣ένου ῥάχου	[to have contracted from him] all the viticultural works of the thicket (?) regardless of its condition
	[ἐν τῶι ὑπάρχοντι] Μ̣ελαγκόμαι τῶι ἀρχισ̣ω̣ματ̣οφύλακι καὶ στρατηγῶι ἀμπ̣ε̣-	[in the] vineyard [belonging] to Melankomas, the *archisomatophylax* and *strategos*,
	[λῶνι πρότερον Λά]μπ̣ρου λεγομένω̣ι̣ μισθο̣ῦ̣ τὴ[ν ἄ]ρουραν ἑκάστην χαλκοῦ νομίσ-	[formerly] called Lampros' (vineyard ?), at a fee for each aroura of
	[ματος δραχμῶν χιλί]ων ἑπτακοσίων ἐξα̣ρ̣ι̣θ̣μ̣ο̣υμένης τῆς ἀρο̣ύ̣ρ̣η̣ς \`ἐ̣κ̣´ τετρακοσί-	[one thousand] seven hundred copper-coin [drachmae], the aroura being reckoned at (?) four hundred
28	[ων ἀμπέλων, καὶ ποιήσο]ν̣ται Σίμων καὶ οἱ συ̣μμέτοχ̣ο̣ι ....[.....] .ην̣κακα.	[vines, and] Simon and his partners will [do ...]
	[± 16] καὶ τὴν φυτου̣ρ̣γ̣ί̣αν ἀνα.. ....τ..[.......]μερων καὶ τε-	[...] and the gardening ... [...] ... and
	[± 16 τ]ῷ̣ι̣ ἐνάτωι καὶ εἰκοστῶι ἔτει. κατ̣[........]ς οὖν τῆς κατα	[...] twenty-ninth year [...] therefore of the
	[± 16]ωι εὐεργουμένῳ̣ οὐθὲν τῶν φυ̣[τῶν]....	[...] cultivated with care (?) none of the pla[nts ...]
32	[± 13 κεχ]α̣ρακισμένον καὶ φλοῦν ἐν αὐτ.[ ]	[...] staked and bark in [...]
	[...Σίμωνι καὶ τοῖς σ]υ̣μμε̣τ̣ό̣χοις ὑ̣π̣ο̣ν̣...[ ]	[... to Simon and his] partners [...]
	[ ]οισχ̣ι̣μ̣[ ]	

*Ll.*24-26 present a particular difficulty. What is the connection between ῥάχου, the duties contracted by the soldiers (*l.*24) and the vineyard (*l.*25)? The use of the genitive implies that the agricultural duties were directed towards the ῥάχος which the editors take to mean either bush, hedge or brambles[183]; but if so, how can the duties be described as viticultural, i.e. τ̣ὰ ἀμπελικὰ ἔργα π̣ά̣ντα̣ τοῦ εὑρεθησομ̣ένου ῥάχου. In response to this difficulty the editors suggest that the contracted work involved the recultivation of a vineyard which had been neglected and thereby had become a thicket (pp.90-91). Further they restore *ll.*25-6 to read [ἐν τῶι ὑπάρχοντι] Μ̣ελαγκόμαι τῶι ἀρχισ̣ω̣ματ̣οφύλακι καὶ στρατηγῶι ἀμπ̣ε̣[λῶνι κτλ] so that the viticultural duties are directed towards the thicket in the vineyard. Some perplexity concerning the textual status of the future passive participle εὑρεθησομ̣ένου is expressed by the editors and it remained untranslated by them. As the participle indicates a future condition or state of affairs (see *P. Fouad* 35, *P. Sarap*. 25 and *P. Ant*. I 42), how can it be related to an already neglected vineyard? The solution, it seems, is best resolved if the participle is perceived to be spoken from the lessees' aspect. In other words, the lessees acknowledge that they have undertaken all the viticultural duties of the thicket regardless of the condition in which they find it.

183 LSJ gives one example of the term used of a vine and offer the translation 'twig, branch'. However, the difficulty with accepting this meaning in the present context lies in the use of the singular.

The vineyard appears to have belonged to Melankomas,[184] and Euachos either acted as his agent (p.91) or had possibly leased it from him. In turn Euarchos leased the labour of the vineyard to Simon and his partners. See *New Docs* 6 (1992) **§13** for a discussion of the possible advantages of this procedure. If the editors' interpretation of *P. Köln* III 144 is correct, then the neglected condition of the vineyard may explain why it was to be cultivated by contracted labour rather than leased as an income earning property; for leasing the vineyard would not have made commercial sense to a tenant given that most agricultural leases were short term (one to three years) and that the present property (like a new vineyard) would not have produced a return for some time. The editors of *P. Köln* III 144 also note that similar labour contracts are infrequent in Ptolemaic Egypt; however, in terms of content they offer as the nearest example *BGU* IV 1122 (13 BC). This also is a labour contract to undertake viticultural duties. From *ll*.15-16 it may be concluded that the contract involved the establishment of a new vineyard. Again, where the property was not immediately productive the owner opted for a labour contract rather than a lease agreement. *P. Oxy*. IV 707, a report of legal proceedings, may also prove of relevance on this point. The document relates that a vineyard and orchard had been leased for a period of six years with no rent being charged for the first four years. Philinus, the tenant, was to plant (ἀνάξαι – train) vines in the open spaces, to erect walls(?) and to build a brick wheel. For the latter he was to be paid two thousand drachmae. As in *P. Köln* III 144, it appears that the vineyard had been neglected. However, in contrast to *P. Köln* III 144 the property was leased for a relatively long period, with allowance made for an initial shortfall in productivity. Cf. also *P. Tebt*. I 5 *ll*.93-8 which remits all taxes on newly planted vineyards and orchards for an initial five-year period and specifies a reduced rate for the following three years. The edict, which was issued after a period of upheaval and sought to encourage the planting of new vineyards and orchards, recognised the fact that they would be unproductive for the first few years and made allowance for this.

Simon and his partners contracted to perform work with persons bearing court titles. Melankomas' title of chief-bodyguard (*archisomatophylax*) is of a higher order than that of Euarchos (*diadochos*). For a ranking of titles and discussion of the arguments tendered for the relationship between title and function see L. Mooren, *La hiérarchie de cour ptolémaïque* (Leuven 1977), pp.36, 61-73. Similar titles were also used in the court of Herod the Great – see A.H.M. Jones, *The Herods of Judaea* (Oxford 1967), p.83. On the status of Jews in Ptolemaic Egypt see A. Kasher, *The Jews in Hellenistic and Roman Egypt* (Tübingen 1985). Simon and his partners are described as *taktomisthoi*. V. Tcherikover and A. Fuks (see *CPJ* I, p.147) suggest that the *taktomisthoi* performed an administrative function in the army, 'perhaps as paymasters'. *P. Tebt*. III 818 = *CPJ* I, p.24 (dated 16 April 174 BC) records that Agathokles, son of Ptolemy, a Jew, was *taktomisthos*. See also *CPJ* I, p.22 where, as Kasher, op.cit., pp.45 and 52, argues, Theodotos, though designated a Paeonian, was also a Jewish *taktomisthos*. For Jewish soldiers in Egypt see *CPJ* I, pp.11-15 & 147ff. and Kasher, op.cit., pp.38-55. The dating of the document implies that it must be used judiciously in any debate concerning the existence of independent Jewish units in the Ptolemaic army before Onias IV (i.e. before approx. 150 BC).

Another document among the papyri published in 1980/81, namely *BGU* XIV 2381 (2 Aug. 176 BC at Poimenon Kome), appears to be a receipt issued by Ptolemy, son of Sabbataios, a Jew, to [...]θᾶτο[ς] τῆς Φ[...], a Jewess. The latter acts with her guardian, probably her husband, who likewise is described as a Jew. The state of the document does not

184 The reading π̣[ρότ]ε̣ρον Λά̣μ̣π̣ρου (*ll*.7 and 26) is rather insecure but, if correct, indicates that it formerly belonged to an individual called Lampros. Immovable property was frequently described by mention of a former owner, e.g. in census returns (see *P. Oxy*. XLVII 3336 in *New Docs* 6 [1992] **§16**); land lists (see *BGU* IX 1896); and deeds of sale (see *P. Bon*. 24, *P. Gen*. II 116).

allow one to determine whether the receipt was issued with the making of a loan or with its repayment. The document is otherwise of interest as the earliest Greek witness to certain priestly names, i.e. Πτολεμαίου [τοῦ] Πτολεμαίου τοῦ Διονυσίο[υ], priest of Alexander and of the gods *Adelphoi* and of the gods *Euergetai* and of the gods *Philopatores* and of the gods *Epiphaneis* and of king Ptolemy; ['Ασκληπι]άδος τῆς 'Ασκλη[πιάδο]υ, priestess *kanephoros* of Arsinoe *Philadelphos*; and ['Αρτεμοῦς τῆς Θεο]δώρου priestess of Arsinoe *Philopator* .

S.R.L.

ECCLESIASTICA

§25 Ammonios to Apollonios (*P. Oxy.* XLII 3057): The Earliest Christian Letter on Papyrus?

Oxyrhynchus — Late first or early second century AD

Ed.pr. — P.J.Parsons, *P. Oxy.* XLII 3057 (London 1974), pp.144-6.

The editor describes the letter as written in 'a single hand, neat and semi-literary'. On the basis of script he assigns the letter to the late first or early second century.

Bib. – P.J. Parsons, 'The Earliest Christian Letter?', *Miscellanea Papyrologica* (Florence 1980), p.289; O. Montevecchi, *Aegyptus* 55 (1975), p.302; C.J. Hemer, 'Ammonius to Apollonius, Greeting', *Buried History* 12 (1976), pp.84-91; E.A. Judge, *Rank and Status in the World of the Caesars and St. Paul* (Canterbury 1982), pp.20-3; G.R. Stanton, 'The Proposed Earliest Christian Letter on Papyrus and the Origin of the Term Philallelia', *ZPE* 54 (1984), pp.49-63.

Ἀμμώνιος Ἀπολλωνίωι τῶι ἀδελφῶι χαίρειν.	Ammonios to Apollonios, his brother, greeting.
ἐκομισάμην τὴν κεχιασμένην ἐπιστολὴν	I received the crossed letter,
καὶ τὴν ἱματοφορίδα καὶ τοὺς φαινόλας καὶ τὰς	the portmanteau, the cloaks and the
σύνριγγας οὐ καλάς, τοὺς δὲ φαινόλας οὐχ ὡς	poorer quality reeds. I received the cloaks not as
παλαιοὺς ἔλαβον ἀλλ' εἴ τι μεῖζόν ἐστιν και-	second-hand but (as) better than new
νῶν διὰ προαίρεσιν· οὐ θέλω δέ σε, ἄδελφε, βα-	because of your intention. I don't want you, brother,
ρύνειν με ταῖς συνεχέσ{εσ}ι φιλανθρωπίαις,	to weigh me down with your continual acts of kindness
\` . . . ´ οὐ δυνάμενον ἀμείψασθαι, αὐτὸ δὲ μόνον	... (seeing that) I am unable to reciprocate. Only
ἡμεῖς προαίρεσιν φιλικῆς διαθέσεως νομί-	an intention of friendly disposition do we think
ζομεν παρεστακέναι σοι. παρακαλῶ	we have offered you. I ask
δέ σε, ἄδελφε, μηκέτι λόγον ποιεῖσθαι πε-	you, brother, no longer to concern yourself
ρὶ τῆς κλειδὸς τῆς μονοχώρου. οὐ γὰρ θέ-	about the key for the single-room. For I do not want
λω ὑμᾶς τοὺς ἀδελφοὺς ἕνεκα ἐμοῦ ἢ ἄλ-	you, my brothers, on my account or (on) another's
λου διαφοράν τινα ἔχειν· ὁμόνοιαν γὰρ καὶ	to have any difference; for I pray that oneness of mind and
φιλαλλη‹λ›ίαν εὔχομαι ἐν ὑμεῖν διαμένειν	mutual friendship remain among you
ἵν' ἦτε ἀκαταλήρητοι καὶ μὴ [[ἦτε]] ὁμοῖοι	that you may be free from gossip and not like

ἡμεῖν. ἡ γὰρ πεῖρα ἐπάγεταί με προτρέψασ-	us. For experience urges me to persuade
θαι ὑμᾶς εἰρηνεύειν καὶ μὴ διδόναι ἀφορ-	you to live peaceably and not to give occasions
μὰς ἑτέροις καθ' ὑμῶν· πείρασαι οὖν καὶ δι'	against you to others. Try then also for
ἐμὲ τοῦτο ποιεῖν, χαρισάμενός μοι ὃ με-	my sake to do this, gratifying me, which meanwhile
ṭọξὺ ἐπιγνώσῃ ἀγαθόν. τὰ ἔρια ἂν ᾖς εἰλη-	you will recognise as a good thing. If you receive the wool
φὼς παρὰ Σαλβίου πλήρη καὶ ᾖ σοι ἀρεσ-	from Salvius in full measure and are satisfied with it,
τά, ἀντίγραψόν μοι· γελοῖα δέ σοι γέγραφα	write to me. I wrote you nonsense
διὰ τῆς προτέρας ἐπιστολῆς, ἃ παραδέξῃ·	in the previous letter which you will admit.
ἡ γὰρ ψυχὴ ἀνειμένη γείνεται, ὅταν τὸ	For my soul becomes relaxed whenever
σὸν ὄνομα παρῇ, καὶ ταῦτα οὐχ ἔθος ἐχού-	your name is present, and this though it is unaccustomed
σης ἠρεμεῖν διὰ τὰ ἐπερχόμενα· ἀλ‹λ›' ὑπο-	to be at rest because of what is happening. But
φέρει Λεωνᾶς· ἀσπάζομαί σε, δέσποτα, καὶ τοὺς	Leonas bears up. I greet you, master, and
σ[ο]ὺς πάντας· ἔρρωσο, ṭẹιμιώτατε.	all your household. Farewell, most honoured one.
(Back) Ἀπολλωνίωι Ἀπολλω( ) ἐπισκέπ(τῃ) ἀδε(λφῷ).	To Apollonios, son of Apollo() surveyor, his brother.

....

30 τιμιώτατε

Changes in the Use of the Singular and Plural 1st and 2nd Person

The letter is addressed by Ammonios to one Apollonios. However, the letter alternates between the use of singular and plural forms in the 1st and 2nd persons. The use of the 1st person plural cannot be explained as an instance of the literary plural, i.e. the author is not associating his reader with himself in the present letter. The first occurs at *l.*10 with a change to the 1st plural ἡμεῖς ... νομίζομεν. The change must be explained by the fact that the writer at times feels himself, no doubt, to be writing for Leonas (see *l.*29). With *l.*11 the letter returns to the 1st singular παρακαλῶ. In *ll.*14-20 the author changes from the 2nd person singular to the 2nd person plural. The reason is simple. Since the letter now refers to a quarrel in the addressee's community, the author had no option but to associate the addressee with his fellows (see *ll.*29-30 τοὺς σοὺς πάντας). However, the return to the 2nd singular at *l.*20 again recognises the sole addressee as Apollonios and the imperatives are directed to him. A similar phenomenon of alternating singular and plural forms can be observed in early Christian papyri also. H.I. Bell, *Jews and the Christians in Egypt* (Westport 1924 – reprinted 1972), p.76 (= *P. Lond.* VI), notes that in the case of the joint letter, papyrus 1916, 'Herieous sometimes forgets that he is not writing in his own name only and drops into the first person singular'. Inverse cases where a letter between two single individuals uses the 1st and 2nd person plurals can be observed more frequently, e.g. *P. Lond.* VI 1917 *l.*8, 1918 *ll.*10,18-9, 1927 *l.*35, 1928 *ll.*3, 15, 1929 *ll.*4, 6. However, the practice was not confined to Christian papyri. For example, see Zenon's draft letters in *PCZ* 59015 (*New Docs* 6 [1992] **§13**), especially *ll.*2 and 27 which are parallel sentences but where in one μοι was used and in the other ἡμῖν.

The phenomenon is observable in the NT also. For example, though each is addressed to an individual, the letters to Timothy and Titus in their concluding wishes address the communities (see 1Tim.6.21, 2Tim.4.22 and Tit.3.15; also see the textual variant at Tit.1.4). The same practice can be observed in Paul's letter to Philemon (see Phlm.6 as textual variant, 22 (2x) and 25).

The phenomenon for the 1st person in the epistles is more complicated. A partial analysis of the NT epistles indicates, however, that the observed uses of the singular and plural 1st person conform to expectation, once allowance is made for the possibility of a corporate greeting but singular address. Table 25.1 shows the frequencies of the 1st person for the Pauline epistles. The columns entitled 'Singular' and 'Plural' give the count data for each epistle. The column entitled 'Percentage' gives the plurals as a percentage of all first person verbs and pronouns. The dates in Table 25.1 were obtained from R. Jewett, *Dating Paul's Life* (London 1979).

Table 25.1: The Frequency of First Person Verbs and Pronouns[185]

Epistle	Singular	Plural	Percentage	Date
Rom.	223	166	42.7	56-7
1Cor.	295	134	31.2	55-6
2Cor.	228	280	55.1	55-6
Gal.	111	56	33.5	53-4
Eph.	32	53	62.4	-
Phil.	137	13	8.7	55
Col.	28	26	48.1	56
1Thes.	4	119	96.7	50
2Thes.	3	46	93.9	50
1Tim.	31	18	36.7	-
2Tim.	61	15	19.7	-
Tit.	10	27	73.0	-
Phlm.	40	4	9.1	55

As Paul's earliest epistles show the highest percentage of plurals (i.e. 1Thes. 96.7% and 2Thes. 93.9%), the question arises as to whether there is a correlation between the date of writing and the use of the singular or plural 1st person. A closer investigation, however, shows no significant correlation between them.[186] In other words, other variables beside the date of writing affected Paul's usage.

The introductions to the letters indicate that only Romans, Ephesians, 1 and 2 Timothy and Titus carry a greeting by Paul alone to his readers. Looking at 1 and 2 Timothy one finds that all plurals are literary plurals (i.e. the speaker associates the reader with himself). In other words, the use of the plural is not problematic. The other letters include opening greetings from Paul together with Timothy or Silas or Sosthenes or unnamed brothers. Yet in the latter case it

---

185 The variable counts were obtained by a search of the morphologically tagged NT text (UBS 3) kindly supplied by CCAT (Centre for Computer Analysis of Texts at the University of Pennsylvania).

186 The Spearman rank-order correlation coefficient of - 0.2647 for 7 degrees of freedom gives a p-value of 0.49. In calculating the coefficient undated letters were omitted and 1Cor. and 1Thes. were dated before 2Cor. and 2Thes. respectively.

is clear that sometimes the message is from Paul alone. For example, Philippians, though the opening greetings are by Paul and Timothy, must be considered the most individual of Paul's letters. All plurals with the exception of one (Phil.3.17) must be classed as literary plurals.[187] Paul and Timothy never (apart from the introduction) address the Philippians together. The same change from a corporate greeting to a singular address can be observed in other epistles also. However, in 2 Corinthians the plural extends beyond the greeting itself (see 2Cor.1.3-14). At the other pole of the Pauline corpus are the letters to the Thessalonians. The opening greetings are made by Paul, Silas and Timothy and the plurality of writers is maintained throughout the epistles. Where the singular is used (1Thes.2.18, 3.5 (2x), 5.27, 2Thes.2.5 (2x), 3.17), it refers to a particular act of Paul. The question naturally arises as to why the epistles to the Philippians and Thessalonians should be so different in their use of the singular and plural 1st person and what this may tell us about Paul's perception of his apostleship.

Determining Christian Authorship

Since its first publication, the question has arisen as to whether or not *P. Oxy*. 3057 is Christian. In this connection P.J. Parsons, *P. Oxy*. XLII (London 1974), pp.144-6, drew attention to three elements of the text. The first concerns the mention of a former crossed letter and its receipt. Parsons entertains three possible interpretations, i.e. a) to indicate the cancellation of a contract – see *New Docs* 6 (1992) §14 for a discussion of the practice; b) to indicate the place of fastening across the letter's address; c) to fill in a blank line as a precaution against unauthorised additions. In view of the fact that *P. Oxy*. 3057 was a private letter Parsons doubts options a) and c). Equally, option b) is thought doubtful since 'the usage should be too common for comment' (p.145). In view of this impasse Parsons suggests a possible reference to the Cross. The second element concerns the use of the title 'brother', the context of internal quarrels and the threat of external attack. Parsons suggests a possible Christian context here, cf. 1 Clement for a parallel context of internal quarrels. The sentiments of *P. Oxy*. 3057 and to a lesser degree its vocabulary, in so far as they have Christian parallels (e.g. compare *ll*.15-16 above with τὴν ὁμόνοιαν καὶ τὴν φιλαλληλίαν in Nilus Ancyranus, *PG* 79.144a), comprise Parsons' third element. However, in his initial publication Parsons drew back and concluded that 'it would be temerarious to look for a Christian context'. Against his three elements argued above he notes that:

a. to see in the crossing of the letter (χιάζειν) a reference to the cross (σταυρός) is forced (see again discussion in *New Docs* 6 [1992] §14);
b. the sentiments of *P. Oxy*. 3057 are likely to have had a wide currency;
c. the early date weighs against Christian authorship.

However, in a later publication (see id., 'The Earliest Christian Letter?', p.289), Parsons adduces new parallels of sentiment between *P. Oxy*. 3057 and the letters of Constantine to Chrestus, Bishop of Syracuse and to Aelafius, Vicar of Africa (both dated AD 313/14). He considers that these parallels strengthen the case for understanding the letter as Christian. He concludes:

> The date of *P. Oxy*. 3057 rests entirely on the hand-writing. Either this palaeographical date is too early ... or this letter is the earliest Christian document surviving in Egypt.

Hemer, op.cit., argues that though Christian authorship is possible, the issue is whether this can be shown to be the case. Against Christian authorship he contrasts the Christian's need to conceal his/her faith in a public inscription and the supposed use of concealment in *P. Oxy*. 3057, a private letter; he sees no reason for the concealment of the author's faith in *P. Oxy*. 3057, if the letter was penned by a Christian. The difficulty with this, however, is that a

187 Twelve of the thirteen occurrences of the plural fall within the section Phil.3.1b-4.20, which is sometimes assumed to be interpolated.

particular circumstance, of which we are now unaware, may well explain the need for concealment. Let me suggest a possible interpretation of the letter where this might be the case. As discussed above Parsons argued that the function of crossing a letter to indicate the place of fastening across its address was 'too common for comment'. The practice alluded to is that of a letter's sealing. The letter was folded and across the exposed verso the address was written. A fibre of papyrus was then tied around the folded letter (alternatively a seal might be used) and a mark (e.g. the shape X) or design made around and over it. When the tie (or seal) was removed the design was disturbed or partly removed. The editors of *P. Oxy.* 3396 comment:

> The purpose of the design was apparently to enable any unauthorized opening of the letter to be detected, since it would have been difficult to match the original freehand design on a new fastening or to replace the old fastening in exactly the right place.

Now by the use of the perfect participle κεχιασμένην Ammonios may have wished to inform Apollonios that his letter was received in its sealed state. In other words, he wished to assure him that the letter had not been opened and read by someone else. But why should Ammonios or Apollonios be concerned about this? The letter itself suggests a possible reason, for Ammonios was subjected to harassment by others (*ll.*15-18, 27-28) and warned Apollonios 'not to give occasions against you to others' (*ll.*18-20). The context of internal quarrels and the threat of external attack may thus have provided an adequate circumstance to explain the need for concealment.

Judge, op.cit., raises a more general question as to how any letter can be identified as Christian. In the case of *P. Oxy.* 3057 he sees only marginal evidence for Christian authorship. The only vocabulary which is parallel to NT usage appears in *ll.*15-16, where the author enjoins Apollonios 'to live at peace and not to give others a handle against you'.[188] Against Christian authorship Judge notes the following:

- **a.** the absence of a distinctive Christian greeting;
- **b.** the term 'brother' may mean no more than colleague, i.e. one of equal rank as in other papyri;
- **c.** the sentiments expressed in the letter were widespread; Parsons' use of similar expressions in Constantine's letters is historically improper as by that time 'an extensive fusion of traditions had occurred', i.e. the fusion of Christian and classical traditions;
- **d.** the letter's vocabulary is problematic in two respects:
  - i. whereas the letter uses the words φιλανθρωπίαις *l.*8, ἀμείψασθαι *l.*9, χαρισάμενός μοι *l.*21 with man as subject, the NT uses them only of God;
  - ii. the word πείρασαι *l.*20 lacks a moral sense in the NT.

However, Judge finds the most important difference between the letter and the NT to be the former's ethics of contractual friendship, i.e. the system of gift and counter gift which weighs down the writer. He concludes:

> The absence of any trace of the ideal of spending for no personal return makes it difficult to put this circle of brothers very close to that tradition.

The difficulty with this observation is that it assumes that the early Church universally accepted the ethics of the Jesus-tradition and Paul. This may not have been the case at all. For example, P. Marshall, *Enmity in Corinth: Social Conventions in Paul's Relations with the Corinthians* (Tübingen 1987), argues that the problem of contractual friendship lies at the heart of Paul's dispute with members of the Corinthian church. Paul had declined to accept the gift of the Corinthian party, it is argued, because this would have placed him under an obligation to its members (see in particular pp.231-3, 397-8). If so, an ethics of contractual friendship was operative amongst members of the Corinthian church.

Stanton, op.cit., argues that since parallels of sentiment do not necessarily imply a shared belief, sentiment alone cannot be used to prove the Christian authorship of *P. Oxy.* 3057. Further, the use of the term 'brother' only implies membership in the same 'social, religious or

---

188 For a discussion of the problem posed by this type of argument see below. Can it be assumed that apart from their cult terms the early Christians had a distinctive vocabulary? Or as G.H.R. Horsley asks (per litt.), is it likely that at so early a date the Christians imitated the language of the NT authors?

economic group'. Though the term φιλαλληλία has some currency in later Christian writings, Stanton observes its use in mathematical works, in Tzetzes' expounding of Democritus and by the Epicurean Diogenes and postulates a more extensive usage than can be documented from extant texts. Accordingly, he concludes that 'the language of the letter is not so distinctive as to suggest Christian authorship'.

Parsons' argument for a Christian provenance rests substantially on the collocation of the terms ὁμόνοια and φιλαλληλία. Is there evidence to suggest that their collocation is a Christian linguistic phenomenon? Here, I believe, the issues of register[189] and lexical cohesion are relevant. For example, the occurrence of terms in two different registers – φιλαλληλία, say, in the mathematical register and ὁμόνοια in the political register[190] – would argue against the possibility of collocation. Was then their collocation a Christian innovation in the language? It is here that the use of φιλαλληλία in the Diogenes fragment (see Stanton, ibid., p.61) and in the description of Democritus' philosophy (see H. Diels, re-ed. W. Kranz, *Die Fragmente der Vorsokratiker* [West Berlin 1952], vol.2., pp.137-138) proves most important. Diogenes describes the utopian ideal of a society 'imbued with justice and mutual love' (φιλαλληλία) which has no need of 'walls or laws and all the things which we devise on account of one another'. Clearly, the register here is one of political discourse. The term φιλαλληλία is also used by Tzetzes to describe the condition of human existence in its primal stages. In the first stage humanity knew neither trade nor farming but grazed as a herd on fruits and vegetables:

φιλαλληλίαν δὲ μόνον ἀσκοῦντες ἀγελαῖον διέζων τὸν βίον δίκην ποιμνίων ἐπὶ νομὰς ἐξιόντες καὶ τοῖς ἀκροδρύοις κοινῶς καὶ τοῖς λαχάνοις τρεφόμενοι.

Practising only φιλαλληλία they lived a gregarious life like a herd going forth to pasture and feeding together on fruits and vegetables.

In the second stage humanity learnt to find shelter and store food. They still lived a simple life without the knowledge of fire, without kings, rulers and masters and without armies, the use of force and robbery. They only knew φιλαλληλία and how to live a free and simple life (ἀλλὰ φιλαλληλίαν μόνον καὶ τὸν ἐλεύθερον καὶ ἀπέριττον τοῦτον βίον ζῆν εἰδότες). Again, the register is clearly political. It follows that within philosophical circles the terms ὁμόνοια and φιλαλληλία shared the same register in the political discourse over the ideal society. Thus, though a pre-Christian or secular collocation of both ὁμόνοια and φιλαλληλία cannot be cited, the collocation is nevertheless probable.

How can a document be recognised and assigned as Christian? The question is not irrelevant to considerations of authorship in the NT itself. For example, if the reference to Christ at Jam.1.1 and 2.1 is a later interpolation (see M. Dibelius, *James*, revised by H. Greeven [Philadelphia 1981], pp.21-2), the question must be asked whether the epistle is Christian or Jewish *paraenesis*. Stanton, op.cit., pp.55f., lists the following indicators of Christian belief which bear on a decision regarding Christian authorship in the papyri:[191]

---

189 As other items of vocabulary span several registers, attention has generally not been paid to them. For example, προαίρεσις (*ll*.7 and 10) occurs in rhetorical (e.g. Aeschines and Anaximenes, fourth century BC), historical (e.g. Appian, first to second centuries AD), medical (e.g. Aelius Aristides, second century AD) and philosophical (Alex. Aphrodisiensis, second to third centuries AD) discourses as well as personal letters (e.g. *P.Oxy*. I 76 of AD 179), petitions (e.g. *P.Oxy*. II 237 vi.30 of AD 186) and legal deeds (e.g. in *P.Berl. Zilliacus* 6 of AD 527-565, where a sale is acknowledged to have been ἑκουσίᾳ γνώμῃ καὶ προαιρέσει).

190 A frequent context for the use of ὁμόνοια is the debate over political concord. It is of interest to note that ὁμόνοια, like φιλαλληλία, had a mathematical referent, i.e. the numbers 3 and 9. This suggests a possible collocation of the terms in the mathematical register. The observation may not be entirely irrelevant as in both cases the terminology of social/political relationship (see below) is applied to number theory.

191 It should not be assumed that all indicators apply concurrently. Clearly many of them would not apply in the case of the earliest Christian writers, as indeed *P.Oxy*. 3057 purports to be. For example, a reference to the Christian community, its officials or particular liturgical practices is absent from many NT texts. One must instead speak of a configuration of indicators. See also M. Naldini, *Il Cristianesimo in Egitto* (Florence 1968), pp.7-32, who discusses these and other indicators of Christian authorship.

a. the author's self-identification as Christian or explicit expression of adherence to Christ;
b. the use of the *nomina sacra*;
c. the use of the bible or other Christian work;
d. reference to the Christian community, its officials or particular liturgical practices;
e. the use of particularly Christian language.

P. Oxy. 3057 provides no evidence on which to base arguments from points **a** to **d**. In their absence, Christian authorship must be determined by point **e** alone. In the above discussion arguments based on vocabulary and its collocation (i.e. the way that words associate) have been adduced in support of Christian authorship (e.g. Parsons) and against it (e.g. Judge). However, it needs to be reiterated that in the case of *P. Oxy.* 3057 vocabulary and collocation are not sufficient in themselves either to prove or refute Christian authorship. The arguments which are adduced are linguistically tenuous. For them to succeed in either proving or refuting Christian authorship two things will need to be demonstrated. First, it must be shown that Christian believers did indeed form a distinct linguistic group. Their distinctiveness needs to extend beyond such factors which mark them out as a particular socio-religious group, i.e. points **a** to **d** above, to such factors which affect their linguistic performance more generally.[192] However, the existence of such a distinct linguistic group seems somewhat remote given the wide ethnic, social and geographical backgrounds of its members. For a similar observation concerning the absence of a distinctive Christian language in early inscriptions see R.A. Kearsley's discussion of the Aberkios inscription in *New Docs* 6 (1992) §26. Second, it must be shown that the vocabulary and collocation in *P. Oxy.* 3057 is such as to determine the author's membership of this linguistic group. Neither of these points is demonstrated.

The papyrological evidence of the fourth century AD can be used to illustrate the dilemma posed by the attempt to deduce belief from vocabulary usage. For example, H.I. Bell, V. Martin, E.G. Turner and D. van Berchem, *The Abinnaeus Archive* (Oxford 1962), p.31, describe the expression ἀγαπητὸς ἀδελφός as 'characteristic of Christian vocabulary' and state that the expression τὸν παντοκράτορα θεόν can hardly be doubted as Christian; however, it is precisely these expressions which are found in the so-called archive of Theophanes (see *P. Herm. Rees* 4 and 5), a member of a pagan circle worshipping Hermes Trismegistus. As B.R. Rees observes on *P. Herm. Rees* 4 (p.7; cf.also on *P. Herm. Rees* 5):

> The similarity of some of the phraseology to that which is usually described as Christian is again striking; indeed, but for the absence of Christian salutations, &c., the letter might well deceive the reader as to the religious affiliation of its writers.

So far the discussion has produced an indefinite result. The objections of Hemer and Judge against the possible Christian authorship of *P. Oxy.* 3057 have been answered. In these matters the way is open to accept a Christian authorship. However, the study of vocabulary items and collocation fails to give any concrete indication of such authorship. Must then the question remain unanswered? Montevecchi, op.cit., has noted the change in the title of Apollonios from 'brother' in *ll.*2, 7, 12 to 'master' in *l.*29. She interprets the latter as reminiscent of Paul's inversion of rank. In particular, she is reminded of Paul's plea that Philemon receive Onesimos no longer as a slave but as a brother (Philemon 15-16). Another example is the advice given to slaves (e.g. 1Tim.6.2 – οἱ δὲ πιστοὺς ἔχοντες δεσπότας μὴ καταφρονείτωσαν, ὅτι ἀδελφοί εἰσιν). Here, as in the Ammonios letter, the issue concerns the attitude of the lower to the higher-status individual – in Paul's advice to Philemon the order is reversed. Does this incidental feature of *P. Oxy.* 3057 give any indication of Christian authorship? To answer this question the evidence needs to be cited (see Table 25.2 below). The most frequent positions for the 'master/brother' designation are either in the opening address, the final salutation or the address on the back of a letter. However, this is not the only position; it can also occur in the body of a letter, e.g. *P. Herm. Rees* 6 (*l.*4).

---

192 In particular vocabulary and collocation must be considered. However, phonology and syntax might also be included.

The evidence is interesting. First, it will be seen that the 'master/brother' designation only began to appear in the century when Christianity became the state religion. Can one assume that there was a causal nexus between the two? To answer that question a more detailed look at the earliest examples is necessary. I leave aside Athanasios and Basil as their religious affiliation is clear.

Table 25.2

Century	Letters with δεσπότης and ἀδελφός
IV	*P.Abinn*. 30, 32, *P.Herm. Rees* 2 (?) and 6, *P.Strass*. IV 286, *SB* VIII 9683, Athanasios, *contra Arian*. 51.4, Basil, *Epist*. 363, 364
IV/V	*P.Ant*. II 92, *P.Ross. Georg*. V 8, *SB* XIV 11882
V	*CPR* V 23, *P.Harr*. I 112
V/VI	*SB* V 7635
VI	*P.Laur*. II 44, *P.Mich*. XI 624, *P.Oxy*. VI 943, VIII 1165, XVI 1933, *SB* VI 9608, *SB* XIV 11492, *PSI* XIV 1429, *P.Ant*. II 95 (ἡ ἀδελφικὴ δεσποτεία)
VI/VII	*P.Laur*. II 46, *P.Oxy*. I 158, VI 942, *SB* VI 9107, 9376

P.Abinn. 30: Zanathos (merely described by the editors as a petitioner p.24) writes to Abinnaeus about some camels bringing a delivery of wine asking him to look after them and to send money. Abinnaeus is addressed as δεσπότης, κύριε ἄδελφε,[193] ἡ ἀμίμητος καλοκαγαθία and ἡ σὴ εὐγενία. Of relevance is the wish that Abinnaeus' house be protected from the evil eye. The suggestion that the wish may be from a Christian pen is rather tenuous for it is based on a reconstruction of *P.Oxy*. XX 2276 *l*.28. It is possible that Zanathos was not a Christian.

P.Abinn. 32: The priest Kaor writes to Abinnaeus to ask him to forgive a soldier who had deserted. Abinnaeus is addressed as δεσπότης, ἀγαπητὸς ἀδελφός, κύριος and κύριέ μου ἄδελφε. The writer is clearly a Christian but the religious position of Abinnaeus in unclear. Two points suggest that he may not have been a Christian: a) the petition makes no appeal to God, Providence or Christ; and b) in the camp under Abinnaeus' control the statue of Fortune occupied a prominent place (see *P.Abinn*., p.33). In all probability only Kaor was a Christian.

P.Ant. II 92: In this memorandum John writes to Anastasios, addressed as δεσπότης ἀδελφός, regarding certain business matters which he will need to attend to. The persons' names together with the repeated use of the expression σὺν θεῷ and the mention of fasting indicates a Christian authorship.

P.Herm. Rees 6: The letters *P.Herm. Rees* 2 to 6 come from a pagan religious circle. In letter 6 Besodoros addresses Theophanes as δεσπότης καὶ ἀδελφός, ἀδελφὸς κύριος, ἀδελφός and ἀδελφὸς ψυχῆς. He prays for the safe return of Theophanes and asks most affectionately for news from him. The expressions of brotherly affection and religious sentiments of the letter could easily be mistaken as Christian. *P.Herm. Rees* 6 thus highlights the difficulty inherent in any use of the master/brother terminology to determine the religious belief of the writer and his reader.

P.Ross. Georg. V 8: The text is very fragmentary but the restoration of the formulaic address [Τῷ δεσπ]ότῃ μου ὡς ἀλη<θῶ>ς [καὶ ἀγαπητῷ ἀδελφῷ ... seems assured. Only one other fragmentary address survives, i.e. ἄδε]λφε *l*.8. The letter seems to be a request by Arios to Eudoxios to send a ὁλοκόττινος (?). There is no indication of the persons' religious beliefs.

P.Strass. IV 286: Demetrios addressed a letter requesting acquittal for a person called Stephanos. The person addressed in not named but is addressed as δεσπότης (μου τῆς ψυχῆς), ἀδελφός, ἡ φιλαδελφικὴ διάθεσις, ἡ σὴ τελειότης, ἡ σὴ τιμιότης and σεμνολόγημα ἐμόν. There is no indication of a Christian authorship for this letter.

SB VIII 9683: Timotheos, a monk, addressed a written complaint to Heron. The complaint concerns an anchor stolen by a soldier by the name of Paul. Heron is variously addressed as δεσπότης, πάτρων and ἀδελφός.

SB XIV 11882: The letter from Dorotheos to John is described as Christian, though there is no clear indication

193 Κύριος ἀδελφός as a form of address occurs frequently in the papyri, e.g. *P.Abinn*. 4, 5, 9-15, 17, 18, 32, 33, 43; *P.Neph*. 1, 2, 8, 10; *P.Oxy*. XII 1424, XXXIV 2728, LV 3813-15, *SB* VI 9138, XVI 12663. The editors of *P.Abinn*. note of this address: 'when they were of equal or nearly equal seniority, members of the army and of the civil administration applied the phrase κύριοι ἀδελφοί to each other in their official or semi-official correspondence' (p.25). He continues: 'the feelings of the writer have no influence on these stereotyped phrases'. *P.Oxy*. LV (p.201) describes the expressions κύριος πατήρ and κύριος ἀδελφός as 'terms of respect and affection'.

of this in the text apart from the names themselves. The latter is addressed as δεσπότης ... ἀδελφός and δεσπότης. Dorotheos asks him to do what is possible to procure a quantity of twenty gold objects (the text breaks off).

Two conclusions follow from the evidence. First, it appears to be important to distinguish between the use of the master/brother designation in the opening address, the final salutation or the address on the back of a letter and the use of either term in the body of the text. The former use is formulaic and gives no indication of the relative status of the persons concerned. For example, in *P. Ant.* II 92 John appears to be either of equal or higher social status than Anastasios whereas in *SB* VIII 9683, XIV 11882 and *P. Strass.* IV 286, for example, the writers are clearly of lower status. Instead, the indication of relative status must be looked for in the types of address in the body of the text. For example, see the use of the titles δεσπότης in *SB* VIII 9683, XIV 11882 and *P. Strass.* IV 286. Interestingly *P. Oxy.* 3057 uses both titles in the body of the letter. Second, it appears that the master/brother distinction is not sufficient to indicate Christian authorship in the fourth century AD as both pagan and Christian authors could use it. Evidence is wanting for the earlier period. Another factor also makes any affirmative answer to the question of Christian authorship hazardous. We have already noted (see *New Docs* 6 [1992] §21) how the familial titles of father, mother, brother and sister were used in a metaphorical sense. The titles of father and mother seem to have been used as a title of respect for persons older than oneself. The titles of brother and sister seem to have been used to address persons of a similar age. Because of this looser use of the familial titles any conclusion as to the authorship of *P. Oxy.* 3057 on the basis of the use of the title 'brother' is questionable. We conclude that the letter gives no indication that the correspondents were Christian. But equally no evidence stands in the way of its being so accepted.

S.R.L.

§26 The Epitaph of Aberkios: The Earliest Christian Inscription?

Hierapolis/Hieropolis, Phrygia c.200
Ed.pr. — W.M. Ramsay, *JHS* 4 [1883] pp.424-427 (*ll.*.7-15 of the full text only).

'Ε]κ̣λεκτῆς πόλε̣ως ὁ πολεί[της] τ̣οῦτ' ἐποίη[σα	Of a chosen city the citizen, this I made
ζῶν ἵ]ν̣' ἔχω φανερ̣[ὴν] σώματος ἔνθα θέσιν,	[during my lifetime] so that I might have here a notable place to lay down my body.
οὔνομ' ‹'Αβέρκιος ὢν ὁ› μαθητὴς ποιμένος ἁγνοῦ,	By name <I am Aberkios>, disciple of the holy shepherd
[ὃς βόσκει προβάτων ἀγέλας ὄρεσι πεδίοις τε,]	[who feeds the flocks of sheep on the heights and on the plains,]
[ὀφθαλμοὺς ὃς ἔχει μεγάλους πάντῃ καθορῶντας.]	[who has great eyes keeping everything within view.]
[Οὗτος γάρ μ' ἐδίδαξε . . . γράμματα πιστά,]	[For he was the one who taught me ... trustworthy letters,]
εἰς Ῥώμη[ν ὃς ἔπεμψεν] ἐμὲν βασ̣ι̣λ[ίδ' ἀναθρῆσαι]	to Rome [he sent] me [to look] upon the capital

καὶ βασίλισσ̣[αν ἰδεῖν χρυσό]στολον χρυ̣[σοπέδιλον.]	and [to see] the queen with the [gold] garment and golden [sandals.]
Λαὸν δ' εἶδον̣ ἐ̣[κεῖ λαμπρὰν] σφραγεῖδαν ἔ[χοντα]	A nation I saw [there which had a brilliant] seal
καὶ Συρίης πέ[δον εἶδα] καὶ ἄστεα πάν[τα, Νισῖβιν]	and the plain of Syria [I saw] and all the cities, [Nisibis]
Εὐφράτην διαβ[άς· πάν]τῃ δ' ἔσχον συνο̣[μαίμους]	after crossing the Euphrates. I had kindred spirits all around
Π̣α̣ῦ̣λο̣ν̣ ἔ̣χω̣ν̣ ἐ̣π̣' ὀ̣[χω̣·] Πίστις π̣[άντῃ δὲ προῆγε]	having Paul in the carriage. Pistis [led the way everywhere]
καὶ παρέθηκε̣ [τροφὴν] πάντῃ ἰχθὺν ἀ[πὸ πηγῆς]	and prepared [nourishment] everywhere, a fish from [the spring],
πανμεγέθη καθ[αρόν, οὗ] ἐδράξατο παρθέ[νος ἁγνή,]	immense, spotless, [which a pure] maiden caught.
καὶ τοῦτον ἐπέ[δωκε φι]λ̣ί̣ο̣ι̣ς̣ ἐ̣σ̣θ̣ε̣[ῖν διὰ παντός,]	And she gave this to her friends to e[at continually]
[οἶνον χρηστὸν ἔχουσα, κέρασμα διδοῦσα μετ' ἄρτου.]	[having (also) good wine, giving mixed wine with bread.]
[Ταῦτα παρεστὼς εἶπον 'Αβέρκιος ὧδε γραφῆναι.]	[Having been present at these things, I, Aberkios, said they should be written in this way.]
[ἑβδομηκοστὸν ἔτος καὶ δεύτερον ἦγον ἀληθῶς.]	[I have lived genuinely for the seventy-second year.]
[Ταῦθ' ὁ νοῶν εὔξαιτο ὑπὲρ 'Αβερκίου πᾶς ὁ συνῳδός.]	[May the whole community who understand these things pray on behalf of Aberkios].
Οὐ μέντοι τύμβῳ τις ἐμῷ ἕτερόν τινα θήσει.	Let no one put anyone else in my tomb.
Εἰ δ' οὖν, Ῥωμαίων ταμείῳ θήσε‹ι› δισχείλια ‹χ›ρυσᾶ	But if he does, let him pay the treasury of the Romans two thousand gold pieces
καὶ χρηστῇ πατρίδι̣ Ἱεροπόλει χείλια χρυσᾶ.	and to my beloved native land Hieropolis, a thousand gold pieces.

The unusual history of the restoration of this inscription is succinctly summarised in the most recent treatment of it by W. Wischmeyer ('Die Aberkiosinschrift als Grabepigramm', *JbAC* 23 [1980], pp.22-24). Originally the text stood as a verse epitaph on a stone cippus c.1.10-1.20m high. Of this only 57cm remains, preserving *ll.*7-15 in two unjoining sections. These are now held in the Vatican Museum in Rome. A factor in the identification of the Aberkios text was the comparison of the inscription with the *Vitae* of Aberkios which survive in over thirty copies in codices of the tenth to the fifteenth centuries and it was by this means, too, that *ll.*1-3 and *ll.*20-22, originally published by W.M. Ramsay as part of the 'Alexander' inscription (*BCH* 6 [1882] p.518), were linked with that of Aberkios. L. Duchesne ('L'épitaphe d'Aberkios', *MEFR* 15 [1895], p.155) proposed that these lines must have been copied from the actual epitaph of Aberkios to be used in that of Alexander, whose name appears in the original lines of the epitaph which is inserted between two sections taken from that of Aberkios. Certainly the 'Alexander' inscription could not have been erected long after that of Aberkios because it is datable to the year AD 216. Published photographs of the Aberkios stone can be found in M.Guarducci, *EG* IV (1978), figs. 111a-b and of the 'Alexander' inscription, now held in the Archaeological Museum in Istanbul, in L.Duchesne, *MEFR* 15 (1895), pl.1.

The Aberkios epitaph stands in twenty-two hexameters of sometimes imperfect form (Guarducci, *EG* IV [1978], p.382), and varying opinions have been advanced on detailed aspects of restoration in the lacunae of the epigram over the many years it has been the object of scholarly attention (on which see M.Guarducci, *EG* IV [1978], p.378). These are comprehensively identified by Wischmeyer in a very extensive *apparatus criticus* to the text (pp.24-26). He makes two supplements of his own to the *lectio communis* of the text: *l*.7 βασιλ[ιδ' (lapis: ΒΑΣΙ̣ Λ̣[ ) and *l*.12 ἐπ' ὄ[χω̣] (lapis: Ε̣ΠΟ̣[ ).

The text given below is that of Wischmeyer apart from two changes to his punctuation. The full-stop has been removed at the end of *l*.11 in order to provide a main verb for the initial clause of *l*.12. Elsewhere (see διαβάς at *l*.11 and ἔχουσα ... διδοῦσα at *l*.16) the author shows a similar liking for placing a participial expression at the end of a sentence. Second, a full-stop replaces the comma at the end of *l*.17 in order to avoid a lack of co-ordination between the two main verbs εἶπον ... ἦγον in *ll*.17-18 and to produce a more definite break between these two lines.

Wischmeyer's commentary focuses particularly on epigraphic parallels for the language of the epitaph which he believes have been neglected over the years in favour of literary comparisons. Following him, the text may be viewed in the following five thematic sections, all of which fall within the conventional *topoi* of the epigraphic genres of the time. Some points from his extensive commentary, and other observations, follow.

Ll.1-2: The identification of Aberkios' native-city and the reason for erecting his grave monument. These two verses are unremarkable in themselves in theme and vocabulary, except for the use of θέσις for the monument in *l*.2. Wischmeyer points out this word is not used to describe grave monuments during the early imperial period but that it is a typically Christian term at a later period. On the other hand the frequency with which the phrase ἐ]κλεκτῆς πόλεως is to be found as a formula in the epigram tradition and the absence of the formula in patristic literature leads him to reject the possibility that this is a reference to Jerusalem.

Ll.3-6 are based on the theme of the shepherd as teacher, one encountered elsewhere in poetic and literary works as well as on tombstones in Asia Minor. The use of ἁγνός to describe the shepherd links the theme to one of deep cultic significance because of the common usage of the word as an epithet of the gods. According to a study of Attic prose epitaphs by M.N.Tod (*BSA* 46 [1951], pp.182ff) ἁγνός is rarely applied to humans. Only three texts using the designation ἁγνός were cited by Tod, one of which reads however: θ(εοῖς) κ(αταχθονίοις) Μάξιμαν τὴν καὶ Εἰρήν[η]ν, παρθένον ἁγνήν, ἐτῶν κʹ (*IG* XIV, 1829 = Moretti, *IGUR* II, 2.768 from Rome and its neighbourhood). The text is not dated by Tod or Moretti, however elsewhere Moretti, probably on the basis of the girl's second name, queries whether it may not be Christian (*Epigraphica* 21 [1959], p.75 n.1). In Asia Minor, however, ἁγνός is to be found in honorific decrees of the first three centuries AD as an epithet for a range of imperial and civic officials at Ephesus. Of these the *agoranomos* is most frequently described as ἁγνός or said to have carried out his duties in the market ἁγνῶς (*I.Eph.* III, 712b; 927-8; 932; V, 1575; VII,1.3011-3, 3015-6), but others include the secretary of the people (*I.Eph.* II, 412), *prytanis* (*I.Eph.* IV, 1066), proconsul of Asia (*I.Eph.* IV, 1312) and quaestor (*I.Eph.* VII, 1.3039).

The same divine connotation also surrounds the phrase ὀφθαλμοὺς μεγάλους πάντη καθορῶντας (*l*. 5), a long-established attribute of deities in Greek culture (M.Guarducci, *EG* IV [1978], p.383). The lacuna in the middle of *l*.6 remains unfilled, although Wischmeyer suggests that an adjective such as ἱερός may have once stood there as in 2Tim.3.15: καὶ ὅτι ἀπὸ βρέφους ἱερὰ γράμματα οἶδας ('and how from infancy you have known the Holy Scriptures'). The description of the γράμματα as πιστά (*l*.6) calls to mind a similar description of the church's teaching as faithful/trustworthy in the pastoral epistles (Tit.1.9, 3.8; 1Tim.1.15, 3.1, 4.9 etc), so, even with the lacuna, the nature of Aberkios' γράμματα would have been clear to a Christian reader.

Ll.7-11 are occupied by the *topos* of 'the journey' or 'travel', for which Wischmeyer is able to draw extensive parallels from inscriptions. *Ll*.12-16, on the other hand, contain the rarest and least familiar *topoi* or themes in the epigram: those of 'the meal' and 'the provision of food'. Nevertheless, Wischmeyer anchors both these firmly within the traditional themes of inscriptions, preferring to view them not as directly symbolic of the eucharist, as suggested by Guarducci earlier (*Anc. Soc*. 4 [1973], p.271 and *EG* IV [1978] p.382), despite the presence of vocabulary which suggests this to be the case. He believes instead that an attempt is being made to represent eucharist theology at that point in the existing language and themes of the epigrams. One such inscription of the Augustan period from Eresos on Lesbos (*IG* XII, Suppl.1, nr.124) is cited in this connection by Wischmeyer (p.42). In it a benefactor of the imperial cult in the city is honoured because at a celebration and banquet (εὐωχία καὶ ἀνακλίσις) he provided 'meat and a jar of wine and three minae of bread' (ἄρνα καὶ κεράμιον οἴνω καὶ ἄρτω μναῖς τρεῖς).

Wischmeyer transcribes πίστις in *l*.12 with an initial capital, thus indicating his belief that the word is a personification of the quality of trust or faithfulness. However, Aberkios may have used the word in its secondary meaning attested in *LSJ* : that which gives confidence or a pledge of good faith, for letters of recommendation to churches in other places are known to have been carried by Christians in Egypt of III/IV when they travelled. That such letters were used in the Graeco-Roman world also is indicated by Paul's comments in 2Cor. 3.1-2: Ἀρχόμεθα πάλιν ἑαυτοὺς συνιστάνειν; ἢ μὴ χρῄζομεν ὥς τινες συστατικῶν ἐπιστολῶν πρὸς ὑμᾶς ἢ ἐξ ὑμῶν; ('Are we beginning to commend ourselves again? Or do we need, like some people, letters of recommendation to you or from you?'); and it is possible, therefore, especially in the context of the travel *topos*, that Aberkios' reference to πίστις may be construed as an allusion to such letters of recommendation. (The lacuna in the text immediately preceding the word leaves open the question of whether or not an article preceded it.) A number of these letters are discussed in *New Docs* 4 (1987), pp.250-5. In these (ibid., p.253, no.6) a reference to scripture is included by way of indicating the level of instruction attained by the person carrying the letter. It is again possible that Aberkios' description of Paul in the carriage with him should be interpreted in this way.

Ll.17-22 represent the final section of the epigram which falls into three parts: a) the 'dictation' formula, here connected with the old age of Aberkios; b) the request for prayer, and, finally c) the imprecation against disturbance of the grave. In the opinion of Wischmeyer these verses (17-22) are so thoroughly conventional and without any underlying poetic structure. Even in b) there is no specific Christian allusion made. Despite the likelihood that συνῳδός refers to the Christian community, it is an old poetic word for which a specifically Christian character cannot be demonstrated.

Ll. 20-22, the imprecation against violators of the tomb, is identical in form to many other epigraphical examples known from Phrygia in particular, but also from many other parts of Asia Minor (W.M.Calder, 'Early Christian Epitaphs from Phrygia', *Anat. Stud.* V [1955], pp.26-8). One example from Bithynia has already been discussed in this series - *New Docs* 4 (1987), pp.25-27 and for further discussion of Phrygian inscriptions of this type, see L. Robert, 'Malédictions funéraires grecques', *OMS* V, pp.710-22).

Wischmeyer's new text of the Aberkios epitaph and his detailed commentary are important in clarifying the extent to which current vocabulary and imagery could be and was drawn on for Christian purposes without the adoption of overt Christian symbols. Wischmeyer argues that the Aberkios text is a fumbling, and at times mannered attempt, e.g. the repetitions of πάντῃ in verses 11-13, to synthesize traditional formulae and themes of grave epigrams with the scarcely developed Christian language and experience. He singles out as Christian elements the stylistic parallel with the Bible in the repeated use of the ὅς sentences in verses 4-7 (cf. Proverbs 17.9-16a), a paraphrase of Psalm 45.10b, and 14b (LXX, 44) in verse 8, and the assimilation of biblical words such as ποιμήν (Matt.25.32), πιστός (Matt.25.21), and the name of Paul. But, he stresses, the cryptic nature of the text is preserved by the fact that all its phraseology and vocabulary is to be found, even if in a different context, in traditional texts and epigrams. Thus while never throwing the Christian character of the Aberkios epitaph into doubt, Wischmeyer clearly demonstrates the pervasive use of conventional formulae and *topoi* within it.

The Aberkios text has been widely recognised as the earliest datable epitaph which attempts to register Christian belief. The scholarly consensus about its character of the Aberkios epitaph is in strong contrast to the controversy surrounding the papyrus, *P. Oxy.* XLII 3057, which some have argued to be the earliest surviving Christian letter (see the discussion by S. Llewelyn in §25 above). Yet over the years the Christian relevance of the Aberkios text has sometimes been denied by others because of the veiled terms in which it is expressed (see M. Guarducci, 'L'iscrizione di Abercio e Roma', *Anc.Soc.* 2 [1971], pp.174-203 for the most recent defence against the denial of its Christian character and *EG* IV [1978], pp.380-86 for detailed discussion of what she believes to be the Christian symbolism throughout the epigram). The text must, however, be viewed against the cultural background in which it was set. In his article Calder (ibid., pp.25-38) goes some way to explaining this in terms of the prevailing absence of a distinctive Christian language in the first two centuries and, in the latter part of the second century, the possibility of persecution of Christian communities. Calder's discussion underlines the fact that some five generations of Christians must have lived and died since Paul's missionary journeys to the region without leaving a trace on their tombstones.

Aberkios himself has been the subject of some discussion. He was identified by Calder (ibid., p.25) with Avircius Marcellus (Eusebius, *H.E.* 5.16.3), a man who is described as the writer of an anti-Montanist tract of the late second century. However Guarducci (*EG* IV [1978], pp.381-2) underlines that the differences in both nomenclature and spelling create difficulties in such an equation and, in his recent study of Montanism, A. Strobel (*Das heilige Land der Montanisten* [1980], p.55) omits any identification of the two men. This debate in turn raises the wider question of the relationship between such Christian inscriptions of the second half of the third century in Phrygia and Montanist beliefs, particularly those texts commonly known as 'the Christians for Christians' inscriptions. This is a topic dealt with already in *New Docs* 3 (1983), pp.130-3.

R.A. Kearsley

§27 Monastic Orthodoxy and the Papyri of the Nag Hammadi Cartonnage

Nag Hammadi 7 Oct.(?) AD 348

Ed.pr. — J.W.B. Barns, G.M. Browne, J.C. Shelton, *P. Nag Hammadi* G65 (Leiden 1981), pp.57-8.

[± 12]ωνι ἐνάρχῳ προέδρῳ	[To NN], authorised city councillor,
[± 13]β´ Αὐρήλιος Μέλας	[ ] Aurelius Melas
[± 13]οσ̣[. . .] χαίρειν.	[ ] greeting.
[ὁμολογῶ ὀμνὺ]ς̣ τὴν θείαν καὶ οὐράνιον	[I acknowledge, swearing] by the divine and heavenly
[τύχην τῶν δεσπ]οτῶν ἡμῶν αἰωνίων	[fortune of our [lords] eternal
[Αὐγούστων ἐγγ]υᾶσθαι μονῆς καὶ ἐμφα-	[Augusti, that I guar]antee for presence and appearance
[νείας Αὐρηλίαν (?)] Θ̣εοδώραν Μαξίμου	[Aurelia] Theodora, daughter of Maximus,
[μητρὸς ± 6 ἣ]ν καὶ παραστήσω ὁπόταν	[her mother being ..., whom] also I will deliver up whenever
[ἐπιζητῆται ἄνευ πάσ]ης ἀντιλογίας.	[she is sought without any] argument.
[ἐὰν δὲ μή, ἔνοχος εἴην τ]ῷ θείῳ ὅρκῳ	[If not, may I be liable] to the divine oath
[καὶ τῷ ἐπηρτημένῳ τούτῳ] κινδύνῳ.	[and its attendant] risk.
[κύριον τὸ χειρόγραφον] ἁπλοῦν γραφὲν	[The *cheirographon*] written in single copy [is valid]
[± 7 ἐξεδόμην σ]οι πρὸς ἀσφάλιαν,	[... I have given] you for security
[καὶ ἐπερωτηθεὶς ὡμο]λόγησα.	[and being asked] I acknowledge.
[ὑπατείας Φλαυίου Φιλίππ]ο̣υ̣ τοῦ λαμπροτάτου	[In the consulship of Flavius Philippus], *clarissimus*
[ἐπάρχου τοῦ ἱεροῦ πραιτωρί]ου καὶ Φλαυίου Σαλιᾶ	[*praefectus sacro praetorio*], and of Flavius Salia,
[τοῦ λαμπροτάτου μαγίστρου ἱππέ]ω̣ν̣, Φ̣α̣ῶ̣φ[ι] ῑ̣.	[*clarissimus magister equitum*], Phaophi 10.

Nag Hammadi Fourth Century

Ed.pr. – J.W.B. Barns, G.M. Browne, J.C. Shelton, *P. Nag Hammadi* G72 (Leiden 1981), pp.69-70.

Σανσνῶτ̣ι̣ κ̣α̣ὶ̣ Π̣σ̣ᾶτος	To Sansnos and Psas,
μοναχοῖς̣ Πρ̣ο̣τ̣η̣ρ[ία] χ̣έ̣ρ(ειν).	monks, Proter[ia] greeting.
εἰ δυνατὸν παρ᾽ ὑμ̣ῖ̣ν̣ ἐστιν	Can you, where you are, possibly
τὸ ἐραυνῆσαι ὀλίγον	look for a little
ἄχυρον πρὸς τὴν ὑπη-	chaff for
ρεσίαν τ̣ῶ̣ν ἐμῶν κτηνῶν	my animals

διότι ὑστεροῦσι, κα̣ὶ οὐ-	because they are in need and
χ εὑρίσκω ἐνταῦθα ἀγο-	I cannot buy (any) here?
ράσαι; ἐπὴν δὲ εὕρη̣τε,	When you can,
πέμψατέ με ὑπ̣ὲ̣ρ τὴν	send me about the
τιμὴν ὅτι πόσον τὴν	price, how much the
ἅμαξαν ἀχύρου, κα̣ὶ ἵνα	wagon (load) of chaff and where (?)
ἔρχεται τὸ πλοῖο̣ν̣	the boat comes ...
[. . πλ]ί[στ]ας χάριτας ὑμ̣ε̣ῖ̣ν̣	[...] utmost thanks to you.
(Back) Π̣ρ̣ο̣τ̣ε̣ρ̣ία Σανσνῶτι καὶ	Proteria to Sansnos and
Πσ̣άτος.	Psas

....

1 Πσάτι 2 χαίρειν 10-11 τῆς τιμῆς 14 πλείστας, ὑμῖν 16 Πσάτι

Shelton translates the infinitive of *P. Nag Hammadi* G72 *l*.4 as imperatival but notes that Proteria had contaminated it by her use of the article as though it were the subject of ἐστιν. He translates: 'If it is possible where you are, seek out a little chaff for the use of my ass etc.'. Another grammatical understanding is possible. The infinitive can be construed as the subject of ἐστιν and the sentence as a direct question introduced by εἰ. This translation has been opted for in the above text and the papyrus at *l*.9 repunctuated accordingly. The use of εἰ to introduce a direct question is found in the LXX (e.g., Gen.17.17, 1K.10.24, 2Macc.7.7, 15.3) and NT (e.g. Matt.12.10, 19.3, Mark 8.23, Luke 13.23, 22.49, John 6.62, Acts 1.6, 22.25, Rom.9.22-24) and is generally considered to be a Hebraism (N. Turner, *A Grammar of New Testament Greek* 3 [Edinburgh 1963], p.333 and BDF §440.3). However, the usage can also be illustrated from non-literary texts (see further the discussion in *New Docs* 5 [1989], pp.57-58). Construed as a question, the sentence has the illocutionary (or intended) force of polite request. On the use of εὑρίσκω (*P. Nag Hammadi* G72 *l*.8) to mean 'I am able' in koine Greek see J.A.L. Lee, 'A Non-Aramaism in Luke 6.7', *NovT* 33 (1991), pp.28-34.

The leather covers of eight of the twelve Nag Hammadi codices, which were found in a sealed jar by Egyptian agricultural workers in 1945, had been strengthened by wads of waste papyri. The above documents come from the richest of these cartonnages, i.e. the cartonnage of Codex VII. The importance of *P. Nag Hammadi* G65 resides in the fact that it provides the *terminus a quo* for the binding of Codex VII and thus a rough date for the making of the Codex itself. The document (dated AD 348) is an acknowledgement by Aurelius Melas to guarantee the appearance, when required, of Theodora. The other contracts of the cartonnage, where dated, are all earlier (*P. Nag Hammadi* G63 dated AD 341; *P. Nag Hammadi* G64 dated AD 346). The letters of the cartonnage to Codex VII are also important as they contain some of the earliest references to monks and offer information on their daily life. *P. Nag Hammadi* G72 is reproduced here as an example.

To whom did the Nag Hammadi codices belong? The proximity of their find to the Pachomian monasteries has suggested to some a possible monastic involvement. If so, were these fourth-century monasteries centres of heretical monks? Indeed, can the mere use of a text be used as a criterion to determine the orthodoxy (or otherwise) of its reader? Alternatively, were the monks involved in some apologetic function which required the reading of heretical texts? Answers to these questions have in part focused on the cartonnages and what they can tell us about the owners of the codices. More particularly, the debate centres on the cartonnage of Codex VII (the other seven cartonnages appear to be secular) and the private letters contained within it. J.W.B. Barns, 'Greek and Coptic Papyri from the Covers of the Nag Hammadi

Codices', *Essays on the Nag Hammadi Texts: In Honour of Pahor Labib, a Preliminary Report*, ed. M. Krause (Leiden 1975), pp.9-17, attempted to reconstruct the ownership of the codices from the wadding in their covers. His argument rests on the premises that: i) the writing and binding of the codices would occur in the same establishment; ii) the binders would use wadding connected with their business. He concluded that the codices belonged to the Pachomian monastery at Chenoboskion for several reasons. First, the documents of the cartonnages appear orthodox. Indeed, the titles of persons, which are used in the documents, imply 'normal and orthodox Egyptian religious life'. There is then no clear impediment against their provenance in an orthodox Pachomian monastery. Second, the documents contain names identical with known Pachomian individuals. That is, the association in names implies a common provenance. Third, the proximity of their find to the Pachomian monastery at Chenoboskion argues a probable connection. Because of the prevalence of documents concerning a certain Sansnos, Barns concluded that it was his monastic department which was responsible for the preparation of the covers. The major problem which Barns had to address was the ownership of heretical texts by an orthodox monastery. He suggested that they were prepared for the purpose of refuting the heresy and that they were disposed of later when the heresy was no longer a live issue.

Shelton, op.cit., pp.1-11, and C. Scholten, 'Die Nag-Hammadi-Texte als Buchbesitz der Pachomianer', *JbAC* 31 (1988), pp.144-72, assume a more cautious position with regard to the relationship of the papyri of the cartonnages and the ownership of the codices. Shelton argues that the documents of the cartonnages are 'dogmatically quite neutral' (i.e. they do not allow one to decide between orthodox or heterodox belief) and that the identification of individuals with known Pachomian individuals is unconvincing. Scholten considers such evidence as the association in names, the titles of persons (e.g. *P. Nag Hammadi* G68 and G75), the Christian authorship of some letters (i.e. *P. Nag Hammadi* G72 and C8) and an indication of community membership (i.e. *P. Nag Hammadi* C4) to be inconclusive.

Shelton adduces further arguments against an association between the documents of the cartonnages and the Pachomian monastery. Chiefly, he notes that the documents indicate a way of life which is inconsistent with known Pachomian practice, e.g. ownership of money and property, free contact with the secular world and its concerns (see especially the secular dealings with a woman in *P. Nag Hammadi* G72 above). Against this, Scholten argues that the business dealings of Sansnos are not *eo ipso* inconsistent with monastic practice. In other words, the dealings may have been undertaken by Sansnos on behalf of the monastery in order to secure its financial independence. Shelton, however, notes two further inconsistencies. First, whereas Pachomian monasteries were predominantly Coptic speaking, the majority of documents in the cartonnages were written in Greek. Second, the majority of documents are secular in nature. In particular, as seven of the eight cartonnages contain only secular material, it is more probable that the bookbinder's source of papyri was the rubbish heap. To sum up, Shelton argues that there is no nexus between the contents of the documents and the ownership of the codices, as was assumed in Barns' initial premise. As a result, the papyri of the cartonnages do not permit an answer to the questions of production and ownership.

The above arguments have been confined to the contents of the cartonnages. Do the contents of the codices and other factors provide an answer to the questions of production and ownership? As this is a much larger question, only a cursory response can be considered here. For example, J.M. Robinson, *The Nag Hammadi Library* (Leiden 1984 – but cf. also 3rd ed. 1988), pp.1-26, tends to agree with Barns' assignment of the codices to the Pachomian monastery but disagrees with the opinion that they were used to refute heresy. Several factors are brought to bear in his argument. Such internal factors as the mixed nature of the texts (i.e. both heretical and non-heretical texts are present in the codices), the apparent way in which the codices have been formed by the combining of smaller collections of tractates and the care involved in the codices' production (i.e. the quality of the codices, scribal notes and corrections) and in their final method of preservation[194] indicate to Robinson that the texts had a religious value other than the mere refutation of heresy. Other external factors confirm this.[195] Robinson tentatively concludes that the picture of fourth-century monasteries as orthodox may be anachronistic. In other words, fifth-century orthodoxy may have been read back into the founding years of the monasteries.

Scholten, op.cit., though following Shelton's caution with regard to the relationship of the papyri of the cartonnages and the ownership of the codices (see above), continues to argue for a Pachomian ownership; this is based on an analysis of the codices as a whole. On the one hand, Scholten maintains that the argument that the codices belonged to a gnostic circle inside or outside the monastery is inconclusive. Its proponents either read too much into the evidence, neglect regional and chronological considerations, disregard the heterogenous nature of the codices' content or suffice themselves with gnostic traces, which may themselves be residuals of an earlier tradition, without showing the existence of a gnostic system. On the other hand, Scholten finds evidence to support Pachomian ownership. First, book usage and production at Pachomian monasteries is consistent with their ownership of the codices. Second, the paleographical and dialectic similarities between the Bodmer papyri and the Nag Hammadi texts suggest the same monastic provenance. Third, indications in the texts themselves (e.g. the colophons to Codices II and VII and the wording of the title to Codex VIII) point to monastic production. Scholten concludes that the codices belonged to a Pachomian monastery. Unlike Robinson, however, he maintains that possession gives no indication as to the owner's unorthodoxy. But how then does one explain the lack of relationship between the papyri of the cartonnages and the assumed Pachomian production and ownership of the codices? Scholten suggests that the monastery declined the demeaning use of monastic papyri for wadding, preferring instead to use waste papyri from the bureau of the *praeses Thebaidos*. For him the significance of the cartonnages lies in their locating the production of the codices in the vicinity of the monasteries, a region in which there is no evidence for the presence of heretical circles in the fourth century.

As discussed above, Shelton has argued that the papyri of the cartonnages indicate a way of life which is inconsistent with known Pachomian practice. Against this Scholten alleges that the business dealings of Sansnos are not *eo ipso* inconsistent with such practice. Another papyrus document in the culling for years 1980/81 also raises the issue of the seeming inconsistency between monastic ideals/rules and the literary evidence on the one hand and actual monastic practice on the other. The document *P. Köln* III 157 concerns a monk's manumission of his slave, Menas.[196]

---

194 The codices were preserved in a jar. C.H. Roberts, *Manuscript, Society and Belief in Early Christian Egypt* (London 1979), pp.7-8, argues that Christians in Egypt may have adopted the Jewish custom of preserving manuscripts either in jars or in a genizah.

195 The external factors are that:

a. the heresy debate was conducted in Greek not Coptic;

b. known Pachomian literature is more pedestrian rather than concerned with the doctrinal debates;

c. the codices were found near a possible place of solitary retreat for the monks.

196 *P. Köln* III 157 is of further interest in that it is one of a few texts of late antiquity providing evidence for the slave's lot in Egypt. In the period the increased use of impressed labour (i.e. the labour of free persons who were bonded to the land or a village) had decreased the reliance on slave labour. For the Roman Empire more generally, see G.E.M. de Ste.Croix, *The Class Struggle in the Ancient Greek World* (London 1981), pp.249-59.

Apollonopolis AD 589

Ed.pr. – B. Kramer, M. Erler, D. Hagedorn and R. Hübner, *P. Köln* III 157 (Opladen 1980), pp.150-161.

Βασιλείας τοῦ θειοτ[άτου καὶ εὐσεβ]εστάτου ἡμῶν δεσπότο[υ Φλ(αουίου) Μα]υρικίου Τιβερίου τοῦ αἰωνίου	In the reign of our most godly [and pious] lord [Flavius Ma]uricius Tiberius, the eternal
Αὐγούστου Αὐτοκ[ράτορος ἔτου]ς ἑβδόμου καὶ ὑπατείa[ς το]ῦ αὐτοῦ ἔτους ἕκτου Ἐπεὶφ κ̄	August Imperator, in the seventh [year] and in the consulship of the same in the sixth year, Epeiph 20
[ἐν Ἀ]πόλλωνος πόλει Μικ[ρ]ᾷ.	[in] Apollonopolis Parva.
Βίκτωρ υἱὸς τοῦ [τῆς . . . . . .] . . μνήμης Κορνηλίου [μη]τρὸς Μαρίας μονάζων σὺν θεῷ	Victor, son of Cornelius of ... memory, my mother being Maria, a monk with God's help
τοῦ εὐαγοῦς μονασ[τηρίο]υ ἄπα Μαχροβίου ὁρμώμε[νος] ἀπὸ τῆς κώμης Τερύθεως	of the holy monastery of Apa Macropios hailing from the village of Terythis
τοῦ Ἀπολλωνοπολ[είτ]ου Μηνᾷ υἱῷ Βίκτορος μη[τρ]ὸς Εἰρήνη ἐμῷ οἰκέτῃ	in Apollonopolis to Menas, son of Victor, your mother being Eirene, my slave,
ὁρμωμένῳ ἀπὸ τ[ῆς κώ]μης Πούχεως τοῦ Ἀνταιοπ[ολί]του νομοῦ χ(αί)ρ(ειν). βουλόμενος εὑρεῖν	hailing from the village of Puchis in the nome of Antaiopolites, greeting. I, wishing to find
ἔλεος ἐν καιρῷ τῆς [ἐμῆς τ]ελευτῆς ἐν τῷ φρεικτῷ β[ήματ]ι τοῦ δεσπότου ἡμῶν Ἰησοῦ	mercy at the time of [my] death before the awful judgement s[eat] of our Lord Jesus
Χριστοῦ κατέστησά [σε τὸν] προγεγραμμένον Μην[ᾶν ἐλ]εύθερον ἀπὸ παντὸς ζυγοῦ δουλίας	Christ, have set [you, the] aforementioned Menas, free from every yoke of slavery
πρὸς τῷ με τυχεῖν [ὡς προ]είρηται ἐλέους εἰς ἄφεσι[ν] κ[αὶ λύ]τρωσιν τῶν ἐμῶν ἁμαρτιῶν.	that I might chance, [as afore]said, mercy for the forgiveness for and ransoming from my sins.
κατὰ τοῦτο ὁμολογῶ [ἐγὼ ὁ] προγεγραμμένος Βίκτω[ρ ἑκ]ὼν καὶ πεπεισμένος ἄνευ βίας	Accordingly [I, the] aforementioned Victor, willingly and persuaded without force,
καὶ ἀπάτης καὶ ἀνάγ[κης κ]αὶ φόβου καὶ οἱασδήποτε [συνα]ρπαγῆς τε καὶ περιγραφῆς	deceit, compulsion or fear and (acting without) any [dec]eption whatsoever, fraud
καὶ πάσης νομί[μου παρ]αγραφῆς καταστῆσαί σε τ[ὸν] προγεγραμμένον Μηνᾶν	or any leg[al counter-]plea, acknowledge that I have set you, the aforementioned Menas,
[ἐλ]εύθερον ἀπὸ παντὸς ζυγο[ῦ] δουλίας ἀπὸ τοῦ νῦν ἐπ[ὶ τὸν δι]η[νεκῆ χρόνον]	[free from every yoke] of slavery from this moment [for perpetuity]

καὶ ειστ.[........]του μὴ δύνασθαί τινα διαφ[± 20]	and ... no one to be able ...
εμους παντὶ καιρῷ [ἢ χ]ρόνῳ ἕλκειν σε εἰς οἱανδή[ποτε δουλείαν ± 7 μήτε]	... at any moment [or t]ime to drag you into any [slavery whatsoever ... nor]
ὑπομνῆσαί σε μ[ήτε πα]ρενοχλῆ[σ]αι μή[τ]ε κ.. [± 18]	to remind you [nor to an]noy nor ...
περὶ οἱουδήποτ[ε πράγμ]ατος τὸ σύνολον ἀνήκοντος [...].ο..[ἐν δικαστηρίῳ]	concerning any [matter] whatsoever in general appertaining [... in court]
ἢ ἐκτὸς δικαστη[ρίου] ἐπιχωρίω ἢ ὑπερορίου, μικ[ροῦ ἢ] μεγάλο[υ], μήτε [διὰ]	or out of court, at home or abroad, small [or] great, neither [through]
ἐμῶν κληρονόμ[ων], μὴ διὰ ἐντολέως, μὴ δι[ὰ π]αρενθέτου οἱουδήποτε	my heirs, nor through an agent, nor through anyone whatsoever
προσώπου δι[ὰ τό μ]ε ἑκόντα καὶ πεπει[σμέν]ον τὴν παροῦσαν	[as I], willingly and persuaded, on the present
[ἐλ]ευθερίαν συν[τεθεῖσ]θαί σοι. εἰς ἀσφάλειαν [σὴ]ν καὶ ὅτι ταῦθ' οὕτως	manumission have [agreed] with you. For [your] security and that these (matters) are so
ἔχει καὶ οὐκ ἀπ[οστή]σομαι ἐπωμοσάμην [τό]ν τε τῆς ἁγίας καὶ	and I will not [renege], I have sworn [the] oath of the holy and
ὁμοουσίου τριάδ[ος καὶ] τοῦ περιβεβλημμένου [μ]οι εὐαγοῦς σχήματος	*homoousios* Trinity [and] of the holy vestments which envelop me
καὶ τῆς σωτηρί[ας καὶ] νίκης καὶ διαμον[ῆς] τῶν γαληνοτάτων	and of salvation [and] of victory and of the perseverance of our most serene
ἡμῶν δεσποτῶ[ν Φ]λ(αουίου) Μαυρικίου Τιβερίου κ[αὶ] Αἰλίας Κωνσταντίνας	lords Fl(avius) Mauricius Tiberius [and] Aelia Constantina,
τῶν αἰωνίων Αὐγ[ούσ]των Αὐτοκρατόρων ‹ὅρκον› στ[έργ]ειν καὶ ἐμμένειν	the eternal August Imperators, to a[cquiesce] and to abide
διαπαντὸς τῇ δυν[άμ]ει ταύτης τῆς ἐλευ[θερί]ας καὶ κατὰ μηδένα	always by the authority of this manumission and in no
τρόπον παρασα[λεύειν α]ὐτὴν ἢ μέρος αὐ[τ]ῆς. εἰ δέ ποτε καιρῷ	way to under[mine it] or part thereof. If ever at some moment
ἢ χρόνῳ τολμ[ήσειέν τις τῶ]ν ἐμῶν κλ[ηρο]νόμων ὑπεναντίον	or time [any of] my heirs [should] attempt to proceed against
[ταύτης τῆς ἐλευθερίας χω]ρεῖν, παρέξ[ει] [.]..........	[this manumission, he] will pay ...
[± 16 παρα]βάσεως χρυσοῦ οὐ[γκίας]	[... for the transgression] X gold u[ncia ...]

[ἔργῳ καὶ δυνάμει ἀπαιτο]υμένας παρ' αὐτοῦ καὶ [μηδὲν ἧττον]	[demanded by deed and authority] from him and [no less]
[ἀρραγῆ καὶ ἀσάλευτ]ον εἶναι διαπ[αντὸς]	that it is [unbroken and unshaken always ...]
[ ].[ ]	[...]
[καὶ ἐπερωτηθ]εὶς εἰς πρόσωπον	[... and being ask]ed in person
[ταῦθ' οὕτως ἔχειν ποιεῖν ἐμμέν]ειν φυλάττειν ὡμολό(γησα).	I have acknowledged [these matters to be so, to do, to abide by] (and) to guard.
(m. 2) [ ].	(m. 2) [...]
[ἐθέμην ταύτην τὴν ἐ]λευθε-[ρίαν]	[... I have made this] manumission ...

....

8 φρικτῷ 10 πρὸς τό με 19 ἐπιχωρίου

The slave Menas is called 'son of Victor' (another Victor than the monastic slave-owner). Since legally only a slave's maternal relationship was recognised, a problem arises because of the mention of Menas' father. The editor suggests that the use of the father's name arose either as a misuse or from the possibility that Menas was sold into slavery after birth.

The reason for the manumission is that Victor might receive mercy at the last judgement. Such a belief was widespread. The editors, ibid., pp.159-60, list the following parallels of religiously motived manumission:

a. *MChr.* 361
ὁμολογῶ ἑκουσίως καὶ αὐθαιρέτως καὶ ἀμετανοήτως ἀφικέναι ὑμᾶς, ἐλευθέρους τοῦ ἐπιβάλλοντός μοι μέρους ὑπὸ Γῆν καὶ Οὐρανὸν κατ' εὐσέβειαν τ[ο]ῦ πανελεήμονος θεοῦ κτλ
I acknowledge willing, freely and without reserve to have set you free, under Earth and Heaven, in reverence of the all merciful God, from the portion falling to me etc.

b. G. Giannelli, *Vat. gr.* 1554, f.100
διὸ καὶ ὁ δεῖνα τὸν ἀργυρώνητον αὐτοῦ δοῦλον ... ὑπὲρ λύτρου καὶ ἀφέσεως τῶν αὐτοῦ ἁμαρτημάτων ἐλεύθερον ποιεῖ κτλ
Wherefore also so and so makes free his slave who was bought with silver ... for the ransom and forgiveness of his sins etc.

c. *Formula Bituricensis* 9 (*MGH*, Legum Sectio V, p.172, 12)
ut, quando de hac luce migravero, anima mea ante tribunal Christi veniam merear accipere ...
that, when I depart this light, I may be worthy to receive mercy before the judgement seat of Christ ...

d. *Senonicarum Appendix* 4 (ibid., p.210, 19f.)
pro remissionem peccatorum meorum te ab [om]ne vinculum servitutis absolvo ...
for the forgiveness of my sins I free you from every bond of servitude ...

e. *Formula extravagans* 18 (ibid., p.544, 26f.)
pro remedio animae meae vel aeterna retributione ...
for the healing of my soul or eternal restoration ...

f. *Carta Senonica* 1 (ibid., p.185, 25ff.)
pro animae meae remedium vel pro meis peccatis minuendis, ut in futurum Dominus veniam mihi praestare dignetur ...
a cure for my soul or for the diminution of my sins, that in future the Lord may deem to show mercy to me ...

Of particular interest in *P. Köln* III 157 is the fact that the monk (whether a hermit or a member of a *koinobion*) owns property and a slave at that. Other papyri witness to the ownership of property by monks (*SB* I 5174, 5175 and *P. Lond.* V 1729) but till now none witnessed to the ownership of a slave. A question naturally arises concerning the apparent inconsistency between ownership of property and the novice's renunciation of possessions on entry to the monastic life. Of related interest also is the fact that despite the owner's religious affiliation the deed of manumission is in the form of a *cheirographon* (i.e. a private document addressed by the master to his slave) and not of a *manumissio in ecclesia*.

Other papyri of the fourth and later centuries witness to monastic ownership of property and commercial involvement. In the case of the apotactics of the fourth century this may have resulted from their continued residence in the village and involvement in its civil and church affairs (see further E.A. Judge, 'The Earliest Use of Monachos for "Monk" and the Origins of Monasticism', *JbAC* 20 [1977], pp.72-89). Of the seventeen documents listed as witnesses to fourth-century monasticism by E.A. Judge, 'Fourth-Century Monasticism in the Papyri', *Am. Stud. Pap.* XXIII (Chico 1981), pp.613-20, fifteen are said 'to indicate a close involvement of monastics with property'. The Nag Hammadi papyri also witness to this same monastic involvement. The question naturally arises as to how one balances the picture of monastic life gathered from the papyri with that derived from the literary sources. The answer to this question will depend on one's weighing of several other possibilities. First, the monastic's involvement with property may not necessarily imply in all cases his personal ownership of that property. For example, he may have acted for his community or monastery, which in order to support itself was involved in agricultural production. Second, the papyri may present a biased picture of monastic involvement. Since the predominant subject matter of the papyri is commercial, it should not be surprising then that when monastics are mentioned they will be implicated in some commercial transaction or other. One's appraisal of the matter naturally turns on whether or not monastics as a group are under-represented in the papyri. Unfortunately, this is a question which cannot be answered as the proportion of monastics in Roman Egypt can only be guessed at. Be that as it may, the apparent inconsistency between ownership of property and the renunciation of possessions resembles other inconsistencies between theory and practice already noted with respect to slavery – see *New Docs* 6 (1992) §6 and §11. How was a theory to be applied in a particular social situation or context? Often its application entailed compromise and therein lay the potential for inconsistency. To understand this better one needs to be aware of the strictures of culture which in practice acted to modify and to change theory.

S.R.L.

MAGIC, MEDICINE AND CULTS

§28 Ailments and Remedies

1. Chalcis, Euboea Undated

Ed.pr. — A.K. Choremis, *Arch.Deltion* 28 (1973), Chron. 1, p.300.
Bib. – Claude Meillier, *ZPE* 38 (1980), p.98.

Ἀσκληπιάδης Ἀναξίππου Ἐφέσιος	Asklepiades, son of Anaxippos of Ephesus,
εἴκοσι καὶ δύ᾽ ἔτη ζήσας πολὺν οἶνον	having lived twenty-two years, drinking a lot
ἀπνευστί	of pure wine in one draught,
ἄκρατον πίνων αἱμαναγῶν ἔθανον	I the son of Anaxippos died bringing up
υἱὸς Ἀναξίππου· κλήζοντ᾽	blood. If anyone calls
Ἀσκληπιάδην	Asklepiades,
οὔνομα καὶ πατέρων ἦν γένος ἐξ	the name and the family of my ancestors was
Ἐφέσου.	from Ephesus.

Herodotos (VI. 84) reports that the Spartans believed the madness of their king, Kleomenes, was due to his having acquired the Scythian habit of drinking his wine undiluted and in the Asklepios text a detrimental effect is also attributed to pure wine. However wine is more commonly suggested to be of benefit. According to C. Meillier, the practice of drinking pure wine for digestive troubles had been established since the time of the Greek physician Hippocrates of Cos (second half of fifth century BC), and a papyrus dated to the second half of II (L.C. Youtie & H.C. Youtie, 'A Medical Papyrus', *Scritti in onore di Orsolina Montevecchi*, ed. E. Bresciani et al. [Bologna 1981], pp.431-35) refers to the use of new wine mixed with water as a remedy for constipation. The use of medicines and prescriptions to facilitate recovery from illness is found in several places in the NT. Particularly noteworthy is the advice to Timothy to 'stop drinking only water and use a little wine because of your stomach and your frequent illnesses' (1Tim. 5.23).

2. Provenance unknown II BC

Ed.pr. — R.S. Bagnall, P.J. Sijpesteijn, K.A. Worp, *Greek Ostraka in Leiden* (Zutphen 1980), pp.1-2, F 1901/9.166.

(Convex side)	
Ὅταν βούληι	Whenever you wish
τῆι διανοίᾳ	to be calmed
καταστορῆναι	in spirit
καὶ εἰδῆις ὅ τι τε	and you know what is
5 ταράσσει, πρὸ δί-	troubling you, drink
πνου πίης	before dinner,
καὶ ὅταν διπνήσεις	and when you eat your dinner
⟦το⟧ ἅμα ἐπὶ τῶι δίπ-	at the same time with dinner
νῳ ὠιὰ φάγε	eat eggs
10 καὶ τὸ πλεῖον τοῦ δίπ-	and most of your dinner
νου ἀπέρασαι	vomit up
καὶ τῇ ἐφαύριον ἐκ-	and on the next day

σειασμὸν ποί- ησαι.	carry out an ἐκσειασμός.
(Concave side)	
ὑπολαμβ`ά΄νω,	I suppose
ὅτι συμφέρει ἀπ' ὄψου.	you may profit from fish.

The text is written on both sides of an *ostrakon* (8.6 x 12 cm). Five lines of an unrelated text, an account, appear above the final two lines of the prescription on the concave side. The word ἐκσειασμός does not appear in lexical sources hence its exact meaning remains unclear. It is suggested, however, that if it is related to the verb ἐκσείω, it could refer to a purgation of the body. Some uncertainty also surrounds the exact nature of the substance to be drunk, although it is most probably wine. Finally, it may be noted that the editors also point out that the text is particularly interesting because it deals not with a physical malady, as the majority of medical prescriptions, but with an emotional or spiritual problem (ibid., pp.1-2).

3. Hermopolis Magna — Late III – early IV AD

Ed.pr. — M-H. Marganne, 'Une étape dans la transmission d'une prescription médicale: *P. Berl.Möller* 13', *Miscellanea Papyrologica* (Florence 1980), pp.179-183.

Πρὸς τὸ μ]ὴ̣ ἀπορρ̣ε̣ῖ̣ν̣ τ̣ὰ̣ς ἐν τῇ κε- φ̣α̣λ̣ῇ [τρ]ί̣χας.	For the prevention of the loss of hair from the head.
λάδανον ἀποβρέχων̣ ἐ̣ν̣ οἴνῳ αὐστη-	Soaking resin in bitter wine
ρῷ λέαινε ἐναλλὰξ παρεπιχέων μύρ-	smooth it on, alternately pouring oil of myrtle
σινον καὶ οἶν[ον] ὡς μέλιτ[ο]ς̣ σχεῖν πά-	and wine so that it has the thickness of honey
χος καὶ χρεῖε τὴν κεφαλὴν πρὸ βαλανεί-	and smear it on the head before a bath
ου καὶ μετὰ βαλανε[ίον]. Βέλτειον δέ ἐσ-	and after a bath. But it is better
τιν καὶ πολυτρί̣[χ]ου, ὅ τινες καὶ ἀδίαντον	to add also in half the quantity of the resin, polytrichos,
καλοῦσι, τὸ ἥμ̣ι̣σ̣υ μέρος τοῦ [λ]αδάνου προσ-	which some people call adiantos,
βάλλειν καὶ χρῆσ]θ̣αι μετὰ το[ῦ] μυρσίνου	and to use it with the myrtle oil
δ	
ἢ μετὰ νάρτου.	or nard.

Other previously unpublished prescriptions on papyrus, this time for an ointment to be used in the case of eye disease and dating to the second or third century AD, are included among the twenty-two papyri from the Austrian National Library collected in H. Harrauer and P.J. Sijpesteijn, *Medizinische Rezepte und Verwandtes* (Vienna 1981). The application of oil as a remedy may, perhaps, call to mind the injunction of James, 'Is any one of you sick? He should call the elders of the church to pray over him and anoint him with oil in the name of the Lord' (5.14), and the prescriptions for eye ointment, the manner in which Jesus applied a salve of clay and spittle to the blind man's eyes in John 9.6.

4. Kula, Lydia — Roman Imperial

Ed.pr. — H.W. Pleket, 'New Inscriptions from Lydia', *Talanta* 10-11 (1978-81), pp.88-90, no.13.

Γλυκία Ἰουλί-	Glykia daughter
ου τοῦ Ἀγρίου	of Iulius Agrius
κολασθεῖ-	having been punished
σα ὑπὸ τῆ-	by
ς Ἀναείτιδος	Anaeitis
τῆς ἐγ Μητρῷ τ-	from Metro
ὸν γλουθροῦν ἐ-	(with a disease) in the buttock,
π̣ιζητήσασα ἀν̣[έθ]-	asked her (what to do) and then dedicated
ηκεν.	this stone.

5. Alasehir, Lydia — Undated

Ed.pr. — Pleket, ibid., p.90, no.14.

[ ] . . Ο . [ ] Φ̣[....]	[ ]. . Ο . [ ] Φ [. . . .]
ηνοῦ κολασθ-	have been punished by the god ---enos;
εὶς, διὰ τὸ μὲ ἕτ-	however because I
οιμον εἶνε	was willing (to ask the God which sin I
κὲ κ̣-	committed) and
εκληδονίσθε	have received an omen telling
με ὅτι· "Μεμολυ-	me: "You are defiled",
μένος εἶ", εὐξάμε-	after having made a vow
νος ἀνέθηκα.	I have dedicated this stone.

The expansion of *ll.*3-4 is that of the editor. However G.H.R. Horsley suggests to me that if for μέ we read μή then the text would be translated 'because of not being ready to ask the god ...'.

In these two texts from Lydia no other method of healing is sought than the intervention of the deity. They also introduce the concept that illness was a divine punishment, a belief attested in the NT (Acts 12.20-23; 28.1-10) as well as the OT. The inscriptions are examples of a quite extensively known class which have emerged from north eastern Lydia and southern Mysia. More recently published texts of this kind and discussion of the class as a whole may be found in G. Petzl and H. Malay, *GRBS* 28 (1987), pp.459-472 and H. Malay, *EA* 12 (1988), pp.147-52. H.W. Pleket, 'New Inscriptions from Lydia', *Talanta* 10-11 (1978-81), pp.88-90, no.13; Pleket, ibid., p.90, no.14.

6. Unknown provenance — III AD

Ed.pr. — R. Kotansky, 'Two Amulets in the Getty Museum: A Gold Amulet for Aurelia's Epilepsy An Inscribed Magical Stone for Fever, "Chills", and Headache', *J. Paul Getty Museum Journal* 8 (1980), pp.180-4.

Ὁ Θεὸς Ἀβραάμ, ὁ Θεὸς	The God of Abraham, the God
Εἰσάκ, ὁ Θεὸς Ἰακώβ, ὁ Θε-	of Isaac, the God of Jacob, the

ὸς ἡμῶν· ῥῦσαι τὴν	God of us, rescue
[Αὐ]ρηλ[ί]αν	Aurelia
ἐκ παν-	from every
τὸς πν[ε]ύματος	evil spirit
πονηροῦ	
καὶ ἐκ πάσης ἐπιλημψί-	and from every epileptic fit
ας καὶ πτωματισμοῦ,	and seizure,
δέομαί σου, κύριε Ἰάω	I implore you Lord Iao,
Σαβαώθ, Ἐλωαῖον, Οὐ{υ}-	Sabaoth, Eloaion, Ou-
ριήλ, Μισιχαήλ, Ῥαφαήλ, Γα-	riel, Misichael, Raphael, Ga-
β̣ριήλ, Σαραήλ, Ῥασοχήλ{ς}	briel, Sariel, Rasochel,
Ἀβλαναθαναλβα Ἀβρασάξ̣	Ablanathanalba, Abrasax,
ξξξξξξνννννα	xxxxxx nnnnnna
ωααιιιιιιιιιξουυυυυ	oaaiiiiiiiiiixouuuuu
υυααοοοοοοοοωνω	uuaaoooooooono
(symb. *chi-rho* symb.) Σεσενγεν-	(symb. chi-rho symb.) Sesengen-
βαρφαρανγης, διαφύ-	barpharanges, pro-
λασσε, ηπφ̣ιν ἰὼ Ἐρβηθ̣	tect, ephin, io Erbeth
(11 characters)	. . .
(10 characters)	. . .
(9 characters)	. . .
(2 characters), διαφύλασσε τὴν	... , protect
Αὐρηλίαν ἀπὸ παντὸς πτω-	Aurelia from every seiz-
ʽματισμοῦʼ	ure,
ἐκ παντὸς πτωματισ-	from every seiz-
μοῦ, Ἰάω, Ἰεοῦ, Ἰηω̣	ure, Iao, Ieou, Ieo
λαμμω Ἰάω χαρακοω	lammo Iao charakoo-
πο̣υ Σεσενγενβαρφαραν-	pou Sesengenbarpharan-
γης Ἰάω α̣ιε̣ι̣υα̣ι̣ Ἰηου Ἰάω,	ges Iao aieiuai Ieou Iao
Σαβαώθ, Ἀδωναῖε, Ἠληληθʼ	Sabaoth, Adonaie, Eleleth,
[Ἰ]ά̣κω.	[I]ako.
Written to the left side of the text and at right angles to it:	
διαφύλασσε ο̣ω [--]	Protect ...

This text, of which a slightly revised version of that published is given here on the basis of the drawing included at the time of publication, was inscribed with a sharp instrument on a thin piece of gold-foil measuring approximately 4.2 x 2.0 cm. It was originally rolled up and was probably placed in a container to be suspended around the neck. The charm, or *phylakterion*, belongs to a class of magical texts against illness which is relatively common on papyrus. Over twenty examples are known (*New Docs* 3 [1983], p.114) and to these may be added a considerably lesser number on other materials such as gold. See, in particular, the recently published *phylacterion* of IV AD which contains [*ll.*5-6] a version of the Aramaic phrase *mry t* – an expression similar to the well-known early Christian liturgical acclamation *μαράνα θᾶ*, Aramaic for '(our) lord come!' (1Cor.16.22) - published by C.A. Faraone and R. Kotansky, 'An Inscribed Gold Phylactery in Stamford, Connecticut,' *ZPE* 75 (1988), pp.257-66. A gold charm is held in the collection at Macquarie University (MU 2755) and a lead one is reported in *New Docs* 2 (1982) , pp.45-6.

Amulets of this kind are characterized by a mixture of elements which makes it difficult and sometimes impossible to ascertain the context from which they originated. The cultural mixing in Egypt of Greeks, Jews and Egyptians from the Hellenistic period on, led to the borrowing and sharing of religious ideas, belief and magical practices. The syncretistic nature of the amulets was one result. It is common to find in the texts, as in this example, Jewish, Christian, Gnostic and Egyptian religious elements as well as letters and vowels used in the manner of Egyptian magical spells (A.D. Nock, 'Greek Magical Papyri', *JEA* 15 [1929], pp.219-35, reprinted in his *Essays on Religion and the Ancient World* [Oxford 1972], pp.176-94. For other examples, see *The Greek Magical Papyri in Translation,* H.D. Betz ed., [Chicago and London 1986] and also *Supplementum Magicum* Vol. I [Opladen 1990] edited with translations and notes by Robert W. Daniel and Franco Maltomini).

Judaism is clearly represented in the Getty text by the names of a variety of angels (*ll.*11-13) and by possibly divine names such as Sabaoth, Adonai, Iao and Elaion (*ll.*10-11; 32). The phrase 'The God of Abraham, the God of Isaac, the God of Jacob, our God' (*ll.*1-3) might also be attributed to this religious tradition (so Kotansky, ibid., p.183). However, there is no certainty for, as Martin Rist points out in his study of this formula ('The God of Abraham, Isaac and Jacob: A Liturgical and Magical Formula', *JBL* 57 [1938], pp.289-303), it may be observed in a variety of contexts. Not only is it to be found in the LXX (e.g. Ex.3.6, 3.15-16 and 4.5) and in extra-canonical Jewish prayers and liturgies, it is also used in a number of inscriptions in Samaria which had a purely magical function.

It is not only the appearance of the patriarchal formula in Acts 3.31 and 7.32 that indicates it was taken over by Christians. It has been found on a silver amulet from Beirut which, according to Rist (ibid., p.299), came from a Christian tomb. There, as in the Getty amulet, it was used against fits. Furthermore, πνεῦμα πονηρόν, the phrase used here (*ll.*6-7), is a phrase which may well have a Christian affiliation because of its occurrence in the gospel of Luke (7.21, 8.2, 11.26). (On this phrase in a Christian context in V/VI AD, see also *New Docs* 3 [1983], p.115.)

Another apparently Christian element, the *chi-rho* symbol, is present in the Getty text, but its inclusion among the vowels and *voces magicae* of the spell (*l.*18) makes it impossible to be sure of the symbol's significance. Patrick Crasta has observed ('Graeco-Christian Magical Papyri', *Stud.Pap.* 18 [1979], pp.31-40) that the inclusion of Christian elements in a text is not necessarily an indication of the religious persuasion of the wearer of the phylactery. And in this context the *chi-rho* is perhaps most likely to be simply an example of the spell-maker's tendency to accumulate names of divinities from all sources in order to reinforce the spell's effectiveness (on this topic see E.A. Judge, 'The Magical Use of Scripture in the Papyri', *Perspectives on Language and Text: Essays and Poems in Honor of Francis I. Andersen's Sixtieth Birthday,* Edgar W. Conrad and Edward G. Newing edd., [Winona Lake, Indiana 1987], pp.339-49). In this respect it may be noted again that the name of the Hebrew god is included in a variety of forms on the Getty amulet.

Other linguistic elements may indicate an underlying Christian influence in the text. For example, the verb ῥύομαι, found here in line 3, is found in other magical texts in a distinctively Christian context where the reference is to the Lord's prayer in Matt. 6.13: καὶ μὴ εἰσενέγκῃς ἡμᾶς εἰς πειρασμόν, ἀλλὰ ῥῦσαι ἡμᾶς ἀπὸ τοῦ πονηροῦ. Elsewhere, for example, in *P. Mich.inv.*6666 (ed.pr. R.W. Daniel, '*P. Mich.inv.*6666: Magic', *ZPE* 50 [1983], pp.147-

54) which does not appear to be Christian, the more literal θεραπεύω is used when seeking to dispel fits of shivering and fever.

Although there is only one clearly Gnostic deity mentioned in the Getty text, Eleleth (*l.* 32), it is not impossible that the text has emerged from that creed rather than the Judaic or Christian. From the beginning of the Christian era there was a growth of Gnostic movements both inside and outside the Christian framework and, in Egypt particularly, considerable borrowing of patterns of expression, formulae and images resulted. So it was that the Gnostics too used the names Iao, Sabaoth, Adonaios, applying them to elements within their own system of belief (H. Jonas, *The Gnostic Religion* [1963], pp.25ff.. See also the translations of Gnostic texts in *The Nag Hammadi Library in English*, J.M. Robinson ed., [Leiden and San Francisco, 1977]) and therefore even the appearance of the name of the OT God does not mean necessarily that Jewish practice is represented in this amulet.

The fourth cultural strain recognisable in the text is Egyptian. Most obvious in this respect is the pervasiveness of Egyptian magical gibberish in the form of groups of vowels (*ll.*15-17) and *voces magicae*, such as Abrasax (*l.*14 – a name, incidentally, which may also be interpreted as that of a Gnostic deity [Kotansky, ibid., p.183]). Probably too, an allusion to the Egyptian deity Seth (in Greek, Typhon) is to be recognised in Ιώ Ἐρβηθ at *l.*20 (Kotansky, ibid.), however in general Egyptian religious elements are far less prominent than in certain other papyri such as *P. Mich.inv.*6666 (Daniel, ibid., p.149) and it seems unlikely that the amulet would have been written for an Egyptian.

The syncretism of this text will now be obvious and identification of individual elements does not assist the interpretation of its specific cultural and religious context in the absence of any information about its provenance. The date too must remain somewhat uncertain. Although Kotansky (ibid., p.181) dates it to the third century on palaeographic grounds and on the basis of its owner's name, i.e. Aurelia, the fact that the Gnostic appellation Eleleth (*l.*32) is not known previously in Greek magical texts, despite its occurrence in those of Coptic origin, may mean the amulet belongs to a slightly later period, as should the *chi-rho* monogram which, if Christian, generally belongs to IV AD or later (*New Docs* 2 [1982], p.171).

In his book, *The Ruling Class of Judaea* (Cambridge 1987), Martin Goodman (pp.100ff.) enlarges on what he believes to be a marked difference between Greeks and Jews to medicine and healing in his discussion of the link between attitudes towards an individual's physical well-being and attitudes towards the well-being of society generally. He particularly emphasizes the fact that, while not denying the power of magic and demons, the Greeks (as evidenced in the teaching and practice of Galen, the physician of II AD) attempted healing predominantly through the application of drugs or water-treatments with a view to readjusting the body's forces which had become unbalanced. However, the Jews, he argues, viewed illness as the work of outside forces and ascribed sickness to divine punishment for sins. For the Jews physical sickness came from pollution and could be cured by purification and exorcism and hence Jewish healers were famous throughout the Greek world for their magical medicine which promised simple cures rather than the restoration of internal balance demanded by Greek medical theory. For a possible difference of attitude to illness between Greeks and Christians as judged from their letters on papyrus, see R.J.S. Barrett-Lennard, 'Request for Prayer for Healing', *New Docs* 4 (1987), pp.245-250.

Reference to magicians and magical healers is not infrequent in Acts and illustrates the existence of animosity between them and the early church (Acts 8.9-13, Acts 13.6-12; 16.16-18; 19.13-19). On the other hand, it has been observed that at several points in both the gospels and Acts, magical belief impinges on the miraculous nature of healing by both Jesus and the apostles (Howard Clark Kee, *Miracle in the Early Christian World* [New Haven 1983] p.215; David E. Aune, 'Magic in Early Christianity, *ANRW* II 23.2 [Berlin 1980] p.1536). One may cite as examples the account of the woman who touched Jesus' cloak and was healed in Mark

5.25-34 and Luke 8.43-48; or the people in Ephesus who recovered from illness after handling handkerchiefs and aprons which had touched Paul (Acts 19.11-12). But none of the characteristic features of magic is found in the actions of the apostles themselves or the beliefs expressed in the NT documents and it is through the reaction of others to the miracles of healing performed by Jesus and the apostles that the element of magic enters the NT world. A wide-ranging study of the relationship between medicine and magic in the Graeco-Roman world and the NT may be found in Howard Clark Kee, *Medicine, Miracle and Magic in New Testament Times*, Cambridge 1986.

R.A. Kearsley

§29 The Mysteries of Artemis at Ephesus

Ephesus 92/93

Ed.pr. — *I.Eph. IV*, 1012.

Inscribed on the drum of a column from the doric porch of the Prytaneion, the chief civic building of Ephesus. Later reused and found to the south of the Scholastika Baths. Of white marble, ht.: 1.76 m; diam. 1.15 m; ht. of letters: 0.02-0.024 m.

Bib. – D. Knibbe, *Der Staatsmarkt. Die Inschriften des Prytaneions, Forschungen in Ephesos IX/1/1* (Vienna 1981), B 12.

	ἐπ[ὶ] π[ρ]υτάνεως Κλαυδίας Τροφίμης	In the *prytany* of Claudia Trophime,
	ἱερᾶς κουρῆτες εὐσεβεῖς φιλοσέβαστοι·	priestess, the pious, emperor-loving *kouretes* (were):
	Θεόφιλος Δημητρίου Μᾶρκος · Λούκιος	Theophilos Markos, son of Demetrios; Lucius
4	Ταρουτείλιος Τύραννος· Ἀλέξανδρος Τρύ-	Tarutilius Tyrannus; Alexandros
	φωνος Σαβεῖνος · Τιβέριος Κλαύδιος	Sabinos, son of Tryphon; Tiberius Claudius
	Ἀγαθόπους ὁ Ἀλεξᾶ · Γάιος Σέλλιος Μακεδών·	Agathopous, called Alexa; Gaius Sellius Macedon;
	Τιβ. Κλαύδιος Εὔπορᾶς· Μᾶρκος ἱεροσκόπος·	Tiberius Claudius Europas; Markos, inspector of the victims;
8	Μηνόδοτος ἱεροκῆρυξ · Ἀττικὸς ἐπὶ θυμιάτρου·	Menodotos, sacred herald; Attikos, incense-bearer;
	Τρόφιμος σπονδαύλης	Trophimos, flute-player at the drink-offering.

Dieter Knibbe's publication of the ninety-four *kouretes* inscriptions (dating from IV BC to III AD) with extensive commentary, has opened up for study one further aspect of the worship of Artemis. (For earlier discussions of the cult in *New Docs* see Vol.4 [1987], pp.74-82, 127-29; Vol.5 [1989], pp.104-5; and elsewhere in this volume, **§30**. See also R.E. Oster, *ANRW* II, 18.3 [1990], pp.1669-1726 most recently for an extended treatment of the evidence.)

The bulk of the inscriptions from the Prytaneion contain lists of the names of those who served as *kouretes* and they provide a basis for the exploration of the group referred to by Strabo (14.1.20) in his description of the ritual surrounding the annual celebration of Artemis' nativity on Mt Solmissus above the grove of Ortygia at Ephesus:

where, it is said, the Curetes stationed themselves, and with the din of their arms frightened Hera out of her wits when she was jealously spying on Leto ... A general festival is held there annually; and by a certain custom the youths vie for honour particularly in the splendour of their banquets there. At that time also, a special college of the Curetes holds symposiums there and performs certain mystic sacrifices (Loeb trans.).

Even in ancient times it was known that the worship of Ephesian Artemis had altered over the many centuries of the cult's existence (Strabo 14.1.23) and Knibbe's analysis of the inscriptions relating to the *kouretes* shows that they were no exception to this process. Nevertheless, despite certain changes, their fundamental link with Artemis and the mysteries was maintained.

In one of only two inscriptions belonging to the fourth century BC (*I.Eph.* V, 1449 = Knibbe, ibid., A2), the *kouretes'* connection with the temple of Artemis is so close that, together with certain *neopoioi* (on these see *New Docs* 4 [1987], pp.127-29), they are acting as representatives of the temple in the civic council of the Ephesians. The matter under consideration concerns the award of citizenship to a benefactor of the sanctuary.

Despite its fragmentary state it is possible to establish from the second inscription of approximately the same date (IV – III BC, *I.Eph.* VII.2, 4102 = Knibbe, ibid., A1), that certain *kouretes* and *neopoioi* were acting as witnesses to a leasing agreement between the Artemision and a second party. Hence the evidence for the pre-imperial period indicates that the *kouretes* played a role within the administrative structure of the Artemision which was additional, we may suppose, to their religious functions.

However, it is only in these two pre-imperial texts that a link between the *kouretes* and the administration of the sanctuary of Artemis is displayed. The remainder of the inscriptions, those of the imperial period, do not refer to the Artemision and were not displayed there. They were inscribed on the walls and columns of the porch of the Prytaneion. This building, central to the religious life of the city as the location of the city's hearth was consecrated to Hestia, not to Artemis. In the hearth the sacred fire of the city, symbolising its continuing well-being, was kept burning by an official known as the *prytanis*. Thus a marked change in the physical arrangements of the *kouretes* appears to have occurred. They must have moved from the Artemision outside the city and made the Prytaneion within the city-walls their base instead. Yet, despite this there does not appear to have been any interruption to their participation in the actual cult of Artemis.

The shift of the *kouretes* from the Artemision to the Prytaneion is estimated by Knibbe to have occurred in late I BC when the Augustan Prytaneion was constructed. The cause is unknown but may have been a result of the weakening of the political influence of the Artemision in the affairs of the city at the time. Once there the epigraphic evidence reveals that, if they were not so before, the *kouretes* became a συνέδριον (guild) comprising some six to nine active members with, in addition, former members who belonged for life (Knibbe, ibid., p.96f).

The text given and translated above is typical of the long sequence of inscriptions from the Prytaneion which records membership of the college of *kouretes* year by year and is dated by the name of the annual *prytanis* in Ephesus. Among the six *kouretes* listed here there are two men who bear purely Greek names while the other four have the Roman *tria nomina* and are therefore probably Roman citizens. Several of the names are of interest. The first on the list, Theophilos, is attested in the NT (see the discussion on occurrences of this name in *New Docs* 3 [1983], pp.38-39) and the inclusion of the name here with a patronymic would appear to support the view (*New Docs* 4 [1987], p.178) that, although the name is attested on several occasions as a servile name, it should not be considered exclusively as such.

The identity of the name Tyrannus with that of the owner of the hall used by Paul when he could no longer teach in the synagogue (Acts 19.9) has already been noted (*New Docs* 4 [1987], p.186 [k], and *New Docs* 5 [1989], p.113, for another first-century Tyrannus in

Ephesus). Tarutilius Tyrannus is also notable as one of only two men who are known to have been *kouretes* three times. The fourth name on the list, Tiberius Claudius Agathopous, called Alexa, is a mixture of Greek and Roman forms since it combines the Roman *tria nomina* with a Greek by-name. By-names of various kinds occur in the NT also although none exactly parallels this in form (see the survey in *New Docs* 1 [1981], pp.89-96).

In addition to the relevance of the names for NT onomastics, this list of *kouretes* is of interest for the information it provides on the social standing of participants in the college. The predominance of Roman names reflects the relatively high social rank of the *kouretes*. This list contains a slightly higher proportion than the average of the period which is based on a total of seventeen lists dating up to the beginning of III AD. With the passage of time, however, the proportion of *kouretes* bearing Roman names increases, so that, by the period of Commodus in late II AD, in an inscription naming over seventy *kouretes* there are around three Roman names to every Greek one (*I.Eph.* Ia, 47; Knibbe, ibid., p.98) and the *kouretes* are sometimes men who have held other important offices within the city (*I.Eph.* IV, 1060 = Knibbe, ibid., C1). Although the increase in college members bearing Roman names may simply be due to the greater prevalence of Roman citizens in Ephesus by late II AD, the inclusion of those who hold high office at this period does suggest an increasing importance for the *kouretes*.

There are also structural changes within the college during this period. By the end of II AD some ranking among the *kouretes* is evident in the appearance of a πρωτοκούρης (*I.Eph.* IV, 1061 = Knibbe, ibid., C2) and two ἄρχοντες (*I.Eph.* Ia, 47 = Knibbe, ibid., B54, *ll* 5-6), while the number of cult assistants increased steadily between late I – early III AD indicating an elaboration of the ritual performed by the college. Three assistants are named in the earliest inscriptions, changing to four by late I AD, while by late II – early III, five or six servers are commonly found.

Since the four cult-servers who appear at the end of the above inscription have Greek names without patronymic they may have been slaves rather than citizens of Ephesus. For a similar situation among the cult-servers of Zeus Kresimos among whom there is also a Trophimos see *I.Eph. VII.1*, 3415, although the evidence discussed by H.W. Pleket, ''Ἱερουργοὶ βου(λευταί): A note on the status of cult servants in the Ephesian Prytaneion', *EA* 1 [1983], pp.104-6) indicates this was not always the case. However, difference in status between themselves and the members of the college certainly appears to exist in that the same cult assistants continued to serve over many years and thus were not chosen annually for their position as were the *kouretes*. Trophimos the flute-player listed above, for example, appears in more than a dozen inscriptions ranging over a 25- to 30-year period. Another flute-player, designated Trophimos B′, appears in an inscription of late II AD (*I.Eph.* IV, 1045 = Knibbe, ibid., B45) and seems likely to be a son of the earlier Trophimos, perhaps indicating that family traditions of service even became established. If this is the case the indication B′ after Trophimos the younger's name suggests either that his father had not been, or was no longer, a slave. The name Trophimos was identified in 1983 by Horsley as one used almost exclusively by those of past or present servile status (*New Docs* 3 [1983], pp. 91-93) and it may be noted that evidence for use of the name among those of non-servile status is now increased by the attestation of four citizens with the name Trophimos in other inscriptions of Ephesus (*I. Eph.VIII.2, Verzeichnis der Eigennamen*).

The only other person named in this inscription is the *prytanis* who was both a high religious official (R. Merkelbach, *ZPE* 37 [1980], p.81) and simultaneously a magistrate of the highest rank (Dionysius of Halicarnassus II.65). The importance of the duties of the *prytanis*, particularly the maintenance of the sacred fire in the hearth of the city and the completion of all the sacrificial requirements of the office is reflected in several poems inscribed in the Prytaneion (Knibbe, ibid., p.101; Merkelbach, ibid.). Of these epigrams one of two written by Claudia

Trophime, the *prytanis* in the above inscription, may be given as an example (*I.Eph.* IV, 1062 = Knibbe, ibid., F1):

Κλαυδία Τροφίμη ἱερῆ ἡ πρύτανις Ἑστίῃ ἔπαινον ἔγραψε·	Claudia Trophime priestess (of Artemis) and *prytanis* wrote a poem of praise to Hestia:
Αὔτα καὶ μακάρεσσιν ἐπήρκεσ' ἐν εὐφροσύναισιν,	She bestows on the blessed gods happiness,
αὔτη καὶ θαλερὸν φῶς κατέχει πατρίδος·	and she also maintains the luxuriant flame of the native city;
ἀδυτάτα δαῖμον, κόσμου θάλος, ἀέναον φῶς	Sweetest spirit, offspring of the universe, eternal flame,
ἃ κατέχεις βωμοῖς δαλὸν ἀπ' οὐρανόθεν.	you who preserve the light from heaven on the altars.

As time passed the relationship between the functions of the *prytanis* and the college of *kouretes* became very close. Artemis' statue as well as that of Hestia stood in the Prytaneion and the cultic functions of Hestia, goddess of the city's hearth, and Artemis, patron-goddess of the city, merged to some extent as, for example, in the following inscription of II – III (*I.Eph.* IV, 1068 = Knibbe, ibid., F5; and see also *I.Eph.* IV, 1064 = Knibbe, ibid., F3; *I.Eph.* IV, 1078 = Knibbe, ibid., F13):

Ἑστία Βουλαία καὶ Ἄρτεμι Ἐφεσία, σώζε-	Hestia in the Council-house and Artemis of Ephesus, preserve
τε Πλούταρχον τὸν πρύτανιν καὶ γυμνα-	Ploutarchos the *prytanis* and gymnasiarch
σίαρχον καὶ τὰ τέκνα αὐτοῦ, τὰς ἱερείας τῆς	and his children, the priestesses of
Ἀρτέμιδος, καὶ τὴν σύνβιον αὐτοῦ, τὴν Μενάνδρου	Artemis, and his wife, Nymphidia daughter
Νυμφιδίαν, καὶ Νεικόπολιν, τὴν ἀδελφὴν αὐτῆς,	of Menander, and Neikopolis, her sister,
γυναῖκα Νυμφίου, ἀδελφοῦ τοῦ πρυτάνεως καὶ π[	wife of Nymphios, brother of the *prytanis* and p...

According to the evidence of surviving inscriptions, this merging occurred without the *kouretes* giving up their part in the mysteries of Ortygia celebrating the birth of Artemis. The *kouretes* became officials of Hestia as well as of Artemis and, in turn, the *prytanis* (not infrequently priestess of Artemis at the same time) and the *kouretes* together undertook the mysteries (Knibbe, ibid., p.101). By early III AD the names of other deities in addition to Artemis are associated with the celebration of the mysteries (*I.Eph.* IV, 1060 = Knibbe, ibid., C1; see also *I.Eph.* IV, 1061 = Knibbe, ibid., C2):

Φαβωνία Φλακκίλλα πρύτανις καὶ γυμνασίαρχος ἡ	I, Favonia Flaccilla, *prytanis* and gymnasiarch,
ἀρχιέρεια εὐχαριστῶ Ἑστίᾳ Βουλαί‹ᾳ› καὶ Δήμητρι	high priestess, give thanks to Hestia of the Council-house and to Demeter

καὶ Δήμητρος Κόρῃ καὶ Πυρὶ ἀφθάρτῳ καὶ Ἀπόλλωνι	and to the daughter of Demeter and to incorruptible Fire and to Apollo
Κλαρίῳ καὶ Σώπολι καὶ πᾶσιν τοῖς θεοῖς, ὅτι	of Klaros and to Sopolis and all the gods because
ὁλοκληροῦσάν με μετὰ τοῦ συμβίου μου Ἀκακίου	in good health with my husband, Akakios,
καὶ τῶν τέκνων μου καὶ τῶν ἀνθρώπων μου	and my children and my people
τὸν ἐνιαυτὸν ἐκτελέσασαν τὰ μυστήρια πάντα	after I performed all the mysteries for a year
εὐτυχῶς ἀποκατέστησαν.	they have happily restored me.
οἵδε ἐκουρήτευσαν·	The following served as *kouretes* : (list of names).

Although the name of Artemis Ephesia is not listed separately in this inscription, she may be assumed to be included in the phrase πᾶσιν τοῖς θεοῖς.

The number of fathers and grandfathers of *prytaneis* who appear suggest that the college of *kouretes* contained a substantial number of older men. Knibbe concludes that the reference to young men (νέοι) by Strabo in the extract above must have been only a relative indication of age (ibid., p.97) but it is possible that Strabo's reference is rather to a formal association of young men (Guy Rogers, *The Sacred Identity of Ephesus: Foundation Legends of a Roman City* [London – New York, 1991], p.60).

It seems that the *prytanis* in time had the prerogative of selecting the officiating *kouretes* (*I.Eph.* 1a, 47 = Knibbe, ibid., pp.96ff.). By late II AD at least, it appears the *prytanis* had accepted responsibility for the financial viability of the college of *kouretes*. Two inscriptions illustrate the obligations of the *prytanis* in this respect (*I.Eph.* Ia, 10 = Knibbe, ibid., D1; *I.Eph.* IV, 1064 = Knibbe, ibid., F3). And a third text of late II AD (*I.Eph.* Ia, 47 = Knibbe, ibid., B54) records the collection of over 6400 *den* taken up by M. Aurelius Menemachus among eighteen former *prytaneis* on behalf of the college when, it appears, it had become insolvent:

ἐπὶ πρυτάνεως Μ. Αὐρ(ηλίου) Μενεμάχου	In the *prytany* of M. Aur(elius) Menemachus
τοῦ καὶ ἀνανεωσαμένου τὸ ἱερὸν συν-	who renewed the sacred college
έδριον τῶν κουρήτων δόντος διανομὰς	of the *kouretes* and also bestowed largesse on it
ὅσας καὶ τῇ γερουσίᾳ [[Κομμοδιανῇ]]	as much as on the Commodeian *gerousia.*
ἐπὶ ἀρχόντων Φίλωνος β´ τοῦ Ἑρμολάου	In the archonship of Philon the son of Philon and grandson of Hermolaos,
φιλοσεβ(άστου) καὶ Ἑρμείας β´ Ἀπολλωνίου ...	friend of the emperor and Hermeias, the son of Hermeias and grandson of Apollonios

Aurelius Menemachus is honoured in another inscription as *prytanis*, asiarch and as the advocate for the guild of the sacred heralds of the *kouretes* (*I.Eph.* IV, 1075 = Knibbe, ibid., D2). The two men officiating on that occasion are designated *archontes* and bear Roman names. It seems to indicate, therefore, that at least by the later part of II AD cult-servers' positions could be filled by men of free status.

The financial decline of the *kouretes* is also reflected in the disappearance of some of the earlier cult positions from the lists and also in the quality of the inscriptions themselves which in early III AD due, no doubt, to a lack of funds for the purchase of suitable material, begin to be engraved on poor stone (Knibbe, ibid., p.91).

The Mysteries of Artemis

Evidence for the nature of the mysteries of Artemis at Ephesus besides that provided by Strabo is scant (see R.E Oster, *ANRW* 18.3 [1990], p.1711 where references are collected). Only in one inscription, that of Favonia Flaccilla quoted above, is the participation of the *kouretes* actually documented. Nevertheless, the mysteries' continued existence throughout the first three centuries AD at Ephesus is attested in several inscriptions. These primarily concern a priestess of Artemis or a *prytanis*.

The two earliest inscriptions belong, possibly, still in I AD, and each records an honorific decree by the Ephesian council and people for a priestess (the two were most probably sisters) ἱερατεύ[σασαν] τῆς Ἀρτέμιδος [ἱεροπρε]πῶς τά τε μυσ[τήρια κ]αὶ τὰς θυσίας [ἀξίως] ἐπιτελέσασαν – 'who was priestess of Artemis in a holy manner and carried out worthily both the mysteries and the sacrifices' (*I.Eph.*III, 987; also 988). And in a third inscription, this time of II AD (*I.Eph.*III, 989), another priestess also speaks of herself ἐκτελέσασαν τὰ μυστήρια – 'having performed the mysteries' – while as late as the third century AD a priestess is able to speak of herself ἀνανεωσαμένην πάντα τὰ μυστήρια τῆς θεοῦ καὶ καταστήσασαν τῷ ἀρχαίῳ ἔθει – 'having revived all the mysteries of the goddess and restored them to the ancient custom' (*I. Eph.* VII.1, 3059). This latter inscription is of particular interest because there is other evidence that in late II AD, during the time of Commodus, cultic practices associated with the mysteries had fallen into disuse. It was only owing to a financial donation of Tiberius Claudius Nicomedes that the regulations, drawn up by Lysimachos (in III BC) regarding the celebration of the mysteries and sacrifices of Artemis and relating to the involvement of the *gerousia*, were restored (*I.Eph.* Ia, 26; Oliver, *Hesperia* VI, no. 12, pp.96-100).

The varying arrangements for maintenance of the mysteries under financial pressure is also suggested by an inscription from early III AD (*I.Eph.* IV, 1069 = Knibbe, ibid., F9) where the *prytanis*, M. Aurelius Agathapous, was assisted in performing his duties by his family: ἐτελείωσε τὰ μυστήρια σὺν καὶ τῇ συμβίῳ αὐτοῦ. . . καὶ τοῖς τέκνοις καὶ ἐκγόνοις <μετὰ> καὶ τῆς εὐσεβοῦς ὑπηρεσίας – 'he performed the mysteries with his wife ... and children and grandchildren together with reverent service'. Because the reference to them is brief, the possibility exists that in some cases the mysteries referred to were not always those associated with the nativity festival of Artemis, but were additional to those of the *kouretes*. However, reference to the *kouretes*, the priestess of Artemis or the *prytanis* may be an indication that it is these mysteries.

Evidence for the celebration of mysteries in the cult of Artemis Ephesia is not confined to Ephesus. An excellently preserved inscription with relief from Pisidia, shortly to be published by G.H.R. Horsley, contains the names of several generations of a local family who initiated the cult and performed the mysteries there.

The Mysteries of Artemis and the Epistle to the Ephesians

The destination of the so-called letter to the Ephesians has long been a matter of discussion. While there is general agreement that it was intended for Christians living in Western Asia Minor, as distinct from Syria for example, any more closely defined recipient has not been identified with certainty. These issues have been canvassed recently by Clinton E. Arnold (*Ephesians: Power and Magic* [Cambridge 1989], pp.5ff) who concludes that there is little within the text itself to justify the title generally used today. He goes on to point out, however, the central place of Ephesus in both the life of Asia and in Paul's ministry, suggesting that owing to this, the letter may well have been sent first to the various churches in Ephesus itself and the nearby villages, although written with a much wider circulation in view and sent to other cities such as Laodicea, Pergamum and Sardis where churches also existed. See also Andrew T. Lincoln, *Ephesians* (Dallas 1990), pp.1-4.

The importance of Ephesian Artemis in religious life throughout the region of Western Asia Minor, in particular as a focus for magical practices (note in this context Acts 19.19 where a large quantity of magical books are destroyed at Ephesus), is also stressed by Arnold. In this sense the cult of Artemis becomes very relevant for understanding the background to the Epistle to the Ephesians although, it is true, there is no specific reference to Artemis or her cult in the text. The constant emphasis on the existence of 'hostile powers' suggests to Arnold that this preoccupation should be seen as a reflection of the religious milieu created by the practices associated with her (ibid., pp.27).

While the notion of μυστήριον in Ephesians generally appears to arise from the writer's Semitic background (see Deut. 2.19), uninfluenced by pagan religion, yet the passage in Eph. 3.9 where the stewardship of the mystery (ἡ οἰκονομία τοῦ μυστηρίου) is referred to may represent an attempt on the part of the author to draw a deliberate contrast between the 'new mystery' (that revealed in the NT) with the Lydian-Phrygian mysteries and to counter their influence within the Christian churches of the area (Arnold, op.cit., pp.126-7, and see the earlier comments by Francis Foulkes, *The Epistle of Paul to the Ephesians* [London 1963], p.51).

There may well be more specific references to Greek mystery cults elsewhere in the NT according to a study of A.E. Harvey (*J.Theol.Stud.* 31 [1980], pp.331-336). He singles out for special discussion οἰκονόμους μυστηρίων θεοῦ (1Cor. 4.1) a parallel passage to that in Eph. 3.9, pointing out that while it is true that the phrase has an almost exact equivalent in a Jewish context, 'it does not follow that the writer did not intend, and the reader did not pick up, some echo of the Greek mystery-metaphor' (ibid., p.331). Harvey's discussions of 1Cor.14.2: οὐδεὶς γὰρ ἀκούει, πνεύματι δὲ λαλεῖ μυστήρια – 'for no-one understands him; he utters mysteries with his spirit' (p.332) and Mark 4.11: ὑμῖν τὸ μυστήριον δέδοται τῆς βασιλείας τοῦ θεοῦ – 'to you is given the mystery of the kingdom of God' (pp. 332-36), follow similar lines. However Bockmuehl (*Revelation and Mystery* [Tübingen 1990], p.224) takes issue with Harvey on the lack of evidence for echoes of Hellenistic mystery metaphors in the Pauline use of μυστήριον and, with respect to 1Cor.14.2, relates the terminology purely to ancient Jewish mysticism (ibid., pp.168-9). And, taking a similar position, Caragounis (*The Ephesian Mysterion. Meaning and Content* [Lund 1977], p.119) observes that of the twenty-eight times the term μυστήριον occurs in the NT, the singular form is almost five times more frequent than the plural whereas in Graeco-Roman cults the word invariably occurs in the plural.

R.A. Kearsley

§30 Ephesus: *Neokoros* of Artemis

Ephesus — AD 211-212 (?)
Ed.pr. — *I. Eph.* III, 647.

A statue base of white marble found in rubble in the street running in front of the auditorium at Ephesus. Dimensions of block 51cm high, 87cm wide and deep (Engelmann & Knibbe, *ÖJh* 52 [1978-80] p.47 where the two texts honouring Androkles, the mythical founder of Ephesus, which appear on two other sides of the same block are published = *I.Eph.* II, 501.) The second καί in *l.*5 must be an error of the mason since in the identical titulature in *I.Eph.*III, 740 it does not appear.

ἀγαθῆι τύχηι
ψηφισαμένης τῆς κρατίστης
βουλῆς καὶ τοῦ ἱερωτάτου δήμου
τῆς πρώτης πασῶν καὶ μεγίστης
καὶ ἐνδοξοτάτης {καὶ} μητροπόλεως τῆς Ἀσίας καὶ νεωκόρου τῆς
[[Ἀρτέμιδος καὶ τρὶς νεωκόρου
τῶν Σεβαστῶν]]
Tib. Cl. Sereṇ[o proc.]
rationis pṛ[ivatae pro-]
vinciae Asiạ[e et Phrygi-]
ae et Cariae, tribuno
cohort. VI civium
Romanorum, praef.
cohortis secundạẹ
Hispaniorum
Severus Augg.nn. verna
exactor praeposito
iustissimo

By God's help.
According to the vote of the most excellent
council and the most holy people
of the foremost of all and greatest
and most highly esteemed metropolis
of Asia and temple-warden of
Artemis and three times temple-warden of the emperors,
to Tiberius Claudius Serenus procurator
of the private account of the province of Asia and Phrygia
and Caria, tribune
of Cohort VI of Roman
citizens, prefect
of the second cohort
of Spaniards.
Severus, house-born slave of our two Augusti,
rent-collector, to his most just chief.

This inscription documents the fact that Ephesus was both *neokoros* of Artemis and three times *neokoros* of the emperors. There is an extensive background to the linking here of the two *neokoriai*, one which throws light on the importance of Artemis to Ephesus and therefore also assists understanding of the incident recorded in Acts 19 when the Ephesians rioted and accused Paul's companions of causing harm to their patron deity.

From the late first century BC temples of a cult of the emperors organised by the provincial assembly of the province of Asia began to be erected. Pergamum was the first city to be honoured by the emperor with permission to build a temple (Dio LI.20.6); Smyrna was the second (Tacitus, *Ann.* IV.55). In the late first century AD, under the Flavian emperors Ephesus too was permitted to build a temple of the cult (D. Knibbe, 'Ephesos vom Beginn der römischen Herrschaft in Kleinasien bis zum Ende der Principatszeit', *ANRW* II, 7.2 [1980], pp.772-3). The construction of such temples was always preceded by a fiercely competitive atmosphere as cities bid against each other for the honour. Sardis and Cyzicus joined the other three cities as the possessors of temples of the provincial imperial cult in the second century and none of the five was content with only one temple but persisted in their attempts to increase this total. The rivalry continued until the first half of the third century after which the imperial cult appears to have declined in vitality.

Ephesus gained its second temple in the reign of Hadrian (D. Knibbe, *ANRW* II, 7.2 [1980], p.785) and inscriptions reveal that by this time the term *neokoros* was embedded within the city's titulature in two forms. Either it was used with direct reference to the name of the city: ἡ πρώτη καὶ με[γί]στη μη[τρό]πολις τῆς Ἀσίας καὶ δὶς [νε]οκόρος τῶν Σεβαστῶν (*I.Eph.* VI, 2039; *I.Eph.* VII.1, 3005 is an example belonging to the Domitianic period); or to the citizens: Ἀρτέμιδι Ἐφεσίᾳ καὶ αὐτοκράτορι Νέρουᾳ Τραιανῶι Καίσαρι Σεβαστῶι Γερμανικῶι Δακικῶι καὶ τῶι νεωκόρωι Ἐφεσίων δήμωι (*I.Eph.* III, 857). This terminology is paralleled in three of the other temple cities as well (*I.Pergamon* VIII.3, 30; *I.Smyrna* II.1, 657, 696; Sardis: *BASOR* 158 [1960], p.8).

It was not until the early third century that the neokorate titulature of Ephesus was expanded to include that of both the imperial cult and of Artemis. This was a development exclusive to Ephesus and due to the emperor Caracalla's decision to respond to Ephesus' request to himself and his brother Geta for further neokorate temples, in an unusual way. He granted the city only one imperial neokorate, in Geta's name, and gave his own to Artemis (*I.Eph.* II, 212, see discussion by L. Robert, *Rev.Phil.* 41 [1967], pp.49-50).

It is exactly this situation which the above inscription represents. However, it was short-lived because with Caracalla's murder of Geta in 212 and the resultant *damnatio memoriae* Ephesus' titulature was reduced to twice *neokoros* of the emperors and once of Artemis: δὶς μὲν τ[ῶ]ν Σεβαστ[ῶ]ν, ἅπα[ξ] δὲ τῆς Ἀρτέμιδος (*I.Eph.*II, 300). It is the *damnatio* which is the explanation for the erasure in *l.*7 of our inscription.

Caracalla's deference to the cult of Artemis is not surprising in view of the copious evidence for the goddess' world-wide veneration. Independent literary and epigraphic evidence confirms that it was no exaggeration on the part of the *grammateus* of Ephesus when he said to the rioting citizens: ἄνδρες Ἐφέσιοι, τίς γάρ ἐστιν ἀνθρώπων ὃς οὐ γινώσκει τὴν Ἐφεσίων πόλιν νεωκόρον οὖσαν τῆς μεγάλης Ἀρτέμιδος ... – 'Men of Ephesus, doesn't all the world know that the city of Ephesus is the guardian of the temple of the great Artemis ...?' (Acts 19.35).

His words are endorsed by Pausanias writing in the middle of the second century: 'All cities worship Artemis of Ephesus and individuals hold her in honour above all the gods. The reason, in my view, is the renown of the Amazons who traditionally dedicated the image, also the extreme antiquity of this sanctuary. Three other points as well have contributed to her renown, the size of the temple, surpassing all buildings among men, the eminence of the city of the Ephesians and the renown of the goddess who dwells there' (4.31.8). Recognition of the importance of Ephesian Artemis in Roman administrative policy in Asia is also well documented from I BC onwards (ibid; and R. Oster, *JbAC* 19 [1976], pp.24-44 for a comprehensive discussion of the cult's economic as well as religious importance in the ancient world). R. Oster, *New Docs* 4 [1987] **§19** contains a list of the possible locations of cults of Artemis Ephesia outside Ephesus.

In an inscription of mid-II (*I.Eph.* Ia, 24 = *New Docs* 4 [1987] **§19**) which records the Ephesian people's attempt to ensure the traditional festivals and sacrifices to Artemis were endorsed by the Roman proconsul, the importance of the cult to the city is illustrated. Artemis is described as the tutelary goddess of Ephesus: [ἡ π]ροεστῶσα τῆς πόλεως (B, *l.*8) and, in the words of the council and people of Ephesus: οὕτω γὰρ ἐπὶ τὸ ἄμεινον τῆς [θεοῦ τιμωμένη]ς ἡ πόλις ἡμ[ῶν ἐ]νδοξοτέρα τε καὶ εὐδ[αιμονεστέρα] εἰς τὸ[ν ἅπα]ντα διαμενεῖ χ[ρόνον] – 'in this way, with the improvement of the honouring of the goddess, our city will remain more illustrious and more blessed for all time' (B, *ll.* 32-34). In other words, the people of Ephesus appear to have believed that their own lives were deeply affected by the degree of reverence accorded Artemis. The Ephesian people identified the city's role in the relationship as that of ἡ τροφὸς τῆς ἰδίας θεοῦ τῆς Ἐφ[εσί]ας – 'the nurturer of its own Ephesian goddess' (B, *l.* 22). An inscription which originally stood in the Artemision at Ephesus and dates to the 4th century BC provides an excellent illustration of the fierce protectiveness felt by the Ephesian people towards Artemis and her cult (*I.Eph.* Ia, 2). The text records the fact that when a sacred embassy, sent from Ephesus to the shrine of Ephesian Artemis at Sardis, was insulted and rites of the cult were violated, it was decided that those who committed the sacrilege should be punished by death.

The process by which the offending Sardians were punished, with formal legal proceedings, a public verdict and publication of the decision on stone, is in strong contrast to what happened to Paul's companions at Ephesus. It perhaps serves to emphasize that the affront to Artemis on that occasion was at a personal level, not a cultic one. The fundamental opposition was economically based (see *New Docs* 4 [1987], p.9. A parallel incident occurs at Philippi: Acts 16.16-22). The secretary of the people, in attempting to calm the crowd, specifically denies any offence against the temple itself or the cult of Artemis (Acts 19.37). A far closer parallel to the way the Christians were treated than the orderly punishment of the Sardians is provided by the account in Acts 21.27-32. After seeing Paul at the temple in Jerusalem some Jews from Asia stirred up a violent mob against him to such an extent that the very Roman intervention which the Ephesian secretary feared (Acts 19.40), did in fact occur (Acts 21.31-33).

Neokoros, the term which later appears in the titulature of the imperial cult, was that which earlier expressed only Ephesus' function as τροφός of Artemis. The relationship is documented as early as the mid-1st century by a coin of Neronian date (*RE* Suppl.12, col. 330) in addition to Acts 19.35. The religious bond between the city and the Artemision overlapped into the civic sphere. Nowhere is this more apparent than in the group of inscriptions recording details of the endowment of Vibius Salutaris in early II (*I.Eph.*Ia, 27, see discussion in *New Docs* 4 [1987] §14 and Guy Rogers, *The Sacred Identity of Ephesus: Foundation Legends of a Roman City* [London 1991]) where city and temple officials are both involved in the distribution of money for the celebration of Artemis' birthday. The frequency and solemnity of the festal days devoted to Artemis (R. Oster, *New Docs* 4 [1987], p.77) also make apparent the tangible impact of the cult on all Ephesian citizens as does the practice of erecting texts of decisions of the Ephesian council and people in the Artemision (see, for example, *I.Eph.* VI, 2004). It was no doubt this close link between city and sanctuary which led to the first element of imperial worship in Ephesus, the Sebasteion, placed within the *temenos* of the Artemision (*I.Eph.* V, 1522) and led to the probable inclusion of the high-priest of the imperial cult as an agent for the monetary distributions of the bequest of Vibius Salutaris also (*I.Eph.* Ia, 27, *l.*259).

Long before the city's role as *neokoros* of Artemis had crystallised, individuals are known with this title. The application of the term *neokoros* of Ephesian Artemis to an individual dates back to the fourth century BC, in both literary and epigraphic sources. In Xenophon's *Anabasis* (5.3.6) it is recorded that Xenophon gave into the charge of 'Megabyzus warden of Artemis' (παρὰ Μεγαβύζῳ τῷ τῆς 'Αρτέμιδος νεωκόρῳ) part of the booty which was ostensibly to be given to Artemis but which he hoped to recover for himself later. An honorary base from the city of Priene (*I.Priene* 231) dated to 334/333 BC also bears the words: [Μεγάβυζος] | Μεγαβύζου | νεωκόρος τῆς |'Αρτέμιδος τῆς | ἐν Ἐφέσωι – 'Megabyzos, son of Megabyzos, warden of Artemis in Ephesus'. However, at least by the later centuries BC the term *neokoros* is recorded over a wide area, including Egypt and Palestine as well as Asia Minor, and in a variety of cults. There is no reason, therefore, to suppose that the term applied *exclusively* to those who served Artemis.

The derivation of *neokoros* is thought to be from κορέω (to sweep) and νεώς (temple) (*MM*, s.v.), hence the assumption that the original meaning and function of a *neokoros* was merely 'temple-sweeper'. If this were the case originally, however, there was an undoubted increase in his importance during the later centuries BC and the imperial period. In the Fourth Mime of Herondas/Herodas(*floruit* 270-60s BC), which is set in the sanctuary of Asklepios on Cos, the *neokoros* of the temple arranges for the offering to be sacrificed and reports afterwards on the good results of it to those making the offering (*ll.* 79-85 Loeb. ed.; on Herondas, see *New Docs* 3 [1983], pp.59-60; also the more recent translation by Ian C. Cunningham [ed.], *Herodas*: *Mimiambi* [Oxford 1971] and the discussion in G. Mastromarco, *The Public of Herondas* [English translation, Amsterdam 1984]). According to Aristeides, *HL* I, 11 (mid II) a *neokoros* was in possession of the keys of the temple of Asklepios at Pergamum.

An undated text from Carian Stratonikeia indicates the *neokoros* was acting as assistant to the priest of Zeus Panamaros: Ἱεροκλῆς Διονυσίου .... προϊερατευκὼς τοῦ μεγίστου θεοῦ Παναμάρου . . . ἐνεω[κόρη]σεν δὲ ἱερῖ Θεοφίλῳ (*I.Stratonikeia* I, 272). At Scepsis in the Troad, regulations for a cult of Dionysos contain the provision: 'He who buys the priesthood ... shall be exempt from ... military service, poll tax, billeting ... in the court necessarily ... and the warden of the temple (*neokoros*) shall have the same exemptions' (Taslikliog̃lu and Frisch, *ZPE* 17 [1975], pp.106-107), thus also indicating the importance of the position relative to the priesthood. Members of elite families in Ephesus at the peak of their public career include the title among the list of their achievements. Tib. Claudius Aristio of late I – early II had been *archiereus* of Asia in the years immediately preceding his post as *neokoros* (*I.Eph.* II, 234-5, 237, 241). After that the title remained among his list of achievements (*I.Eph.* II, 424a; III, 710; VII.1, 3057).

Although the earliest *neokoroi* of Artemis, known by the generic name Megabyzos, were eunuchs (Strabo 4.1.23) there is strong reason to doubt that this requirement, if such it ever was, was extended to the imperial cult as some of those known to have been *neokoroi* were married with families. Both the wife and son of Tib. Claudius Aristio can be identified in inscriptions (see *New Docs* 4 [1987] §14), and another family of important office-bearers at Ephesus, the Pompeii, included the claim to be *neokoroi* as an hereditary right among their honours: νεωκόρου διὰ γένους ναοῦ θεοῦ Οὐεσπασιανοῦ (*I.Eph.* VII, 1, 3038). Five generations of this family are known from Ephesus, the first of which achieved the pinnacle of provincial success by attaining the high priesthood of Asia and the second raising the family to senatorial rank. Other examples of eminent *neokoroi* are found at Smyrna (*I.Smyrna* II, 1, 644) and at Pergamum (*I.Pergamon* VIII, 3, 29; 31).

One further aspect of the ancient evidence for the office of *neokoros* may be noted. Despite the fact that women served the city in public offices such as *prytanis* and priestess of Artemis, and the provincial high priesthood, there is no woman's name among those known to have been *neokoroi*.

R.A. Kearsley

§31 Angels in Asia Minor: The Cult of Hosios and Dikaios

Phrygia, Upper Tembris Valley. After 212
Ed.pr. — A.R.R. Sheppard, 'Pagan Cults of Angels in Roman Asia Minor', *Talanta* 12-13 (1980-81), pp.87-88, no. 8, pl.1.

Within pediment containing radiate head:

Ạὐρ(ήλιος)	Aur(elius) ...

Below figures:

Φιλανγέλων συνβί-	the Association of Friends of the Angels
ωσις Ὁσίῳ Δικέῳ εὐ-	(made) to Holiness and Justice
χήν.	a vow.

A.R.R. Sheppard reports that this is only one of some forty dedications to Hosios and Dikaios, Holiness and Justice, mostly in fragmentary condition, which were recovered at the same spot, perhaps indicating the existence of a sanctuary there.

On the monument, beneath the pediment containing the radiate head, two standing figures are represented in relief in addition to the inscription. On the right, a male with a long staff in his right hand and to the left of him a figure, possibly a woman, who bears in her right hand a pair of scales. The iconography is familiar from other dedications belonging to the Hosios and Dikaios cult. However the reference in the inscription to angels in association with the cult is uncommon among the many texts now known, mainly, from Phrygia and Lydia. In 1981 *TAM* V, 1 (edited by P. Herrmann) also appeared and in it may be found thirteen new or previously published texts of the same cult from various locations in Lydia.

The first indication of angels within the cult emerged from a Lydian text which bears the words Ἀνγέλῳ Ὁσίῳ [Δικ]αίῳ (published in 1958 by L. Robert and reproduced by Sheppard, ibid., no.9 = *TAM* V, 1 [1981], no. 185. See *New Docs* 3 [1983], p.28). When he published the text Robert expressed the belief that it referred to Hosios and Dikaios as a messenger god or intermediary between the human and divine worlds. While the new text from Phrygia now confirms the association of angels with the cult, Sheppard (ibid., p.77) argues instead that angels in the pagan cults of Asia Minor designate a particular type of supernatural being rather than simple messengers of the gods. See, for example, the inscription from Carian Stratonikeia dedicated to [Δ]ιὶ Ὑψίστ[ῳ] καὶ Θείῳ Ἀγγέλῳ (Robert, *OMS* I, p.414) and the two new texts from the same site, published by E. Varinlioğlu (*EA* 12 [1988], pp. 85-6, nos. 7-8 = *I.Stratonikeia* II, 2, 1307-8) dedicated to Διὶ Ὑψίστῳ καὶ Θείῳ Ἀγγέλῳ Οὐρανίῳ. In such cases Θεῖος Ἄγγελος is clearly a separate deity. (See New Docs 5[1989], p.136 and, on the ambiguities associated with *angelos* in inscriptions, ibid., pp.72-3.)

A third stone, published by G. Petzl in 1978 (*Studien zur Religion und Kultur Kleinasiens: Festschrift für F.K. Dörner* [1978], p.757 = *SEG* 28.929; see *New Docs* 5 [1989], p.136), may perhaps contribute to the discussion. The stone is a dedication to the deity Hosios and Dikaios:

Θείῳ Ὁσίῳ καὶ Δικαίῳ	To the Holy and Just Deity,
Γ(άιος) Ἰ(ούλιος) Ἀνείκητος εὐχήν,	Gaius Iulius Anicetus made this as a dedication;
προνοήσαντος Ἀμ-	supervision of its erection was borne
φιλόχου β̄ ἱερέος (sic)	by Amphilochos during his second term as priest.

The text may read alternatively in its last line: Amphilochos, son of Amphilochos, priest.

The stone bears in relief on its upper surface a male figure who resembles Hermes since he is carrying a winged herald's staff in his left hand. The association of such iconography with Hosios and Dikaios would provide confirmation of Robert's interpretation of the role of the angel Hosios and Dikaios as a messenger between the divine and the human world if it could be assumed that the figure on the stone was directly related to the dedicatory inscription. However Petzl (op.cit., pp.758-9) believes it is uncertain whether the figure and the deity to whom the dedication is made are one and the same because of the example of another Lydian stone bearing a similar figure with a herald's staff whose dedicatory inscription is clearly made to a quite separate deity, namely the goddess Μήτηρ Νοτηνή.

Many dedications to Hosios and Dikaios alone are attested (recently published examples in addition to that above include G. Petzl, *ZPE* 30 [1978], p.268, no.14 = *SEG* 28.889; *MAMA* IX [1988], p.24, no.63). Very frequently also, however, Hosios and Dikaios are associated with other deities such as Men (Drew-Bear, *ANRW* II, 7.2 [1980], p.939;

Sheppard, op.cit., p.90); the Rider God with the double axe whose affinity to Helios is sometimes indicated by the radiate crown he wears (Robert, *Hellenica* X, p.104 – relief only; *MAMA* IX, p.25, no.64a [?], p.59 no. 171 – relief only; see too Sayar, *ZPE* 49 [1982] pp.191-2 for relief and inscription); Cybele/the Mother of the Gods (*BSA* 49 [1954], p.12 no.2 – relief only; E. Haspels, *The Highlands of Phrygia*, Vol. I [1971], no. 116); Zeus Bronton (Drew-Bear, *Nouvelles inscriptions de Phrygie*, p.40, no.6 and, for a relief only, L. Robert, *OMS* II, p.1359); Zeus Hypsistos (Drew-Bear, op.cit., p.41 no.8), and Apollo (Drew-Bear, op.cit., p.40, no.7; Robert, *OMS* V, p.724 – relief only; S. Mitchell, *R.E.C.A.M.* II. *The Ankara District. The Inscriptions of North Galatia* [1982], no.44). It is Helios or perhaps radiate Apollo which is likely to be the deity represented in the pediment of the text published by Sheppard and a good comparison for the relief is afforded by a dedication to Hosios and Dikaios from Cotiaeum (*JRS* 15 [1925], p.161, no.150). Hosios and Dikaios also appear as the child, new-born of Herakles (L. Robert, *OMS* I, p.420 referring to an unpublished inscription).

Elsewhere Hosios and Dikaios are associated with 'the One and Only God':

‹Σ›τρατόνεικος Κακολεις τοῦ ἑνὸς
καὶ μόνου θεοῦ ‹ἱ›ερεὺς καὶ τοῦ Ὁ-
σίου καὶ Δικαίου μετὰ τῆς συμβίọụ
Ἀσκληπιαίας εὐξάμενοι περὶ τῶ[ν]
τέκνων εὐχαριστοῦντες ἀνέσ-
τησαν ἔτους τμα'.

Stratoneikos Kakoleis, priest of the one
and only god and of
Hosios and Dikaios with his wife
Asklepiaia having prayed about their
children giving thanks, ded-
icated (this) in the year 256/7.

In their commentary on this inscription from the neighbourhood of Kula in Lydia, Herrmann & Polatkan (*SAWW* 265 [1969], pp.52-3) dismiss the possibility that reference to εἷς θεός constitutes evidence for monotheism in the local cults of Asia Minor. On the basis of an epigraphic study of this and related phrases incorporating μόνος and μέγας by E. Peterson (*Εἷς θεός*, Göttingen, 1926), they argue that it is more likely related to a widely attested terminology of acclamation, such as μέγα τὸ ὄνομα τοῦ θεοῦ, μέγα τὸ ὅσιον, μέγα τὸ ἀγαθόν. Such acclamations, Herrmann and Polatkan point out, emphasize the greatness of a deity and a sense of his uniqueness rather than indicating the existence of a 'single' or 'sole' deity in an exclusive sense. In this inscription, moreover, the formulation suggests that the εἷς καὶ μόνος θεός should probably be considered a separate deity from Hosios and Dikaios. The vagueness of the god's name recalls that of the θεὸς ὕψιστος, a deity widely attested in eastern Lydia (see, for example, the inscription in Robert, *OMS* I, p.411, dated 181/2).

Similarly Sheppard (op.cit., pp.91-92) does not believe that the wording of such inscriptions is evidence of genuine monotheistic belief, but in accordance with his interpretation of angels in the cult as lesser deities rather than messengers, he does view it as evidence of an hierarchical arrangement where one god is proclaimed supreme over others in the Pantheon.

Dedications frequently portray Hosios and Dikaios in human form, as here, with Justice represented by a woman with a pair of scales and Holiness as a man with a staff – which Drew-Bear (*GRBS* [1976], p.263) takes to be a measuring rod or cubit rule. But in the texts the name of the deity takes various forms. Most frequently it is masculine (either singular or plural – *TAM* V, 1, no. 586 – Θεοῖς Ὁσίῳ [καὶ Δικαίῳ]; *OMS* II, pp.1358-60) with, in some texts, Hosios honoured alone (Drew-Bear, *Nouvelles inscriptions* [1978], p.39, no.5; *MAMA* IX, p.25, no. 64), but the neuter form also appears (Petzl, *Dörner Festschrift*, p.758) together with, on occasion, the two virtues united in the single 'Holy and Righteous Divinity' (*MAMA* IX, p.24, no. 63). Sometimes the deity is feminine, Hosia and Dikaia together (Herrmann & Polatkan, op.cit., p.50, no.8; Robert, *Hellenica* X, p.104 [relief only]); or simply Hosia alone (L. Robert, *OMS* V, p.724; Robert, *Hellenica* X, p.106 – relief only). All this suggests to

Sheppard (op.cit., p.91) that Holiness and Justice were only vaguely conceptualized in the Anatolian cult.

Sheppard also believes that the term *angelos* was borrowed from Hellenistic Jewish communities of the area, albeit in a very loose fashion without any real understanding of the monotheistic background of such terms. He points out (op.cit., p.82) that so far there is evidence for at least fourteen organised Jewish communities in western Asia Minor, at cities in the regions of Phrygia, Lydia, Caria and also on the coast, such as Ephesus, Smyrna and Miletus. 'Hosios' and 'Dikaios' are two of the standard attributes of God of the Septuagint, according to Sheppard (op.cit.., 91), some of the inscriptions of the cult contain language which is very reminiscent of Judaism. L. Robert (*OMS* V, pp.724-5) points out elsewhere also that the apparent deification of the virtues of holiness and justice themselves by the use of the neuter forms Hosion and Dikaion (with or without Θεῖον) may be compared to a similar practice among the Jews. In addition, the texts now known mentioning angels in the cult of Hosios and Dikaios, though relatively few, may provide an insight into the cautionary comment of Paul to the Colossians (2.18). Certainly the importance of these virtues is not foreign to the NT either in relation to God or to his followers according to Rev. 16.5: δίκαιος εἶ, ὁ ὢν καὶ ὁ ἦν, ὁ ὅσιος – 'You are just in these judgements, you who are and who were, the holy one'; Eph. 4.24: καὶ ἐνδύσασθαι τὸν καινὸν ἄνθρωπον τὸν κατὰ θεὸν κτισθέντα ἐν δικαιοσύνῃ καὶ ὁσιότητι τῆς ἀληθείας – 'and to put on the new self, created to be like God in true righteousness and holiness'.

Although the cult's concern was frequently a moral one, this is not always so. Alongside the stone bearing the images of Hosios and Dikaios and a confession of perjury by Telesphoros and Hermogenes of the Stallaenoi (see *New Docs* 1 [1981], p.32 = Drew-Bear, *GRBS* [1976] no.17), must be placed another in which the dedication to the same deities is made for the success of a crop – Θελεσφορία τῶν καρπῶν (Drew-Bear, *Nouvelles inscriptions* [1978], p.38, no.3). In an inscription first published by Herrmann (*TAM* V, 1 [1981], no. 598) a request for healing is directed to Hosios and Dikaios: Γλυκία ὑπὲρ ὀφθαλμῶν Ὁσίῳ κ‹α›ὶ Δικαίῳ εὐξαμένη ἀνέθηκα – Glykia on behalf of my eyes vowing to Hosios and Dikaios dedicated (this).

Even greater diversity within the cult of Hosios and Dikaios is indicated by the report of Robert (*Villes d'Asie Mineure,* 2nd ed., 1962, p.387 n. 2) that a dedication from Mysia contains the epithet κριτής (judge) associated with Hosios and Dikaios and that in a second inscription from the region an epitaph bears the words: [Θεῷ Ὁ]σίῳ τε Δικαίῳ χεῖρας ἀεί[ρω] – 'I lift my hands to the God Hosios and Dikaios (for help)' – at the beginning of an imprecation to protect the tomb.

R.A. Kearsley

§32 Acts 14.13: The Temple Just Outside the City

With the publication, posthumously, of Colin J. Hemer's comprehensive study *The Book of Acts in the Setting of Hellenistic History* (Tübingen 1989) questions surrounding the historicity and date of composition of Luke-Acts have once more been brought to the fore. In the context of this discussion the following small item relating to the passage in Acts 14.13 which mentions ὅ τε ἱερέυς τοῦ Διὸς τοῦ ὄντος πρὸ τῆς πόλεως ('the priest of Zeus, whose temple was just outside the city') may be of interest.

New Docs 4 [1987], p.156 cited *I.Ephesos* V, 1595, referring to a priestess who served διὰ βίου τῶν πρὸ πόλεως Δημητριαστῶν καὶ Διονύσου Φλέω μυστῶν (ll.3-6) as a parallel for the terminology in Acts. This inscription is not alone in containing the phrase πρὸ πόλεως and some half-dozen more from other cities in Asia Minor including Smyrna, Thyatira and Aphrodisias are known and listed in the note to *CIG* 2963c. Their testimony surely roots the language of Acts even more firmly within the epigraphic tradition of Asia Minor.

The wording of the phrase in Acts, πρὸ τῆς πόλεως, with the definite article between the preposition and its dependent noun, leaves little doubt that it is the position of Zeus' temple outside the city gate which is being described. Where the phrase is found elsewhere, however, it is not always free of interpretative problems. It has been argued that in some cases the phrase refers not to the location of the deity's sanctuary but to his or her function as patron of the city (L. Robert, *Et. Anat.*, p.25).

Where the phrase contains the definite article (πρὸ τῆς πόλεως) it clearly refers to the location of the deity's sanctuary or temple. If, however, the article is absent (πρὸ πόλεως), either meaning seems possible.

In his discussion of two inscriptions from Ephesus Robert (*BE* 1977, 420) drew attention to some apparent examples of the second meaning of the phrase. In *I.Eph.* II, 276, which contains the words: οἱ τὸν [χρύ]σεον κόσμον βαστά[ζον]τες τῆς μεγάλης θεᾶς ['Αρτέ]μιδος πρὸ πόλεως ἱερεῖς [καὶ] ἱερονεῖκαι; and in *I.Eph.* III, 650, where a certain Claudius Tuendianus is described as: ὁ πρύτανις καὶ ἀγωνοθέτης τῶν πρὸ πόλεως ἱερέων καὶ ἱερονεικῶν, Robert concluded that in neither of these inscriptions did the phrase refer to a location. On the contrary, in them, πρὸ πόλεως was being used in the manner of an additional title of Artemis, or, in *I.Eph.* III, 650, of her priests.

The question arises therefore whether *I.Eph.* V, 1595 indeed offers a parallel for the NT passage for in it the definite article is not included, thus leaving open the possibility that the phrase is being used in the second sense. However, the indisputable fact that Artemis alone was the patron deity of Ephesus makes it unlikely that Demeter and Dionysos Phleus could be so described in *I.Eph.*V, 1595. The purpose of πρὸ πόλεως in the text must be to signify the location of the cult of those two deities (see the discussion by J. & L. Robert in *Fouilles d'Amyzon en Carie*, vol.I. [Paris 1983], pp.171-72). An identical dual use of the phrase has already been observed among the inscriptions of Thyatira (Robert, *Hellenica* VI, p.79).

R.A. Kearsley

APPENDIX

i) Statistical Tables to *New Docs* 6 (1992) §10

Conclusions **6** to **10** in *New Docs* 6 (1992) **§10** were derived by a log-linear modelling of the count data of Tables 10.1 and 10.2. On log-linear modelling see S.E. Fienberg, *The Analysis of Cross-Classified Categorical Data* (Cambridge, Mass. 1980) or A. Agresti, *Analysis of Ordinal Categorical Data* (New York 1984). Likelihood-ratio statistics (G^2), degrees of freedom (d.f.) and probabilities (p-values) for all possible models of Table 10.1 are given below.

Likelihood-ratio statistics for Table 10.1
[1] sex; [2] age; [3] period

Model	G^2	d.f.	p value
[1][2][3]	79.50	10	0.0000
[23][1]	9.12	7	0.2442
[13][2]	75.07	7	0.0000
[12][3]	78.23	9	0.0000
[12][13]	73.80	6	0.0000
[12][23]	7.85	6	0.2493
[13][23]	4.68	4	0.3217
[13][12][23]	2.56	3	0.4646

For Table 10.1 at the 0.05 level of significance the preferred model is [23][1], i.e. **age** and **period** are conditionally dependent given sex but sex is conditionally independent of both age and **period**. The model permits an analysis of the association between any two variables by collapsing the data over the remaining variable.

The adjusted residuals for the **age** by **period** marginal table are given below. If the absolute value of the adjusted residual is greater than 1.96, then its cell shows a significant difference between observation and theory.

Adjusted residuals: age by period marginal table

	Period (BC)			
Age	201 – 153	153 – 100	100 – 53	53 – 1
Adult	6.41	- 0.07	- 5.47	- 5.83
Child	- 6.41	0.07	5.47	5.83

Likelihood-ratio statistics (G^2), degrees of freedom (d.f.) and probabilities (p-values) for all possible models of Table 10.2 are given below.

Likelihood-ratio statistics for Table 10.2
[1] sex; [2] type of release; [3] period

Model	G^2	d.f.	p value
[1][2][3]	28.27	10	0.0016
[23][1]	5.99	7	0.5409
[13][2]	26.06	7	0.0005
[12][3]	27.76	9	0.0011
[12][13]	25.55	6	0.0003
[12][23]	5.48	6	0.4839
[13][23]	3.77	4	0.4380
[13][12][23]	2.96	3	0.3978

For Table 10.2 at the 0.05 level of significance the preferred model is [23][1], i.e. **type of release** and **period** are conditionally dependent given **sex** but **sex** is conditionally independent of both **type of release** and **period**. The model permits an analysis of the association between any two variables by collapsing the data over the remaining variable.

The adjusted residuals for the **type of release** by **period** marginal table are given below. If the absolute value of the adjusted residual is greater than 1.96, then its cell shows a significant difference between observation and theory.

Adjusted residuals: type of release by period marginal table

	Period (BC)			
Type of release	201 - 153	153 - 100	100 - 53	53 - 1
Unconditional	- 0.72	3.07	0.36	- 4.35
Conditional	0.72	- 3.07	- 0.36	4.35

ii) Statistical Tables to *New Docs* 6 (1992) §17

Likelihood-ratio statistics (G^2), degrees of freedom (d.f.) and probabilities (p-values) for all possible models are given below. Account has be taken for the presence of structural zeros in Table 17.1.

Likelihood-ratio statistics for Table 17.1
[1] region; [2] source; [3] marriage

Model	G^2	d.f.	p value
[1][2][3]	5.86	2	0.0534
[23][1]	5.55	1	0.0185
[13][2]	0.23	1	0.6315
[12][3]	5.86	2	0.0534
[12][13]	0.23	1	0.6315
[12][23]	5.55	1	0.0185
[13][23]	0.00	0	-
[13][12][23]	0.00	0	-

For Table 17.1 at the 0.05 level of significance the preferred model is [13][2], i.e. **region** and **marriage** are conditionally dependent given **source** but **source** is conditionally independent of both **region** and **marriage**. Since the p value of G^2([1][2][3]|[13][2]), i.e. 5.63 for one degree of freedom, is 0.0177, [1][2][3] is not the preferred model. The model permits an analysis of the association between any two variables by collapsing the data over the remaining variable.

INDEXES

SUBJECTS

Aberkios **177-181**
Absenteeism n.75
Acts of God **82-86**
Addressees of Paul's letters n.165
Administration of Palestine
  Census **123**
  Reintegration edicts **118-119**
  Sources of influence **91-92**
  The Herods **99**
  The Ptolemies **100-104**
  Toparchies **129**
Agoranomion **39, 42**
Agoranomos **42, 66, 107**
Allotment after death **27-39**
  Relation to testament **38-39**
  Homologia **32-33, 38**
  Formal structure n.34
  Jewish adaptation of **36-38**
  Jewish practice **43-47**
  Obligations and charges **31**
  Ownership of property **33-36**
  Parable of the wicked tenants n.49
  Revocability of **32-36, 43,** n.39
  Right of usufruct **31**
Amulet
  Magical **192-196**
Anakrisis n.61
Antoninus Pius **148**
Archelaus **128**
Archisomatophylax **167**
Artemis of Ephesus **196-201, 203-206**
Augustus **149**
Auxilia n.173
Avircius Marcellus **181**
Baienus Blastianus **113**
Bonded labour **51**
Burial and the collegium funeraticium n.62
Caracalla **117, 118**
Census **31, 119**
  Census period **121**
  Dates of edicts n.137
  Declaration as proof of status **137**
  Duration in Egypt **136**
  Form of declaration **120-121**
  Fouteen-year cycle (Egypt) **121**
  Idia **125-126, 127**
  In Herod's kingdom **129**
  In Judaea by tribe? **127-129**
  Luke's dating of Jesus' birth **123**
  Official use of declarations **121-122**
  Personal details n.131
  Personal presence at lodgement **126-130**
  Persons lodging a declaration **3, 124-125**
  Place of declaration's lodgement **124-130**
  Proof of registration n.136
Census (continued)
  Roman administrative structures **127-129**
  Six-year cycle (Herod) **129**
  Twelve-year cycle (Syria) **127**
  Types of declarations n.127, n.129
Census-motif
  Gospel of Luke n.153
Cheirographon **11, 61, 62, 63, 105-111, 115, 189**
Christian Households
  Ownership of slaves **54-55**
Claudius **51, 148, 153**
Claudius Lysias **152-154**
Cohabitation
  Jewish practice n.32
Collocation
  As indicator of belief **174-177**
Confessional texts **192**
Contractual friendship **173**
Copying an exemplum **49-50**
Corruption n.177
Court titles **167**
Crossing
  Of letters **172-173**
  Of loan documents **107-110**
Dative
  For duration of time **62**
Delphi
  Sacral manumission **72-76, 79-81**
Deutero-Pauline letters **22**
Diadochos **167**
Diagraphe **5-6, 11,** n.8
Διαθήκη in LXX and NT **43**
Diploma **48**
Dismission **37**
Divorce
  Deeds of divorce **6**
  Initiating divorce **15-16,** n.25
Divus n.155
Documentary evidence
  Bias in data **143**
Domestic code or Haustafel **18-19**
Doric dialect **23**
Dowry **1-18,** n.38
  LXX n.16
  Metaphor fo n.30
  Παράφερνα **4-5**
  Προίξ to Φερνή **2-4**
  Προσφορά **4**
  Provision of **2, 10**
  Return of **2-3, 13**
  Roman practice n.6
  To regulate marriage **3-4**
Ellipsis **67-69, 132**
Ephebe **145**

Ephesians
Epistle to **201-202**
Epikrisis **126, 132-140, 145,** n.162
Education **136**
Form of **135**
Military epikrisis n.162
Proof of ancestry **136-139**
Taxation **136**
Epistrategos **142, 144,** n.160
Eschatology
And celibacy **16-17**
And slavery **54, 55**
Exegetes **142**
Freedman
Jewish n.31
Lex Junia **51,** n.168
Junian Latinity **151-152**
Freedom
Four types of **62**
Gabinius **129**
Genitive absolute **132**
Gnomon of the Idios Logos **39, 107**
Gnosticism (?) n.65
Goliath **162-164**
Grant of citizenship n.163
Grapheion **7, 61, 110, 127**
Greek ethical tradition **18**
Gymnasium class **136-139**
Hadrian **148, 149**
Herod **42, 99, 129, 130**
Herod Antipas **99**
High-priestess of Asia **25-27**
Holiness and Justice **206-209**
Homologia **32, 38**
Hosios and Dikaios **206-209**
Hypographe **107**
Ḥazaqah **37, 95-98, 105,** n.106, n.112
Date of **97-98**
Illiteracy **30**
Impressed labour n.196
Influences on legal systems
Disposition of property **32-33, 36-38**
Marriage **4, 6-9, 12-14**
Inheritance **27**
NT metaphor **39**
Roman law and custom **39-40**
Heir **38-39**
Iunia Theodora **24-25**
Jewish gifts in contemplation of death **36-38,** n.107
Jewish knowledge of ancestry **128**
Judaea
Hellenization **164**
Judaism
Influences on **36-38, 91-92**
Law of inheritance **32, 45**
Marriage **12-14**
Koine paraphrase **23**
Kouretes **196-201**
Labour contracts – see paramone
Language
Christian **85, 174-177**
Nature of metaphor **40, 43, 53**
Leases
Duration of n.108
Leasing
Agricultural land **86-105**
Duration of agricultural leases **89**
Duty of care (Egypt) **89**
Duty of care (Palestine) **89-90**
Maritime **82-85**
New vineyards **96**
Letters
Christian **169-177**
Crossing and sealing **172-173**
Filial respect **157**
Identification as Christian **173-177**
Lex collegii funeraticii Lanuvini n.62
Loans **105-111**
Cancellation of **107-109**
Interest rate **107**
Paramone **61**
Log-linear modelling **211**
Luke's dating of Jesus' birth **31, 118-119, 123**
Manumission **63-70** (see also paramone)
1Cor.7.21 **67-70**
Analysis of data **73-75**
Christian slaves **55**
Cost of **66, 74**
Delphi **52, 72-76, 79-81**
Economic effects of **80**
Exploitation of **50, 66, 80-81**
Formal and informal n.168
Jewish practice **37, 66**
Origins of sacral manumission **73**
Patrons **79**
Proportions of sexes released **79-81**
Sacral manumission **70-76**
'Slave of god' (Delphi) **72-73**
'Slave of God' (Paul) **75-76**
Slave's patronym **79**
Tax on **66**
Thessaly **76-81**
Under Zeus, Earth and Sun **66**
Marriage **1-18**
Vows n.21
As agreement **12, 14**
Bride's guardian **5, 15**
Celibacy **16-17**
Consanguinity **137**
Egyptian marriage **6-9**
In Roman period **4-6**
Jewish (kethubah) **12-18**
Jewish terminology **13-14**
Lex Minicia **17**
Maintenance of widow **2, 13, 31,** n.37
Marital duties **3-4, 14-15**
Ownership of property in **3-4, 10, 13**
Roman law **4, 14, 15, 16, 17**
Social function **2-4, 8, 18**

Marriage (continued)
Unwritten marriage **4, 16, 18**
Virtue in a woman **18-19**
Metropolites n.161
Midrash **18**
Monks
Orthodoxy **182-185**
Ownership of property **182-189**
Mortgage n.100
Municipal magistracy n.157
Mysteries of Artemis **196-201**
Nag Hammadi library
Ownership of **182-185**
Name
As indicator of status **62, 149-152**
Neokoros of Artemis **203-206**
Nero **113**
Notification of birth **122-123**
As proof of status **122, 137-139**
Notification of death **122**
Official corruption n.114
Oikonomia **19**
Oil for anointing **191**
Ordinal adjectives **132**
Orthography **61-62**
Parable and allegory
Definition **92-93**
Parable of the wicked tenants **93-105**
Paramone **60-63, 66**
At Delphi **74, 75, 80-81**
Loans without interest n.71
Prepayment for services **61**
Release from **61**
Services unspecified **61**
Slave of God in Paul **75**
Paratactic καί n.105
Paul **53**
Advice on marriage **14-18**
Attitude to slavery **53-55, 59-60**
Evaluation of status **139-140**
κατὰ ἄνθρωπον **44-45**
Letter to Philemon **54**
Manumission **70**
Metaphor of inheritance **39**
Metaphor of the testament **42-47**
Roman citizenship **39, 41, 154-155**
Slave of God **75-76**
Paul and Seneca n.64
Petitions **96, 99**
Form of **140-141**
Pretence n.66
Social history **140-146**
Addressees of **143**
Threats and appeal to pity **142-143**
Verbs of **145-146**
Plurality of laws n.11
Poll-tax
Variations in n.156
Possession and ownership **33-36, 37, 43-44**
Prefect n.160
Priestesses in Roman Egypt n.77
(see also under High-priestess of Asia)
Propraktikon **66**
Proselyte
Jewish n.31
Prostatis **24-25**
Prozbol **92,** n.100
Pseudepigraphy **19, 22**
Publication of decrees **110-111, 115**
(Neo-) Pythagorean letters **19**
Quirinius **31, 123, 124, 127, 130, 131**
Qumran
Administrative organisation of n.147
Receipts **107-109**
Reciprocal obligation n.176
Reintegration edicts **115-119**
Right of execution **90-92**
Egypt **90-91**
Palestine **91-92**
Self-help **91-92, 98-104**
Roman administration
Perception of **141-142, 145**
Roman testaments n.52
Root fallacy **114**
Rounding of ages **30-31**
Runaway slaves **55-60**
Apprehension of **57**
Assistance of **56**
Destinations of flight **58**
Master's reputation **58, 60**
Need to explain flight **59-60**
Paul's letter to Philemon **59-60**
Response of masters **57-60**
Theft of property **58, 59**
School exercises **23**
Self-help in Graeco-Roman Egypt n.115
Sempronius Liberalis **117**
Septimius Severus **117, 148**
Shipping contracts **82-86**
Duration of leases **83**
Limitation of liability **83-85**
Singular and plural
First and second person **170-172**
Slavery (see also slaves)
Moral dilemma of **53, 54, 59**
NT attitude to **53-55**
NT metaphor of **53**
Stoic attitude to **52-53**
Slaves (see also manumission and paramone)
In Christian housholds **54-55, 70**
Compliance of **57-58**
Discipline and coercion **50, 54**
Discontent of **51-52, 55**
Familial relationships **50, 79, 188**
Fictitious sale of **72**
Funerary inscriptions **51-52**
Joint ownership of **79**
Legal capacity of **50, 66**
Legislation improving lot **51**
Lot of slaves **50-52**

Slaves (continued)
- Management slaves **51**
- Manumission of **186-189**
- Murder of master n.67
- Names of n.72
- Origins of **58**
- Paramone n.69
- Permit of movement **60-63**
- Prisoners of war n.63
- Rebellion n.67
- Relationship to master **58**
- Runaways **101-104**
  - see also runaway slaves
- Sale of **48, 53**
- Slave of God (Delphi) **72-73**
- Slave of God (Paul) **75-76**
- State slaves **79**
- Taxes on n.141
- Terminus technicus σῶμα n.94

Soldiers
- Claudius' reform **148**
- Discharge **147-148**
- Epikrisis **135, 148**
- Expenses (clothing) **158-159**
- Grant of citizenship n.171
- Jerusalem garrison **159-161**
- Jewish **167**
- Letters **156-159**
- Marriage and family **148-149, 152-153**
- Pay **157-158**
- Settlement on retirement **152-153**
- Size of units **159-161**
- Status advancement of **153-154**
- Taktomisthoi **167**
- Tax exemption **147-148**

Souchos **71**

Status
- Epikrisis **132-139**
- Freedmen **151-152**
- Indicated by name **149-152**
- Notification of birth **122**
- Paul **139-140**
- Petitioners **143**
- Role of marriage **18**
- Soldiers **149, 152-154**
- Titles **175-177**

Stoicism
- Attitude to slavery **52-53**

Storms at sea **85-86**

Strategos **42, 56, 113, 114, 116, 129, 141, 142**

Subatianus Aquila **117, 118**

Syngraphe **107**

Taxation
- Absenteeism **112-119**
- Abuses **144-145**
- Ages of liability to **121**
- Assessment of **113-115**
- Cancellation of **114**
- Census declarations **121-122, 124**

Taxation (continued)
- Epikrisis **136**
- Exemption of veterans **147-148**
- Herod **129**
- Idia **113**
- Judaea **129**
- Lists **126, 136**
- On manumission **66**
- Notification of birth **122-123, 137-139**
- Notification of death **122**

Tiberius **31**

Titles n.178
- Brother **175-177**
- Father **177**
- Master **175-177**
- Mother **177**
- Sister **177**

Trajan **148**

Twelve tables of Roman law **111**

Tyrannus **197-198**

Usufruct **31, 33-37, 43, 46**

Valerius Datus **117, 118**

Vibius Maximus **115-119, 126**

Vineyards **167**

Vows n.21

Wife
- As property n.18

Wills **38-39**
- Annulment by others **42**
- Annulment of **41-47**
- Conditions and regulations **39**
- Jewish legal instruments **43-46**
- Paul's metaphor **42-47**
- Ways to revoke **42**

Wine
- Medicinal use **190-191**

Women authors **19-22**

Women in public life **24-27**

Work contracts **95, 164-167**
- See also paramone

Zenon **98-105**

WORDS

Greek

ἀγαθός 157
ἀγαπητος ἀδελφός 175
ἀγράφως συνεῖναι 4
ἀγώγιμος 8
ἀδελφός 175, 177
ἀθετει 43
ἄμφοδον 125
ἄξιος 157
ἀξιῶ 141, 145
ἀναγράφειν 107
ἀναχώρησις 113, 126, n.75, n.119
ἀνακεχωρηκότες 113, n.139
(ὁ ἔσω) ἄνθρωπος 53
ἀντίρρησις 90
ἀπεδήμησεν n.102
ἀπέχειν 3
ἀποδίδωμι 3, 157, n.176
ἀπόλυσις 61
ἀπόλυσις n.69
ἀποπομπή 11
ἄποροι 113-114, n.139
ἄρχοντες 99
ἄρχων 92
ἀφαίρεσις n.25
βιάζεται 98
βία n.113
βία θεοῦ 82-86
βιβλιοθήκη ἐγκτήσεων 9
βλάβης δίκη 90
δάνειον 6
δεδανεικέναι 7
δεξιολάβοι 160, n.181
δέομαι 141, 145-146
δεσπότης 175-177
δημοσία βιβλιοθήκη 121
δημόσιος χρηματισμός 107
διαγράμματα 90
διαθήκη 37, 38-39, 41-47, n.51, n.60
διαστολικόν 90
δική 90
διπλώματα 48
δόγμασιν 110-111
δόμα n.16
δοῦλος Χριστοῦ 75
δωδεκάδραχμος 138
ἔγγραφος γάμος n.25
ἐγδεδομένη 10
εἰ (direct question) 183
εἰ καί 69
εἰκονίζειν 127
εἰκονισμός 127, n.146
εἰς 157-158
ἐκδιδόναι 15
ἐκδόσιμον 39
ἔκδοσις n.10
ἐκουσία ἀπαλλαγή 11
ἐκουσίως 10-11
ἐκτίθημι 110
ἑλληνικῷ νόμῳ n.27
ἐμβαδεία 90
ἔνδειξιν 115
ἐνεχυρασία 90
ἐξέτασις 121
ἐξουσιάζω n.22
ἐξουσία n.74
ἔπαρχος 160
ἐπιδιατάσσεται 43
ἐπίκρισις 132, 139, n.127, n.146
ἔργα ἀγαθά 19
ἐργάζεσθε ὡς τῷ Κυρίῳ 19
ἐρωτῶ 145
εὐκοσμία τῆς ψυχῆς 18
εὑρεθησομένου 166
εὑρίσκω 183
εὐταξία 19
εὐτύχει. 141
ἐφέστιον n.122, n.123
θεός (= divus) n.155
(τὸν παντοκράτορα) θεόν 175
ἰδία 113-114, 115-119, 125-126, 127, n.122, n.123
ἱερός 72
ἱκονισθέντες 126
καθάπερ ἐκ δίκης 91
καλοκαγαθία 19
καλῶς ἄν ποιήσαις 104
κατὰ ἄνθρωπον 44-46, n.56, n.57
καταγραφη 90
κατ' οἰκίαν ἀπογραφή 119
κληρονόμος n.49
κόλλημα 9, 121, n.13
κοράσιον 49, 61-62
κρίτης 92
κύριος 2, 15, 34, n.9, n.143
κεκυρωμένην 43
κύριος ἀδελφός n.193
κύριος πατήρ n.193
κωμάρχης 129
κωμογραμματεύς 129
λαογραφία n.156
λεύκωμα 115
λοιποῖς 16
μᾶλλον 69-70
μεμερικέναι ... μετά 32
μερισμός 113-115, n.139
μεριτεία 34
μετάβασις 125-126
μισθοπρασία 83
μισθός n.71
νεανίσκος 100
νόμοι 90, n.27
νοῦς 53
οἱ χωρὶς οἰκοῦντες 63
οἶκος 2
ὁμολογεῖ n.50
ὁμολογία 32
ὁμόνοια 173-174, n.190
ὅμως n.55
οὐδείς 46
πάλιν 98
παράδειξις 90
παρακαλῶ 145
παραμονή 60-63, n.69
παράφερνα 3, 4-5
Πέρσης τῆς ἐπιγονῆς 7, 9, n.12
πόλις 2
πορνεία 16
πράκτωρ ξενικῶν 90
πρᾶξις 90-92
πρό 157
προαίρεσις n.189
προέθετο 115
προίξ 2, n.2, n.38
πρός 10, 157-158
προσβολή 90, 92
πρόσδοσις 8
προσηλῶσαι n.118
προστάγματα 90
προσφορά 4
προτίθημι 110
πρωτοπραξία 4, 13
πρῶτος – πρότερος 130
ῥάχος 166
σάρξ 53
σταυρός 109
στέρεσθαι 3
στρατηγός 129
συγχώρημα 35
συγγραφη 34
συγγραφη τροφῖτις 6-9
σωφροσύνη 18
τελειοῦσθαι κατ' ἀρετήν 18
τιμιώτατος 157
τόμος 121, n.13

τοπάρχης **129**
τοπογραμματεύς **129**
ὑπέρθεσις **114**
ὑποθήκη n.100
ὑπόμνημα ἐπιγεννήσεως **122, 137**
ὑποτασσόμενοι ἀλλήλοις **19**
φερνή **1-18**, n.2, n.16
φιλαλληλία **173-174**, n.190
φιλοκαλεῖν **19**
χάρις **157**
χιάζειν **108, 109**
  κεχιασμένην **173**
χιλίαρχος **160**, n.180
χώρα **118, 137**

Latin

album **115**
annona **83**
auxilia **149, 159-161**
avaritia **58**
beneficium abstinendi n.52
cives Romani **127**
cohors equitata **160**
cohors equitata milliaria **160**
collegium funeraticium n.62
conubium **17, 148**
corpus **53**
cum manu n.20, n.24
diploma **147**
divus (= θεός) **122**, n.155
donatio mortis causa n.52
fideicommissum n.52
fiscus **83, 113, 118**
heres n.52
institutio heredis n.52
interior pars **53**
ius civile **40**, n.52
ius praetorium **40**, n.52
iustum matrimonium **17**
manumissio inter amicos; per epistulam; censu; testamento; vindicta n.168
mens **53**
militia secunda **154**
milliaria **159-161**
missio **147**
modus n.52
nemo est heres viventis **40**
nomina sacra **175**
paterfamilias **14, 15, 40**, n.24
peculium **50, 66**
persona **40**
potestas **14, 15**, n.22, n.24
praefectus **160**
praefectus alae **118**
quingenaria **159-161**
receptum nautae **83**
sacra **40**
saevitia **58**
senatus consulta **110-111**
stipendium **157**
successor in locum defuncti **40**, n.52
sui heredes **40**
sui iuris **14, 15**
tria nomina **149-151, 154**
tribunus militum **160**
turma **159**
tutor **14, 15**
vis maior **83**

Hebrew

ארוסין n.33
בית דין **92**
בעל **13**, n.18
ברית **14**
דיאתיקי **37, 43**
חליצה **12**
חקוה **95-98**
כתובה **12-18**, n.3
מהר **12**, n.16
מהיום ולאחר מיתה **33**
מכר **13**
מלוג **13**
משלים **105**
מתנת בריא **37, 43-47**
מתנת שכיב מרע **37, 45**
נשואין n.33
עם הארץ **128**
פורנא **12**
פרוזבול **92**
צאן ברזל **13**
קדש **14, 18**
קל וחומר **69**
קנה **13**, n.22
שלחים n.16
שלימן למלקח לך **91**

GREEK AND LATIN WRITERS

Aelian, *De nat.anim.* 8.12 **131**
Aelius Aristides, *Pan. in Kyz.* 240 n.57
Anon., *In ethica Nicomachea* 54 n.57
Appian, *Illyr.* 30.88 n.74
Aristeides, *HL* I 11 **206**
Athanasius, *Contra Arian* 51.4 **176**
Contra Sab. 28.112 n.57
Athenaeus, *Deipn.* 4.19 **157**
4.630c **131, 132**
Basil, *Epist.* 363, 364 **176**
Carta Senonica 1 **188**
Cicero, *Ad fam.* 13.77.3 **58**
Democritus **174**
Demosthenes, *In Tim.* 202 **69**
Digest 4.9.3.1 **83**
11.3.1.5 **56**
19.2.15.1, 19.2.25.6 **83**
19.2.25.6 **85**
19.5.17.4 **83**
48.15.6.2 **56**
50.15.3 **127**
Dio Cassius, *Hist. Rom.* 46.25.2 **69**
51.20.6 **203**
59.1 **42**
60.17 **154**
62.4.3 **69**
67.3.5 **157**
68.25.5 n.57
69.9 **149**
Dion. Hal., *Antiq. Rom.*9.17.1 **157**
9.36.2 **157**
9.59.4 **157**
Diod. Sic., *Hist.* 1.42.1 **131**
11.25.1 **111**
12.26.1 **111**
12.70.5 **111**
13.19.3 **111**
Eusebius, *Hist.Eccl.* 3.20 **130**
5.16.3 **181**
Eusebius, *De incarn.* 1013 n.57
Formula Bituricensis 9 **188**
Formula extravagans 18 **188**
G. Giannelli, Vat. gr. 1554, f.100 **188**
Galen, *In Hipp.* 18b.315 n.57
Herodian 1.3.1 n.74
3.8.5 **148**
Herondas/Herodas, Fourth Mime **206**
Herodotus 4.84 **190**
Homer, *Il.* 13.502 **131**
18.92 **131**
2. 617-670 **23**
4.349-363 **23**
Ignatius, *Epist.* 3.2.1 n.57
Isocrates, *Aegin.*12, 15 **42**
Busiris 48 **69**
De pace 1 **69**
John Chrystostom, *Hom.18.4 in Ac.* n.30
Josephus *AJ* 13.10.5.292 n.172
14.197-8 **111**
16.9-10 **91**
17.195, 202 **42**
18.3 **128**
20.135 **163**
20.251 **128**
20.6.2.132 n.180
BJ 1.669 **42**
2.12.6.244 n.180
2.273 **91**
2.405 **128**
2.427 n.109
2.571 **99**
3.359 **69**
3.67 n.180
Vita 1-6 **128, 139**
Lucian, *Syr.D.*60.12 **111**
M. Aurelius, *Med.* 9.3.1 n.57
Manetho, *Apotel.* 1.329-30 **131**
Melissa **18-23**
Methodius, *Symp.*6.5 n.30
Pausanias **204**
Philo, *De spec. leg.* 2.5 **66**
Leg. ad Cai. 4.26, 8.54 n.74
Leg. ad Cai. 23.155 n.172
Virt. 217 n.57
Plato, *Leg.* 922 **42**
Pliny, *Epist.* 2.4 n.52
8.14 n.67
9.21 **60**
Plutarch, *Cato Minor* 18 **131**
Plutarch, *Lyc.*12.2, 82.222 **157**
Polyb., *Hist.*1.72.6, 5.89.4 **157**
Quintilian, *Inst. Or.* 10.5.4-11 **23**
*Script.Hist.Aug., Had.*10 **149**
Seneca
De clem. 1.26.1 n.67
Epist. 107.1 **58**
Strabo, *Geog.* 4.1.23 **206**
6.4.2 n.74
14.1.20 **196**
14.1.23 **197**
Suetonius, *Dom.* 7.3 **157**
Tacitus, *Ann.* 1.17.6 n.177
4.55 **203**
13.32.1 n.67
14.42-45 n.67
Tertullian, *Adv.Marc.* 4.19.10 n.152
Xenophon, *Anabasis* 5.3.6 **205**
Hell. 3.3.1 n.57

PAPYRI AND OSTRACA

Aramaic Papyri
15 **13**, n.26
10 **91**
BGU I 86 **31, 35-36**, n.45, 50
I 140 **148**
I 159 **117, 118**
I 168 **141**
I 183 **35**, n.39, n.45, n.50
I 251 **35**, n.39, n.45, n.50
I 252 n.50
II 372 **114, 117**
II 562 **127**
III 719 **35**, n.39, n.50
III 887 **48, 49**
III 903 **114**
III 913 **62**
III 993 **33**, n.39, n.44, n.50
III 994 **33**
IV 1050 **3**
IV 1098 n.50
IV 1122 **167**
IV 1126 **61**
IV 1153, 1154 **61**
IV 1157 **83**
V 1210 **39, 107**
IX 1896 n.184
VIII 1836 **142**
XII 2133 **11**
XIII 2245 **11**
XIV 2376 **90**
XIV 2381 **167**
XV 2472-3 **90**
XV 2475 **127**
XV 2476 **34**
Brooklyn Aramaic Papyri
2 **13**, n.26
7 **13**
CPJ 128 **15** 6 n.116
CPR I 27 **10**
I 28 n.50
V 19 **157**
V 23 **176**
VII 20 n.46
DJD II 18 **92**, 18 n.100
19 **14, 16, 17**, n.28
20 **14, 15**, n.27
24 **90**
114, 115 **92**
116 **13**
MChr 289 **10**
306 n.45
312 n.50
341 n.96
P. Abinn. 4, 5, 9-15, 17, 18, 33, 43, n.193
30 **176**
32 **176**, n.193
P. Amst. 32b **122**
40 **1, 9-11, 158**, n.13
P. Ant. I 42 **166**
II 92 **176, 177**
II 95 **176**
P. Berl. Zilliacus 6 n.189
P. Berl.Leihg. 7 **113**
16 **125**, n.145
*P. Berol. inv.*16546 (*Am. Stud. Pap.* XXIII) **140-143**
P. Bibl.Univ.Giss. inv. 311 **42**, n.53
P. *BM* 10591 recto X n.42
P. Bon. 21 **57**
24 n.184
P. Cair. Isidor. 4, 5 **30**
P. Cair. Preis. 42 **34**, n.39
P. Cattaoui II (= SB I 4284) **117**
P. Coll. Youtie II **2**
P. Colon. XII **12, 15**
P. Cornell 16 **125**
P. Diog. 11-12 **31**, n.39, n.44, n.50
P. Dura 20 **61**
30 **2**
P. Fam. Tebt. 7 and 10 **31**
P. Fay. 20 **111**
24 **117**
105 **158**
P. Flor. 6 **117, 118**
44 **61**
61 and 65 **108**
P. Fouad 26 **101**
35 **166**
P. Gen. 16 **117, 118**
116 n.184
P. Gen. lat. 1 **158**
4 **157**
P. Giss. I 2 **2**
II 40 col. ii **117, 118**
P. Graux 2 **142**
P. Grenf. II 43 **158**
P. Gron. 10 **34**, n.39
P. Harr. 70 **125**
112 **176**
P. Haun. II 13 **18-23**, n.23
P. Heidelberg (n.f.) III 13 **57**
P. Herm. Rees 2 **176**
4 **175**
5 **175**
6 **175, 176**
P. Iand. VIII 146 **157**
P. IFAO II 24 **62**
P. Ital. II 30 (l.50), 37 (l.5) **50**
P. Köln III 144 **96, 164-167**
147 **82-85, 158**, n.14
157 **185-189**
P. Kron. 50 **31**, n.44, 50
P. L. Bat. XXII 32, 34 **107**
P. Laur. I 6 **84**, n.97
II 44 **176**
II 46 **176**
P. Lille I 8 **142**
P. Lond. II 220 col. II **107**
II 261 **126, 127**
II 311 n.43
III 904 **115-119, 126**, n.123
III 924 (= WChr.355) **117**
III 1164 **83**
V 1714 **85**
V 1729 **189**
VI 1917, 1918, 1927, 1928, 1929 **171**
VII 1951 **58**
P. Lond. inv. 2196 **127**
P. Med. I 7 **61**
P. Mert. III 105 n.50
P. Mich. II 121 recto II ii **7, 9**, n.50
II 121 verso XII **7**
II 123 XI **61**
III 209 n.178
V 238 IV (l.167) **61**
V 321 **34**, n.50
V 322a **34**
V 339 l.5 **9**
V 340 **11**
V 340 recto I/II **7, 8**
VI 579 **122**
VIII 467 **158**, n.178
VIII 468 **158**, n.177, n.178
X 580 **114**
XI 624 **176**
XIV 676 **132-137**
XV 700 **5-6**
P. Mich. inv. 5262a (*ZPE* 42) **144-145**
5806 **127**
P. Mich. Zen. 18 **58-59**
P. Mil. 33 **157**
P. Monac. 8 n.39
P. Muraba'at 24 n.109
P. Nag Hammadi C4 **184**
C8 **184**
G63 **183**
G64 **183**
G65 **182-183**
G68 and G75 **184**
G72 **182-183, 184**
P. Neph. 1, 2, 8, 10 n.193
P. Ness. III 89 **62**
P. Oslo I 3 **11**
II 31 **11**
III 111 n.123
*P. Oslo inv.*1518 (*Am. Stud. Pap.* XXIII) **62, 147-152**
P. Oxy.
I 76 n.189
I 106, 7 **84**
I 144 **84**
I 158 **176**

I 178 n.53
II 237 **33**
II 237 n.10, 25
II 237 vi.30 n.189
II 251-3 **114**
II 265 n.50
II 281-282 **11**
II 282 **57**
II 362, 363 **108**
III 491, 494 **36**
III 601 n.53
IV 707 **167**
IV 713 **34**
VI 904 **69**
VI 942 **176**
VI 943 **176**
VIII 1132 **10, 11**
VIII 1157 **126**
VIII 1165 **176**
IX 1205 **71**
X 1282 **108**
X 1296 n.178
XII 1423 **57**
XII 1424 n.193
XII 1463 n.61
XIV 1631 **95**
XIV 1643 **56**
XIV 1643 **57**
XVI 1933 **176**
XVII 2106 n.123
XVII 2131 **141**
XVII 2136 **83**
XX 2276 **176**
XXII 2347 **84**
XXIV 2413 **114**
XXVII 2479 **142**
XXXIV 2710 **111**
XXXIV 2721 **85**
XXXIV 2728 n.193
XXXVI 2759 n.53
XLII 3057 **169-177**
XLII 3057 **181**
XLVII 3333 **158**
XLVII 3336 **119-120, 124**, n.184
XLVII 3354 **95**
XLVIII 3396 n.178
XLIX 3464 **98**
XLIX 3477 n.61
XLIX 3491 n.50
XLIX 3500 **2**
XLIX 3510 n.141
L 3593 **62**
LV 3813-15 n.193
LVI 3859 n.178
P. Oxy. inv. 21 3B25G **84**, n.97
P. Petrie II 2 1 **142**
P. Rein. I 18 **142**
P. Ross. Georg. II 12 **127**, n.138
V 8 **176**
V 154/6 **157**
P. Ryl. 119 **142**
141 **142**
154 **11**
P. Sarap. 25 **166**
P. Strassb. I 239 **113**
II 122 **62**
IV 286 **176, 177**
P. Tebt. I 5 **167**, n.11
I 6 **98**
I 41, 50, 53 **142**
II 381 **31, 38**, n.50
II 384 **61**
II 386 **7**
III 776 n.42
III 782, 786, 787 **142**
III 818 **167**
P. Tor. 13 **7**
P. Turner 17 **108-109**
18 **156-159**, n.14
19 **63-66, 70**
22 **48-52, 62**
26 **66, 70-72**
29 **123**
41 **51, 55-60**
P. Ups. Frid 1 **27, 32, 39**, n.1, n.2
2 **8-9**
3 **105-108**
6 **137-139**
7 **60-63**
P. Vindob. Tandem 27 **31**, n.44, 45
P. Wash. Univ. 3 n.162
13 **41-42, 43**
P. Yadin 10 **15**
11 **92**, n.100
18 **12, 13, 15, 92**, n.27
19 **46**
21 **92**
*P. Yale inv.*1535 **2**
PCZ 59015 **101-104, 171**
59018 **100-101**
PGM II, p.113 **131**
PSI X 1112 **125**
XII 1276 **23**
XIV 1429 **176**
SB
I 2133 **11**
I 5174, 5175 **189**
I 5217 **148**
III 6263 n.178
III 7246 **111**
IV 7427 **145**
IV 7457 **111**
V 7559 **35**
V 7635 **176**
V 7642 **157**
V 8033 **98**
V 8267 **111**
VI 9107, 9376 **176**
VI 9138 n.193
VI 9373 n.50
VI 9377 **31**, n.44
VI 9528 **111**
VI 9608 **176**
VIII 9642 **31, 35**, n.44, n.50
VIII 9683 **176, 177**
X 10572 n.50
XII 10786 **11**
XII 10888 **31**, n.50
XIV 11270 **137**
XIV 11277 **50**
XIV 11279 **86-89**
XIV 11374 **112-115**
XIV 11492 **176**
XIV 11548 **11**
XIV 11552 n.96
XIV 11575 **10**
XIV 11577 **3**
XIV 11586, 11587 **122**
XIV 11882 **176, 177**
XVI 12334 n.50
XVI 12663 n.193
Stud. Pap. II, p.27 **127**
Stud. Pap. XX 75 n.177
UPZ I 65 n.178
II 158a **157**

R.S. Bagnall, P.J. Sijpesteijn, K.A. Worp, *Greek Ostraka in Leiden* (Zutphen 1980), pp.1-2, F 1901/9.166 **190**
R.W. Daniel, 'P. Mich.inv. 6666 Magic', *ZPE* 50 [1983], pp.147-54 **194**
M-H. Marganne, 'Une étape dans la transmission d'une prescription médicale P. Berl. Möller 13', *Miscellanea Papyrologica* (Florence 1980), pp.179-183 **191**
L.C. Youtie & H.C. Youtie, 'A Medical Papyrus', *Scritti in onore di Orsolina Montevecchi*, ed. E. Bresciani et al. (Bologna 1981), pp.431-35 **190**

INSCRIPTIONS

CIL III 12074 **157**
CIL XIII 1042-5 **160**
CIL XVI 30 n.182
CIL XVI 31 **159, 160**
CIL XVI 31 n.182
CIL XVI 33 **157**
CIL XVI 48 **161**
GDI 2327 n.69
I. Eph. Ia 2 **204**
Ia 10 **200**
Ia 20 I. **150**, n.167
Ia 24 **204**
Ia 26 **201**
Ia 27 **205**
Ia 27 **205**
Ia 47 **198, 200**
II 212 **204**
II 234-5, 237, 241 **206**
II 276 **210**
II 300 **204**
II 412 **179**
II 424a **206**
III 647 **203**
III 650 **210**
III 712b **179**
III 857 **204**
III 987 **201**
III 989 **201**
IV 1012 **196**
IV 1045 **198**
IV 1060 **198, 199**
IV 1061 **198, 199**
IV 1062 **199**
IV 1064 **199, 200**
IV 1066 **179**
IV 1068 **199**
IV 1069 **201**
IV 1075 **200**
IV 1078 **199**
IV 1312 **179**
V 1449 **197**
V 1522 **205**
V 1595 **209**
V 1595 **210**
VI 2004 **205**
VI 2039 **204**
VII 1 3038 **206**
VII 1 3039 **179**
VII 1 3005 **204**
VII 1 3059 **201**
VII 1 3415 **198**
VII 2 4102 **197**
I. Pergamon VIII 3 29 **206**
VIII 3 30 **204**
I. Priene 231 **205**
I. Smyrna II 1, 644 **206**
II 1 657, 696 **204**
I. Stratonikeia I 272 **206**
II 2 1307-8 **207**
IG 12 (5) 590 5 **131**
XII, Suppl.1, nr.124 **180**
XIV, 1829 **179**
IGRR I 881 **72**
IGUR II, 2.768 **179**
ILS 1418 **159**
MAMA IX, p.24, no.63 **207**
IX, p.24, no. 63 **208**
IX, p.25, no. 64 **208**
OMS I, p.414 **207**
SEG 28 889 **207**
28 929 **207**
30 531a,b n.91
31 577 n.91
31 543 **72**
35 593, 599 and 600 n.91
Syll.[2] 694 **110**
764 **111**
TAM V 1 185 **207**
V 1 586 **208**
V 1 598 **209**

J. Bousquet, *BCH* 95 (1971), pp.277-82 n.91
W.H. Buckler, W.M. Calder and C.W.M. Cox, *JRS* 15 (1925), p.161, no.150 **208**
T. Drew-Bear, *ANRW* II, 7.2 (1980), p.939 **207**
T. Drew-Bear, *Nouvelles inscriptions* (1978), 3 **209**
5-8 **208**
K.I. Gallis, *AAA* 13 (1980), pp.256-261 **76-81**
R. Hachlili, 'The Goliath Family in Jericho Funerary Inscriptions from a First Century AD Jewish Monumental Tomb', *BASOR* 235 (1979), pp.31-73, nos. 3, 9, 14 **162-164**
E. Haspels, *The Highlands of Phrygia*, Vol. I (1971), no. 116 **208**
P. Herrmann & K.Z. Polatkan, *SAWW* 265 (1969), pp.50, 52-3 **208**
S.E. Johnson, *BASOR* 158 (1960), p.8 **204**
D. Knibbe, Der Staatsmarkt. Die Inschriften des Prytaneions, Forschungen in Ephesos IX/1/1 (1981), A1 **197**
A2 **197**
B12 **196**
B45 **198**
B54 **198, 200**
C1 **198, 199**
C2 **198, 199**
D1 **200**
D2 **200**
F1 **199**
F3 **199, 200**
F5 **199**
F9 **201**
F13 **199**
pp.96ff. **200**

R. Kotansky, 'Two Amulets in the Getty Museum: A Gold Amulet for Aurelia's Epilepsy. An Inscribed Magical Stone for Fever, "Chills", and Headache', *J. Paul Getty Museum Journal* 8 (1980), pp.180-4 **192**

A. Latyschev, *Inscriptiones Antiquae* II 52, 53, 400 and 401 **66**, n.89

P. Lazaridis, *Praktika* (1972), p.31 **62**

S. Mitchell, *R.E.C.A.M. II. The Ankara District. The Inscriptions of North Galatia* (1982), no.44 **208**

J.H. Oliver, *Hesperia* VI, no. 12 **201**

G. Petzl, *Studien zur Religion und Kultur Kleinasiens. Festschrift für F.K. Dörner* (1978), p.757 **207**

G. Petzl, *ZPE* 30 (1978), p.268, no.14 **207**

H.W. Pleket, 'New Inscriptions from Lydia', *Talanta* 10-11 (1978-81), pp.88-90, no.13 **192**

J. Pouilloux, *BCH* 79 (1955), pp.442-66 n.91

W.M. Ramsay *BCH* 6 (1882) p.518 **178**

W.M. Ramsay, *JHS* 4 (1883) pp.424-427 **177**

J. Reynolds, *Aphrodisias and Rome* (1982) §8 **110**

J.& L. Robert, *Fouilles d'Amyzon en Carie* (1983), pp.259-66 n.67

L. Robert, *OMS* I, p.411 **208**

M.H. Sayar, *ZPE* 49 (1982) pp.191-2 **208**

A.R.R. Sheppard, 'Pagan Cults of Angels in Roman Asia Minor', *Talanta* 12-13 (1980-81), pp.87-88, no. 8, **206**

Arch. Deltion 28 (1973), Chron. 1, 300 **190**

M. Speidel, *ANRW* II 7 2 (1980) **152-153**

G.-J. M.-J. Te Riele, *ZPE* 27 (1977), pp.259-62 n.91

G.-J. M.-J. Te Riele, *ZPE* 49 (1982), pp.161-176 n.91

W. Wischmeyer, 'Die Aberkiosinschrift als Grabepigramm', *JbAC* 23 (1980) **178**

OLD TESTAMENT, QUMRAN AND RABBINIC LITERATURE

Old Testament

Genesis
2.24 n.22
17.17 **183**
20.3 **13**
31.15 **13**, n.16
34.12 **12**, n.16

Exodus
3.6 **194**
3.15-16 **194**
4.5 **194**
18.13-27 n.147
20.17 **13**
22.16-7 **12**
22.16-7 n.16
30.11-16 **128**

Numbers
27.8-11 **43**

Deuteronomy
2.19 **202**
17.17 n.15
21.13 **13**
21.14 n.18
21.16-17 **43**
22.22 **13**
23.15-16 **54**
24.1 **13**
24.2 n.28

Joshua
15.18-20 n.16
16.10 n.16

Ruth
4.5, 10 **13**

1Samuel
18.25 **12**, n.16

1Kings
9.16 n.16
10.24 **183**

1Chronicles
24.7-18 **129**

Ezra
9 **17**

Nehemiah
10.31 **17**
13.23-28 **17**

Psalms
45.10b, 14b (LXX, 44) **181**

Proverbs
2.17 **14**
17.9-16a **181**

Isaiah
5.1-2 **94**

Jeremiah
3.19 **40**

Ezekiel
16.8 **14**
Malachi
2.13-16 **14**

Tobit
5.2-3 **108**
7.12-14 **12**
7.13 **15**
8.21 **46**, n.16
10.10 **46**

2 Maccabees
1.14 n.16
7.7, 15.3 **183**

Qumran

1QM
2.3-4 n.147
5.12-13 n.147

1QS
2.19-24 n.147

11QTemp.
57.17-19 **16**

CD
4.19-5.5 n.15, n.29
4.5-6 **128**
13.1 n.147
14.3-6 n.147
16.10-13 n.21

Mishnah

'Arak.
5.6 **15**

B. Bat.
3.1 **97**
3.2 **96, 97**
3.3 **96, 97**, n.106
4.9 n.106
8-9 **43**
8.1 **13**
8.7 n.47
10.4 n.109

B. Meṣ.
1.6 **92**
5.3 n.110
9.1-10 **89**
9.11 **96**
9.13 **92**
9.2, 3, 4, 5,6 **89**
9.8-9 **90**

'Ed.
1.12 **13**, n.37
8.2 n.172

Git.
5.1-3 **13**
5.6 n.112
7.5 **16**
9.2-3 **16**
9.2 **17**
9.3 **14**, n.28
9.8 **12, 15**
9.10 **15**

Hor.
3.7 n.172
3.8 **128**

Ket.
1.4 n.172
2.2 **97**
2.9 n.172
4.12 **13**, n.37
4.4 **12**, n.21, n.32
5.5 **14**
5.6 **14**
5.7 **13, 15**
5.8-9 **14**
6.3 **13**
7.4-5 **15**
7.6-7 **13, 15**
7.9-10 **15**
8.1 **13**
9.1 **13**
9.9 **12**
12.3-4 **13**
13.1 **91**
13.7 n.111

Kil.
7.6 n.112

Ned.
10.2 n.21
11.1-2 n.21
11.4 **14**

11.10 **12**, n.21
11.12 **15**

Nid.
5.4 n.32
5.7 n.21
11.10 n.21

Qid.
1.1-6 **14**
1.1 n.32
1.5 n.106
2.1, 3.2 **12**
3.12 **17**
4.1-7 **17**
4.1 **128**
4.4 **128**
4.9 **14**

Sanh.
11.4 **91**

Sheb.
10.4 **91**

Shev.
10.3-4 **92**

Soṭa
1.3 **91**
8.2, 4 **96**

Yad.
4.4 **128**

Yeb.
4.3 **13**
4.7 **13**
7.5 **17**
11.2 n.31
12.6 **12**
13.1, 2 **12**
13.6 **12**
14.1 **15**

Tosefta

B. Bat.
9.14 **47**

B. Meṣ.
9.1-33 **89**
9.8 **89**
9.13 **90**
9.33 **89**

'Ed.
1.6 **13**

Git.
5.1 n.112

Ket.
3.2 n.172
4.9 **15**
4.16 n.106
12.1 **13**

Ned.
7.1 n.21

Qid.
3.7 **14**
4.15, 5.1-13 **17**

Yeb.
13.1 **12, 14**

Palestinian Talmud

B. Bat.
3.3 **97**
16c **16**
3.3 **96, 97**
3.5 **96**

Ket.
30b **16**
4.8.28d **15**

Kil.
7.4 **96**

Qid.
3.4 **108**

Sanh.
2.6 **46**, n.15, n.29

Yeb.
15.3.14d **15**

Babylonian Talmud

B. Bat.
135b **46**
35b **96**

Git.
9a **37**

Ket.
84a **13**

Qid.
66a n.172

Others

Mek. Nez. 3 **12**
SifNum 134 n.120
*Tg. Exod.*21.11 **14**

NEW TESTAMENT

Matthew
2.1, 3 **123**
5.25-26 **92, 99**
5.32 **16**
6.13 **194**
6.30 **68, 69**
7.11 **69**
8.27 **85**
10.25 **68, 69**
11.12 **98**
12.10 **183**
14.22-33 **86**
18.30 **99**
19.3 **183**
19.9 **16**
19.12 **16**
20.20-28 **50**
21.28 **131**
21.33-44 **93-105**
21.33-46 **39**
21.37 **95**
25.21 **181**
25.32 **181**
27.35 **159**

Mark
4.11 **202**
4.41 **85**
8.23 **183**
10.11-12 **16**
10.35-45 **50**
11.1- **37**
12.1-12 **39**
12.1 n.105
12.7 n.49
13.9 **91**
13.34 **62-63**
14.29 **68**
15.24 **159**
15.26 **115**

Luke
1.5, 26, 39-41 **123**
1.26, 36, 59 **132**
2.1-3 **119, 123**
2.1-5 **124**
2.1 **111**
2.2 n.154
2.3 **112-119**
2.7 **130**
2.39 **119, 123**
3.1, 23 **31**
3.14 n.177
6.7 **183**
7.21 **194**
8.2 **194**
8.25 **85**
8.43-48 **196**
9.22 **132**
11.13 **69**
11.26 **194**
12.13 **39**
12.28 **68, 69**
12.38 **132**
12.57-59 **92**
12.58-59 **99**
13.23 **183**
13.32 **132**
15.11-32 **37**
16.18 **16**
18.1-8 **98**
18.33 **132**
20.9-19 **39**
22.49 **183**
23.34 **159**
23.44 **132**
24.7, 21, 46 **132**

John
1.11 n.126
1.15 **131**
2.20 **62**
6.19 n.35
6.62 **183**
9.6 **191**
12.1 **157**
15.4 n.79
19.23-24 **159**

Acts
1.1 **131**
1.6 **183**
2.15 **132**
3.1 **132**
3.31 **194**
5.37 **131**
7.12 **131**
7.32 **194**
7.8 **132**
8.9-13 **195**
10.1 **159**
10.3, 9, 30, 40 **132**
12.10 **131, 132**
12.20-23 **192**
13.6-12 **195**
14.13 **209**
16.4 **111**
16.16-22 **205**
16.37 **154**
17.7 **111**
19.9 **197**
19.11-12 **196**
19.19 **202**
19.35 **204, 205**
19.37, 40 **205**
20.18 **132**
21.27-32 **205**
21.27 – 23.35 **159-161**
21.31-33 **205**
22.22-29 **154**
22.25-8 **153**
22.25 **154, 183**
22.28, 30 **154**
23.23 **132**, n.181
27.1-44 **85**
27.1 **159**
27.19, 27, 33 **132**

Romans
1.3 n.57
3.5 n.56
3.25 **115**
4.1 n.57
5.3 n.57
5.10,15,17 **69**
6.8 n.56
6.12ff. n.64
6.18, 22 **75**
7.13-15 **53**
8.4 n.56
8.12 n.57
9.22-24 **183**
11.12 **68, 69**
11.16 **68**
11.24 **69**
12.1 **146**
13.1-7 **145**
15.30 **146**
16.13 n.178
16.17 **146**

1 Corinthians
1.10 **146**
3.3 n.56, n.57
4.1 **202**
4.6-13 **139**
4.8ff n.78
4.15 **68**, n.178
4.16 **146**
6.13-20 n.64
6.16 n.22
6.20 **75**
7.1-16 **14**
7.3 **14**
7.4 **15**, n.22
7.5 **15**
7.10-11, 12, 15 **16**
7.12-13 **17**
7.12-16 **17**
7.14 **18**
7.20 **53**
7.21 **67-70**
7.23 **75**
7.24, 35 **75**
7.25-40 **14**
7.29-31 **17**
7.32-35 **15**
7.36-38 **14**, n.19

7.39 **17**
9.2 **68**
9.8 n.56, n.57
9.12 **68, 69**
9.27 n.64
10.2-3 n.56
11.3 **15**
11.11 **15**
12.13 **54, 59**
14.2 **202**
14.7-9 n.55
15.32 n.56, n.57
16.15 **146**
16.22 **194**

2 Corinthians
1.3-14 **172**
2.8 **146**
3.1-2 **180**
3.9,11 **69**
4.10ff. n.64
4.16 **69**
5.13 **68**
5.16 **68**
5.20 **146**
6.1 **146**
6.14-16 **17**
7.12 **68**
8.12 **68**
10.1-2 **146**
11.2 n.30
11.6 **68**
11.15 **69**
11.22 **139**
11.24-5 **154**
11.26 **85**

Galatians
1.11 n.56, n.57
3.15-19 **43**
3.15 **37, 41-47**
3.18 **68**
3.26-8 **59**
3.27-28 **54**
3.28 **15, 152**
4.1 **39**
4.12 **146**
4.23 n.57
5.1,13 **75**
6.1 **69**

Ephesians
3.9 **202**
4.1 **146**
4.24 **209**
5.21-33 **15**
5.21, 22-6.9 **19**
5.27 **19**
6.5 **53, 55**

Philippians
1.20 n.64
2.6-8 **140**
2.17 **69**
3.1b-4.20 n.187
3.4 **68, 69**
3.5-8 **139**
3.5 **128**
3.17 **172**
4.2, 3 **146**

Colossians
1.5, 12-13, 13-15, 23, 27-29 **110**
2.13-14 **115**
2.14 **105-111**
2.18 **209**
3.18-4.1 **19**
3.18-19 **15**
3.23 **19**
4.7-8, 9, 10 **110**

1 Thessalonians
2.18 **172**
3.5 **172**
4.1,10 **146**
4.4 n.64
5.12, 14 **146**
5.27 **172**

2 Thessalonians
2.1 **146**
2.5 **172**
3.12 **146**
3.17 **172**

1 Timothy
1.15 **180**
2.1 **146**
2.8-15 **19**
3.1 **180**
3.14-15 n.82
4.9 **180**
5.23 **190**
6.1-2 **19**
6.2 **175**
6.21 **171**

2 Timothy
2.3-4 **149**
3.15 **180**
4.22 **171**

Titus
1.4 **171**
1.9 **180**
2.2-10 **19**
2.3-5 **22**
3.1 **145**
3.8 **180**
3.15 **171**

Philemon
6 **171**
9,10 **146**
15-16 **60, 175**

1 Peter
2.11 **146**
2.13-17 **145**
2.18-20 **53**
2.18-3.7 **19**
3.3-5 **19**
3.14 **69**
4.11 **68**
5.1 **146**

James
5.14 **191**

Hebrews
12.25 **68**
13.19,22 **146**

Jude 3 **146**

Revelation
16.5 **209**
17-18 **145**
20.5 **131**
21.1 **131**
21.2 n.30